Essays in Real Estate Research
Band 5

Edited by
N. B. Rottke, Eschborn, Germany
J. Mutl, Wiesbaden, Germany

Die Reihe „Essays in Real Estate Research", herausgegeben von Professor Dr. Nico B. Rottke FRICS und Professor Jan Mutl, Ph.D. umfasst aktuelle Forschungsarbeiten der Promovenden der Lehrstühle und Professuren des Real Estate Management Institutes der EBS Business School. Forschungs- und Lehrschwerpunkte des Institutes bilden die interdisziplinären Aspekte der Immobilientransaktion sowie die nachhaltige Wertschöpfungskette im Immobilienlebenszyklus. Die Kapitalmärkte werden als essenzieller Bestandteil der Entwicklung der Immobilienmärkte aufgefasst.
Die in der Regel empirischen Studien betrachten transaktions- und kapitalmarktnahe Themenbereiche aus dem Blickwinkel der institutionellen Immobiliengewerbe- und -wohnungswirtschaft, wie bspw. Finanzierung, Kapitalmarktstruktur, Investition, Risikomanagement, Bewertung, Ökonomie oder Portfoliomanagement, aber auch angewandte Themen wie Corporate Real Estate Management, Projektentwicklung oder Unternehmensführung. Die ersten 11 Bände der Reihe erschienen bis 2014 auch im Immobilien Manager Verlag, Köln.

The series "Essays in Real Estate Research", published by Professor Dr. Nico B. Rottke FRICS and Professor Jan Mutl, Ph.D., includes current research work of doctoral students at the chairs and professorships of the Real Estate Management Institute of EBS Business School. The research and teaching focus of the Institute constitutes the interdisciplinary aspects of real estate transactions as well as the sustainable value creation chain within the real estate life cycle. The capital markets are regarded as essential components of the development of the real estate markets.
The mostly empirical studies consider transactional as well as capital market topics from the point of view of the institutional commercial and residential real estate industry, such as finance, capital market structure, investment, risk management, valuation, economics or portfolio management, but also applied topics such as corporate real estate management, real estate development, or leadership issues in the property industry. The first 11 volumes of the series appeared up until 2014 in Immobilien Manager Publishing, Cologne, as well.

Edited by
Nico B. Rottke
Ernst & Young Real Estate GmbH
Eschborn, Germany

Jan Mutl
EBS Business School
Wiesbaden, Germany

Simon Kempf

Development of Hedonic Office Rent Indices

Examples for German Metropolitan Areas

With a Preface of the Editors by Prof. Dr. Matthias Thomas and Prof. Dr. Nico B. Rottke

Springer Gabler

Dr. Simon Kempf
EBS REMI
Wiesbaden, Germany

Unchanged Reprint 2015
Up to 2014 the title was published in Immobilien Manager Verlag, Cologne, in the series "Schriftenreihe zur immobilienwirtschaftlichen Forschung".

Essays in Real Estate Research
ISBN 978-3-658-11169-4 ISBN 978-3-658-11170-0 (eBook)
DOI 10.1007/978-3-658-11170-0

Library of Congress Control Number: 2015954810

Springer Gabler

Printed on acid-free paper

Springer Gabler is a brand of Springer Fachmedien Wiesbaden
Springer Fachmedien Wiesbaden is part of Springer Science+Business Media
(www.springer.com)

PREFACE OF THE EDITORS

Office rents are prices for heterogeneous goods and are determined by various criteria: location, lease factors, building quality, equipment and layout of the office rental unit. On the one hand, this heterogeneity causes difficulties the aggregation and implementation of office rents into one index value; on the other hand, this same heterogeneity makes a reliable index even more valuable.

In practice, the prevailing methodology to compute office rent indices is to calculate average office rents. This methodology assumes homogeneity among all office rent determinants. It goes without saying that such an assumption does not hold true neither in practice nor in theory, and that the explanatory power of such office rent indices for real estate analysis is inappropriate when one looks beyond indicating a general trend in real estate markets.

Against this background, the author Simon Kempf has developed hedonic office rent indices for German metropolitan areas. These indices are useful for real estate practitioners as well as academics who are looking for trustworthy market and economic indicators.

His work is structured in seven chapters. Subsequent to the concise introduction, chapter two outlines the theory of the construction of the hedonic office rent indices. Thereafter, chapter three gives an insight on the general functioning of the office market, thereby identifying and elaborating the implications on developing office rent indices for the German property market.

Chapter four analyses the influencing factors of office rents. After an extensive literature review the explorative survey carried out by Simon Kempf among over 1,700 real estate professionals sheds light on the topic of drawing lease contracts. So far this issue has been largely neglected in German property research as it has only been analysed on the level of strategic portfolio management. In chapter five, the hedonic analysis of German office rents is undertaken representing the main empirical analysis and the nucleus of his thesis. Before the hedonic analysis based on a data set comprising more than 22,000 office leases is conducted, the author has to deal with the problem of missing data. Instead of using the single imputation method to solve this problem - a common, but misleading way in statistical analysis - he breaks ground by introducing the multiple imputation method to the German property research community. In chapter six, hedonic office rent indices for Berlin, Düsseldorf, Frankfurt, Hamburg and Munich based on the Laspeyres and Paasche index formulae are elaborated and compared. Finally, the last chapter summarizes the results, points out the limitations of his research and thereby indicates the direction of future work .

The thesis, which has been accepted at European Business School (EBS) in summer 2008, is both innovative and creative. We sincerely hope that this thesis will be well appreciated by property researchers and real estate practitioners alike.

Wiesbaden, September 2008

Prof. Dr. Matthias Thomas MRICS
Executive Director
Real Estate Management Institute
Stiftungslehrstuhl Immobilienmanagement

Prof. Dr. Nico Rottke MRICS
Executive Director
Real Estate Management Institute
Aareal Professur Real Estate Banking

Real Estate Management Institute
European Business School (EBS)
International University Schloss Reichartshausen

Preface of the Author

The judgement of rental level development plays a fundamental role in any real estate investment decision. One would expect established and consistent office rent indices to be available in all mature office markets. So far quite the opposite is the case in Germany. The development of office rent indices is particularly difficult due to the heterogeneity of office leases as well as the sheer absence of available data. The fact, that - despite the aforementioned problems - I was able to develop hedonic (i.e. quality adjusted) office rent indices for German metropolitan areas and finish my thesis, is due to many friends and persons who accompanied me along my "thesis-project". To these people I want to direct my preface.

For the numerous consultations during the monthly meetings, annual proposal defences as well as the review of my thesis, I want to thank Prof. Dr. Matthias Thomas MRICS and Prof. Dr. Schiereck of the Real Estate Management Institute (REMI) of the European Business School (EBS). For the support during the quantitative statistical analysis I am very thankful to Prof. Dr. Steffen Sebastian of the University of Regensburg. Special thanks I owe to Prof. Dr. Kurzrock of the University of Kaiserslautern, Lars Dierkes of IPD GmbH as well as Justus Vollrath who provided and retrieved all relevant office lease data out of the IPD rental databank. For the explanation of the difficulties in gathering office rental market as well as office lease data in Germany, I owe my gratitude to Günther Muncke and Ulrich Denk, BulwienGesa.

For assistance and moral support, I am very thankful to my employer and my colleagues of Savills Immobilienberatungs-GmbH Corporate Finance - Valuation.

I want to express my thanks to all my friends who supported me with helpful comments but even more important with their patience. Here, I am specifically grateful to Jeffrey King and Fenja Winkelmann who proofread the thesis from the beginning to the end and, improved the quality of my thesis significantly with their comments and remarks.

Last but not least, I am thankful to my family and to my girlfriend Anais Cosneau.

Berlin, September 2008

Simon Kempf

CONTENT OVERVIEW

CONTENT

LIST OF FIGURES

List of Tables

List of Abbreviations

AC	Available Case Analysis
BAFA	Bundesamt für Wirtschaft und Ausfuhrkontrolle
BGB	Bürgerliches Gesetzbuch
BIIS	Bundesverband der Immobilien-Investment Sachverständigen
CBD	Central Business District
CCA	Complete Case Analysis
Cf.	Confer
CPI Method	Characteristic Price Index Method
DDIV	Dachverband Deutscher Immobilienverwalter
DID	Deutsche Immobilien Datenbank
DIN	Deutsches Institut für Normung
EM	Expectation Maximization
ERP	Entreprise Resource Planning System
EUR	Euro (€)
GIF	Gesellschaft für immobilienwirtschaftliche Forschung (German Society of Property Researchers)
GVIF	Generalized Variance Inflation Factor
HORIX	Hedonic Office Rent Indices
IPD	Investment Property Databank
IVD	Immobilienverband Deutschland
LD	Listwise Deletion Analysis
L-HORIX	Hedonic Office Rent Indices based on the Laspeyres Index Formulae
MAR	Missing At Random
MCAR	Missing Completely at Random

MI	Multiple Imputation
MICE	Multiple Imputation with Chained Equations
MNAR	Missing Not At Random
MPT	Modern Portfolio Theory
MPE	Mean Percentage Error
MPT	Modern Portfolio Theory
MSE	Mean Square Error
P-HORIX	Hedonic Office Rent Indices based on the Paasche Index Formulae
RESET	Regression Equation Specification Error Test
RICS	Royal Institution of Chartered Surveyors
RIWIS	Regionales Immobilienwirtschaftliches Informationssystem (Bulwien Gesa)
RMSE	Root Mean Square Error
Sqm	Square metre (m^2)
TAB	Transaction-based Approach
TDV Method	Time Dummy Variable Method
UK	United Kingdom
USA	United States of America
VAT	Value-added Tax
VIF	Variance Inflation Factor

List of Symbols

α	Vector of socio-economic characteristics
α, β, λ,δ, γ	Regression coefficients
β	Shift parameter
B	Between-imputation variance
$b_1, b_2, \ldots b_N$	Fixed effects
C	Total costs
$C_{0,1,2}$	Capitalization function in period 0, 1 and 2
λ	Variable in Box-Cox transformation
D	Time dummy
$D_{0,1}$	Demand function of office space (or land) in time period 0 and 1
df	Degrees of freedom
∂	First order moment
θ	Bid function
θ	Likehood function
€	EUR
g	Non-parametric shape function
γ	Fraction of information
h	Hedonic function
i (as subscript)	Characteristic index
K	Capital
	Kurtosis
k	Number of characteristics
	Number of variables in regression function
L	Labour

log	Logarithm
ln	Logarithm naturalis
M	Materials
	Number of office units produced by a firm
m	Number of imputed datasets
N	Number of observations
n	Number of varieties of an product
	Number of observations
Π	Profit
π	Profit level
ϕ	Offer function
P	Vector of prices
	Probability
p	Price
Q	Utility (or Output)
$\overline{Q}$	Combined regression estimate of multiple imputd regression analysis
$\hat{Q}_i$	Regression estimate of multiple imputed dataset *i*
$q_{0,1}$	Quantity of office space (or land) supplied in time period 0 and1
R	Missingness
r	Relative increase in variance due to nonresponse
$r_{0,1,2}$	Office Rent in time period 0,1 and 2
S	Skewness
$S_{0,1}$	Supply function of office space (or land) in time period 0 and 1

S^2	Variance
Σ	Sum
Σ, Ψ	Covariances matrices
T	Total variance
t	Production function
t (as subscript)	Time index
$\overline{U}$	Within-imputation variance
$\hat{U}_i$	Estimated variance of multiple imputed dataset *i*
u	Disturbance or error in the regression model
x	Vector of other, homogeneous consumption goods (or inputs)
Y_{com}	Complete dataset
Y_{mis}	Missing part of complete dataset
Y_{obs}	Observed part of complete dataset
y	Total budget of a company
$y_1, y_2, \ldots, y_N$	Random effects
$\overline{y}$	Population mean
Z	k x n matrix of characteristics of a product
	Set of dummy variables
$z_{1..N}$	N- Characteristic of an office unit
z_i	i- Characteristic of an economic good

1 Introduction

1.1 Research Problem

As in most developed countries, German office properties play a significant role in the overall economy and in the real estate market. Office buildings not only shape the structural environment but also perform various functions.

First, office property is a factor of production, as it provides the space to house the activities of business and industry.[1] In 2006, the total number of office employees in Germany was estimated at approximately 12.5 million.[2] Its importance as a factor of production increased substantially with the rising number of employees working in the tertiary sector. In 1965, 40 percent of total number of employees were working in the tertiary sector; in 2005, it was more than 72 percent in 2005.[3] Due to the increasing tertiarisation of jobs and diversification of the economy, the office property sector gains in importance for the employment market and also increases the value-creation potential of Germany's national ecomomy.[4]

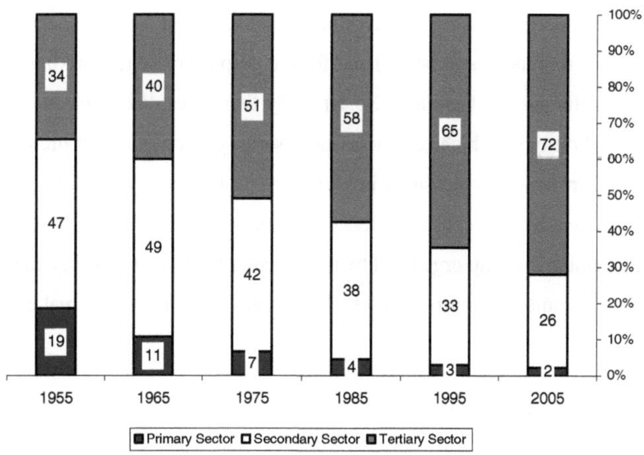

Source: Federal Statistical Bureau of Germany

Table 1: Distribution of Employees in Germany according to Economic Sector

[1] Cf. Hall, J. M. (1985), p. 25

[2] Cf. BulwienGesa Online Databank (2008), w/o pages [Online Database]

[3] See Table 1

[4] Cf. Heyser, H. (2006), p. 29-30

Second, it is a financial asset and an investment medium, generating revenue for its holders on the basis of value and forming a significant part of the asset market.[5] More than 31 billion EUR, constituting more than 50 percent of all real estate investments in 2007, have been placed in German office properties (19 billion EUR in 2006 and 10 billion EUR in 2005).[6] The increasing interest in office properties led to a significant compression of net initial yields in the major office markets. Whereas in the past investors mainly purchased office properties in the biggest office markets (i.e. Berlin, Düsseldorf, Frankfurt, Hamburg, and Munich), they started to invest in regional office markets because of the lack of investment opportunities.[7] [8] Furthermore, it is worth mentioning that their fixed assets at net book value amount to approximately 300 billion EUR.[9]

Office properties are primarily income-producing assets. The value of any income-producing asset is a function of its expected future cash flows and an appropriate discount rate.[10] Whereas the discount rate is dependent on the risk of the investment,[11] the future cash flows are primarily determined by office rents. Therefore, office rents are of the utmost importance in property valuation, investment, and portfolio management.[12]

Because of the importance of rent in investment decisions, one would expect robust and consistent office rent indices to be on hand for the purpose of benchmarking. However, the opposite is the case in Germany. So far, only two types of office rent indices are available. The first type, which represents time series of average or prime office rents for the major German cities measured in EUR per square metre per month, is published by real estate agencies and consultancies.[13] The second type is formed by expert judgments. At an annual meeting organized by the German Society of Property Researchers, Gesellschaft für Immobilienwirtschaftliche Forschung (gif), the major real estate agen-

---

[5] Cf. Wilson, T. (1985), p. 121-132, Ball, M., et al. (1998), p. 18-40, Slade, B. A. (2000), p. 357

[6] Cf. ATIS Real (2006e), w/o pages, ATIS Real (2007), w/o pages, ATIS Real (2008), w/o pages

[7] Regional office markets comprise cities with an office stock of less than 4 million sq m. BulwienGesa (2008), w/o pages [Online Database]

[8] Cf. Beyerle, T. (2007), p. 20-26

[9] Cf. ifo Institut für Wirtschaftsforschung (2005), p. 39. According to the Federal Statistical Bureau of Germany the fixed assets at net book value are at 5.533 billion EUR and office buildings represent approximately 13 percent.

[10] Cf. Janssen, C., et al. (2001), p. 342, Webb, B. R., et al. (1992), p. 329

[11] Cf. Ball, M., et al. (1998), p. 265

[12] Cf. Crosby, N. /Murdoch, S. (2000), p. 13

[13] Cf. Dröge, F. (2005), p. 89-90, Kauffmann, A. /Nastansky, A. (2007), p. 57

cies and consultancies for each metropolitan area[14] reach a consensus on the average and prime office rents. However, this consensus does not imply that the participants in the aforementioned meeting are bound to publish exactly these figures themselves. Rather it presents the least common denominator.[15] On the contrary, the participants still publish different figures from which they agreed upon[16] resulting in further discussion about the reliability of office property market data.[17] In fact, one could argue whether the figures published by the German Society of Property Researchers confuse more than clarify.[18]

		Berlin	Düsseldorf	Frankfurt	Hamburg	Munich
Prime Office Rent per Month in EUR / sq m	**Atisreal**	20.05	21.50	35.00	23.50	29.50
	BulwienGesa	20.50	20.50	32.00	21.00	28.00
	Catella Property Group	20.02	21.50	n.a.	n.a.	n.a.
	CB Richard Ellis	21.00		34.50	23.00	30.50
	Colliers	20.50	21.10	35.00	21.00	30.00
	Cushman Wakefield	20.05	21.00	34.00	21.00	29.00
	DEGI	n.a.	21.00	31.00	20.70	26.50
	DTZ	23.00	22.00	35.00	23.00	30.00
	Engel & Völkers (gif)	21.20	21.00-23.00	n.a.	n.a.	n.a.
	Eurohypo	12.00-21.00	n.a.	n.a.	n.a.	n.a.
	gif e.V.	20.50	21.20	34.60	21.50	30.00
	HVB	n.a.	n.a.	n.a.	n.a.	n.a.
	Jones Lang LaSalle	20.50	21.50	35.00	22.00	28.50
	NAIapollo	21.00	19.50	34.70	23.50	28.50
	Savills*	20.00	n.a.	34.00	22.13	29.50
	*based on 3-5% of transaction volume					

		Berlin	Düsseldorf	Frankfurt	Hamburg	Munich
Average Office Rent per Month in EUR / sq m	**Atis Real**	n.a.	n.a.	n.a.	n.a.	n.a.
	BulwienGesa	15.30	15.70	18.00	15.10	17.25
	Catella Property Group	10.13	12.71	n.a.	n.a.	n.a.
	CB Richard Ellis	11.84		17.45	12.36	14.28
	Colliers	10.60	12.70	15.50	12.35	14.42
	Cushman Wakefield	n.a.	n.a.	n.a.	7.90	n.a.
	DEGI	n.a.	n.a.	15.00	n.a.	14.00
	DTZ	11.00	n.a.	n.a.	n.a.	n.a.
	Engel & Völkers (gif)	10.50	12.50	n.a.	n.a.	n.a.
	Eurohypo	8.50-15.50	n.a.	17.00	12.40	15.20
	gif e.V.	10.50	12.70	17.00	12.40	15.20
	HVB	n.a.	n.a.	n.a.	n.a.	n.a.
	Jones Lang LaSalle***	12.63	12.33	18.23	12.14	13.84
	NAIapollo	10.50	12.50	17.00	12.10	13.60
	Savills***	10.18	n.a.	16.20	11.54	13.73
	*** Weighted Average					

Source: Thomas Daily 2008

Table 2: Comparison of Published Office Rents

[14] Metropolitan areas are the primary geographic units of space segmentation. A metropolitan area encompasses a central city and its surrounding suburbs and tends to be relatively integrated economically, culturally and socially. Cf. Geltner, D. M., et al. (2007), p. 4

[15] See Appendix A.10

[16] See Table 2

[17] Cf. Rohmert, W. (2008), p. 12-13

[18] See Section 6.1.3 for an in-depth discussion about the research methodology of the consensus meeting organized by the German Society of Property Researchers, its advantages and disadvantages.

A comparison of average and prime office rents by different real estate agents and consultancies demonstrates significant variances. The absolute and relative differences are depicted in the following tables.[19] For instance, the published average office rents for Berlin in 2006 differ by up to 51 percent and for Hamburg even by up to 91 percent. These differences cause confusion among participants in the real estate market, especially foreign investors.[20]

		Min	Max	Difference (absolut)	Difference (relative)
Prime Office Rent per Month in EUR / sq m	**Berlin**	20.00	23.00	3.00	15.00%
	Düsseldorf	19.50	22.00	2.50	12.82%
	Frankfurt	31.00	35.00	4.00	12.90%
	Hamburg	20.70	23.50	2.80	13.53%
	Munich	26.50	30.50	4.00	15.09%
Average Office Rent per Month in EUR / sq m	**Berlin**	10.13	15.30	5.17	51.04%
	Düsseldorf	12.33	15.70	3.37	27.33%
	Frankfurt	15.00	18.23	3.23	21.53%
	Hamburg	7.90	15.10	7.20	91.14%
	Munich	13.60	17.25	3.65	26.84%

Table 3: Comparison of Published Office Rents (Summary)

One source of these variances is the different delimitations of the regional office market.[21] The major shortcoming of these office rent indices,[22] however, is that they fail to account for the influence of the office rent determinants.[23] These determinants influence the level of office rent and can be broadly categorized as follows: location of the office property, building factors, equipment and layout of the office unit, lease factors, and the current market situation.[24]

---

[19] See Table 2 and Table 3

[20] Cf. Rohmert, W. (2002), p. 5

[21] Cf. Deutsche Gesellschaft für Immobilienfonds (2008), w/o pages, Schulte, K.-W. /Wiffler, M. (2006), p. 418

[22] Strictly speaking, a time series of average or prime office rents cannot be categorized as an index, but rather as a comparative measure. Cf. Thomas, M. (1997), p. 36

[23] Cf. Maurer, R. /Sebastian, S. (2000), p. 13-14

[24] See Figure 1

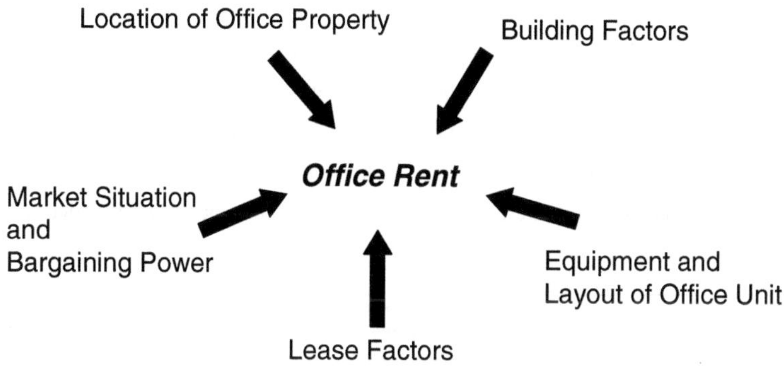

Figure 1: Office Rent Determinants[25]

Office rent is the price a tenant pays for the right to use a given amount of office space for a particular time period.[26] This right is embedded in an office lease agreement. Therefore, it is possible to classify an office lease agreement as an economic good that embraces the various office rent determinants. Because the office rent determinants take different values, it becomes clear that office leases are heterogeneous goods. In other words, each office lease consists of a bundle of characteristics (office rent determinants), each of which is integral to the office property and lease. Hence, each office lease agreement has its own quality.[27]

The following examples have been chosen for their simplicity but will illuminate the problem and most of its basic issues that real estate practitioners are currently facing when it comes to German office rent indices. For the sake of simplicity, it is assumed that only two lease agreements were concluded per time period and that all lease agreements differ only in their lease length, in the building age of their underlying property, and in the level of office rent. As mentioned, the majority of office rents indices are calculated using simple averages of contract rents. Table 4 shows the effect of this methodology. The average office rent in both time periods (i.e. t and t+1) amounts to 12.50 EUR per month per sqm. Real estate practitioners (e.g., investors) would therefore conclude that the office rental market is stable and that no price changes occurred between the time periods. A closer investigation, however, reveals that the average lease

[25] Adapted from Heyser, H. (2006), p. 17
[26] Cf. Ball, M., et al. (1998), p. 19
[27] Cf. Dunse, N. /Jones, C. (1998), p. 299

term in time period t+1 is 2.5 years shorter and the office properties four years newer. In other words, the office rental market changes and office rents were not stable as in time period t+1, therefore office users could let office space with a higher quality and to more flexible conditions (shorter lease length) than in the time period t. Obviously, the office rental market is a downturn. A landlord holding an office property with the average quality of time period t, therefore, cannot expect to successfully let his office space at 12.50 in time period t+1.

Time Period	Lease Contract	Lease Length (in years)	Building Age (Building Quality)	Office Rent per Month in EUR per sqm
t	A	5	10	10.00
t	B	10	5	15.00
Average in t		*7.5*	*7.5*	***12.50***
t+1	C	2	5	10.00
t+1	D	8	1	15.00
Average t+1		*5*	*3*	***12.50***

Table 4: Example 1

This problem is not only restricted to intertemporal comparison but also to interregional comparison of office rents. The same figures and assumption are used in the following example which represents a comparison of the office rental market in Berlin and Frankfurt.[28] From the comparison of the average office rents, one would come to the conclusion that the level of office rent for Frankfurt and Berlin is the same. Again, a closer look would reveal that office tenants in Berlin have to pay the office rent for older office space and have less flexible lease conditions. In other words, the office rental market is more attractive for landlords and developers in the Berlin than in Frankfurt.

Time Period	Lease Contract	Lease Length (in years)	Building Age (Building Quality)	Office Rent per Month in EUR per sqm
Berlin	A	5	10	10.00
Berlin	B	10	5	15.00
Average in Berlin		*7.5*	*7.5*	***12.50***
Frankfurt	C	2	5	10.00
Frankfurt	D	8	1	15.00
Average in Frankfurt		*5*	*3*	***12.50***

Table 5: Example 2

These examples illustrate the problems of office rent indices based on a simple or weighted average methodology as they cannot distinguish between movements in prices

[28] See Table 5

and changes in the characteristics. The fact, that the publishers of these office rent indices neither give any information about the quality of underlying office buildings nor any details about the underlying lease agreements which has important for the various users of the index, including appraisers, investors and public.sector policy makers aggravates the problem.[29]

The office rents published so far, respectively the office rent indices, based on simple or weighted average are therefore inappropriate for any use in real estate analysis (e.g., portfolio analysis, valuation, and lease negotiations)[30] [31] beyond indicating a trend in real estate rental markets. *Drummer (2007)* points out that office rent indices published at present have limited meaningfulness because of incentive packages that include rent-free periods, takeover of removal costs, and liabilities assumed by the landlord.[32] In addition, from a statistical point of view, these office rent indices contradict "[…] the fundamental principle of price statistics that 'like' shall be compared with 'like' only."[33] Therefore, a more robust index construction methodology - one that takes the different qualities of office leases into account - is needed for the compilation of office rent indices.

The aim of this thesis is one of the classic goals of price statistics: the quantification of the true price change of a given good with a certain quality. As *Brachinger (2003)* points out, "[…] the problem is that qualities change in time and the goods of today are no more the same as yesterday. So the goods actually available on the market are no more directly comparable with those which were available before. Therefore for price comparisons, prices have to be quality adjusted."[34]

[29] Cf. Tu, Y., et al. (2004), p. 307

[30] See Section 1.4 for the different applications and uses office rent indices in the field of real estate.

[31] See Section 6.2.3 for the different application of the developed hedonic office rent indices (HORIX) in this thesis.

[32] Cf. Drummer, M. (2007), p. 41

[33] Hoffmann, J. /Lorenz, A. (2006), p. 2

[34] Brachinger, H. W. (2003), p. 1

In summary, the following problems regarding office rent indices in Germany are observed:

- Published office rent indices show significant differences and inconsistencies. Consequently, rather than making the real estate market more transparent, they cause confusion among its participants.
- Office rent indices are compiled by computing the average of contractual rents or expert judgments. These methodologies neglect the fact that office leases are heterogeneous goods; therefore, they contradict the basic principle of price statistics, which requires that prices be quality adjusted for price comparisons.
- Because of the lack of robust and consistent index construction methodologies, market participants, using current office rent indices, obtain a broad trend rather than an exact price movement of office rental space.
- Due to the aforementioned reasons, the application of these office rents and office rent indices in any real estate analysis should be discouraged.
- In a nutshell, the German real estate market lacks of office rent indices that can be used for real estate analyses in which office rents play a key role (e.g., valuation, investment, project development, and lease negotiations).

1.2 Aim and Objectives

The aim of this dissertation is to develop rent indices for office properties in German metropolitan areas that take into account the heterogeneity of office leases and are thus considered to be constant quality indices, so-called hedonic office rent indices (HORIX). In less technical terms and at the risk of anticipating the results, this thesis attempts to provide office rent indices in which the influence of office rent determinants is controlled and adjusted. Two types of office rent indices based on common index formulae (Laspeyres and Paasche)[35] have been developed for each metropolitan area.

[35] See Section 2.2

	Laypeyres (L-HORIX)	Paasche (P-HORIX)
Berlin **(BER)**	*BER-L-HORIX*	*BER-P-HORIX*
Düsseldorf **(DUS)**	*DUS-L-HORIX*	*DUS-P-HORIX*
Frankfurt **(FRA)**	*FRA-L-HORIX*	*FRA-P-HORIX*
Hamburg **(HAM)**	*HAM-L-HORIX*	*HAM-P-HORIX*
Munich **(MUC)**	*MUC-L-HORIX*	*MUC-P-HORIX*

Table 6: Preview of Hedonic Office Rent Indices (HORIX)

The following objectives are derived from the aim of this dissertation:

I. to identify the significant determinants of office rent in Germany in regard to physical accommodation, location, and term structures;

II. to quantify the significant determinants of office rent in Germany in regard to physical accommodation, location, and term structures;

III. to construct constant quality rent indices for the major German real estate office markets, which are Berlin, Düsseldorf, Frankfurt, Hamburg, and Munich;

IV. to apply the developed rent indices and to identify the intertemporal and interregional pure rent changes.

1.3 Research Approach and Methodology

1.3.1 Research Approach

The aim and objectives make it clear that this thesis falls within the category of Applied-Science.[36] It uses the knowledge from fundamental and theoretical sciences and from practical experiences to solve problems and can be placed between fundamental research and practice. Moreover, the origin of the research problem lies between the practical and scientific worlds. From the practical world originates the research problem that office rent indices based upon average rents are biased and imprecise and might lead to false decisions. From the scientific world originates the research problem that homogeneous and heterogeneous goods have to be treated differently when it comes to index construction. It is inappropriate to apply to heterogeneous goods an index construction methodology designed for homogeneous goods.

---

36 See Figure 2

In general, the object of experience of this thesis is the office market in Germany, and the object of understanding is office rents. However, this classification is too broad, and therefore the thesis is categorized using a more specific approach to real estate research.

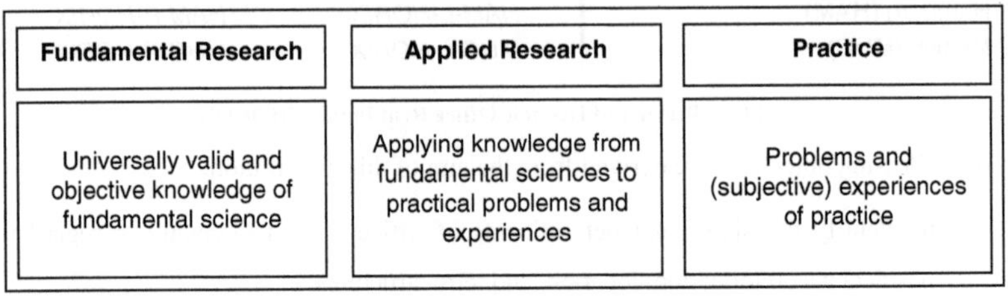

Figure 2: Classification of Applied Research[37]

The task of specifically classifying the adopted research approach is challenging. Many different approaches, from interdisciplinary to multidisciplinary to transaction based, have been introduced.[38]

In this thesis, the transaction-based approach (TAB) introduced by *Rottke (2007)* is adopted.[39] The TAB defines the real estate discipline as part of business administration and takes three different perspectives, namely, the management perspective, the institutional perspective, and the generic perspective. The ***management perspective*** has four subdivisions: the leadership perspective, which covers planning, organization, and control; the genesis perspective, which comprises real estate development, project management, and facility management; the strategic perspective, which focuses on the planning, regulation, and monitoring of real estate; and, finally, the functional perspective. The ***institutional perspective*** looks at the parties involved in the real estate management process, including developers, investors, construction companies, financiers, service companies, managers, agents, and users. The ***generic perspective*** looks at the different types of real estate assets (e.g., residential, office, retail, industrial, and special). Moreover, ancillary disciplines - namely, real estate law and real estate economics - and adjacent disciplines flank the real estate discipline. The main difference between ancillary and adjacent disciplines is that the latter form disciplines of their own.[40]

---

[37] Adapted from Breidenbach, M. (2005), p. 16

[38] Cf. Rottke, N. B. (2007), p. 1-19 gives a concise, but complete overview of different approaches.

[39] See Figure 3

[40] Cf. Rottke, N. B. (2007), p. 13-14

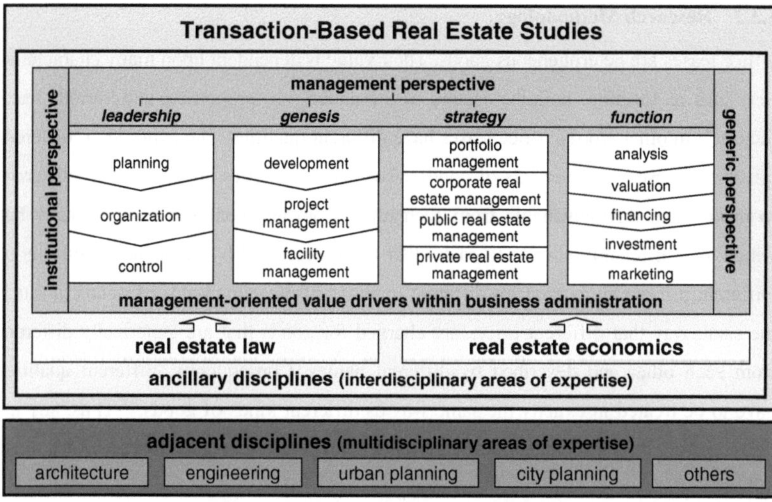

Figure 3: Transaction-based Real Estate Approach[41]

As evidenced by the summary of its aim and objectives, this thesis refers to several perspectives. Beginning with the institutional perspective, this thesis covers all participants involved in the real estate management process. However, the analysis specifically focuses on the user of office space (tenant). The only type of real estate asset that this thesis analyses from the generic perspective is the office market with office rent as the object of experience. Therefore, all aspects of the management perspective are concerned. Nevertheless, the focus is on the function of the management perspective, especially that of analysis and valuation.

As stated previously, each office lease contract has its own quality. The quality of an office lease contract is determined by the office building and by the content of the lease contract. Therefore, this thesis uses the knowledge from adjacent disciplines, especially architecture and engineering, and from ancillary disciplines, namely, real estate law and real estate economics. The latter become relevant because office rents are a function of supply and demand.[42]

---

[41] Ibid., p. 14

[42] See Section 3.3

1.3.2 Research Methodology

Office leases are heterogeneous goods. Their value is dependent upon many characteristics, such as location, building factors of the underlying properties, and various lease factors.[43] In other words, office leases have different qualities. The expression 'different qualities' is used to cover sets of goods whose characteristics are sufficiently different to make them distinguishable from each other from an economic point of view but which are sufficiently similar to each other to be described by the same generic term. Different prices are charged for different qualities of the same kinds of goods in much the same way that different prices are charged for goods that are generically different from each other and described by different names. Consequently, different qualities have to be treated in exactly the same way as different kinds of goods.[44] Thus, any index construction methodology that attempts to map office rents has to account for these different qualities inherent in office leases.

The construction of price indices for heterogeneous products is a well-known and frequently addressed problem. The hedonic method has been recommended as a reasonable approach to solving this problem.[45] For instance, the hedonic method has been used to develop price indices for computers, cars, and houses, and it is even used in official statistics.[46]

Although this approach was first developed to track automobile prices in the 1940s, it is well suited to real estate.[47] In this thesis, the office rent indices will be constructed using the hedonic method. Although the hedonic method will be explained in more detail later,[48] a brief presentation of its underlying theory is given here so that the research methodology can be better understood.

The starting point of the hedonic method is the hedonic hypothesis. The core of this hypothesis is that each good is determined by the set of all its characteristics. It is assumed that the corresponding characteristics vector determines the preferences of the

---

[43] Cf. Dunse, N. /Jones, C. (1998), p. 297-299

[44] Cf. Beer, M. (2006), p. 14-15

[45] Cf. Heckman, J., et al. (2003), p. 1-3, Brachinger, H. W. (2003), p. 1

[46] Cf. Sirmans, G. S., et al. (2005), p. 3-43, Hoesli, M., et al. (1997), p. 93-109, Wolverton, M. L. /Senteza, J. (2000), p. 235-253, Conniffe, D. /Duffy, D. (1999), p. 403-423, Maurer, R., et al. (2001), p. 1-25, Case, B. /Szymanoski, E. J. (1994), p. 483-496, Fenwick, D. /Ball, A. (2003), p. 11-15, Kokoski, M., et al. (2000), p. 1-52, Jonker, N. (2001), p. 1-4

[47] Cf. Hoesli, M. /MacGregor, B. D. (2000), p. 62, Gerhard, J. (2003), p. 117

[48] See Chapter 2

economic actors with respect to any good. Furthermore, it is assumed that a functional relationship exists between any good's price and its characteristics. The function is specified using the typical multiple regression technique.[49] If this approach is applied to office rents, the regression analysis enables researchers to estimate the implicit price of each attribute by relating the rent of a real estate unit to its individual attributes.[50]

$$\text{Rent} = f\,(\textit{location, building characteristics, and lease characteristics})$$

Equation 1-1: Basic Hedonic Rent Model

It can be concluded from the above formula that the hedonic method has two significant applications in real estate, depending on whether the analysis is concentrated on the right-hand side or the left-hand side of the equation.[51] If the analysis focuses on the right-hand side, it can be used to estimate the rental value of a property on the basis of its characteristics (see Objective I & II). As can be seen from the function, the characteristics of a property (its lease contract) are valued using its regression coefficients, and the rental value can be estimated by summing the price of the characteristics. The left-hand side can be used to construct real estate rent indices (see Objective III). The price coefficient of each characteristic is estimated by means of a cross-section regression. Such a regression is reestimated for each time period t. Then a lease contract with standard characteristics is valued for each time period, and an index is constructed.[52] The goal is to develop a real estate rent index, not a performance index or total return index.[53]

As this thesis seeks to utilise hedonic analysis to develop a constant office rent index, some methodological issues raised by the hedonic theory and by the use of the multiple regression techniques have to be overcome and clarified. First, it is essential that the rent data sample provide a fair representation of what real tenants are paying. Second, the appropriate set of variables has to be selected and included in the analysis.

The representation of rent data sample is often beyond the researcher's influence. However, this thesis uses over 22,000 office leases provided by the Rental Database of In-

---

[49] Cf. Fletcher, M., et al. (2004), p. 89, Beer, M. (2006), p. 49-51

[50] Cf. Dunse, N. /Jones, C. (1998), p. 297, Hoesli, M., et al. (1997), p. 68, Slade, B. A. (2000), p. 2, Hoesli, M. /MacGregor, B. D. (2000), p. 62 Wheaton, W. C. /Torto, R. G. (1995), p. 133

[51] Cf. Björklund, K., et al. (2002), p. 67

[52] Cf. Plewka, T. (2003), p. 174-181, Hoesli, M. /MacGregor, B. D. (2000), p. 62-66

[53] Performance indices or total return indices include not only the income but also capital returns.

vestment Property Databank Germany (IPD Germany). Given the number of leases, it can be assumed that the data is probably representative.[54]

This thesis tackles the issue of the appropriate set of variables for the regression equation from different angles. Because research on German office rents is scarce, an international literature review that aims to identify all possible variables is provided. The question of whether these variables also determine the level of office rents in Germany so far remains unanswered. Therefore, a survey among German real estate professionals has been conducted.[55] This survey indicates which variables believed to be driving office rents and, thus, should be included in the hedonic rent model.

1.3.3 Theoretical Framework

From this brief description of the hedonic method, as well as from later stages of this thesis,[56] it becomes clear that the theoretical underpinnings of the hedonic theory and, therefore, of this thesis lies in the field of consumer demand theory. The theory is based on the *homo economicus*[57] and builds up on the following assumptions:[58]

- All goods possess objective characteristics relevant to the choices people make among different collections of goods.
- It is the characteristics, rather than the goods, that are the ultimate objects of consumer satisfaction. The consumers are endowed with preferences for collections of characteristics, and the preferences for goods are indirect or derived in the sense that goods are required only to produce characteristics.

In addition, the hedonic theory itself amounts to a description of competitive market equilibrium in a plane of several dimensions on which both producers and consumers

---

[54] The question of to what extent the rent data sample is representative of the overall office rental market will be discussed in chapter five. See Section 5.1.1

[55] See Section 4.3

[56] See Sections 2.1 and 3.3

[57] The term "homo economicus", or "economic man", is used for an approximation of a human that acts to obtain the highest possible well-being for himself given available information, about opportunities and other constraints, both natural and institutional, on his ability to achieve his predetermined goals. He is seen as rational in the sense that well-being as defined by the utility function is optimized given perceived opportunities. In other words, the individual seeks to attain very specific and predetermined goals to the greatest extent with the least possible cost. Cf. Persky, J. (1995), p. 221-231, Gowdy, J. M. /Polimeni, R. I. (2005), p. 924-926, Bowles, S. /Gintis, H. (1993), p. 83-85, Badeen, D. (1999), p. 62-65, Bishop, M. (2004), w/o pages [Online Database]

[58] Cf. Bowbrick, P. (1994), p. 2-3, Drèze, J. H. /Hagen, K. P. (1978), p. 493

allocate. It is determined by some market-clearing conditions, as defined by *Rosen (1974)*:[59]

- Amounts of characteristics offered by producres at every point on the plane must equal amounts demanded by consumers choosing to locate there.
- Consumers base their decisions on maximising behaviour and producers base their decisions on maxisming profits
- Equilibrium prices are determined so that buyers and sellers are perfectly matched.
- No individual can improve his position, and all optimum choices are feasible.

From the assumptions and conditions defined above, it becomes clear that as in most real estate studies,[60] the hedonic theory is nested in the broad field of neoclassical economics,[61] with its emphasis specifically on perfect competition and equilibrium.[62]

It goes without saying that, due to the fact that the hedonic theory relies on the neoclassical foundations, some critiques have evolved, as almost every market suffers from "imperfection" and experiences of rapid dynamic change, which seem the contrary to stability and equilibrium.[63] As *Dunse /Jones (1998)* point out, "[...] in the light of market imperfections, disequilibrium could be a more realistic assumption but the data required for this form of modelling places this out of the scope of most research. Despite these failings, the technique has been widely applied to housing market analysis and has become well established."[64] Nevertheless, this thesis acknowledges these critiques,

---

[59] Cf. Rosen, S. (1974), p. 35-36

[60] Cf. Gibler, K. M. /Nelson, S. L. (2003), p. 63

[61]. The term "neoclassical economics" refers to the introduction of the economic theory in the late 19th century by W. Stanley Jevons, Alfred Marshall, Carl Menger and Leon Walras. Neoclassical economics is the grouping of a number of schools of thought in economics. There is not complete agreement on what is meant by neoclassical economics; in particular, vision, problem domains, and particular concerns vary among neoclassical economists. However, neoclassical economics basically rest on three assumptions although some branches of neoclassical economics may have different approaches: (1) Peoples have rational preferences among outcomes that can be identified and associated with a value; (2) individuals maximise utility and firms maximise profits; and (3) people act independently on the basis of full and relevant information. Cf. Shiller, R. J. (2006), p. 2

[62] Cf. Berliant, M. /McMillen, D. P. (2006), p. 118-131, Drèze, J. H. /Hagen, K. P. (1978), p. 498-509, Nesheim, L. (2006), p. 11-14, Nitzan, J. (1992), p. 155-178, Rosen, S. (1974), p. 34-55

[63] Cf. Bowbrick, P. (1994), p. 42-45, Nitzan, J. (1992), p. 155-177

[64] Dunse, N. /Jones, C. (1998), p. 301

elaborates on them,[65] and derives their implications and consequences for the development of hedonic rent indices.[66]

1.4 Relevance of the Study

The relevance of this study can be explained by the different applications of office rent indices (focus on the left-hand side of the hedonic function) and by the analysis of office rent determinants (focus on the right-hand side of the hedonic function). Like stock price indices, real estate rent indices have descriptive and operational fields of application.[67]

Descriptive Applications

Because rent is a significant variable in determining the value of income-producing real estate, rent indices can be seen as value indices that map the periodic movements of asset prices. Therefore, rent indices serve as a **market indicator** and provide useful information not only to those who study the market but also to practitioners and investors who participate in the market.[68] Furthermore, as market indicators, rent indices enhance the transparency of the real estate market.[69]

Because an increase in real estate rents can be interpreted as a sign of inflation, real estate indices that track rent changes can serve as an **economic indicator.**[70]

Furthermore, rents are forward-looking indications of market conditions and result from negotiated lease contracts that commit market participants to future cash flow.[71] Therefore, a real estate index that measures the changes in rent also can be useful as a **forecasting tool.**

Operational Applications

A real estate index that is based on rents and adjusts for different qualities allows for a comparison between the rental incomes of an individual property and the real estate index. Therefore, it is possible to analyse whether the property is under- or over-rented.

[65] See Sections 3.4.1, 3.4.2, 3.5.1.1 and 3.5.2
[66] See Sections 3.4.3 and 3.5.2.3
[67] Cf. Plewka, T. (2003), p. 136
[68] Cf. Gatzlaff, D. /Geltner, D. (1998), p. 2
[69] Cf. Thomas, M. (1997), p. 13
[70] Cf. Ibid.p. 14
[71] Cf. Webb, B. R. /Fisher, J. D. (1996), p. 16

Such a real estate index can be considered a **benchmarking instrument** in the field of portfolio management.

In addition, a constant quality rent index provides for the building of a theoretical forward-lease contract. Because the actual market conditions are reflected in such an index, the real estate market risk is quantified and is therefore tradable. In other words, the introduction of real estate **derivatives**[72] **(future and options)** would be possible.[73]

Rent plays an important role in any real estate valuation or investment decision. Therefore, a constant quality rent index is beneficial to real estate developers, investors, service providers, and real estate users alike.[74] In addition, because it is no longer certain that well-located offices lease up quickly, it is essential that all market players fully understand and develop methods for anticipating changing market conditions.[75] Some examples highlight the importance and usefulness of this study:

Real estate developers will benefit in two ways from this research. First, they will gain knowledge of which factors have the greatest influence on rent. Based upon this knowledge, they can focus on the value-driving factors during the project development process. Second, as the estimation of the market rent becomes more precise, this research will enhance their development calculations.

Real estate investors will likewise have better insight while making investments. For instance, by using a constant quality rent index, they can benchmark different investment alternatives of office buildings. Moreover, understanding the underlying rent determinants allows investors to develop better price expectations and make more informed investment decisions. This research satisfies the demands of *Webb /Fisher (1996)*, who point out that "more accurate [...] information is needed for the capital markets to favourably respond to financial requests from this asset class in future."[76]

This research is of great value **for real estate service providers** - especially valuation companies. Although valuation is based on professional judgment, it is a subjective

---

[72] The term derivative refers to any investment with an underlying value that is dependent in another security, pool of securities or index. Cf. Brueggeman, W. B. /Fisher, J. D. (2007), p. 583

[73] Cf. Plewka, T. (2003), p. 200-201

[74] Cf. Mills, E. S. (1992), p. 273

[75] Cf. Dowall, D. E. (1988), p. 34

[76] Webb, B. R. /Fisher, J. D. (1996), p. 2

opinion of value.[77] The comparison method in valuation is also biased, as it is impossible to have properties that have exactly the same characteristics.[78] This valuation technique breaks down, especially in overbuilt markets, because real rents are changing rapidly, and rent incentives are widespread and variable.[79] The findings of this research will support valuers because the hedonic regression analysis allows them to quantify and to price the different attributes of the property. They will no longer have to rely solely on their extensive knowledge of the local market.[80]

Real estate users will have a method for analysing whether they pay rents that are over or under the market rent. Hence, a constant quality rent index is a helpful tool in lease negotiations.

Finally, **scholars** and **practitioners** in real estate will profit from this research, for it will contribute to a more transparent office market in Germany. Such a market is desperately needed.[81] Transparency is a general prerequisite for successful real estate investments, and only transparent markets can create confidence among professional investors.[82] It should also be kept in mind that, in the recent past, the German office market experienced unexpected volatility in rental rates, which resulted in significant financial losses. There is still much to learn about the determinants of office rental rates.

---

[77] Cf. Dunse, N. /Jones, C. (1998), p. 297
[78] Cf. Bone-Winkel, S., et al. (2005), p. 16-19
[79] Cf. Hendershott, P. H. (1996), p. 57-58
[80] Cf. Dunse, N. /Jones, C. (1998), p. 297
[81] Cf. Degener, A. (2005), p. 7-8
[82] Cf. Schulte, K.-W., et al. (2005b), p. 90

1.5 Outline of the Research

This thesis is divided into two parts and has seven chapters. In the first part, it provides the theoretical background on hedonic office rent indices and the office market, and then it presents empirical analyses resulting in the application of the hedonic office rent indices. In the second part, the thesis offers an international analysis of the office property market and of office property rents and, at a later stage, focuses on German office property markets. This thesis is also built on the following sequence of questions:

Chapter 2: What constitutes the hedonic theory?

Chapter 3: Why is the hedonic theory suited to office leases, and why is the variable office rent important in real estate economics?

Chapter 4: What are the determinants that influence office rent?

Chapter 5: How can a hedonic office rent index be developed?

Chapter 6: What interregional and intertemporal rent changes are observed in the major office rental markets?

Chapter two introduces the theory of the construction of hedonic office rent indices. The construction follows a two-stage process, namely, the estimation and the composition. The estimation stage (section 2.1) demonstrates the underlying concept of the hedonic theory and identifies which set of characteristics is important. The composition stage (section 2.2), building on the knowledge gained from the estimation stage, explains and compares various index formulae to develop the actual hedonic office rent index.

Chapter three lays out the fundamentals for the thesis. It not only provides the rationale for why office leases are heterogeneous goods (section 3.1) but also, gives an overview of the various principles, namely, price, rent, value, and worth (section 3.2). In addition, this chapter looks at other fields of real estate research and analyses their implications for the development of hedonic office rent indices. Section 3.3 explains through office market dynamics why rent, not price, was chosen as the centre of the analysis. Finally, while section 3.4 considers the market efficiency of office property, section 3.5 outlines the cycle of real estate office theory and examines the different behaviour it causes among office users and landlords. Both issues have different implications for the development of hedonic office rent indices. The changing behaviour of office users and landlords during the cycle stages affects the estimation stage, whereas the degree of market efficiency of office property indicates the level of expectation for hedonic office rent indices (a result of the composition stage) as compared with the indices of other assets.

Chapter four represents the preparatory work for the estimation stage. Beginning with a review of international literature, it scrutinizes which factors influencing office rents have been shown to be important in other office property markets (section 4.1). The review is not limited to quantitative research studies but also embraces qualitative studies. Section 4.2 describes the German office rental markets and analyses whether the results of the preceding section can be transferred to Germany. Moreover, a survey among German real estate professionals sheds further light on this matter (section 4.3). Finally, the implications for the empirical analysis are discussed (section 4.4).

Chapter five represents the main empirical analysis and is the nucleus of this thesis. It consists of two main parts. The first part deals with the data-mining process and the transformation process (sections 5.1 to 5.3). The second part constitutes the estimate stage of the hedonic function. Here, regression analysis is conducted and its result interpreted (5.3 to 5.5).

Before any office rent index is developed, it is necessary to analyse whether the underlying data source is reliable and the office leases are representative - in other words, whether the data sufficiently covers the market (section 5.1). Thereafter, the data has to undergo a screening process (section 5.2). This process includes plausibility checks and data transformations. Although the problem of missing values remains unmentioned or ignored in most real estate research studies, this thesis takes up this important topic (section 5.3), outlines the types of missing values (section 5.3.1), presents the strategies for handling them (section 5.3.2), performs a missing values analysis on the underlying data (section 5.3.3.), and replaces the missing data using the multiple imputation method (section 5.3.4). The purpose of the extensive discussion of the missing values problem is not only to provide insights into the data-mining process but also to increase the awareness among real estate practitioners and researchers of this important, but often neglected, issue.

Once the missing values have been replaced, the data enter the main empirical analysis and estimation stage of the construction of hedonic office rent indices (section 5.4). Based on the findings of chapter four, the hypotheses, econometric models, and statistical tests are formulated and explained (section 5.4.1). After the regression analysis is run and its assumptions checked (section 5.4.2), the regression results are interpreted, and their implications for the final construction of the indices in the composition stage are discussed (section 5.4.3).

In *chapter six,* the thesis enters the composition stage and uses the results of the previous chapter to develop two different types of hedonic office rent indices (section 6.1). Thereafter, these indices are applied so as to discover the interregional and intertemporal rent changes of the largest German office property markets, namely, Berlin, Düsseldorf, Frankfurt, Hamburg, and Munich (section 6.2). Finally, the hedonic office rent indices (HORIX) are evaluated and compared with the office rent indices published by the German Society of Property Researchers (GIF-ORIX), a market representative (section 6.3), giving a final assessment of the necessity and usefulness of hedonic office rent indices for real estate market participants.

Chapter seven summarizes the results of the previous chapters (section 7.1) and points out the limitations of the study, thus indicating the direction in which real estate research should continue. The following figure pcitures the outline of the research.[83]

[83] See Figure 4

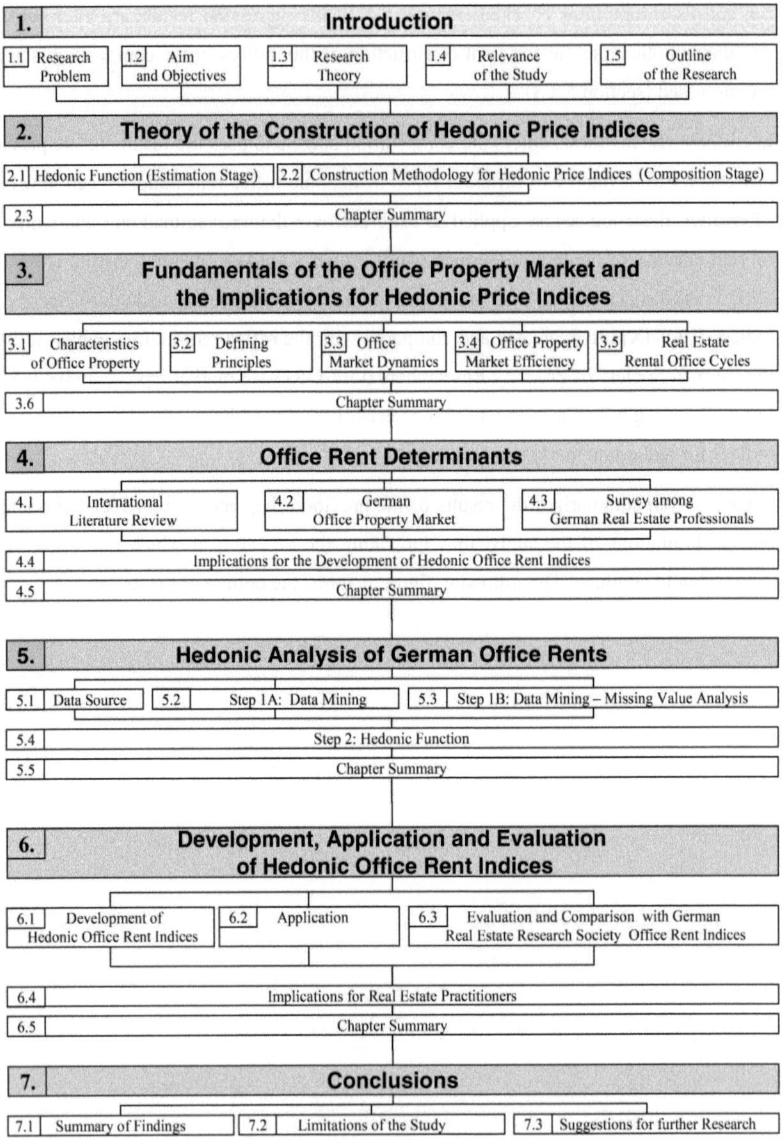

Figure 4: Outline of the Research

2 Theory of the Construction of Hedonic Price Indices

In order to fully understand what the strengths and weaknesses of the hedonic method are and how it provides a more robust methodology for the development of office rent indices, an in-depth discussion of its theoretical underpinnings is necessary. *Triplett (2004)* points out that each hedonic price index study has two empirical parts. The researcher has to first estimate the hedonic function and then decide how to use the hedonic function to calculate the price index.[84] *Wallace (1996)* likewise states that "[...] it is useful to view the theoretical implications by distinguishing between the estimation stage concerning the appropriate specification of the hedonic price function [...] and the composition stage in which the estimated hedonics are used to obtain the price indexes."[85] This chapter is organized in a corresponding manner. First, the underlying theory of the hedonic function is explained, and second, a price index[86] is developed from the hedonic function. Thereafter, some practical issues that will be addressed later in this thesis are highlighted.

2.1 Hedonic Function (Estimation Stage)

The hedonic function relates the prices of heterogeneous goods with the quantities of characteristics contained in them:

$$P = h(Z)$$

Equation 2-1

P is an *n*-element vector of prices and (Z) is a *k x n* matrix of characteristics. Hence, there exist *n* varieties of the product and *k* characteristics. This is the basic hedonic function and accounts for all heterogeneous goods.[87] In the context of this thesis, the product is a lease contract for an underlying office rental unit.[88] The term 'hedonic' is used because it is determined by the different qualities of the heterogeneous good and

---

[84] Cf. Triplett, J. E. (2004), p. 136

[85] Wallace, N. (1996), p. 38-39

[86] The purpose of this thesis is to develop hedonic office rent indices. In chapter 3 it will be shown, that rent is the price paid by tenants in order to obtain a certain amount of space over a specific time. As in most academic literature the term price is used to explain the hedonic theory, the same terminology will be used.

[87] Cf. Brachinger, H. W. (2003), p. 2-3

[88] An office rental unit comprises the area unit that is usable by the tenant and lettable by the landlord. Cf. Flüshöh, C. /Stottrop, D. (2005), p. 75

by the 'pleasure' these would bring to the purchaser. In economic terms, 'pleasure' should be translated as 'utility.'[89]

The economic interpretation of hedonic functions lies in the hedonic hypothesis. The hedonic hypothesis states that the heterogeneous goods are aggregations of their characteristics. The economic behaviour does not relate simply to the goods but also to the characteristics. In addition, the hedonic hypothesis postulates that the transaction of a heterogeneous good is a tied-in sale of a bundle of characteristics. In other words, the price of a good is the aggregation of the prices and quantities of its characteristics. *Triplett (2004)* illustrates this notion with his example of a grocery cart. If one imagines that a heterogeneous good is a filled shopping cart, then the groceries in the cart are the characteristics of the heterogeneous good. The consumer does not buy the cart but rather the groceries in the cart. When the groceries are purchased at the checkout line of a store, the aggregation of prices paid for groceries multiplied by the quantities purchased yields the total expenditure on groceries.[90] In the office property market, a tenant pays for the flow of services derived from the characteristics of the office rental unit per period of time.

The hedonic hypothesis implies that the characteristics of heterogeneous goods are the true variables in utility functions. Thus, the consumer utility function can be written as

$$Q = Q(Z, x)$$

Equation 2-2

where Q is utility, x is a vector of other, homogeneous consumption goods, and, for expositional simplicity, only one heterogeneous good in the system is specified with characteristics, (Z).[91]

Equation 2-2 also can be interpreted as a production function, where Q is the output, which has some heterogeneous inputs, with characteristics, (Z), and other, homogeneous inputs, x. If a production function is intended, then the hedonic function has to be rewritten as

[89] Cf. Triplett, J. E. (2004), p. 223, Day, B. (2001), p. 25
[90] Cf. Triplett, J. E. (2004), p. 223-224
[91] Cf. Ibid., p. 224-225, Jonker, N. (2001), p. 5-7

$$t(Z,K,L,M) = 0$$

Equation 2-3

Because the production of heterogeneous goods can be seen as transformation, the characteristics Z are produced with the standard inputs of capital K, labour L, and materials M. As a matter of fact, the inputs can be heterogeneous.[92]

So far, it is understood that hedonic functions can be interpreted either from the demand, or user, side (demander for office space) or from the supply, or producer, side (landlords). The following two sections illuminate both sides and explain why the approach of one side will be followed in this thesis.

2.1.1 Demand or User Side

In general, the user's choice of characteristics is determined in a two-stage budgeting process. A company looking for new or additional office space first decides on the budget for office rent expenses. After the level of office rent expenses is determined, the company decides how this budget will be allocated among the characteristics.[93] In other words, as in consumer theory, utility is maximized subject to a budget constraint.[94]

$$MaxQ(x,Z,;\alpha)$$
$$s.t.y = x + P(Z)$$

Equation 2-4

where y is the total budget of the company, Q is the utility, x is the composite good representing all other goods outside the office-property market, Z is a vector of office characteristics of the office rental unit $(Z = z_1,...z_n)$, and α is a vector of socioeconomic characteristics.[95] The latter is necessary because office users can no longer be considered one monolithic group.[96] Companies choose levels of x and Z to maximize utility. The following equation is the first order condition of equation 2-4 and states that the

---

[92] Cf. Triplett, J. E. (2004), p. 224-225

[93] Cf. Ibid., p. 226-228

[94] Thereby, the hedonic price functions are always nonlinear, since office space demanders are unable to repackage the offered office rental unit. In other words, office users cannot break up the office rental unit into its constituent characteristics and enjoy the benefit of each characteristic separate from the whole. The possibility of repackaging is referred to as arbitrage opportunity. If an arbitrage is not possible, the budget constraint is nonlinear. Cf. Day, B. (2001), p. 26

[95] Cf. Clauw, F. (2005), p. 5, Rosen, S. (1974), p. 38-39

[96] Cf. Dowall, D. E. (1988), p. 35

ratio of marginal utilities equals the marginal implicit price of the characteristic. In other words, the ratio of marginal utilities is the marginal rate of substitution between z_i and x, which describes the preparedness of a company to give up a certain quantity of one good to obtain an extra unit of another good, ceteris paribus. In addition, the term $h_i(z, y-P(Z);\alpha)$ can be seen as the marginal rate of substitution function and as the hedonic demand function.[97]

When the marginal utility of money is constant, y-P(Z) will disappear in the marginal rate of substitution functions, and they will revert to traditional demand functions. When the marginal utility of money is not constant, y-P(Z) will appear in the demand functions.[98]

$$\frac{Q_{z_i}}{Q_x} = \frac{\partial Q/\partial z_i}{\partial Q/\partial x} = \frac{\partial P}{\partial z_i} = P_i = h_i(Z, y-P(Z);\alpha)$$

Equation 2-5

In this context, the term 'utility,' rather than 'profit,' is used because office rental units not only represent a cost factor to the company but also provide benefits.

Rosen (1974) formulates a user's action by defining a bid function $\theta(Z,q,y;\alpha)$ to stress the spatial context of the problem. In the context of the office property market, this function indicates the willingness to pay rent for an office rental unit with characteristics Z, given a variable for budget y and a level of utility. It is defined by $Q(y-\theta,z_1...z_n;\alpha)=q$. The bid function can be demonstrated by bid curves, which are the inverted indifference curves. For a certain characteristic z_1 the optimal bundle $(\hat{x},\hat{z}_1)$ will be found on the tangency point between the highest indifference curve and the nonlinear budget constraint.[99] Similarly, a company maximizing its utility will choose the bundle of characteristics on the bid curve with the highest level of utility whilst still being able to fulfill the market conditions given by the hedonic price function.[100]

The slope of the hedonic price function and the slope of the bid function are the same. If a company wants an extra unit of characteristic z_1, its willingness to pay for that unit

[97] Cf. Bartik, T. J. (1987), p. 82, Clauw, F. (2005), p. 5, Rosen, S. (1974), p. 38-40, Day, B. (2001), p. 29-37

[98] Cf. Clauw, F. (2005), p. 5

[99] See Figure 5

[100] Cf. Clauw, F. (2005), p. 6, Rosen, S. (1974), p. 38

equals the market price of that extra unit. In addition, the chosen bundle of characteristics must be purchased by the market price as defined by the hedonic price function. This forms an upper envelope of different optimising bid functions.[101]

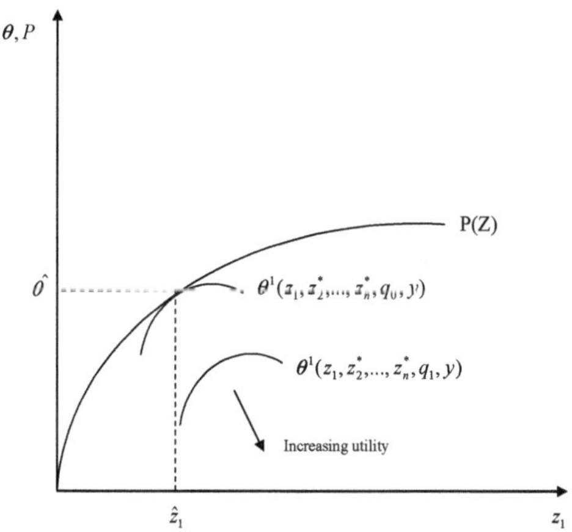

Figure 5: User Choice of Characteristic[102]

2.1.2 Supply, Producer, or Landlord Side

The landlords represent the supply side. They maximize their profits as follows:

$$Max \prod = M.P(Z) - C(M, Z; \beta)$$

Equation 2-6

where $C(M, Z; \beta)$ represents the total cost derived from minimizing factor costs to a joint production function constraint relating *M*, *Z*, and factors of production. *M(Z)* is the number of office units produced by a firm of designs offering specification *Z*. The shift parameter β reflects underlying parameters in the cost minimization problem, namely, factors prices and production function parameters. *C* is assumed to be convex with *C (0,Z)*, and the first derivatives to, respectively, *M* and z_i strictly positive. Furthermore, the production process is characterized by constant returns to scale.[103]

---

[101] Cf. Clauw, F. (2005), p. 6, Rosen, S. (1974), p. 40, Day, B. (2001), p. 38-45

[102] Clauw, F. (2005), p. 5

[103] Cf. Triplett, J. E. (2004), p. 229-330, Clauw, F. (2005), p. 7, Rosen, S. (1974), p. 41-43

The first order conditions of the optimal choice of M and Z require

$$P_i(Z)=\frac{\partial P}{\partial z_i}=\frac{\partial C}{\partial z_i}/M$$
$$P(Z)=C_M(M,z_1,...,z_n)$$

Equation 2-7

In other words, this implies that, in the optimal design, the marginal price for each characteristic equals the marginal cost per unit of increasing the amount of that characteristic. Furthermore, quantities are produced up to the point where unit revenue *P(Z)* equals marginal production costs, evaluated at the optimal bundle of characteristics.[104]

In his seminal paper, *Rosen (1974)* formulates an offer function $\phi(Z,\Pi;\beta)$. This function shows the price at which the producer will offer the office unit to obtain a particular profit level π, given a particular value of Z. The offer function can be solved for by using the following first order conditions:[105]

$$\Pi=M\phi-C(M,z_1,...,z_n)$$
$$C_M(M,z_1,...,z_n)=\phi$$

Equation 2-8

The offer function can be depicted by offer curves. A certain optimal bundle $(\hat{\phi},\hat{z}_1)$ will be found on the tangency point between the offer curves with the highest profit level whilst still being able to fulfill the market conditions given by the hedonic price function.[106] Differentiating both equations given the marginal reservation supply price for attribute i, increasing in z_i:[107]

$$\frac{\partial\phi}{\partial z_i}=\frac{C_{z_i}}{M}>0$$
$$\text{and}\quad\frac{\partial\phi}{\partial\pi}=\frac{1}{M}>0$$

Equation 2-9

---

[104] Cf. Clauw, F. (2005), p. 7
[105] Cf. Rosen, S. (1974), p. 42
[106] See Figure 6
[107] Cf. Clauw, F. (2005), p. 7-8

In general, there is a distribution of β across all potential suppliers. The producer equilibrium is then characterized by a family of offer functions that envelop the market hedonic price functions. The empirical content of β is anything that shifts cost conditions among firms.[108]

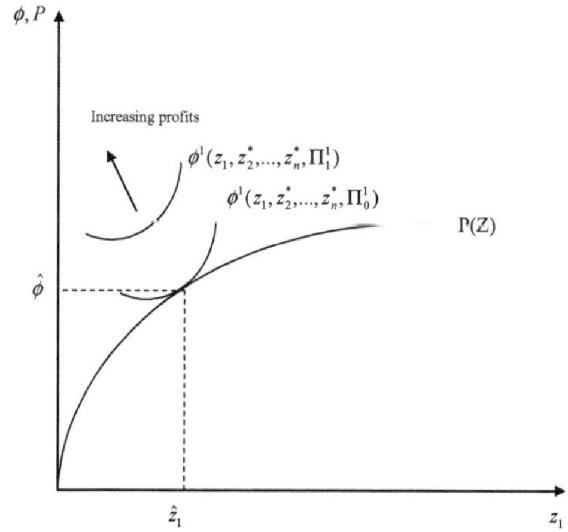

Figure 6: Landlord Choice of Characteristic[109]

2.1.3 Market Equilibrium

Different office users have different sets of bid curves, and different landlords have different sets of offer curves. Office users maximize their utility and look for the lowest possible bid, and landlords attempt to maximize their profits and look for the highest possible offer. Therefore, different choice points exist along the hedonic price function. Moreover, each point along the hedonic price function corresponds to tangency between the bid function of an office user and the offer function of a landlord.[110]

On the one hand, the requirement that the amount the consumer is willing to pay must be equal to the price (P(Z)) makes the optimal point between the bid function and price function. On the other hand, the requirement that the amount the landlord is willing to offer must be equal to the price (P(Z)) makes the optimal point to be the tangency point between the offer function and the price function. Therefore, it can be said that the ob-

---

108 Cf. Rosen, S. (1974), p. 43

109 Clauw, F. (2005), p. 8

110 Cf. Rosen, S. (1974), p. 44, Clauw, F. (2005), p. 8-9, Day, B. (2001), p. 46-48

servations that constitute P(Z) represent a joint envelope of a family of bid functions and a family of offer functions. In addition, it can be concluded that the hedonic model assumes a market equilibrium throughout the property market.[111]

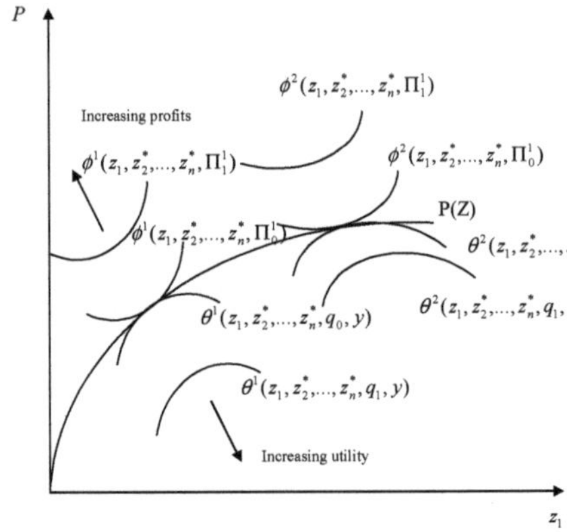

Figure 7: Market Equilibrium[112]

From the above discussion it can be deducted that one can model the hedonic price function by modeling either the supply side or the demand side. In this thesis, a demand side approach is followed. Because the stock of existing office rental units dominates the office property market in most areas and the supply of office rental units is fixed in the short run, it is assumed that office rent is demand determined.[113]

Some researchers go beyond the estimation of the hedonic function and attempt to identify supply and demand parameters for individual characteristics. This undertaking, which is often referred to as 'the second stage' hedonic price model, constitutes a separate field of research, as different methodological problems have to be tackled.[114]

2.1.4 Interpretation of Regression Coefficients in Hedonic Functions

The hedonic price function is determined using the common multiple regression technique. Thereby, the dependent variable price is regressed against the characteristics that are thought to be of highest value to the user. The regression coefficients measure the

---

111 Cf. Clauw, F. (2005), p. 8-9, Rosen, S. (1974), p. 44-45, Day, B. (2001), p. 46-48

112 Clauw, F. (2005), p. 9

113 Cf. Geltner, D. M., et al. (2007), p. 6-7, Ball, M., et al. (1998), p. 22-24, Kurzrock, B.-M. (2007), p. 88, Jedem, U. (2006), p. 32, Day, B. (2001), p. 47

114 Cf. Brasington, D. M. /Hite, D. (2005), p. 4-5, Malpezzi, S. (2002), p. 59

implicit prices for characteristics. From a user's perspective, the implicit prices ought to have some relation to what the users are paying for units of the characteristic. In hedonic studies, it is common to inspect estimated hedonic functions for the plausibility of the estimated coefficients.[115] This undertaking again implies that the appropriate set of characteristics has been included in the hedonic function. In other words, the search for the characteristics for which the user is willing to pay is of utmost importance. If the wrong variables have been selected, then the hedonic function and, as a consequence, the hedonic price index are wrong and useless. *Triplett (2004)* underscores this point: "[...] the first principle for conducting a hedonic study is: Know your product."[116]

Besides the in-depth search for the correct set of characteristics, which will be undertaken separately,[117] the interpretation of the regression coefficient depends on the choice of the functional form of the hedonic function. In hedonic price studies, the following four functional forms are widely used:[118]

The simplest functional form is the ordinary linear approach given by

$$p=\beta+\sum_{i=1}^{K}\beta_i z_i+u$$

Equation 2-10

with hedonic prices

$$\frac{\partial p}{\partial z_i}=\beta_i$$

Equation 2-11

The regression coefficient β_i (i=1,...,K) indicates the marginal change of the price with respect to a change of the i-th characteristic z_i of the good. The term u represents a disturbance or error in the regression model.

---

[115] Cf. Triplett, J. E. (2004), p. 137-138

[116] Ibid., p. 138

[117] See Chapter 4

[118] Cf. Maurer, R., et al. (2001), p. 4-6, Li, W., et al. (2006), p. 13-14, Brachinger, H. W. (2003), p. 3-4

Another functional form is the semilog form given by

$$\ln p = \ln \beta_o + \sum_{i=1}^{K} \beta_i z_i + u$$

Equation 2-12

with the hedonic prices

$$\frac{\partial p}{\partial z_i} = \beta_i p$$

Equation 2-13

Here the regression coefficients can be interpreted as growth rates. The coefficient β_i (i=1,...,K) indicates the rate at which the price increases at a certain level, given the characteristic z.

In addition, a double log form can be chosen as the functional form given by

$$\ln p = \ln \beta_o + \sum_{i=1}^{K} \beta_i \ln z_i + u$$

Equation 2-14

with the hedonic prices

$$\frac{\partial p}{\partial z_i} = \frac{\beta_i}{z_i} p$$

Equation 2-15

The regression coefficients can be interpreted as partial elasticities. The coefficient β_i (i=1,..., K) indicates how much in percent terms the price p increases at a certain level if the i-th characteristic z_i changes by one percent.

Few hedonic studies recommend the Box-Cox form given by

$$p^{\lambda} = \beta_0 + \sum_{i=1}^{K} \beta_i z_i + u$$

Equation 2-16

where the Box-Cox transformation is defined as

$$p^{(\lambda)} = \begin{cases} \dfrac{p^{\lambda}-1}{\lambda} & if\ \lambda \neq 0 \\ \ln p & if\ \lambda = 0 \end{cases}$$

Equation 2-17

The linear model results if λ equals 1, whereas a log-linear or semilog model results if λ equals 0. The interpretation of regression coefficients of the Box-Cox functional form is difficult, as the regression's coefficients are artificial.[119]

More recently, some hedonic studies have questioned whether the hedonic function must follow a parametric form. Instead, they suggest a semi-parametric model:

$$\ln p = \beta_0 + \sum_{i=1}^{K} \beta_i z_i + g(z_1, z_2, \ldots z_n) + u$$

Equation 2-18

The terms β_0, $\sum_{i=1}^{K} \beta_i z_i$ and u represent the linear part of the model and are interpreted as in Equation 2-12, and the term $g(z_1, z_2, \ldots z_n)$ is the nonparametric shape function.[120]

An *a priori* choice for one of the above-mentioned functional forms does not exist. The functional form has to be determined empirically.[121] Nevertheless, the research objective partly influences the choice. If the research objective scrutinizes the impact of specific characteristics on the price, then the Box-Cox or semi-parametric model is not appropriate, due to the problematic interpretation of the regression coefficients. However, if the research objective attempts to develop an index, then the Box-Cox model provides the best statistical fit and therefore might be appropriate.[122] Because this thesis aims at identifying the influencing characteristics on office rent <u>and</u> at developing constant quality office rent indices, no functional form is determined beforehand.

---

[119] Cf. Huh, S. /Kwak, S. (1997), p. 989-998, Maurer, R., et al. (2001), p. 5

[120] Cf. Clapp, J. M. (2003), p. 303-320, Bao, H. X. A. /Wan, A. T. K. (2004), p. 487-507, Hodgson, D., et al. (2006), p. 151-168

[121] Cf. Triplett, J. E. (2004), p. 181-182

[122] Cf. Maurer, R., et al. (2001), p. 6

2.2 Construction Methodology for Hedonic Price Indices (Composition Stage)

Once the correct set of characteristics has been obtained and the best functional form has been estimated, the issue of which index construction methodology is appropriate must be resolved.

2.2.1 Time Dummy Variable Method

The time dummy variable method is the most widely used methodology to construct a hedonic price index. With this method, the observations for all periods are pooled into one regression, which holds constant all coefficients with the exception of the intercept. For instance, if the estimation stage concludes that the semilog model is the more appropriate form, the price index formula will look like the following:

$$\ln p = \beta_0 + \sum_{j=1}^{K} \beta_j Z_j + \sum_{i=2}^{t} \gamma_i D_i + u$$

Equation 2-19

where p represents the price of a product for all the periods, β_j measures the logarithms of implicit prices for characteristic j, and Z_j represents the quantities of characteristic j. D_i is the time dummy variable and takes the value of 1 if the transaction occurs at the certain period i or 0 otherwise. The variable u represents the error term. The coefficient γ_i measures the logarithm of the price index for each period, with the first period as the base period. The price indices are obtained by taking the antilog for coefficients of each time dummy variable γ_i.[123]

However, as *Triplett (2004)* clarifies, "[...] pooled regressions are not the best way to construct a time series of hedonic indexes."[124] The main criticism lies in the fact that the regression coefficients are not allowed to vary between the time periods. This interperiod parameter stability is questionable.[125]

---

[123] Cf. Slade, B. A. (2000), p. 362-363, Li, W., et al. (2006), p. 10, Triplett, J. E. (2004), p. 48-51, von Auer, L. (2004), p. 4-5

[124] Triplett, J. E. (2004), p. 50

[125] Cf. Slade, B. A. (2000), p. 363, Munneke, H. /Slade, B. A. (2001), p. 62, von Auer, L. (2004), p. 5

2.2.2 Adjacent Period Dummy Variable Method

Closely related to the time dummy variable method is the adjacent period dummy variable method. Instead of pooling all observations into one regression, this method pools the observations of only two adjacent periods. In this method, all observations are divided into subintervals of time, which are then pooled into subsamples. The first pooled subsample contains periods one and two, the second subsample two and three, and so on. Similar to Equation 2-19, for each subsample a regression is run given by

$$\log p = \beta_0 + \sum_{j=1}^{K} \beta_j Z_j + \gamma D + u$$

Equation 2-20

P denotes the prices for the adjacent periods. D represents the time dummy variable for the comparison period. The price change within a subsample can be obtained by taking the antilog for γ. The price change for a given period relative to the first period, denoted as $\lambda_{0,i}$, is found by multiplying the antilogs over the desired interval.[126]

$$\lambda_{o,i} = 100 * \prod_{i=1}^{t} \exp(\gamma^i) \qquad t = 1,2,...T$$

Equation 2-21

where, by definition, $\gamma^1 = 0$.

The adjacent period dummy variable method relaxes the restrictive assumptions of the time variable dummy method by holding the regression coefficients constant only for two subsequent periods. Therefore, it allows for the presence of structural change across time. However, as *von Auer (2004)* cautions, overlapping time periods usually lead to estimation bias.[127]

2.2.3 Characteristics Price Index Method

Another approach is referred to as the characteristic price index or time varying parameter method, which uses the implicit price characteristics from the hedonic function in a conventional weighted index number formula. Here, a regression for each period is car-

---

[126] Cf. Slade, B. A. (2000), p. 364, von Auer, L. (2004), p. 5-6, Triplett, J. E. (2004), p. 50-51, Li, W., et al. (2006), p. 11

[127] Cf. von Auer, L. (2004), p. 6

ried out separately, allowing the intercept and the regression coefficients to change over time.

$$p_t = \beta_{t,0} + \sum_{i=1}^{K} \beta_{t,i} Z_{t,i} + u_t$$

Equation 2-22

where p_t denotes the price in period *t*, subscript *i* represents each characteristic with value $Z_{t,i}$, and $\beta_{t,i}$ denotes the implicit price of characteristic *i* for period *t*. The intercept term $\beta_{t,0}$ can be interpreted as a group of characteristics not included in the regression.

In comparison to the aforementioned index construction methodologies, the characteristic price index method places no restrictive assumption. However, the data requirement is substantially higher.[128]

Three varying parameter techniques for construction of the price index of heterogeneous goods (so-called index number formulae) exist: the Laspeyres index, the Paasche index, and the Fisher index.

The Laspeyres can be written as

$$P_{Laspeyres} = \frac{\beta_{t,0} + \sum_{i=1}^{K} \beta_{t,i} Z_{i,0}}{\beta_{0,0} + \sum_{i=1}^{K} \beta_{i,0} Z_{i,0}}$$

Equation 2-23

As can be derived from Equation 2-23, the Laspeyres index uses the mean value of each characteristic from the base period (t=0). Thus, it does not account for any substitution effect or for changes in consumer preferences. It therefore has an upward bias. More generally, a hedonic office rent index using the Laspeyres formula answers the question of how much it would cost an office user in the current period to rent the same average office rental unit in the base period.[129]

The Paasche index can be written as

---

[128] See Section 5.4.1.2

[129] Cf. Thomas, M. (1997), p. 39-41, Jonker, N. (2001), p. 10, Lum, S. K. (2004), p. 33

$$P_{Paasche} = \frac{\beta_{t,0} + \sum_{i=1}^{K} \beta_{i,t} Z_{i,t}}{\beta_{0,0} + \sum_{i=1}^{K} \beta_{i,0} Z_{i,t}}$$

Equation 2-24

The Paasche index uses the subsequent period as a reference point. Here, a hedonic office rent index using the Paasche index answers the question of how much it would cost an office user in the base period to rent the same average office rental unit that he can rent in the current period. Hence, the Paasche index has a downward bias. It is important to note that two index numbers are not directly comparable as the index weights have changed.[130]

A third method is the Fisher index, which can be written as

$$P_{Fischer} = \sqrt{P_{Laspeyres} * P_{Paasche}} = \sqrt{\frac{\beta_{t,0} + \sum_{i=1}^{K} \beta_{i,t} Z_{i,t}}{\beta_{0,0} + \sum_{i=1}^{K} \beta_{i,0} Z_{i,t}} * \frac{\beta_{t,0} + \sum_{i=1}^{K} \beta_{t,i} Z_{i,0}}{\beta_{0,0} + \sum_{i=1}^{K} \beta_{i,0} Z_{i,0}}}$$

Equation 2-25

Whereas the Paasche index underestimates and the Laspeyres index overestimates the cost of renting an office rental unit, the Fisher index should be nearer to an accurate price index but it further complicates the interpretation.[131]

2.2.4 Comparison and Evaluation of the Index Construction Method

The characteristic price index method has two theoretical advantages. First, in the time dummy variable method, the hedonic functional form commands the index number formulae. This is a problem, as "[...] the index number formula depends on the usual theoretical conditions from index number theory, not on the statistical relation established empirically by the hedonic function."[132] The characteristic price index breaks this connection and allows the functional form of the hedonic function and the functional form of the index formula to be determined separately. Second, as opposed to the characteristic price index, the time dummy variable method and the adjacent period time

---

[130] Cf. Thomas, M. (1997), p. 41-42, Jonker, N. (2001), p. 10, Lum, S. K. (2004), p. 33

[131] Cf. Jonker, N. (2001), p. 10, Lum, S. K. (2004), p. 33

[132] Triplett, J. E. (2004), p. 60

method assume that the regression coefficients do not change over time. This assumption is very restrictive, and it can be assumed that transaction volume influences real estate prices.[133] [134] However, different statistical tests, such as F-statistics, Tiao-Goldberger, and Chow tests, can investigate whether this assumption holds true.[135] Although the characteristic price index method surpasses the time dummy variable method, it has one major shortcoming. For such an index to be constructed, the data sample has to be disaggregated into different time intervals. Hence, large data sets are necessary.[136] Although large data sets are available in many economic areas, the data availability for property markets and especially for the German office property market is scarce.[137]

In summary, from a theoretical point of view, the characteristic price index method has to be used. From a practical point of view, however, only the time dummy variable method or the adjacent period dummy variable method is feasible in most cases, given the scarcity of data for the property market. In other words, data availability determines which index construction methodology one should choose.

2.3 Chapter Summary

The objective of this chapter was to explain the underlying theory of the construction of hedonic price indices. The following points are especially relevant for further proceedings:

- The construction of a hedonic price index comprises two stages: the estimation stage of the hedonic function and the composition stage of the hedonic price index. The estimation stage precedes the composition stage.
- The hedonic function relates prices of heterogeneous goods to the quantities of characteristics contained in them. Thus, the hedonic function is obtained with a multiple regression technique. It has been shown that the estimated regression coefficients can represent the value that the market places upon the various characteristics in terms of both the cost that firms face in producing the characteris-

---

[133] Cf. Hoffmann, J. /Lorenz, A. (2006), p. 5
[134] This point will be elaborated later in chapter 3 and 4.
[135] Cf. Munneke, H. /Slade, B. A. (2001), p. 65-66, Triplett, J. E. (2004), p. 61
[136] Cf. Knight, J., et al. (1995), p. 191
[137] Cf. Schick, J. M. (2005), p. 20

tics (supply or producer side) and the value that buyers place upon the characteristics (demand or user side).

- In this thesis, the hedonic function will be determined from the demand side, as it is assumed that the supply of office rental units is fixed in the short term and that the existing stock of office rental units dominates the office property market in most areas.
- Different functional forms (linear, semilog, double-log or Box-Cox approach) for the hedonic regression function are discussed in the hedonic research literature. However, little theoretical guidance is given as to which functional form is to be used. Rather, the selection of functional form is an empirical matter. Independent of the choice of functional form is the requirement that the appropriate set of characteristics be determined.
- Once the functional form has been estimated, it is possible to enter the composition stage and to construct the hedonic price index. Different construction methodologies have been presented, namely, the time dummy variable method, the adjacent period dummy variable method, and the characteristic price index method.
- The time dummy variable method pools all observations into one regression equation and thereby assumes that the influence of the office rent determinants remains constant over the entire time period. The characteristic price index method relaxes the assumptions, as it computes a regression equation for each time period separately. In addition, it includes the possibility of building indices according to the Laspeyres, Paasche, or Fisher index formula.
- Unfortunately, the choice of which construction methodology to use depends on data availability, as the theoretically more advantageous methodology, namely, the characteristic price index method, has higher data requirements.

3 Fundamentals of the Office Property Market and the Implications for Hedonic Price Indices

The previous chapter explained the theory of the construction of a hedonic price index. Where possible, the office rental unit has been used as an example of a heterogeneous good. However, insufficient justification has been provided thus far as to why an office lease has to be considered a heterogeneous good. In addition, although the importance of an office rent index was explained in the introduction,[138] no theoretical reasons have been given as to why the variable rent should be at the centre of the analysis. Both issues will be addressed in this chapter.

Furthermore, as “the challenge […] is to ensure that techniques imported from other markets are applied appropriately in a property context,”[139] this chapter presents the fundamentals of the office property market and derives the implications for the development of hedonic price indices.

3.1 Characteristics of Office Property

3.1.1 Characteristics of Real Estate

Real estate is different from many other economic goods, and the main differences can be summarized in the following aspects: immobility, heterogeneity, duration of the development process, investment volume, transaction costs, and length of the life cycle.[140] These differences give rise to a number of problems when real-estate-related issues are scrutinized.

Because real estate is location specific, it is an immovable asset. This characteristic, ***immobility***, leads to the observation of regional markets, where different supply and demand situations can arise. For instance, one market may suffer from a considerable oversupply of office space, whereas another market may lack office space. As real estate is immovable by definition and cannot be transported, no short-term mechanism for driving the different regional markets into equilibrium exists. But because location is important, the price of the same building will vary from place to place, and differences

---

[138] See Chapter 1

[139] Morrell, G. (1995), p. 11

[140] Cf. Bone-Winkel, S., et al. (2005), p. 16-21

in location segment the market. Against this background, real-estate-related questions have to be answered on a regional and a local market level.[141]

Directly related to the aspect of immobility is the aspect of ***heterogeneity***. Because it is impossible to construct two buildings at the same location, each property is different.[142] This so-called location problem could be resolved if real estate were homogeneous in all other aspects. However, each property is different due to its architecture and equipment and layout factors. Thus, it can be said that each property comes as a bundle of characteristics.[143]

In addition, the ***investment volume*** and the ***transaction costs*** are significantly high in comparison to other economic goods. These factors represent entry and exit market barriers and prevent real estate from being traded on a frequent basis.[144]

Real estate is considered a durable economic good. On the one hand, the ***long life cycle*** of real estate is due to its physical and technical characteristics. On the other hand, as the ground is unsinkable, so is real estate. Nevertheless, when speaking of the life cycle of real estate, one has to consider the economic life of buildings. The economic life of a building ends normally when the net present value of a new building exceeds the net present value of the existing building.[145]

In summary, real estate is a heterogeneous commodity, and it is now understandable why real estate often has been at the centre of hedonic regression analysis and hedonic price indices.[146]

3.1.2 Office Property and Its Differences from Other Property Types

So far, only the characteristics of real estate in general have been highlighted. However, as this thesis deals exclusively with office real estate, it is necessary to briefly define office property and to outline what differentiates office property from other property types.

---

[141] Cf. Fisher, J. D. (1994), p. 7-9, Kling, J. L. /McCue, T. E. (1987), p. 237, Wernecke, M. (2004), p. 22-23, Evans, A. W. (1995), p. 19-21

[142] Cf. Wurtzenbach, C. H. /Miles, M. E. (1995), p. 10, Bone-Winkel, S., et al. (2005), p. 18-19

[143] Cf. Evans, A. W. (1995), p. 21

[144] Cf. Bone-Winkel, S., et al. (2005), p. 20-21, Evans, A. W. (1995), p. 21-22

[145] Cf. Wurtzenbach, C. H. /Miles, M. E. (1995), p. 10, Bone-Winkel, S., et al. (2005), p. 21

[146] Malpezzi, S. (2002), p. 25-27 gives an overview of different hedonic models applied in the field of real estate.

Unfortunately, a nationwide definition of office property does not exist.[147] *Falk (2002)* defines office properties as properties in which predominantly service companies undertake office activities that imply concentrated and communicative work. The office unit space consists of circulation space and useful area. Falk further differentiates office property from other types of property by the fact that office space must be self-contained and marketable.[148] This definition, however, does not take into account that non-service companies have departments that undertake office work. *De Lange (1989)* proposes another approach by first defining office activities. He states that office activities are all activities related to desk work.[149] A similar definition can be found in *Hall (1985)*. He defines offices as places where "[…] information is collected, sorted, analysed, made secure and transmitted. The 'office' can be a single function room […], a large purpose-built block, or say, simply a small suite of rooms for the board and secretaries in a manufacturing entreprise."[150]

In this thesis, the definition of the German Society of Property Researchers (gif), which is a combination of the above-mentioned office property definitions, is followed. Here, office property is defined as the space where desk work prevails regardless of the business affiliation (e.g., non-service companies and government institutions). In addition, office space must be self-contained and marketable. The requirement of marketability does not mean that the office space has to be lettable at any time. Rather, it excludes office space within apartments, retail shops, et cetera.[151]

The following figure differentiates office property from other types of properties.[152] Four types of properties exist. Office property is classified as commercial property. Besides office properties, commercial property includes retail properties, business parks, and logistic properties. The differences between office properties and retail and logistic properties are apparent. However, because business parks also include office areas,[153] the difference between office property and business parks is not clearly defined, and therefore business parks will be treated as office properties.

---

[147] Cf. Ertle-Straub, S. (2003), p. 13
[148] Cf. Falk, B. (2002), p. Punkt 3.3.2
[149] Cf. De Lange, N. (1989), p. 34
[150] Hall, J. M. (1985), p. 25
[151] Cf. Gesellschaft für immobilienwirtschaftliche Forschung (gif) (2004), p. 7-8
[152] See Figure 8
[153] Cf. Walzel, B. (2005), p. 134-136

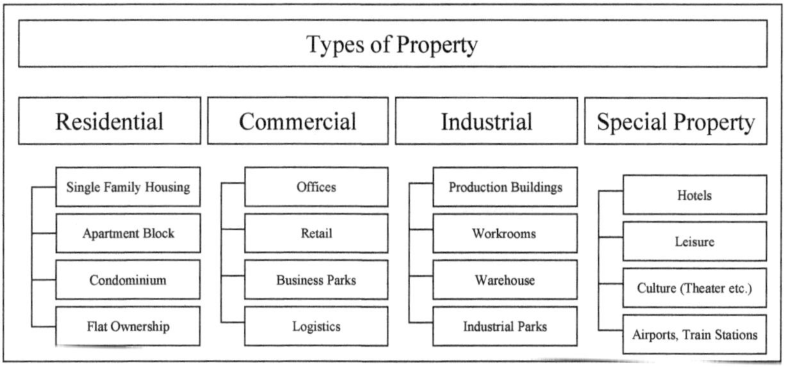

Figure 8: Types of Properties[154]

Although anecdotal evidence suggests that around 75 percent of corporate real estate in Europe, is owned by the occupier, compared to around 30 percent in United States of America (USA), many in the real estate industry anticipate that the trend in Europe will be toward the US model.[155] In fact, in recent years, large portfolios of corporate real estate have been offered on the market in sale and leaseback or similar transactions. Therefore, in addition to considering the above-mentioned classification, it is important to recognize that office properties are primarily investment assets. Because the income generated by the office property determines the value of the investment, the users, or tenants, are at the centre of the analysis.[156] The reasons why companies are leasing rather than buying office properties are manifold. These reasons include taxes, access to credit markets, transaction costs, risk shifting, comparative advantage in asset disposal, asymmetric information, economies of scale, and other agency problems.[157]

The spectrum of users is wide. Figure 9 presents business sectors conducting primarily office activities. Each user is affected differently by changing labour market conditions, rent cost pressures, competition, technology, and corporate restructuring, and expresses different needs and requirements concerning quality and location of office space.[158] In

[154] From Ibid., p. 120
[155] Cf. Hill, M. (2003), p. 313
[156] See Section 3.2.3 and 3.3.1
[157] Cf. Benjamin, J. D., et al. (1998), p. 225-230
[158] Cf. Dowall, D. E. (1988), p. 35-40

addition, because the users of office space cannot be treated as a monolithic group, the complexity of analyzing office property markets increases.[159]

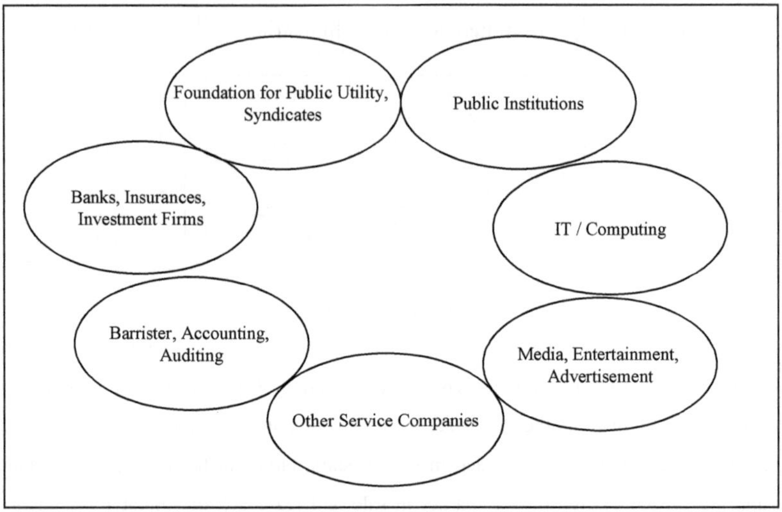

Figure 9: Types of Office Users

Mainly professional organisations undertake the decisions about buying or renting office properties. Nonetheless, rationality and emotions drive the decisions-making process of the market participants. As a consequence, the supply and demand processes and price mechanisms are not transparent. The wide range of product variation and pricing policies exacerbates the situation.[160] For instance, in recent years many landlords granted the tenant incentives (e.g., rent-free periods) and more flexible lease structures. The fact that office properties are mainly let and that different lease structures exist aggravates the problem of heterogeneity mentioned in section 3.1.

Moreover, the transaction costs, construction, and investment volumes are higher in comparison to other types of properties, increasing the importance of banks and other financing institutions.[161]

The development of new offices takes between three to five years, a period that is, in general, longer than that of other types of properties. The lengthy duration of the office

[159] See Section 3.3.1
[160] Cf. Ertle-Straub, S. (2003), p. 36-37
[161] Cf. Ibid.p. 38

development is due to construction periods but also to the time-consuming phases of project initiation and conception and the approval process of various relevant managers.[162]

Because of technical improvement, changes in working conditions, and company structures, the needs and requirements of office users shift quickly, rendering office buildings obsolete more quickly. In other words, the economic life span of office buildings (without renovations) is shorter than that of other types of property (e.g., residential property).[163]

In section 2.1, it has been pointed out that this thesis approaches the hedonic function from the demand side. For the office property market, this approach implies that the correct set of characteristics has to be derived from a tenant's perspective. Because office tenants are companies, the set of characteristics explaining the hedonic function has to be extended to include not only location and building factors but also lease factors.

3.2 Defining Principles

In the previous chapter, the terms rent, price, value, and worth have been used as synonyms. Although accurate and precise definitions of these terms have been avoided to simplify and keep the reader's focus on the explanation of hedonic theory, it is important to resolve this shortcoming for the remaining analysis. In real estate research and practice, these terms are often used loosely. As a consequence, reviews of real estate literature on hedonic analysis often create confusion.[164]

3.2.1 Rent

When one is defining rent, it is important to bear in mind the context in which the term is employed. For instance, different types of rents exist in practice (e.g., gross rent, net rent, effective rent, and asking rent) and in academia (e.g., land rent, building rent, and imputed rent). It is also important to look at which country is being considered, as the definitions of rent differs from country to country.[165]

---

[162] Cf. Ibid.p. 40

[163] Cf. Tu, Y., et al. (2004), p. 300-301

[164] Cf. Malpezzi, S. (2002), p. 16-17

[165] In Section 4.2.3.5 a detailed discussion follows about the definitions of rent employed in the German real estate market.

If the purpose of the research is to describe and analyze the supply and demand in property markets, then academics mostly use the definition of building rent. ***Building rent*** constitutes the costs for users of letting space. In other words, it represents "[...] the payment a firm makes in order to use a given amount of commercial property for a particular time period."[166] In contrast to building rent, the term ***imputed rent*** is used when discussing owner-occupied office buildings and refers to the cost of use that implicitly constitutes rent.[167] Furthermore, in economics and classical political economy, the term ***land rent*** is often employed and is defined as the payments to landowners for the use of a particular piece of land.[168]

When comparing different market reports or studies of rent indices developed by academics or practitioners, one has to look at the underlying definition of rent. As *Dunse, et al. (1998)* observe, rents may be estimation- or transaction-based calculations of top, achievable, expected, or average rents.[169] For instance, many studies developing real estate rent indices use the term ***headline rent***, which is the rent to be achieved with a normal set of incentives, such as rent-free periods and shorter lease lengths, for the particular market at the particular time.[170] Here, the question arises of what constitutes the normal set of incentives. As this set of incentives probably varies with the situation on the rental market, this definition limits the intertemporal comparability of two headline rents. Closely related to the headline rent is the asking rent. ***Asking rent*** represents market valuations undertaken by professionals within their local market and is set at a level that will attract tenants.[171] Other studies refer to ***contract*** or ***negotiated rent***, which is the rent achieved on the basis of negotiations between the landlord and tenant. The problem with these aforementioned types of rent definition is that incentives are not reflected explicitly and are therefore hardly comprehensible.[172] The Red Book of the Royal Institution of Chartered Surveyors (RICS) provides another rent definition. It defines ***market rent*** as "[...] the estimated amount for which a property, should lease on a date of valuation between a willing lessee and a willing lessor on appropriate lease terms, in an arm's length transaction, after proper marketing wherein the parties acted

[166] Ball, M., et al. (1998), p. 19
[167] Cf. Ibid., p.
[168] Cf. Ibid., p. 58-59
[169] Cf. Dunse, N., et al. (1998), p. 461-462
[170] Cf. Crosby, N. /Murdoch, S. (2000), p. 425
[171] Cf. Dunse, N. /Jones, C. (1998), p. 302, Mueller, G. R. (1999), p. 131
[172] Cf. Orr, A., et al. (2003), p. 478

knowledgeably, prudently and without compulsion."[173] Again the problem of this definition is that the proper marketing is rarely quantified. Another set of studies analyse effective rents. In most cases ***effective rents*** are defined as the annual equivalent of the present value of all explicit net cash flows from market-negotiated leases. Escalations in the base rent, months of free rent, tenant improvements, moving allowances, and expense stops are included.[174] But the process of discounting incentives is not without discussion and represents "[...] in itself a major valuation project."[175] Finally, some studies employ ***consideration rents***, which lie between the first year contract rent and the net effective rent.[176]

Although only an overview of rent definitions has been given, it should be clear that researchers and practitioners have to be very careful when discussing rents. The choice of office rent definitions in hedonic analysis depends on the research objective and on data availability.[177] [178]

3.2.2 Price

Two important issues have to be kept in mind when office prices are discussed. First, office price is the actual exchange price for an office building in the marketplace and is different from the value of an office building that is an estimation or proxy of that price.[179] *Peto, et al. (1996)* point out that price is "[...] a figure at which the market is in balance [...] a snapshot in a dynamic market, [...] a function of supply and demand."[180]

Second, the rents and prices of office buildings are directly connected. As it will be shown later, [181]rent fulfills the role that price normally does. The price of an office building depends primarily on income generated by the property, with the price being some multiple of the income.[182] In other words, in the analysis of office rent determinants, it does not matter if one looks at prices or rents. As *Janssen, et al. (2001)* point

[173] RICS (2003), p. 12
[174] Cf. Webb, B. R. /Fisher, J. D. (1996), p. 2
[175] Dunse, N. /Jones, C. (1998), p. 302
[176] Cf. Wheaton, W. C. /Torto, R. G. (1995), p. 4
[177] Cf. Desyllas, J. (2000), p. 34-35
[178] In this thesis contract rent is used as dependent variable. See Chapter 5.2.2
[179] Cf. Fisher, J. D. (1994), p. 24-25, Peto, R. (1997), p. 411-412, Mackmin, D. /Emary, R. (2000), p. 53-55
[180] Peto, R., et al. (1996), p. 81
[181] See Section 3.3
[182] Cf. Lützkendorf, T. /Lorenz, D. (2005), p. 227

out, "[...] prices depend on income [rent], income depends on the features of the property. This creates a direct relationship between market prices on the one hand and property characteristics on the other."[183] This relationship between rent and price is not only limited to property characteristics but extends to other factors like lease terms, market situation and bargaining power.[184] [185]

3.2.3 Value

The concept of value can be applied to price and rent, as rent is the price one pays to use space over a specific period of time. The value of an office building has been defined so far as the estimation of the actual exchange price in the marketplace. This definition of value, however, captures only a part of the concept of value. In a general discussion, *Thomson, et al. (2003)* state that "[...] value is a perception."[186] Furthermore, it has to be differentiated between a subjective and objective interpretation of value and present three different types of values: exchange value, use value, and esteem value. The ***exchange value*** is the estimation of the market price (rent) of an office building, the ***use value*** is the value of a building to the organization performing activities within it, and the ***esteem value*** is the attractiveness and desirability of a building to those who are not using it.[187] The latter definition can hardly be captured, and it will therefore be ignored in the scope of this thesis. The exchange and use value can differ significantly in that the current market development influences the exchange value, whereas the attributes that benefit the existing tenant - attributes that might change with the next tenant - determine the use value.[188] In the long run, the exchange value and use value should be equal, as tenants are unwilling or unable to pay rents that are higher than their use value.[189] Because the first step in building a hedonic rent index is to identify the correct set of characteristics (estimation stage), studies that employ either use or exchange value in their regression function are reviewed.

---

[183] Janssen, C., et al. (2001), p. 343

[184] For example, a risk-adversed buyer is likely to pay a higher price for an office building if the underlying cash flow is based on a long lease term.

[185] See Section 4.1.5

[186] Thomson, D. S., et al. (2003), p. 337

[187] Cf. Neap, H. S. /Celik, T. (1999), p. 184, Thomson, D. S., et al. (2003), p. 338

[188] Cf. Fisher, J. D. (1994), p. 25-26

[189] Cf. French, N. /Wiseman, G. (2003), p. 25-26

3.2.4 Worth

Closely linked with the discussion of price and value is the term 'worth'. In many languages the terms value and worth are interchangeable.[190] However, the difference between these terms is that worth is the assessment of the benefits accruing through ownership to a particular purchaser. In addition, worth can be distinguished from price and value in that it is the value to an individual or organization of an interest judged against defined criteria. *Peto, et al. (1996)* emphasize the important difference by a simple example. They argue that a rational investor will only buy (sell) an asset if the market price is equal or below (equal or higher) his assessment of the present worth of the future cash flow likely to be produced by the asset. Thus, they conclude that investors buy or sell based on their own perception of the future. This perception of worth differs from investor to investor and depends on the negotiating strength of the buyer (tenant) and seller (landlord). Therefore, price and value are different from worth, as they do not recognize the underlying motivation of all financial markets.[191]

This brief description of rent, price, value, and worth is intended to show that these terms, though closely related, have different meanings and cannot be used in an interchangeable manner. In the scope of this thesis, rent is the dependent variable. However, many characteristics that have an impact on office price, value, or worth also have an impact on office rents. Thus, so that the correct set of characteristics (office rent determinants) will be investigated, research studies that use office price, value, or worth as a dependent variable will be reviewed.[192]

---

190 Cf. Mackmin, D. /Emary, R. (2000), p. 52

191 Cf. McParland, C., et al. (2000), p. 95-96, Lützkendorf, T. /Lorenz, D. (2005), p. 219, Peto, R., et al. (1996), p. 82

192 See Section 4.1

3.3 Office Market Dynamics

Most researchers approach the analysis of office market dynamics within the context of market equilibrium, which is achieved through the interaction between the supply of and the demand for office space (so-called static comparative market equilibrium). *DiPasquale /Wheaton (1992)* expand this traditional view by introducing a conceptual framework that divides the real estate market into two markets: the market for real estate space and the market for real estate assets.[193] *Ball, et al. (1998)* follow their conceptual framework, but they differ between four interlinked submarkets: the user market, the financial asset market, the development market, and the land market. These four submarkets constitute the office property market.[194] Modeling the office market entails a significant constraint: unlike the decision to invest in financial assets, the decision to invest in office buildings involves high transaction costs. Furthermore, if office buildings are held as financial assets, substantial costs are involved in buying and selling these assets (e.g., land registry, transfer tax, agent's commission, and notary costs).[195]

3.3.1 User Market

The user market is generally defined as the market in which office space is demanded as an input of the production of goods or services.[196] Naturally, in the case of office space, the importance lies in services. Therefore, the demand for office space is always a derived demand. In other words, if the demand for the services produced in an office space increases, new office space will be demanded. This point is important because it demonstrates the link between the office space market and the general economic activity.[197] Although most offices belong to the service industry, office users should not be considered as a monolithic group, and the user market should not be oversimplified. Users have different requirements regarding the quality and location of office space, and it is impossible for a single building to attract every user.[198] Therefore, it is more realistic to assume that different demand curves for each user, or at least for each user type, exist.

---

[193] Cf. DiPasquale, D. /Wheaton, W. C. (1992), p. 181-197

[194] Cf. Ball, M., et al. (1998), p. 20-41

[195] Cf. Kling, J. L. /McCue, T. E. (1987), p. 238, Colett, D., et al. (2003), p. 205

[196] Cf. Jaffe, A. J. (1995), p. 86, Kling, J. L. /McCue, T. E. (1987), p. 237

[197] Cf. Clapp, J. M. (1993), p. 4, Colin, J. (1995), p. 22

[198] See Section 3.1.2

However, for the sake of simplicity and for the following explanation only, one supply and demand curve for office space is assumed.

The following diagram illustrating a demand and a supply function explains the adjustment process of the user market.[199] Rent is represented on the y-axis and the stock of offices on the x-axis. If all market players act rationally, then it can be assumed that the demand for office space is a negative function of rent. In other words, holding all other variables constant, the higher the rent level is, the lower user demand will be for office space. The supply of office space is fixed in a short-run perspective, which is shown by a vertical line.[200] At the intercept of the supply and demand function an equilibrium point $(q_0;r_0)$ exists. However, as mentioned, demand for office space is always derived and therefore dependent on other exogenous factors. For instance, an increase in office employment will lead to a higher demnd for office space, which can be illustrated by a shift of the demand function to the right (D_0 to D_1). If no supplemental office space is provided, then the new equilibrium is at point (r_1). However, in the long run, new office space is introduced to the market (S_0 to S_1), which causes the rent to fall at point $(q_1;r_2)$, where a new equilibrium point is achieved.

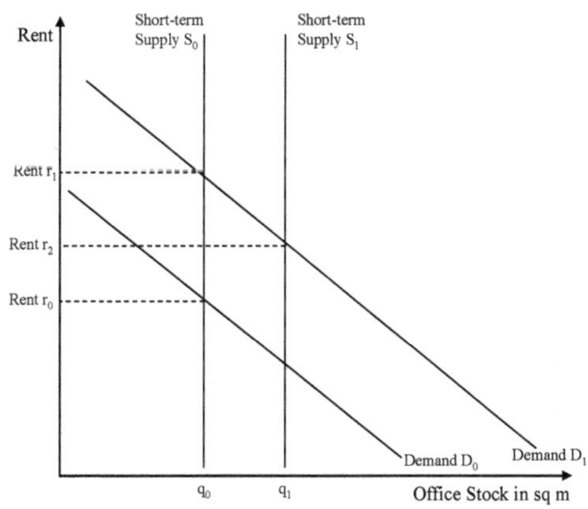

Figure 10: User Market[201]

[199] See Figure 10

[200] Wernecke, M. (2004), p. 66-67 points out that the short-term supply curve is actually not completely inelastic (represented with a vertical line). It is to a certain degree flexible by means of redesignation of areas (e.g. conversion of residential unit to office units) and change of the vacancy rate. This fact, however, is disregarded for the sake of simplicity.

[201] Cf. Ball, M., et al. (1998), p. 25

3.3.2 Financial Asset Market

Office space and office property can be seen as a financial asset for those who retain ownership. If all agents holding office space act in an economically rational manner, they will evaluate the risk and opportunities of office property in comparison to other financial assets.[202]

If office property is to be understood as a financial asset, it is necessary to introduce the concept of basic valuation methods. To determine the value of property, investors multiply the rental cash flow with the inverse of the capitalization rate or initial yield that investors demand to hold real estate assets.[203] The capitalization rate accounts for the long-term interest rate in the economy, the expected growth in rents, the risks associated with that rental income stream, and the tax treatment of holding real estate. The capitalization rate, together with the rental stream of the office property, determines the value (price) of the office property. If the capitalization rate increases, the value of the property declines, and vice versa. The following diagram illustrates this simple fact.[204] The y-axis represents the rent, and the x-axis is the price of the office property. If the rent level increases, then the value of the office property increases as well. The capitalization determines the slope of this function. If the long-term interest rate in the economy increases, the capitalization rate will increase accordingly and cause the function to shift to the left (C_1), whereas a decrease will cause a shift to the right (C_2).[205] For instance, in mid-2007 the U.S. sub-prime crisis hit the real estate market. Banks demanded higher interest rates and were more restrictive about debt financing, which resulted in a significant decrease in property prices.[206]

The demand for office property as a financial asset is mainly influenced by the demand for office space, which determines the rent level. In general, investors in real estate assets purchase a current or future income stream. If the rent level changes in the user market, this change immediately affects the demand for office property in the financial

---

202 Cf. Ibid., p.

203 Cf. DiPasquale, D. /Wheaton, W. C. (1992), p. 187, Hoesli, M. /MacGregor, B. D. (2000), p. 40-42

204 See Figure 11

205 Cf. Ball, M., et al. (1998), p. 25-26, DiPasquale, D. /Wheaton, W. C. (1992), p. 187-188

206 Cf. Gärtner, M. (2007), p. 36-37

asset market. This observation underpins the strategic importance of rent in real estate decisions.[207]

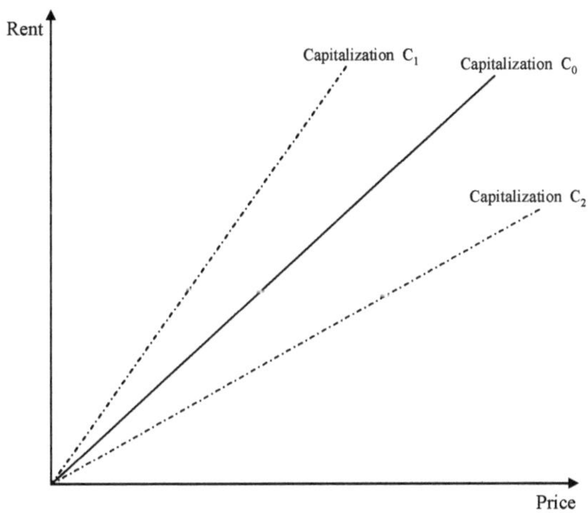

Figure 11: Financial Asset Market[208]

3.3.3 Development Market

The production of new office space takes place in the development market. It is not unusual for many developers to build offices and hold them as financial assets. However, for the sake of simplicity, it is assumed that developers and investors are two separate entities and operate in two separate submarkets. In addition, three further assumptions are assessed: On the one hand, office users are indifferent between new and existing buildings in the absence of technological improvements. On the other hand, no replacement of obsolescent buildings are taken into account, and replacement development would behave similar to market forces as for new developments. The primary motive for developers or any other economically rational agent to start building activity is profit. Thus, the development market is often referred to as being profit driven, which means the development and sale of property must be higher than the replacement cost, including the costs of site clearance, land, construction, and financing. Moreover, the involved risk has to be reflected with an additional profit margin. The following dia-

[207] Cf. DiPasquale, D. /Wheaton, W. C. (1992), p. 187-188
[208] Cf. Ball, M., et al. (1998), p. 26

gram depicts this issue.[209] On the ordinate, the new office space is presented, and on the x-axis, the price for office space. The price level of office space determines the supply of new office space. The intercept with the x-axis fixes the minimum point at which developers are prepared to build. A change in the replacement costs triggered by a change in the costs of site clearance, land, construction, and financing causes the intercept of the supply curve with the horizontal axis to shift (from S_0 to S_1).[210]

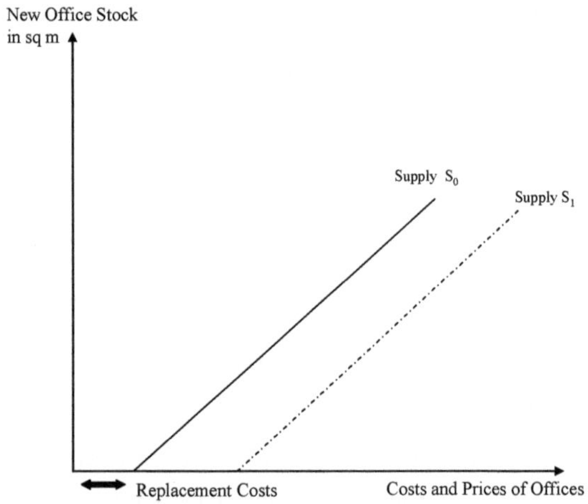

Figure 12: Development Market[211]

As in the financial asset market, the trigger to start or stop the construction of new office buildings in the user market is the rent level. A high rent level causes prices for office properties in the financial asset market to increase. This increase in office prices leads to new office development, as long as the office prices are higher than the replacement costs. If demand is constant, the supply of new office spaces has to be added to the existing stock, which causes the rent level to fall. As a consequence, it can be derived that "the user market [...] stimulates or discourages activity in the development market."[212]

---

[209] See Figure 12

[210] Cf. DiPasquale, D. /Wheaton, W. C. (1992), p. 187-190, Ball, M., et al. (1998), p. 28-32

[211] Cf. Ball, M., et al. (1998), p. 29

[212] Ibid., p. 30

3.3.4 Land Market

Finally, *Ball, et al. (1998)* refer to the land market. According to their argument, the limited availability of land at any location creates competition for its use. New office developments have to compete with old office buildings on the one hand and with other land uses on the other hand. The fact that land prices (costs) are a major part of the developer's calculation illustrates the link between the development market and the land market.[213]

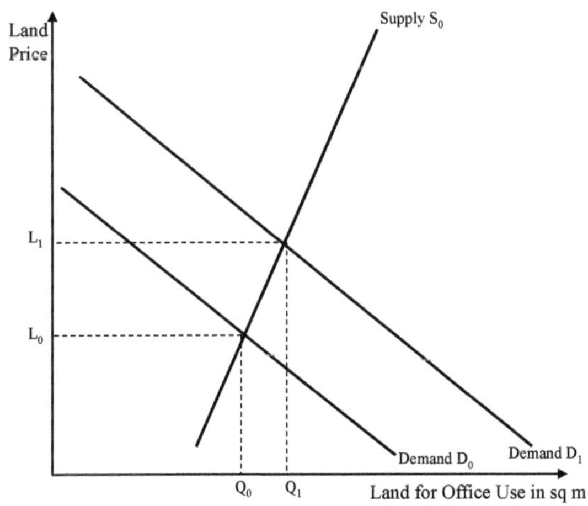

Figure 13: Land Market[214]

The demand for land is downward sloping for two reasons. First, a higher price for land increases the level of replacement costs in the development market, which in turn raises the rent level for office users. The rational reaction of users is to economise on office space. Second, high land prices reduce the relative costs of building high office buildings and thereby increase the intensity with which land is used. Therefore, the demand curve cannot be immediately derived from the user market, and the land market has to be treated separately.[215] However, in the case of the German office property market, this presumption has to be restricted because of strict workplace regulations and building regulations. They set severe requirements and give little leeway to manage the intensity with which land is used. Furthermore, in 2005 a high vacancy dominated all major

[213] Cf. Ibid., p. 32-34
[214] Ibid., p. 33
[215] Cf. Ibid., p. 32

German office property markets. As a consequence, speculative development (i.e., construction that starts before any tenant has signed a lease agreement) is rare. Nowadays, banks or other financing parties often require that a lease contract be signed before new office development takes place. Therefore, the above-mentioned assumption can be relaxed, and it can be assumed that the demand curve in the user market primarily forms the demand curve in the land market.

The different uses for land compete by increasing the price for land. For instance, if the demand is presented by the curve D and the supply by S, then the price for land is L_0, and the quantity Q_0 of land will be supplied. However, if office rents rise, then the demand for new office space increases as well, and a higher price can be paid for land, which is illustrated by a shift to the right of the demand curve D_1. The new price for land is then L_1, and the quantity Q_1 of land is supplied. The problem in modeling the land market is that the land market is regulated by the planning regime and influenced by public expenditure on infrastructure. Both factors affect the position of the demand and supply curves.[216]

3.3.5 Adjustment Processes for the Office Property Markets and the Importance of Rent

It is now important to demonstrate how these different submarkets are interlinked and how equilibrium is again achieved once the markets have been in disequilibrium. Here again the argumentation of Ball et al. (1998) is followed because of its explanatory power.

In this scenario, which assumes that the market is competitive and that, at the point of reference, the office stock, interest rates, and replacement costs are fixed, the user market gets into disequilibrium because new office space is demanded.[217] Because the stock of office space is fixed in the short term, office space users are more likely to pay higher rents r_1 *(Arrow 1)*. A higher rent level increases the value of office space and therefore makes office property as a financial asset more attractive than others. Investors will subsequently articulate this attractiveness in a higher demand for new office space and a readiness to pay higher prices for new developments p_1 *(Arrow 2)*. This encourages developers to build additional office space *(Arrow 3)*, which increases the available office

[216] Cf. Ibid., p. 32-33
[217] See Figure 14

stock, with delay, on the user market q_1 *(Arrow 4)*. As a side effect, the land price required for building offices increases. The production of new office space then ceases for two reasons. First, the additional office space supplied satisfies the demand, and second, the higher rent level discourages potential users. The market reaches equilibrium at point r_2 again *(Arrow 5)*.

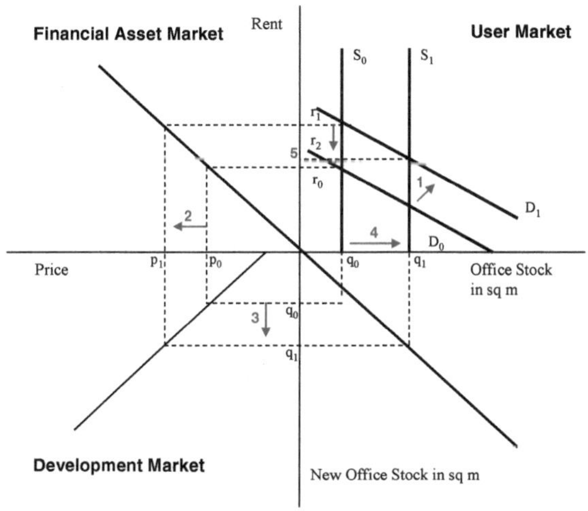

Figure 14: Adjustment Process of the Office Property Market

From the contents of section 3.3.1 through section 3.3.5, one can derive the importance of rent for the economic and hedonic analysis of office property markets. "[…] rent plays the role that price does. It acts as the key signal to agents active in the market, […] and clears these markets by equating the quantity supplied with that demanded."[218] In other words, "[…] rent is considered the most important variable in property economics."[219] In addition, while rent reacts quickly to change, the physical asset and office stock do not.[220] The prospective tenant in the user market determines the level of rent. The tenant also sets the level of rent depending upon the ability of the office space to satisfy his needs and requirements.[221] As a consequence, office rent is the dependent variable in the hedonic function, and the office tenant determines the independent variables (set of characteristics).

---

[218] Ball, M., et al. (1998), p. 19
[219] Karakozova, O. (2004), p. 51
[220] Cf. Wheaton, W. C. (1999), p. 212
[221] Cf. Greer, G. E. (1993), p. 89

3.4 Office Property Market Efficiency

In real estate research, there is a wide range and bountiful quantity of literature on the issue of property market efficiency. However, empirical work has mainly focused on the stock market.[222] The question of whether office property markets are efficient has two important implications for the development of constant quality rent indices using a hedonic approach. First, if office property markets are not efficient, then other factors, such as the role of the agent and the psychology of landlords and users, are important and influence the level of rent. Second, if office property markets are inefficient, then the expected degree of accuracy from the constant quality rent indices is affected and should be reduced.[223]

3.4.1 Definitions and Forms of Property Market Efficiency

Before the causes and consequences of property market efficiency can be discussed, it is necessary to define and explain the concept of property market efficiency. *Keogh /D'Arcy (1999)* identify two perspectives. The first perspective of property market efficiency deals with allocation efficiency and the second perspective with informational efficiency.[224]

Allocation efficiency refers to maximising the total value of the available resources. That means that resources are moved to their highest valued uses, as evidenced by consumers' willingness to pay for the final product. The process of demand and supply leads resources to their most efficient uses.[225]

Informational efficiency refers to the efficient market hypothesis of financial economics, which states that prices fully reflect information quickly and accurately. Therefore, future price changes must depend on information not yet available and so are unpredictable, no matter how informed someone is. According to *Fama (1970)*, there are three forms of market efficiency: weak form efficiency, semi-strong form efficiency, and strong form efficiency. The differences lay in the information set considered. Weak form efficiency requires that all market information be included in the current price. Semi-strong form efficiency requires that all publicly available information be included

---

[222] Cf. Wang, P. (2000), p. 185-186

[223] Cf. Evans, A. W. (1995), p. 5-29

[224] Cf. Keogh, G. /D'Arcy, E. (1999), p. 2402-2406

[225] Cf. Baßeler, U., et al. (2002), p. 42-44, Keogh, G. /D'Arcy, E. (1999), p. 2402-2404, Ball, M., et al. (1998), p. 6

in the current price, and strong form efficiency requires that all information be included in the current price.[226]

3.4.2 Causes of Office Property Market Inefficiency

Many real estate studies indicate that the office property market is inefficient from the perspective of allocation and information inefficiency.[227] *Hutchison, et al. (2005)* argue that property market's inefficiency mainly steems from informational inefficiencies as market participants have different access to available information.[228]

Evans (1995) argues that the inefficiency of property markets arises from the following factors: location, heterogeneity, and economic change.[229] Although he refers to property prices, his findings also can be applied to rent, as explained earlier.[230]

The location is an important characteristic in determining the value of a property. The price of the same building will vary from place to place. Office buildings are heterogeneous products that differ not only in location but also in their building, equipment, and layout characteristics. This fact leads *Evans (1995)* to the conclusion that "[...] the very large number of ways in which properties can differ, even though some of the differences may be small, make it statistically impossible to determine the prices of all characteristics [...].[231] Moreover, because of economic change, the prices for the same property will vary over time. In other words, the features that capture the essence of the property as a product and its market lead to market inefficiency.[232] This view is also shared by *Clayton (1998)* who states that at times property prices paid do not reflect the underlying market fundamental.[233]

Some researchers have challenged the conclusion that office property markets are inefficient. For instance, *Keogh /D'Arcy (1999)* argue that the supporter of inefficient property markets uses an absolute, rather than a relative, concept of market efficiency. They

---

[226] Cf. Fama, E. F. (1970), p. 382-420 quoted in Kulish, V. V. (2007), p. 861-862, Milionis, A. (2007), p. 608-610, Jaffe, A. J. (1995), p. 34-36, Ross, S. A., et al. (2002), p. 342-344, Ball, M., et al. (1998), p. 6, Keogh, G. /D'Arcy, E. (1999), p. 2404-2406

[227] See Keogh, G. /D'Arcy, E. (1999), p. 2402-2406 for a literature review

[228] Cf. Hutchison, N., et al. (2005), p. 155

[229] Cf. Evans, A. W. (1995), p. 18-23

[230] See Section 3.2

[231] Evans, A. W. (1995), p. 21

[232] Cf. Evans, A. W. (2004), p. 52-64, McParland, C., et al. (2000), p. 93, Evans, A. W. (1995), p. 18-23

[233] Cf. Clayton, J. (1998), p. 41-57

state that "[...] it is possible to compare market outcomes against a hypothetical Pareto-efficient world in which no market failures exists, but it is not helpful."[234] Their argument is consistent and clearly points out the theoretical deficiencies of earlier studies of property market efficiency. Nevertheless, the fact remains that, in comparison to other assets (e.g. bonds and stocks), office property markets are less efficient.[235]

3.4.3 Implications of Inefficient Office Property Markets

The previous section explained the causes of office property market inefficiency. Because office property markets can be considered inefficient, various consequences can be derived. *Evans (1995)* concludes that buyer-seller psychology and negotiation abilities and positions influence property prices. He further postulates that property valuations will not be as accurate as share valuations.[236]

According to his argument, office rent indices cannot be as precise and accurate as other indices from other financial assets for which more information is available.[237] Hedonic office rent indices use the notion of implicit price characteristics. However, because the office property market is inefficient, other influencing factors (e.g., negotiating power and experience) are hard to measure and therefore are never collected. As a consequence, these factors cannot be included in the regression analysis and will limit the explanatory power (in terms of explained variance). Any hedonic office rent index based on a regression analysis will therefore carry some noise. As *Triplett (2004)* points out "[...] markets are not 'perfect'; this just implies that hedonic functions have residuals."[238]

---

[234] Keogh, G. /D'Arcy, E. (1999), p. 2403

[235] Cf. Hoesli, M. /MacGregor, B. D. (2000), p. 79 „[...] seem like evidence of the failure of the property market to conform to weak form efficiency."

[236] Cf. Evans, A. W. (1995), p. 27-28

[237] Cf. Jedem, U. (2006), p. 34

[238] Triplett, J. E. (2004), p. 46

3.5 Real Estate Office Rental Cycles

The adjustment process for the office property market presented in the previous section is affected by the theory of expectations adopted.[239] Due to market inefficiency,[240] and behavioural anomalies,[241] it seems unrealistic that all participants (e.g., office users, investors and developers) of the office property markets have the same expectations and can predict the adjustment process correctly. In addition, due to the interactions of the different submarkets,[242] it is unrealistic to assume that an equilibrium is achieved after one period. As *Kurzrock (2007)* points out that, in practice, the equilibrium endures only for a short time period.[243] In fact, property markets are inherently subject to booms and busts.[244] Real estate literature covers this phenomenon under the real estate cycle theory and, as a matter of fact, a broad strand of literature has studied the different causes of real estate cycles and their strategic implications for real estate market participants.[245] The variable rent is cyclical,[246] and, as *Wernecke (2004)* provides strong evidence that the German real estate office rental market also has a cyclical behaviour,[247] it is necessary to briefly review the causes for real estate cycles, the office rental cycle phases, and the behaviour of office users and landlords during the different cycle phases and, to discuss the implications for modeling office rents in German metropolitan areas.

3.5.1 Causes for Real Estate Cycles and Cycle Phases

3.5.1.1 Causes for Real Estate Cycles

In theory, it is possible for office property markets to be in equilibrium and to follow the explained adjustment process in office property markets.[248] The static comparative view of office property markets is important for the understanding of the longterm relationships,[249] but it does not help the understanding of short- or midterm mechanism of the

---

[239] Cf. Ball, M., et al. (1998), p. 37

[240] See Section 3.4

[241] Cf. Wernecke, M. (2004), p. 101-117

[242] See Section 3.3.5

[243] Cf. Kurzrock, B.-M. (2007), p. 28-29

[244] Cf. Fraser, W. D., et al. (2002), p. 355-356, Geltner, D. M., et al. (2007), p. 28-33

[245] Pyhrr, S., et al. (1999), p. 7-68 synthesize relevant research and commentary on real estate cycles in a micro-decision-making context and discusses their strategic implications.

[246] Cf. Ibid.p. 17

[247] Cf. Wernecke, M. (2004), p. 244

[248] Cf. Ibid.p. 80

[249] See Section 3.3

office property markets.[250] Several causes challenge the static comparative approach because they lead to market disequilibrium and therefore, to real estate cycles. In his thesis about real estate office cycles in Germany, *Wernecke (2004)* differentiates between exogenous and endogenous causes for real estate cycles which are briefly summarized as follows.[251]

3.5.1.1.1 Exogenous Causes

The *socioeconomic framework* is constantly changing. Most of theses changes occur gradually (e.g. development of social product). However, unpredicted economic or political events (e.g., changes in taxation laws, German reunification) can result in shocks that unsettle the equilibrium. The *economic situation* is a driving factor for the demand of office space.[252] As the economic situation is also subject to irregular cyclic behaviour, the predictability is hampered; therefore, market participants can misjudge the future demand of office space and reach a wrong decision. Closely related with the aforementioned economic situation is another important cause of real estate cycles: *procyclical credit lending behaviour of banks and financial institutions*. In times of economic upturns the possibility of debt financing is greater than in economic downturns.[253] As a matter of fact, it is even possible to finance real estate projects to 100 percent. Moreover, real estate forms an investment asset,[254] and real estate markets become increasingly integrated in the financial markets.[255] Therefore, it competes with other investment alternatives and is affected by *changes in the capital markets*. For instance, when institutional investors close positions in the stock markets, it automatically leads to an increase in real estate investments. Finally, the *political situation* has a major impact on office property markets (e.g., changes in taxes, regulation of the land supply and credit lending practice, or the decision to privatise public real estate influence the property markets).[256]

---

[250] Cf. Wernecke, M. (2004), p. 123
[251] Cf. Ibid.p. 80-123
[252] See Section 3.3.1
[253] Cf. Meija, L. C. (1999), p. 175-196
[254] See Section 3.3.2
[255] Cf. D'Arcy, E. /Keogh, G. (1999), p. 923-924
[256] Cf. Wernecke, M. (2004), p. 80-94

3.5.1.1.2 Endogenous Causes

The characteristics of office property presented in section 3.1 are reason for several endogenous causes for market disequilibrium. Four categories are identified: time lags, behavioural anomaly, information inefficiences and special factors.

As mentioned, the office property market is subject to a construction time lag.[257] In addition to time lags in construction, time lags in decision making and in price mechanism are inherent in the office property market. While the latter subscribes the time period until changes in demand and supply have an impact on rent (prices), time lags in decision making are the time span between the registration of changes in rent (price) and the decision to invest or disinvest in office property, to let or to terminate a lease contract. Time lags vary between the regional office property markets and are not constant. For the office development market in Germany the time lag is one to four years.[258]

Unlike postulated by the neoclassical theory,[259] market participants are subject to behavioural anomaly due to bounded rationality, which means that market participants cannot process all information correctly.[260] In practice, they have problems in the perception, processing and valuation of information. Therefore, to reduce the amount and complexity of information, they apply different strategies, such as the selective perception or heuristic availability.[261] Moreover, market participants suffer under the winner's curse syndrome. This anomaly states that when the number of participants in an auction or a similar transaction increases, it also increases the probability that the winner of the auction purchased the item above his worth. The behavioural anomaly is not only limited to individual market participants but can also apply to masses. Decision makers in real estate exert influence among each other, the result of which is that the individual thinking is abandoned to follow the masses.[262]

---

[257] See Section 3.1.1 and 3.3.3

[258] Cf. Wernecke, M. (2004), p. 96-99

[259] See Section 1.3.3

[260] Cf. French, N. (2001), p. 401, Bruin, A. d. /Flint-Hartle, S. (2003), p. 272-273

[261] Heuristics is called the phenomenon in which human problem solvers employ cognitive shortcuts because short-term memory has serious limitations in processing capacity and speed. Cf. Hansz, A. J. /Diaz III, J. (2001), p. 553

[262] Cf. Wernecke, M. (2004), p. 101-112

As described in section 3.4, the office property market is not information efficient. Not all relevant market information is incorporated into the valuation or investment decisions that can cause a market disequilibrium.[263]

Finally, special factors, such as institutional discrepancies and game theoretical aspects are inherent in the office property market and challenges the assumptions set by the neoclassical theory. Under the neoclassical assumption, there are many market participants and the individual market participants do not have any dominant role. However, this assumption is invalid for office property. For instance, in the years 2006 and 2007, private equity firms could outbid many of their competitors, such as open-ended funds. While open-ended funds are legally constrained on the amount of debt, private equity investors can engage in high leverage investments.[264] Game theoretical aspects refer to the observations that even if market participants act rationally, their actions sometimes result in an undesired and suboptimal result. For instance, although market participants recognize that too many projects are under construction and will result in an oversupply, they continue to pursue their project. The rationale is that all participants know that if they stop their project the competitors will benefit, and vice versa. Therefore, they attempt to finalize their project ahead of their competitors to still make a profit.[265]

3.5.1.2 Cycles Phases

The aforementioned causes lead to a disequilibrium in the office property submarkets. For the effect of these different forces to be explained, it is necessary to describe the office rental cycles phases. In addition, these causes do not emerge separately, but often in combination or in fast succession. Therefore, the comparative-static model is not suited to explain the different stage of real estate rental cycles, as it allows only the change of one paramater (variable) at a time.[266]

---

[263] Cf. Ibid.p. 112-118

[264] This contention is underpinned by the observation that, in the first half of 2007, debt financing was easily available for investors, and most portfolio and single investment were bought by highly leveraged real estate funds with a short-term investment strategy. In the second half of 2007, due to the credit crunch debt, financing became less available; therefore, equity investors with a long-term investment strategy were more successful in portfolio and singe asset investments. Cf. ATIS Real (2008), w/o pages, Deutsche Gesellschaft für Immobilienfonds (2008), w/o pages

[265] Cf. Wernecke, M. (2004), p. 118-123

[266] Cf. Focke, C. (2005), p. 67-68

3.5.1.2.1 Phase 1: Recovery

In phase 1 (recovery), a state of oversupply characterizes the office property market, and the occupancy level is at its lowest level. The oversupply might be the result of new construction from the previous cycle, or it might be due to negative demand growth.[267] This situation changes, however, as economic activity increases. This upward trend in the economy is further boosted by low interest rates and high capital availability, resulting in a strong user demand for office space. Consequently, available office space is absorbed, vacancy rates decrease, and office rents begin slowly to increase, as does the optimism of real estate market participants (specifically, developers). Because of an environment of low interest rates, a higher-than-expected rental growth, and falling vacancy rates, the capital values for office buildings rise. As the capital values increase, the development of new office buildings becomes profitable again, and new office projects that will reach the market in two to three years are initiated. As the boom continues, lending practices become more relaxed. Banks and other financiers also are willing to finance speculative development projects.[268]

3.5.1.2.2 Phase 2: Expansion and Overbuilding

In phase 2 (expansion and overbuilding), new office space starts to reach the market. Furthermore, the upward trend of the economy slows down due to an increase in real interest rates. While there is no perceived oversupply during the beginning of this phase, because of high occupancy rates, new buildings compete for tenants in the marketplace, and the rental growth rate continues to decline from its highest rate at the peak of the cycle, when space was most difficult to find. Demand for and absorption of new office space level off and then fall. As the vacancy rate rises and the rental growth slows down, the capital values of new office projects fall. When market participants realize that the market has turned downward, new construction slows down or stops completely.[269]

---

[267] Cf. Mueller, G. R. (1999), p. 136

[268] Cf. Downs, A. (1993), p. 167, Ball, M., et al. (1998), p. 196, Mueller, G. R. (1999), p. 136-137

[269] Cf. Downs, A. (1993), p. 167, Wernecke, M. (2004), p. 43, Ball, M., et al. (1998), p. 197, Mueller, G. R. (1999), p. 137

3.5.1.2.3 Phase 3: Contraction

In phase 3 (contraction), the fall in the demand for new office space coincides with the peak in supply. Vacancy rates rise above their equilibrium levels, and rent levels continue to fall. The competition for tenants increases, as does the willingness of landlords to grant more lease incentives. Office buildings that do not meet the latest technical standards or that are located in less favourable locations are especially difficult to let. As a consequence, office developers who are unable to find tenants do not generate the income required to meet the interest payments and go bankrupt. Furthermore, because of the low rent level and the low occupancy rate, the capital values of office buildings decrease, and investors retreat from this financial asset market.[270]

3.5.1.2.4 Phase 4: Recession Stability

Finally, phase 4 (recession) begins when the market occupancy is below equilibrium and the decline of rents bottoms out. The extent of the down cycle in the market will be determined by the difference between the market supply and demand growth rates. [271] Eventually, two effects stabilize the office space market. First, little new office space reaches the market (most comes from the completion of projects started in phase 2). Second, some office buildings that remain vacant for a long time become obsolete.[272] These office buildings are not competitive, and only major refurbishment could make them marketable again.

---

[270] Cf. Wernecke, M. (2004), p. 43-44, Ball, M., et al. (1998), p. 197, Mueller, G. R. (1999), p. 137

[271] Cf. Downs, A. (1993), p. 168, Wernecke, M. (2004), p. 44, Ball, M., et al. (1998), p. 197, Mueller, G. R. (1999), p. 137-138

[272] Cf. Dobberstein, M. (2000), p. 8

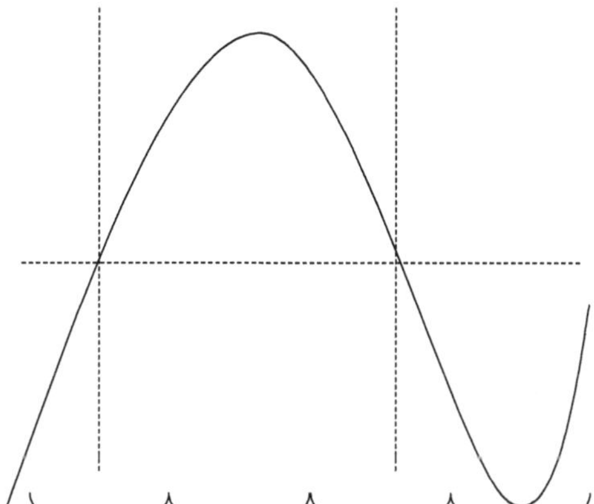

Figure 15: Office Rental Cycle Phases[273]

3.5.2 Office User and Landlord Behaviour during Cycle Phases and its Implication for Hedonic Price Indices

The characteristics of the phases of the office real estate cycle were outlined in the previous section. Now it is necessary to analyse whether the real state cycle phases influence the behaviour and decisions of tenants (office users) and landlords. If they do, then they have a direct impact on the set of characteristics defining the hedonic function.[274]

3.5.2.1 Office Users

In comparison to users in other property markets (e.g., the residential property market), office users are better informed.[275] In addition, they generally employ a real estate agent or consultant in the office-allocation process. Therefore, office users are aware of their bargaining power. When the economy picks up, companies (office users) start slowly to hire new personnel. Employee recruitment, however, does not necessarily imply that new office space will be demanded. The companies will demand additional office space

---

[273] Cf. Rottke, N. B. /Wernecke, M. (2002b), p. 7

[274] See Section 2.2, 5.4.3.3 and 5.4.1.2

[275] Cf. Ball, M., et al. (1998), p. 192, Orr, A., et al. (2003), p. 478-479

only if they are persuaded that the upward trend will last. Otherwise, they will compress the amount of space they use per employee.[276]

If the upward trend has proved to be lasting, then companies will ask for additional office space. Moreover, as the stock of available office space decreases rapidly, companies are willing to pay higher rents and to agree to less favourable lease conditions.[277] Office users who are more sensitive to rent differentials will try to move out, as they favour cheaper rents in lower class buildings. In contrast, when tenants are faced with a downturn in demand and with abundant space and falling rents, they will move to higher quality properties, since they can do so without sustaining any significant rent increases.[278] Alternatively, tenants whose lease contracts are expiring in a short time attempt to renegotiate their lease contract. The result of this renegotiation process might be that they pay less rent, obtain more flexible lease terms, or receive other incentives.[279]

3.5.2.2 Landlords

Landlords also behave in predictable ways during cycle phases. In phases 1 and 2, landlords attempt to receive the highest rent possible and to obtain lease conditions in their favour. In phases 3 and 4, they realize that they will quickly lose tenants if their rental rates are not competitive. Consequently, they lower rents to retain tenants whose leases are expiring and to capture new tenants, even if rents cover only their building's fixed expenses.[280] Therefore, they often offer flexible lease structures and lease incentives.[281]

However, it is also known that some landlords will leave their office properties vacant until market conditions improve. This strategy is referred as stockpiling, and it is possible only because of the long life of office buildings. The rationale behind this strategy is that landlords would rather hold vacant stock in the short term and capitalize on the opportunity of supplying units when rental rates are higher than let properties during periods of low rental value. The decision to adopt this strategy is primarily determined by

---

[276] Cf. Downs, A. (1993), p. 158
[277] Cf. Hahr, H. (2006), p. 24
[278] Cf. Munneke, H. /Slade, B. A. (2001), p. 57
[279] Cf. Mueller, G. R. (1999), p. 138
[280] Cf. Hahr, H. (2006), p. 23-24, Shilton, L. (1998), p. 339, Wernecke, M. (2004), p. 45, Mueller, G. R. (1999), p. 138
[281] Cf. Mueller, G. R. (1999), p. 149, Rottke, N. B. /Wernecke, M. (2002c), p. 5

the landlord's financial strength, since during times of vacancy the owner of the office building still incurs costs.[282]

3.5.2.3 Implications for Hedonic Price Indices

In summary, real estate cycle phases influence the level of rent. Office users and landlords adopt different strategies during the various phases and place different values on the same office rent determinants (e.g., lease incentives) during real estate cycle phases. Therefore, when rent indices are constructed using a hedonic approach, it is likely that the assumption that the implicit prices of quality characteristics are constant across time is probably invalid.[283] Rather, it should be assumed that the implicit prices vary from phase to phase of the real estate cycle and that they are formed by a complex equilibrium process.[284] Consequently, to capture the presence of office rental cycles, this thesis advocates the use of the characteristic price index model for the construction of the hedonic office rent indices.[285]

3.6 Chapter Summary

The purpose of this chapter was to delineate the fundamentals of the office property market and to derive the implications for the development of hedonic office rent indices. The findings can be summarized as follows:

- Real estate and especially office properties are heterogeneous goods. Therefore, they are suited to a hedonic analysis.
- Office properties differ from other property types. The value of an office property depends on its income-generating ability. The ability of the office property to satisfy the needs and requirements of its users determines the income. As a consequence, the variable rent has to be at the centre of a hedonic price index. Moreover, to determine the correct set of characteristics (independent variables) that influences office rent, one must adapt an office tenant's perspective and include lease factors in the hedonic analysis.

---

[282] Cf. Rottke, N. B. /Wernecke, M. (2002a), p. 3, Orr, A., et al. (2003), p. 478
[283] See Section 2.2.1
[284] Cf. Ball, M., et al. (1998), p. 192-193, Hulten, C. R. (2003), p. 11
[285] See Section 5.4.1.2 and 5.4.3.3.

- Confusion reigns when it comes to the choice of the dependent variable in hedonic analysis, since the terms rent, price, value, and worth are often used inappropriately and without proper definition. Different definitions of these terms have been delineated. For the purpose of developing a hedonic price index, the variable rent will be used. However, so that the correct set of characteristics (the independent variables) can be found, the literature review is extended to include hedonic studies, which employ price, value, and worth as dependent variables.
- The office property market can be interpreted as four interlinked submarkets: user, financial asset, development, and land market. Here, rent plays the key signal to all market participants and clears these markets by equating the quantity supplied with that demanded. This finding further underpins the necessity of employing rent as a dependent variable in a hedonic regression analysis.
- Office property markets are inefficient in comparison with other asset markets. This implies that the level of accuracy of a hedonic office rent index cannot be compared to indices of other asset markets, such as stocks and bonds
- Office property markets show cyclical behaviour, which also affects the behaviour and decision of landlords and office tenants. The implication for the hedonic regression analysis is that the assumption that the influence of the office rent determinants remains constant over the entire time period (constant regression coefficients) is probably invalid, because the office user will place different importance on location, building, and lease factors during cycle phases. From a theoretical point of view, therefore, the characteristic price index method is put forward as an index construction methodology.

4 Office Rent Determinants

In this chapter the important characteristics and factors that determine the level of rents are scrutinized. As chapter 2 pointed out, a product has to be known before any hedonic study can be constructed.[286] The first step, a review of international literature, reveals which office rent determinants have been discovered and how they can be measured. The discussion includes research studies that focus on office prices, value, and worth. However, the discussion is not limited to quantitative studies but includes research studies, which are based on interview or surveys. In the second step, the German office property market and its lease structure are described. Thereafter, these findings are used for the conception and development of a survey of German real estate professionals that aims at identifying the factors that determine the level of office rent in Germany. The conception, development, and results of this survey are presented in the third step. Finally, the important key findings are summarized and their implications for the development of hedonic office rent indices for German metropolitan areas are discussed.

4.1 International Literature Review

A broad band of literature has been published that analyzes the factors that determine the level of office rents, prices, value, and worth. In the following section, the main findings are compiled. However, it should be kept in mind that these research studies focus on different office property markets at different times. Furthermore, they use different research methodologies. Therefore, the findings of these research studies often overlap but are sometimes contradictory.[287]

4.1.1 Location Factors and Spatial Relationships

It is a matter of fact that companies are ready to pay higher office rents for some locations over other locations, ceteris paribus. The concept of accessibility explains this phenomenon. Accessibility can be defined as "[...] the ability of individuals to travel [to] and to participate in activities at different locations in an environment."[288] The concept of accessibility is broad. For instance, locations in close proximity to highways, train stations, or airports command higher rents than those that are more remote. An-

---

[286] See Section 2.2.4

[287] See Appendix A.1 for a complete overview of the international literature review

[288] Thériault, M., et al. (2005), p. 23

other aspect of the concept of accessibility is that companies pay higher rents for labour market proximity. Amenity-oriented firms prefer one location to others because it enhances the working environment for employees (quality of the surroundings). In addition, it is argued that it is important for office companies to have close access to their customers and business contacts (so-called face-to-face contacts). Finally, some companies choose their locations on the basis of representativeness and image.

The reasons for location decisions, however, are not considered independently but are intermingled. Furthermore, because the concept of accessibility is broad, different approaches to operationalizing and measuring accessibility have been presented in recent years, which aggravate a clear delimitation. This section attempts to identify office rent determinants and to show how they can be operationalized and therefore included in the hedonic function. This section first presents the different concepts of accessibility. Second, the section challenges the importance of face-to-face contacts in location decisions. Strictly defined, the importance of face-to-face contacts relates to the concept of accessibility. However, because it is discussed extensively in real estate literature, it is presented separately. Third, the representativeness of office address is assessed.

4.1.1.1 Accessibility

4.1.1.1.1 Transportation Modes

In the research on the office property market, only a few studies shed light on the link between office rent and transportation modes .[289] For instance, *Nitsch (2006)* examines the impact on office rents, the distance to the airport, and the accessibility of the office building by different means of public transportation. Here, he computes the walking time between the office building and the nearest point of the public transportation system. Thereby, he accounts between the different means of public transportation (subway, train, tramway, and bus) by adding ten minutes of 'hypothetical' waiting time for buses and tramways because of their lower attractiveness. His study focuses on Munich (Germany) and also includes office building characteristics. His sample size consists of only 46 observations.[290] Aside from the small sample size and the measurement of accessibility, he states that the office rent is mainly explained by the office building's lo-

[289] Most real studies assessing the relationship between property value and transportation modes are limited to residential properties. Cf. Bollinger, C. R., et al. (1998), p. 1097, Ryan, S. (2005), p. 751

[290] Cf. Nitsch, H. (2006), p. 93-107

cation, which itself can be "[...] reduced to the distance between from the airport and from the next access point to public transportation." Both variables are statistically significant and show the expected negative relationship to office rents.[291]

Heyser (2006) also has analyzed the Munich office market. His data sample consists of 30 independent variables and is based on 89 office properties. His regression model is similar to that of *Nitsch (2006)* in that it includes a variable measuring the distance to the airport and a variable measuring the distance to the next access point to public transportation. Both variables are statistically significant and show the expected negative relationship to office rents (the asking office rent). However, their explanatory power is reduced when other location dummies are included.[292] Moreover, from a statistical point of view, some criticism arises because the ratio of the sample size to the number of independent variables is insufficient.[293]

Ryan (2005) conducted an empirical study investigating the influence of transportation modes on office rent in San Diego (USA).[294] Two access variables are introduced. One variable measures the straight-line distance between the office building and the next freeway access, and the second measures the straight-line distance to the closest light transit station. In addition, his office rent model captures building and neighbourhood characteristics. His sample consists of 520 office buildings. He finds statistically significant results for both accessibility variables. The variable measuring the distance to the next freeway access has the expected negative relationship to office rents. However, the variable measuring the distance to the next public transportation access is surprisingly positive. In other words, the closer the office building is to the light railway station, the lower the office rent. *Ryan (2005)* explains the unexpected result by the fact that "[...] much of the San Diego light rail system is located in corridors that were previously rail rights-of-way."[295]

Oven /Pekdemir (2004) focus their analysis on Istanbul (Turkey). Rather than using a standard multiple regression approach, they employ a factor analysis ranking 52 office

[291] Ibid.p. 104

[292] Cf. Heyser, H. (2006), p. 150-154

[293] For testing the multiple correlations a sample size of $N \geq 50+8m$ and for testing individual variables a sample size of $N \geq 104+m$ (where m is the number of independent variables) is recommended. Cf. Tabachnick, B. G. /Fidell, L. S. (2006), p. 123

[294] Cf. Ryan, S. (2005), p. 751-764

[295] Ibid.p. 760

rent determinants for Istanbul, which are later compared with the reported findings of other metropolitan areas. Their analysis also includes the distance to the next underground station. However, this variable is revealed to be statistically insignificant. In the opinion of *Oven /Pekdemir (2004)*, this finding stems from the fact that Istanbul lacks a proper underground transportation network.[296]

In a research study investigating the existence of office submarkets, *Dunse, et al. (2002)* also examine the relationship between the proximity to the nearest railway station and office rents with a dummy variable. The dummy variable takes the value of 1 if the office building lies within 250 metres of a major railway station, and 0 otherwise. Their study concentrates on Glasgow and Edinburgh (both UK), and the sample consists of 539 observations. Controlling for other buildings and location characteristics, their hedonic office rent model implies that proximity to the public transportation system has a positive impact on office rent at a 0.95 significance level.[297]

Bender, et al. (1999) employ a different approach. Rather than analyzing office rent determinants by multiple regression analysis based on rental data, they sent questionnaires to 1,800 office users in Geneva (Switzerland), who answered questions about their perceptions of the environmental quality and location criteria. Using the analytic hierarchy process, a multi-attribute modeling methodology, they determine the importance of the individual criteria. Although their study does not directly focus on office rents, it seems logical to conclude that office users are willing to pay more for important criteria than for less important ones. Their empirical findings confirm that the proximity to local public transportation is of the utmost importance, while proximity to long distance public transportation is less important.[298]

Gat (1998) presents a study of the office market in Tel Aviv (Israel). Using 50 office buildings, he includes location and building characteristics in his office rent model. One location variable measures the distance between the office buildings and the beltway. Although this variable does not remain in his final model, it is statistically significant at the 0.95 level and has the expected negative relationship.[299]

---

[296] Cf. Oven, A. /Pekdemir, D. (2004), p. 1-25
[297] Cf. Dunse, N., et al. (2002), p. 489-506
[298] Cf. Bender, A., et al. (1999), p. 280-296
[299] Cf. Gat, D. (1998), p. 229-247

In a study of Chicago's office property market, *Colwell, et al. (1998)* attempt to identify the determinants that influence the prices of parcels. Using 427 observations that originated between the years 1986 and 1993, they build two hedonic models, controlling for location and building characteristics. Both models use the same set of explanatory variables. The only difference lies in the manner in which the variable time is incorporated. Their set of explanatory variables comprises three variables that measure accessibility in terms of transportation modes. Their models include the distance to the next airport, the percentage of quarter sections devoted to interstates and tollways, and the percentage of quarter sections devoted to rail transportation. All variables prove to be statistically significant at the 0.95 level, though with different coefficients signs. For instance, the parcel's price decreases the farther away it is from the airport. Although the price increases with the increasing percentage of land devoted to interstate highways and tollways, it decreases with the presence of railways. *Colwell, et al. (1998)* attribute this observation to the less attractive surroundings in the vicinity of railroads.[300]

Bollinger, et al. (1998) estimate different hedonic office rent models for Atlanta (USA). Their elaborated models, which control for building characteristics and lease factors, also include location variables. They employ two dummy variables. One variable takes the value of 1 if the office building lies within one mile of a highway interchange; otherwise the value is 0. The second dummy variable takes the value of 1 if the office building lies within a quarter-mile of a train station. Their sample spans the years 1990 to 1996 and consists of 658 to 907 observations per year. Their empirical results demonstrate that proximity to a highway interchange has a positive impact on office rents, while proximity to a railway station has a negative impact. Both variables are statistically significant at the 0.95 level. In the opinion of *Bollinger, et al. (1998)*, the failure of the proximity to the public transportation system to increase office rents arises from the perception that public transportation stations are unsafe.[301]

In a study similar to that of *Bender, et al. (1999)*, *Bottom, et al. (1997)* analyse the importance of 39 location and design characteristics in meeting tenants' requirements, as determined by a postal survey. Their survey targets London tenants of offices located in properties held by institutional investors. Their survey's results demonstrate that the

[300] Cf. Colwell, P. F., et al. (1998), p. 92-99
[301] Cf. Bollinger, C. R., et al. (1998), p. 1097-1118

importance of the proximity to public transportation depends on the tenant's industry background. While those in banks and legal services perceive that the proximity of public transportation is very important, those in insurance and brokering services attribute only moderate importance.[302]

In her study, *Sivitanidou (1996)* analyzes the Los Angeles (USA) office property market. Although her research question focuses on whether large main and secondary service centres play an important role for office companies, her study also sheds light on the impact of transportation modes on property value. Her hedonic model, in which property value is a dependent variable, includes, along with many building, neighbourhood, and location variables, two variables that measure the accessibility to different transportation modes. The first variable measures the distance between the office building and the closest major airport. The second variable measures the distance between the office building and the closest freeway. Using 539 observations, she obtains interesting results. For instance, the empirical results confirm at a 0.95 statistical significance level that the closer the office building is to an airport, the higher its property value. However, the regression coefficient measuring the proximity to the next freeway is not only statistically insignificant but also shows an unexpected positive sign. *Sivitanidou (1996)* attributes this unusual result to the small variation in freeway distances across sample properties and to worsening traffic congestion at locations closer to these freeways.[303]

In a study of the Los Angeles (USA) office market, *Clapp (1980)* introduces one variable measuring the accessibility via transportation modes. The variable measures the distance by road between the office building and the nearest freeway entrance. Moreover, his model is based on 105 observations and also includes building characteristics. Statistical tests confirm the expected results. In other words, the farther away the office building is from the nearest freeway entrance, the lower the level of office rent.[304]

The literature review is inconclusive. Obviously, the importance and impact of accessibility measured by transportation modes on office rent depends on the city structure, its roads, and its public transportation networks. In addition, a survey of office occupiers and office agents conducted by *Leishman, et al. (2003)* and *Bottom, et al. (1997)* pro-

---

[302] Cf. Bottom, C., et al. (1997), p. 195-203

[303] Cf. Sivitanidou, R. (1996), p. 125-149

[304] Cf. Clapp, J. M. (1980), p. 387-399

vides a strong indication that the impact of accessibility is mainly dependent on the office user's business activities.[305]

4.1.1.1.2 Quality of the Surroundings

The importance of accessibility has been reduced so far to transportation modes. Another important location factor is the quality of the surroundings and neighbourhood characteristics. For amenity-oriented office companies, the appeal of the new location to the existing employee base is often rated as more important than financial aspects.[306]

Ihlanfeldt (1990) investigates the intra-metropolitan location of new companies and thereby measures the quality of the surroundings for the Atlanta region by several variables. For instance, the availability of shopping is constructed as a dummy variable indicating whether or not the tract of the office building contained a regional shopping centre. To measure the accessibility to restaurants and entertainment, Ihlanfeldt constructs a gravity variable.[307] In addition, he introduces the per capita police expenditures to measure the perceived exposure to crime. While the latter variable does not prove to have any statistical significance, the accessibility to shopping centres, restaurants, and entertainment is statistically significant at the 0.95 level. In other words, these variables are important to new companies in determining the office location.[308] Consequently, new companies are willing to pay more if these location attributes are present.

In her study on Los Angeles, *Sivitanidou (1996)* constructs several variables as proxies for the quality of the surroundings. As proxy for the quality of the office property's surrounding neighbourhood, she measures the per capita income in the census tract within which each property is located. She also measures the average crime rate, and, as proxies to capture the accessibility to shopping and entertainment, she uses the retail and motion picture employment per resident population at the census tract level. Furthermore, she includes the distance between the office building and the ocean in her hedonic model. This variable serves as proxy for access to recreational and environmental qual-

---

[305] Cf. Leishman, C., et al. (2003), p. 59

[306] Cf. O'Mara, M. A. (1999), p. 382

[307] "Gravity models are accounts for a wide variety of flow patterns in human/economic systems, based on Newton's gravity equation which defines gravity of the flow of potential (between two sites or locations) as directly proportional to the product of their masses (or size) and inversely proportional to the square of the distance between them." Realtors Commercial Alliance (2005), p. 14

[308] Cf. Ihlanfeldt, K. (1990), p. 190-193

ity. The empirical results confirm at a 0.95 statistical significance level that these variables have an impact on the property land value.[309]

In their hedonic model examining the parcel prices of the Chicago office market, *Colwell, et al. (1998)* include different variables accounting for the quality of the surroundings. The percentage of quarter sections devoted to recreational parks, conservation parks, and golf courses is measured. However, only recreational parks increase the value of parcel prices by a statistical significance; the other two variables are statistically insignificant.[310]

In their office rent model for Atlanta's region, *Bollinger, et al. (1998)* include four variables intended to measure the quality of the surroundings and worker utility. In their model, they measure as a dummy variable whether the office building is near a shopping mall. In addition, they also measure the concentration of blue-collar workers employed in the census tract, the percentage of the tract's population that is Black, and the median household income of the tract. It is argued that industrial areas in which the concentration of blue-collar workers is relatively high provide work environments that are less desirable, due to pollution, noise, and negative aesthetics. The percentage of the tract's Black population and the median household income of the tract are supposed to capture dimensions of neighbourhood quality not reflected by other variables of their model. Although the percentage of the tract's Black population is statistically insignificant, all other variables measuring the attractiveness of the work location are significant and in line with their expectations.[311]

For Istanbul, *Oven /Pekdemir (2004)* report completely different results, which "[...] may not be necessarily in line with general common sense."[312] In their study, they use the college-educated household and average household income to measure the desirability and quality of the surroundings, but both variables prove to be statistically insignificant.[313]

In his study of the San Diego office property market, *Ryan (2005)* incorporates only one variable as proxy for the neighbourhood quality. He measures the median household

[309] Cf. Sivitanidou, R. (1996), p. 139-143
[310] Cf. Colwell, P. F., et al. (1998), p. 99
[311] Cf. Bollinger, C. R., et al. (1998), p. 1101-1111
[312] Oven, A. /Pekdemir, D. (2004), p. 17
[313] Cf. Ibid., p. 16-17

income for residents in the census tract where each office property is located. The empirical results imply that, for the majority of San Diego's submarkets, office occupiers pay a premium to be located in neighbourhoods with high-income residents.[314]

The hedonic office rent model by *Nitsch (2006)* assesses the quality of the surroundings differently. He computes a new variable. First he multiplies the distance to the city centre by a dummy variable indicating if the office building contains an in-house restaurant. Second, this product is added to a variable indicating whether the office building has a landscaped terrace. His reasoning is that only office buildings in unattractive neighbourhoods have in-house restaurants and landscaped terraces to compensate for the quality of the surroundings. The computed variable capturing the missing neighbourhood quality is statistically significant and has the expected negative relationship.[315]

Heyser (2006) follows another approach. In his studies, two variables measure the quality of the surroundings. First, he constructs a variable that represents the mean average price of wheat beer and coffee offered by restaurants located within 500 metres of the office buildings. As a sole explanatory variable, it is surprisingly important. However, when other independent variables enter the regression equation, its explanatory power diminishes, but it remains statistically significant.[316] The second variable measures the total rental area in the vicinity of 500 metres of the office building and classifies it into one of three categories. In his opinion, this second variable accounts for the quality of the surroundings in terms of restaurants, service providers, and private postal services.[317] He obtains mixed results. In one regression model, in which the dependent variable is not transformed, this independent variable has a high explanatory power and is statistically significant; however, it becomes insignificant in another regression model, in which the dependent variable is logarithmic transformed.[318]

For most metropolitan areas, the quality of the surroundings is an important aspect. However, the literature review also demonstrates that no consensus concerning what

---

[314] Cf. Ryan, S. (2005), p. 756-760
[315] Cf. Nitsch, H. (2006), p. 93-107
[316] Cf. Heyser, H. (2006), p. 146
[317] Cf. Ibid.p. 108
[318] Cf. Ibid.p. 143-154

constitutes the quality of the surroundings and which variables can serve as proxies has been reached. This question remains unanswered at a city-specific level.

4.1.1.1.3 Labour Market Proximity

In location theory, labour market proximity is often mentioned as an important factor explaining companies' location decisions. However, as *Bollinger, et al. (1998)* point out, this factor is difficult to measure separately, as it coincides with proximity to suppliers and customers.[319] As a consequence, many research studies operationalize this factor by the distance to the cemtral business district (CBD) or by the distance to the public transportation system. In order to avoid repetition, only research studies that explicitly attempt to examine the impact of labour workforce proximity on office location decisions are presented.

In their survey focusing on Edinburgh's office property market, *Leishman, et al. (2003)* ask office occupiers and agents to rank different the location preferences of office occupiers. Their empirical results state that labour workforce proximity gets the highest average mean scores by office users. Although agents also consider this factor important for office users, they do not view it as the most important one.[320]

O'Mara (1999) reports that access to suppliers or customers is seldom the driving force influencing location decisions of information-age companies. Instead, these companies locate where a labour workforce skilled in specific industry knowledge is available.[321]

Clapp (1980) operationalizes the labour workforce proximity by measuring the average commuting time by car from the home to the workplace. The variable has been based on interviews with employees working in the dataset's office buildings. The statistical results strongly indicate that office buildings that are nearer to the residences of employees obtain a premium, and vice versa.[322]

4.1.1.2 Importance of Face-to-Face Contacts

Closely related to transportation modes as a measure of accessibility is the importance of face-to-face contacts for office companies. In many classic theories of urban location, face-to-face contacts are the escrow issue for explaining the city patterns. Formerly, it

[319] Cf. Bollinger, C. R., et al. (1998), p. 1101-1102
[320] Cf. Leishman, C., et al. (2003), p. 49-51
[321] Cf. O'Mara, M. A. (1999), p. 384
[322] Cf. Clapp, J. M. (1980), p. 396

has been argued that business takes place primarily through face-to-face contacts with customers, suppliers, and office workers who have their highest density in the central business district (CBD). Hence, the level of rent that a company is willing to pay declines as the distance from the CBD increases, because the travel costs associated with maintaining contact with other companies increase. Various researchers have criticised these classic theories because of their simplifying assumptions and the influence of modern working structures.[323] For instance, lower transportation costs and better information and communication technologies have raised serious doubts about the importance of the CBD in location choice. Especially in the aftermath of September 11, it has been argued that communication technology will become more important and will take the place of face-to-face contacts.[324] Therefore, the impact of distance to CBD (as proxy for face-to-face contacts) on explaining the level of rent is challenged.

In this tradition, *Nitsch (2006)* includes in his hedonic office rent model for Munich the proximity to the CBD as Euclidean distance. His empirical results confirm at a 0.99 statistical significance level that the greater the distance between the office building and the CBD, the lower the office rent.[325] In his analysis of the office market of Munich, *Heyser (2006)* employs a dummy variable to measure the CBD. His statistical results confirm the importance of the CBD as an explanatory variable.[326] Similar findings are reported by *Dunse, et al. (2002)*. Confirming their earlier work on the Glasgow office property market,[327] they report at a 0.99 statistical significance level that office rent is a declining function of the distance to the CBD for Edinburgh as well.[328] This observation is also empirically tested and confirmed for the Tel Aviv, the Atlanta, and the Los Angeles office property market.[329]

Several research studies have contributed opposite findings, suggesting that the distance to the CBD is not an important or statistically significant determinant of office rent. For instance, *Oven /Pekdemir (2004)* report a statistically insignificant result for their vari-

---

[323] Cf. Wyatt, P. (1999), p. 3 for a literature review.
[324] Cf. Dixon, T., et al. (2003), p. 348
[325] Cf. Nitsch, H. (2006), p. 93-107
[326] Cf Heyser, H. (2006), p. 151
[327] Cf. Dunse, N. /Jones, C. (1998), p. 311
[328] Cf. Dunse, N., et al. (2002), p. 483-506
[329] Cf. Clapp, J. M. (1980), p. 387-399, Ihlanfeldt, K. (1990), p. 182-198, Gat, D. (1998), p. 229-247

able measuring the distance to the CBD for the Istanbul office property market.[330] *Archer /Smith (2003)* assess the Houston (USA) office property market using 647 observations. Contrary to their expectations, their regression results demonstrate a positive sign for the regression coefficient at a 0.99 significance level.[331] *Munneke /Slade (2001)* developed a commercial price index for Phoenix (USA) using 890 office property transactions and report only statistically insignificant results.[332] Previously, *Downs /Slade (1999)* found no statistically significant relationship for the Phoenix metropolitan area.[333] Likewise, in a study of the Chicago office property market, the empirical results of *Colwell, et al. (1998)* show that the effect of distance to the CBD is statistically insignificant.[334] The empirical results of a study by *Hodgson, et al. (2006)*, who focus more on the correct functional form of hedonic office price models, demonstrate that an increase in distance to the CBD leads to an increase in office prices within the Phoenix metropolitan area at a statistically significant 0.95 level. Their hedonic models also incorporate other building characteristics and are based upon 1,846 observations.[335]

In addition, some research studies report mixed results. In his study, *Ryan (2005)* subdivides the San Diego office property market into three parts: Center City, South Bay, and East County. In the results for the Centre City market area, the coefficient for distance to the CBD is significant with the expected positive relationship. However, it is insignificant in the results for South Bay and East County. His explanation refers to the fact that the San Diego office property market is polycentric. In other words, its metropolitan regions have developed subcentres, which reduce the importance of the CBD.[336] Similarly, in a previous study of the Atlanta office property market, *Bollinger, et al. (1998)* report negative, statistically significant regression coefficients for the north side of the Atlanta region and positive, statistically significant coefficients for the south side.[337]

From the above research studies it is evident that no clear answer is given as to whether the level of office rent is a negative function of the distance to the CBD and whether the

---

[330] Cf. Oven, A. /Pekdemir, D. (2004), p. 16
[331] Cf. Archer, W. R. /Smith, M. T. (2003), p. 159-160
[332] Cf. Munneke, H. /Slade, B. A. (2001), p. 67-69
[333] Cf. Downs, D. H. /Slade, B. A. (1999), p. 97-99
[334] Cf. Colwell, P. F., et al. (1998), p. 98
[335] Cf. Hodgson, D., et al. (2006), p. 151-168
[336] Cf. Ryan, S. (2005), p. 757-760
[337] Cf. Bollinger, C. R., et al. (1998), p. 1105-1108

classic theory of the urban location of face-to-face contacts still holds true. Instead, a closer look at the business activities of office occupiers is necessary. For some businesses, face-to-face contacts will prevail, as human interaction at close proximity fosters new ideas, creative insights, formal education, training, and trust, which may in turn result in more innovation, more rapid diffusion of innovation, greater adaptability, and improved management skills.[338] Therefore, proximity is vital for much of the knowledge work that takes place in offices.[339] In contrast, backroom offices and noncritical support activities do not require a CBD location and therefore can be decentralised.[340] It is a matter of fact that many offices are now located outside the CBD (decentralisation) area, causing submarkets to emerge.[341]

In other words, technological changes in information and communications, new working practices, and outsourcing have increased the complexity of modeling office rents and office markets.

4.1.1.3 Representativeness of Location ("Quality of Address")

In addition to the concept of accessibility and the importance of face-to-face contacts, some researchers maintain that the image and prestige of the office location often is the leading factor in managers' decisions concerning office location.[342] This phenomenon is often referred to as seeking "the right address."[343]

At first glance, it seems that the vanity of managers rather than rationality drives this decision factor. However, *Archer /Smith (2003)* propose a convincing argument to the contrary. They state that a representative office location can be part of a company's marketing strategy to establish favourable recognition, client confidence, and brand loyalty. The choice of a representative office location becomes "[...] a capital investment to reduce future marketing expenses."[344] In addition, they interpret that a company's having the right address not only influences the prospective employee's perception of the company but "[...] also facilitates employee retention by serving as a con-

---

[338] Cf. Anas, A., et al. (1998), p. 1426, Wyatt, P. (1999), p. 3
[339] Cf. Gat, D. (1998), p. 235
[340] Cf. Sing, T. F. (2005), p. 495
[341] Cf. Hanink, D. M. (1996), p. 342, Archer, W. R. /Smith, M. T. (2003), p. 140-141
[342] Cf. Gat, D. (1998), p. 238
[343] Cf. Archer, W. R. /Smith, M. T. (2003), p.
[344] Ibid.p. 143

tinuing signal for employees of the personnel policies and the 'quality' of the firm."[345] However, it is difficult to determine if the effect of representativeness results from office location or from the architectural features of the office building. So far, only three quantitative research studies have been found to incorporate explicitly this factor in their analysis.

In her study of the Los Angeles office property market, *Sivitanidou (1996)* measures the representativeness of the office location as a dummy variable, which takes the value of 1 if the office is located in Beverly Hills, and 0 otherwise. Although *Clapp (1980)* has used this approach, Sivitanidou's research focuses on the substitutability of the CBD by secondary centres. She formulates different hedonic rent models under different assumptions of substitutability. In two out of the three models, the variable measuring the prestige of the office location is statistically significant and thereby confirms *Clapp (1980)* earlier findings.[346] Investigating the Munich office property market, *Nitsch (2006)* includes a dummy variable controlling for office buildings near the Marienplatz, which is commonly known as a highly representative area. His empirical results confirm that office companies are willing to pay a rent premium for highly representative locations.[347]

Other research studies tackle the measurement of representativeness differently. For instance, some studies assume that an office location within the CBD area is representative. Therefore, they use the distance of the office location to the CBD as proxy for the representativeness. Another strand of research studies models the effect of representativeness on office rents by including building characteristics. These studies suggest including the building age squared, as older buildings are located in more representative areas.[348] Nevertheless, the measurement of representativeness of an office location and delineation from other factors remains a difficult task.

[345] Ibid.p. 149

[346] Cf. Clapp, J. M. (1980), p. 387-399, Sivitanidou, R. (1996), p. 125-149

[347] Cf. Nitsch, H. (2006), p. 101-102

[348] Cf. Section 4.1.2.1

4.1.2 Building Factors

Real estate researchers and practitioners do not question that building factors have a major impact on the level of office rent. It is imperative to control them in any hedonic office rent models. However, various building characteristics have been analyzed in real estate and engineering literature in the past. Therefore, a review of which building characteristics have been identified as important and how they are operationalized is necessary. First, the topic of quality in terms of building and design quality is presented. Second, how the representativeness and image of an office building are measured is discussed. The section closes with a review of research studies investigating the importance of environmental aspects.

4.1.2.1 Quality

The quality of an office building is a latent concept that is difficult to delineate. To make matters worse, different definitions and measurements of quality are used in the real estate and engineering literature. Here, the following definition by *Thomson, et al. (2003)* is adopted in a real estate context:[349]

The quality of an office building is an assessment of how well its features meet the tenant's requirements and needs.

Many hedonic studies in office rent analysis advocate the employment of the variable building age to measure the quality of an office building. The intuitive reasoning is that office buildings, like other types of production capital, become physically and functionally obsolete. In other words, the building age captures the depreciation of an office building. As a consequence, the level of rent decreases with the age of the building. Because the building age is measurable and easily collected, it is included in many hedonic analyses and proves to be of statistical significance.[350]

Although it is often assumed that many building quality characteristics can be subsumed within the age variable,[351] some researchers question the reliability of age as a building

---

[349] Cf. Thomson, D. S., et al. (2003), p. 337

[350] Cf. Downs, D. H. /Slade, B. A. (1999), p. 97-99, Gunnelin, A. /Söderberg, B. (2003), p. 241-265, Dunse, N. /Jones, C. (1998), p. 297-312, Slade, B. A. (2000), p. 357-380, Colwell, P. F., et al. (1998), p. 83-106, Archer, W. R. /Smith, M. T. (2003), p. 139-164, Bollinger, C. R., et al. (1998), p. 1097-1118, Laverne, R. J. /Winson-Geideman, K. (2003), p. 281-290, Hodgson, D., et al. (2006), p. 151-168, Sivitanidou, R. (1996), p. 125-149

[351] Cf. Dunse, N. /Jones, C. (1998), p. 307

quality estimator. For instance, *Gat (1998)* objects that "[...] as time goes by, various design innovations are tried. Some of them become timeless and others are just passing fads."[352] *Ball (2003)* articulates further criticism. He challenges the assumption that new buildings generally command higher rent due to quality reasons and remarks that "[...] older buildings [...] may develop prestige and status that command higher rent charges."[353] In addition, many office buildings undergo a refurbishment that keeps them modern. Some hedonic analyses attempt to circumvent this problem by adding age square variables in their regression equation.[354]

Nevertheless, a few research studies tackle the measurement of building quality in more detail. *Gat (1998)* interviews several Tel Aviv architects. Each architect has to appraise the quality of the building using a list of different attributes. The average score from these expert judgments generates a summary quality estimator that is included in the regression equation. His findings suggest that building quality is a statistically significant driver of office rents.[355]

In a previous research study of Boston's and Cambridge's office market, *Vandell, et al. (1989)* propose a similar approach. Besides a number of building characteristics, they include a variable in their hedonic model that represents the quality of the office building architecture. In their terms, architecture is the aesthetic pleasure a person experiences looking at the exterior of the structure. A survey of 80 architects generated the data for this variable. The survey's questions distinguished between new and refurbished office buildings and covered aspects such as the quality of materials used, fenestration, massing, the design of the interior public space, the view of the skyline, the design of the exterior space, the relationship to the neighbourhood, and the provision of public amenities. In their regression analysis, however, the design variable remains statistically insignificant, and no influence on rent is reported.[356] Severe criticism arises because the sample size is small (N=56), the study focuses solely on aesthetics, and only architects undertake to measure the architectural quality.[357]

---

[352] Gat, D. (1998), p. 235
[353] Ball, M. (2003), p. 177
[354] Cf. Colwell, P. F., et al. (1998), p. 83-106, Hodgson, D., et al. (2006), p. 151-168
[355] Cf. Gat, D. (1998), p. 229-247
[356] Cf. Vandell, K. D., et al. (1989), p. 235-265
[357] Cf. Kain, J. F. (1989), p. 261-265

In his data sample, *Heyser (2006)* has two categorical variables measuring the quality of an office building: one indicates the type of cladding of the office, and the other classifies the office building entrance. However, the variables are not statistical significant and are not included in his final hedonic model.[358]

Developing an office rent index for Chicago, *Webb /Fisher (1996)* also assess building quality. They include one dummy variable for each building to control for differences across buildings (N=225 leases). In their hedonic model, they also include a quality variable that measures the quality of the office space within the building. As in the studies of the aforementioned authors, this variable is based on interviews. However, property managers, not architects, are interviewed. Unfortunately, they do not clearly specify if these variables are of statistical significance.[359] In a similar study, *Englund, et al. (2004)* include 871 building dummy variables in their hedonic analysis of office leases in Sweden.[360] Both aforementioned research studies control only for building quality. It should be made clear that the aim of their scope of research is not to examine the influence of building quality.

A common approach to operationalizing the quality of an office building is to categorize office buildings into different classes. Leasing agents and appraisers of the respective market mainly provide the definitions of these classes. In their office rent analysis of Baton Rouge (USA), *Glascock, et al. (1990)* incorporate a dummy variable for each class using the following notion, which has become widely accepted in many other office property markets around the world: class A is the best; class D is the worst. Their empirical results are in line with their expectations and are statistically significant.[361] Analyzing the office property market of Cleveland (USA), *Laverne /Winson-Geideman (2003)* likewise incorporate dummy variables for the different office categories. Their regression coefficients have the expected sign and are highly statistically significant.[362] *Bond, et al. (2005)* follow this approach, except that they use a slightly different classification (class A to class C). Their empirical results confirm for the London office property market that class B occurs at a discount in comparison with class A, and class C at

358 Cf. Heyser, H. (2006), p. 115

359 Cf. Webb, B. R. /Fisher, J. D. (1996), p. 1-19

360 Cf. Englund, P., et al. (2004), p. 183-215

361 Cf. Glascock, J. L., et al. (1990), p. 105-119

362 Cf. Laverne, R. J. /Winson-Geideman, K. (2003), p. 281-290

a discount in comparison with class B.[363] *Desyllas (2000)* includes a dummy variable indicating whether it is a new or old office building. In his regression analysis of office rents in Berlin, he finds a statistically significant result but with an unexpected negative relationship.[364] Furthermore, *Hodgson, et al. (2006)* and *Dunse, et al. (2002)* employ dummy variables measuring building condition based upon appraisers' estimations and also find statistically significant results.[365]

In her hedonic model, *Sivitanidou (1996)* applies three dummy variables to the exterior quality of the buildings. The first variable takes the value of 1 if the office building has a metal frame. The second and third variables take the value of 1 if the office building has external glass or external wooden walls, respectively. The regression coefficients of these variables are statistically significant and have the expected sign. Metal frame office buildings and buildings with external wooden walls are discounted, whereas office buildings with external glass walls are valued with a premium.[366]

4.1.2.2 Prestige and Representativeness

The representativeness resulting from an office building's physical characteristics is difficult to measure. As pointed out in section 4.1.1.3, it is hard to delineate whether the representativeness results from its location (quality of address) or from its physical structure.

It is argued that building height can serve as proxy for an office building's representativeness and prestige.[367] The reasoning is that the higher an office building is, the more it shapes its building environment and the more it attracts the attention of the public. *Clapp (1980)* refers to the so-called amenity of view.[368] As a matter of fact, many hedonic models using either office prices or rents as a dependent variable include a variable measuring the height of an office building. While some models use dummy variables, others employ a continuous variable for building height. In both cases, the build-

---

[363] Cf. Bond, S. A., et al. (2005), p. 1-27
[364] Cf. Desyllas, J. (2000), p. 192-228
[365] Cf. Dunse, N., et al. (2002), p. 483-506, Hodgson, D., et al. (2006), p. 151-168
[366] Cf. Sivitanidou, R. (1996), p. 125-149
[367] Cf. Gat, D. (1998), p. 235
[368] Cf. Clapp, J. M. (1980), p. 387-399

ing height shows the expected positive relationship and proves to be of major statistical significance.[369]

Another proxy for the representativeness of an office building is the total floor or building area. The office buildings with a large total floor area are more visible, as they take up more space. Several hedonic studies include building area in their models and find statistically significant results.[370]

As *Slade (2000)* remarks, building height and building area are often highly correlated; therefore, entering both variables might introduce multicollinearity in the regression equation.[371] As a consequence, some researchers use the average floor area or building footprint instead of building area or building height.[372]

Most studies using building height, building size, or other proxies for the representativeness of an office building in their hedonic models find statistically significant relationships. However, surveys of different tenant organizations investigating the importance of different office building characteristics reveal that the importance of a representative office building depends largely on the type and organization of the office users. Whereas banks with many backroom operations considered the quality and exterior of the building unimportant, companies working in the insurance, brokering, or legal industry with many frontroom operations ranked it as very important.[373]

4.1.2.3 Environmental Aspects

In the recent past, the importance of environmental aspects has increased among the population. Similarly, the awareness and recognition of environmentally friendly office buildings, so-called green buildings, have increased. City officials, developers, institutional investors, and tenants recognize that green buildings add value.[374] In an extensive

---

[369] Cf. Downs, D. H. /Slade, B. A. (1999), p. 95-104, Wheaton, W. C. /Torto, R. G. (1995), p. 121-139, Colwell, P. F., et al. (1998), p. 83-106, Munneke, H. /Slade, B. A. (2001), p. 55-84, Archer, W. R. /Smith, M. T. (2003), p. 139-164, Gat, D. (1998), p. 229-247, Bollinger, C. R., et al. (1998), p. 1097-1118, Clapp, J. M. (1980), p. 387-399, Hodgson, D., et al. (2006), p. 151-168

[370] Cf. Downs, D. H. /Slade, B. A. (1999), p. 95-104, Munneke, H. /Slade, B. A. (2001), p. 55-84, Archer, W. R. /Smith, M. T. (2003), p. 139-164, Hodgson, D., et al. (2006), p. 151-168, Nitsch, H. (2006), p. 93-107

[371] Cf. Slade, B. A. (2000), p. 360

[372] Cf. Sivitanidou, R. (1996), p. 125-149, Slade, B. A. (2000), p. 357-380, Colwell, P. F., et al. (1998), p. 83-106

[373] Cf. Bottom, C., et al. (1997), p. 195-203

[374] Cf. Shiers, D. (1999), p. 1-2, Kuls, N. (2006), p. V13

literature review, *Heerwagen (2000)* identifies four potential links between green buildings and organizational performance: financial outcomes, business process outcomes, stakeholder relations, and human resource management.[375] Most links seem to be intuitively logical. Furthermore, if these links exist, then it also logical to assume that office tenants are willing to pay a rent premium for an environmentally friendly office building as compared to a 'standard' office building.[376] Specifically, the fact that green buildings have significantly lower running costs is appealing to many office tenants in times of increasing energy prices.[377] However, it also becomes obvious that these links are hard to quantify and analyze statistically because no comprehensive data are available.[378] As a matter of fact, most studies investigating the impact of the features and organizational performance of green buildings use case studies as the research methodology.[379]

Financial Outcomes •Reduced resource utilization •Reduced operating/maintenance costs •Reduced risks/avoided costs •Increased overall productivity •Increased resale value of property •Reduced absenteeism	Business Process Outcomes •Process innovation •Increased work process efficiency
Stakeholder Relations •Improved public image •Community outreach and education •Improved ability to work with community stakeholders •Increased ability to sell to pro-environmental customers	Human Resource Development •Improved quality of work life •Improved personal productivity •Improved well being •Reduced turnover and increased ability to attract high quality workers

Table 7: Potential links between green buildings and organizational performance[380]

---

375 See Table 7

376 Cf. Ries, R. /Bilec, M. (2006), p. 259-263, Boyd, T. /Kimmet, P. (2004), p. 5, Bartlett, E. /Howard, N. (2000), p. 317-318

377 Cf. Wild, B. /Autenrieth, M. (2008), p. 14-17, Frankfurter Allgemeine Zeitung (2006), p. 49

378 Cf. Ries, R. /Bilec, M. (2006), p. 260

379 A in-depth literature review of case-based studies can be found in Heerwagen, J. (2000), p. 356-364

380 Ibid.p. 356

In a conference paper, *Shiers (1999)* presents some preliminary results of a case study based on 23 commercial projects in the United Kingdom. Semi-structured interviews that include both quantitative and qualitative aspects have been conducted with developers, property managers, letting agents, and representatives of tenant organizations. His findings are in line with the aforementioned advantages of green buildings.[381]

However, the research findings of *St. Lawrence (2004)* cast doubt as to whether office occupiers have recognized and priced in the advantages of environmental aspects. In other words, it is arguable whether environmentally friendly characteristics have yet to influence office rents. The findings of her interviews with developers, government and nongovernment organizations, chartered surveyors, corporate occupiers, and industry bodies in the UK conclude that "[...] office occupiers need to be more vocal about their demands for green buildings."[382] Similarly, *Boyd /Kimmet (2004)* report that tenants do not appreciate some features of green buildings.[383] A study of among 183 German companies reveals that office occupiers are not willing to pay per se a higher rent for office space in green buildings. Among a scale of one (do not agree) to five (fully agree) 63 percent of the respondents crossed one or two when they were asked whether they would pay a higher rent for green office building. Only if the higher rent is linked to lower running costs, the willingness increases. In this case, the average score was 3.7. The research study resumes that at present environmental aspects do not have on letting decisions, but are likely to play an important role in the future.[384]

4.1.2.4 Internal Services / Amenities

Finally, building factors also include internal services, which define the quality of the office space (interior quality) and available amenities. Again, the term 'quality' is difficult to delineate.[385] The *Bottom, et al. (1997)* survey illustrates this difficulty. In their survey, they asked tenant organizations from banking, legal, insurance, and brokering industries to rank the importance of 39 factors that measure the quality of office

---

[381] Cf. Shiers, D. (1999), p. 1-10
[382] St. Lawrence, S. (2004), p. 159
[383] Cf. Boyd, T. /Kimmet, P. (2004), p. 5
[384] Cf Jones Lang LaSalle (2007f), w/o pages, Thomas Daily (2008), p. 1
[385] Cf. Dunse, N. /Jones, C. (1998), p. 298

space.[386] The following research studies that attempt to measure the quality of office space have been identified.

Clapp (1980) captures the internal services with two variables. The first variable is a dummy variable that takes the value of 1 if the office building has exceptional amenities, and 0 otherwise. It must be pointed out that the assessment of whether exceptional amenities are present has been made by the author's observations. The second variable is also a dummy variable and takes the value of 1 if the office building has internal parking, and 0 otherwise. The regression analysis states that both variables are statistically significant and have the expected positive relationships.[387]

In their research study of Baton Rouge's office market, *Glascock, et al. (1990)* capture the variety of services (e.g., open parking, covered parking, janitorial, and security) provided in the lease contract with a categorical variable (full, partial, or no service provided). According to the study, full-service buildings rent about 8 percent more than office buildings that do not provide additional services.[388]

Investigating the office rent determinants for the Chicago area, *Mills (1992)* uses a variety of variables measuring the amenities that office buildings might provide. These dummy variables represent if the office building contains a bank, internal parking, a health club, day care, or a restaurant. However, only a bank and a restaurant prove to be of statistical significance. In his view, office occupiers are willing to pay a premium for restaurants because they keep office employees in the building and shorten lunch breaks.[389]

Sivitanidou (1996) includes only two variables. The first variable measures the number of elevators in an office building, and the second variable denotes if an office building has subterranean parking. Both variables are highly statistically significant and increase the property value.[390]

In their study of the Glasgow office market, *Dunse /Jones (1998)* include 12 dummy variables measuring the amenities and quality of the office space: air conditioning, acoustic tiling, carpeting, cellular layout, double layout, double glazing, private en-

386 Cf. Bottom, C., et al. (1997), p. 199
387 Cf. Clapp, J. M. (1980), p. 387-399
388 Cf. Glascock, J. L., et al. (1990), p. 113
389 Cf. Mills, E. S. (1992), p. 273-287
390 Cf. Sivitanidou, R. (1996), p. 125-149

trance, fluorescent light fittings, internal parking, reception area, raised floors, security systems, and tea-preparation area. Because a stepwise regression procedure is applied, the regression coefficients and statistical significance are not reported for all these variables. Nevertheless, only the variables for double layout, security systems, private entrance, and reception area prove to be statistically insignificant.[391]

Using the aforementioned dataset to test the existence of submarkets, *Dunse, et al. (2002)* conflate the quality variables (lighting type, heating type, lifts, ventilation, security, and car parking) in a summary quality variable with three attributes (poor, good, and excellent). The empirical results confirm statistically that office buildings that are better equipped achieve a rent premium.[392]

Bollinger, et al. (1998) and *Slade (2000)* use the load factor[393] of an office building as proxy for the quality of the building and office space. *Slade (2000)* argues that load factors and office rents are positively correlated because office buildings with higher load factors have greater amenities and more elegant designs. In both research studies, the variable load factor proves statistically to be positively correlated.[394]

Nitsch (2006) uses ten variables to control for the quality of office space. These dummy variables represent if a building has raised floors, external sun protection, air conditioning, water-cooled ceilings, windowsill cable trucking, antiglare light fittings, a kitchenette, a landscaped terrace, an in-house restaurant, and suspended ceilings. If a backward regression procedure is used, only three variables remain in the hedonic regression equation. Raised floors, air conditioning, and suspended ceilings are statistically significant and increase the level of rent.[395]

Similarly, *Heyser (2006)* builds a hedonic model with several variables measuring what types of internal services and amenities are included in the office building. Out of 13 variables, only two variables, namely, air conditioning and cooling ceilings, remain in the hedonic regression equation and are statistically significant.[396]

---

[391] Cf. Dunse, N. /Jones, C. (1998), p. 297-312
[392] Cf. Dunse, N., et al. (2002), p. 483-506
[393] "Load factor is the ratio of rentable area to useable area." Realtors Commercial Alliance (2005), p. 19
[394] Cf. Slade, B. A. (2000), p. 357-380, Bollinger, C. R., et al. (1998), p. 1097-1118
[395] Cf. Nitsch, H. (2006), p. 93-107
[396] Cf. Heyser, H. (2006), p. 113-154

4.1.3 Equipment and Layout Factors of Office Space

It can be assumed that, in addition to building factors, equipment and layout factors of the office space itself are very important to the office occupiers. There is the general belief that a direct relationship exists between the success of a business and the design, equipment, and layout of the workplace.[397] *Gibson (2003)* points out that organisations seek "[...] individual buildings that can accommodate the rapid organizational change and support a range of functions, [...] similar to the way employees are expected to move between tasks."[398] He further clarifies that this flexibility of office buildings is not without costs. Therefore, it can be assumed that equipment and layout factors should have an impact on the level of office rents.

Unfortunately, so far only a limited number of research studies have been found that test the aforementioned contention empirically. Although they do not test it directly, *Leishman, et al. (2003)* indicate that equipment and layout factors of office space are important to office occupiers. According to their study examining office space requirements, tenants and lease agents recognize the floor space layout type to be very important.[399]

In their study of Glasgow's office property, *Dunse /Jones (2002)* include a dummy variable recording a 1 if the office unit contains a cellular layout, and 0 otherwise. The empirical findings state that this variable is statistically significant and is negatively correlated with office rent. [400]

Although it does not explicitly test for the influence on office rents, the research undertaken by *Arge (2005)* finds some interesting results. Applying a comparative case study approach, she examines the importance of adaptability in office buildings and tests whether office buildings built by owner-occupiers are more adaptable than office buildings built by developers. She defines adaptability as a threefold concept that includes generality, flexibility, and elasticity. In this context, flexibility is defined as "[...] the ability of a building to meet changing functional user or owner needs by changing its properties."[401] In her opinion, the most important features of flexibility in office build-

[397] Cf. Hassanain, M. (2006), p. 214
[398] Gibson, V. (2003), p. 13
[399] Cf. Leishman, C., et al. Ibid.p. 51
[400] Cf. Dunse, N. /Jones, C. (2002), p. 174
[401] Arge, K. (2005), p. 121

ings are modularity; plug and play building elements, which allow for fast changes of layout or technical service parts; and soundproof ceilings for rapid and easy moving of internal walls.[402] Her empirical findings state that owner-occupiers' office buildings are more flexible than office buildings constructed by developers. She attributes this result to the fact that owner-occupiers adopt a long-term perspective and are therefore willing to pay for the adaptability in office buildings. Developers, who build property for renting and management, have no incentive to invest extra money in more adaptability in office buildings if the tenant is not willing to pay for it. Consequently, if developers do not invest in adaptability, it can be derived that users are not aware of the benefits of adaptable office buildings. This conclusion challenges the aforementioned contention.[403]

4.1.4 Lease Factors

Whereas location and building characteristics influence the price, rent, value, and worth of an office building, lease factors matter only for office rents. *Crosby /Murdoch (2001)* point out that "[...] the rental value is a product of the terms and conditions of the lease and that the same property can therefore quite justifiably have a variety of rental values at the same time."[404] Consequently, a review of which lease factors influence the level of office rents is necessary.

4.1.4.1 Lease Length

Many quantitative office market studies control for lease length. The hypothesis is that landlords offer lower rents on longer leases in comparison to short leases. On the one hand, the justification is that each tenant movement results in transaction costs. These transaction costs consist of lease agent fees, refurbishment costs, negotiation costs, and vacancy until a new tenant moves in. Specifically, the risk of vacancy is a strong motive for landlords to offer lower rents in a recessionary rental market.[405] In addition, because long leases generally provide a better lending environment and promote capital asset valuations, landlords prefer long leases.[406] On the other hand, from a tenant's point of

---

[402] Cf. Ibid.p. 122

[403] Cf. Ibid.p. 126-127

[404] Crosby, N. /Murdoch, S. (2001), p. 135

[405] Cf. McAllister, P. (2001), p. 365, Englund, P., et al. (2004), p. 186-187, Rowland, P. (2000), p. 181-182

[406] Cf. Crosby, N., et al. (2003), p. 1492

view, longer leases reduce flexibility. Therefore, it is argued that tenants are willing to pay more for shorter leases. In the context of financial leases, longer leases result in higher capitalized liability, which in turn motivates tenants to ask for shorter lease terms.[407]

Although the importance and impact of lease length on office rents are recognized, only a limited number of office market research studies that explicitly include lease lengths in their hedonic models exist. Some researchers attempt to circumvent the problem of a missing variable of lease length by applying asking rent as a dependent variable. In their opinion, asking rent is set at a level of standard lease terms. In other words, it accounts for lease lengths and other questions of tenure rights.[408]

However, another strand of literature specifically focuses on the term structure of office leases, challenging the aforementioned argument that the market environment and market participants' expectations drive the impact of lease length on the level of office rents.[409]

Grenadier (1995) has set the basis of research on term structures of real estate leases. He analyzes the term structures of leases by using an equilibrium model. Similarly to bonds with different maturities he assumes that, in comparison with a lease, an office occupier can obtain the same value by buying the freehold interest in the asset today whilst simultaneously receiving the present value of the freehold interest at the end of the hypothetical lease term. He further puts forward three possible shapes for the lease term structure: downward sloping, upward sloping, and single humped. In a bullish market the shape is downward sloping. As the ratio of capital values to construction costs is high, developers are induced to build new offices. As a result of this potential supply of new office space, market participants expect rent to fall in the future. Therefore, office occupiers prefer short leases to avoid the 'lock-in' effect of long leases. In contrast, landlords prefer long leases to avoid vacancy. In a bearish market, the shape of the term structure is more likely to be upward sloping. Because in the near future capital values are unlikely to exceed construction costs triggering new office space development, market participants expect an increase in rents. Thus, office occupiers try to obtain long leases, and landlords are more willing to agree on short leases to renegotiate

407 Cf. Ibid.p. 1491, Robinson, J. (1999), p. 178
408 Cf. Dunse, N. /Jones, C. (1998), p. 305
409 See Section 3.5.2

the leases at a higher level of office rents. When the supply of new office space is expected in the medium term, the shape of the term structure is single humped.[410]

The empirical findings of *Benjamin, et al. (1992b)*, who examined the Greensboro (USA) office market, confirm that lease length is statistically negatively correlated with office rent. Their model is based on 320 lease contracts and controls for location, building, and other lease characteristics.[411]

The results of a study by *Stanton /Wallace (2002)* of different US metropolitan areas and different property types show that lease length has a statistically positive effect on rents.[412] Unfortunately, each property type is entered as a dummy variable in the regression equation. This procedure makes it difficult to determine whether the results could be confirmed had only office leases been examined. Further doubts are raised because their sample contains only 130 office leases, originating between 1987 and 1996, for three metropolitan areas.

Studying the office market of Berlin, *Desyllas (2000)* also performs a regression analysis that includes lease length as an independent variable. Based on 437 office leases over a period of seven years, the analysis shows a positive but statistically insignificant relationship.[413]

Based upon a database containing more than 4,000 lease contracts between 1998 and 2002, *Englund, et al. (2004)* investigate three Swedish office markets (Stockholm CBD, Stockholm city, Göteburg, and Malmö). Controlling for physical, building, and lease factors, their hedonic regression analysis confirms that the lease length is an important factor influencing office rents. In a further analysis, they find that the term structure is upward sloping for all years in Stockholm CBD and in Stockholm city (except for the year 1998) and for some years in Göteburg and Malmö. However, these results are counterintuitive, given the market conditions at that time.[414]

In another study focusing only on the Stockholm CBD office market, *Gunnelin /Söderberg (2003)* find statistically significant differences in lease terms for 7 out of 15

---

[410] Cf. Grenadier, S. R. (1995), p. 297-331 in Gunnelin, A. /Söderberg, B. (2003), p. 244-245, Bond, S. A., et al. (2005), p. 3-4, Englund, P., et al. (2004), p. 185-188

[411] Cf. Benjamin, J. D., et al. (1992b), p. 259-272

[412] Cf. Stanton, R. /Wallace, N. (2002), p. 1-27

[413] Cf. Desyllas, J. (2000), p. 192-228

[414] Cf. Englund, P., et al. (2004), p. 187-215

years. Their model is based upon more than 1,300 leases and controls for building and lease characteristics. Moreover, they identify an upward-sloping curve in the bullish market and a downward-sloping curve in the bearish market, results that coincide with the market conditions at that time.[415]

Bond, et al. (2005) examine the term structures for the London office market. Using 935 office leases that originated between 1994 and 2004, they find a statistically significant, positive relationship between lease length and office rents controlling for location, building, and other lease characteristics. They scrutinize this finding, as it is opposed to market evidence, and they presume that the lack of control for other factors (e.g., tenant quality, transaction incentives, and unrecorded fit-out costs) is responsible for this odd observation.[416]

Research undertaken by *Crosby, et al. (2006)* demonstrates that the relationship between office rents and lease lengths has to be seen from a different angle. In their study of the office market of England and Wales, they report empirical evidence that lease length is also affected by the size of the tenant organization. They show that small office occupiers negotiate shorter lease lengths in comparison with large and medium-sized office occupiers.[417] As a consequence, in the analysis of term structures, it is necessary to control for the size and type of office tenants. *McCann /Ward (2004)* have previously expressed this view. They point out that "[...] the existence of clientele effects in different lease lengths that will distort the relationship between the term structure of market rents and the expected level of rent in the future."[418] For instance, because headquarters of major companies commit to a site and tend to move infrequently, they prefer long leases. On the other hand, small companies prefer short leases because they want the flexibility to expand or relocate within their planning horizon.[419]

Although little research has been undertaken in this area, sometimes with counterintuitive results, the aforementioned research studies demonstrate that it is of the utmost importance to control for lease length in hedonic rent indices.

---

[415] Cf. Gunnelin, A. /Söderberg, B. (2003), p. 241-265
[416] Cf. Bond, S. A., et al. (2005), p. 1-27
[417] Cf. Crosby, N., et al. (2006), p. 163-188
[418] McCann, P. /Ward, C. (2004), p. 274
[419] Cf. Ibid.p. 273-292

4.1.4.2 Size of Rental Area

Some research studies also measure the effect of the size of rentable area on office rents. However, whether the size of rentable area has a negative or positive influence on rents is still under discussion. On the one hand, it is argued that the long-term costs of operating a building with one large tenant are lower than those for an office building with numerous tenants. Another economies-of-scale explanation suggests that effective rents should decrease as the cost of searching for tenants, negotiating, and servicing lease contracts decreases.[420] Furthermore, the negotiating power of tenants who lease large office space increases. As discussed in chapter 3, in a bearish market with high vacancy rates, the competition for tenants becomes fiercer, and landlords are willing to give large tenants a discount on rents. On the other hand, it is argued that office buildings with large, continuous space are highly valued by large firms and are frequently in short supply. In essence, the effect of the size of rentable area depends on the market and its cycle stage.[421]

Dunse /Jones (1998) and *Gunnelin /Söderberg (2003)* investigate the variable 'size of rentable area.' Although in both studies the variable is highly statistically significant, its effect is negligible.[422] *Wheaton /Torto (1995)* report a positive, as well as a negative, statistically significant relationship for US metropolitan areas. *Bond, et al. (2005)* and *Benjamin, et al. (1992b)* discover a negative, statistically significant relationship for the London office market and for the Greensboro office market.[423] *Desyllas (2000)* finds a negative, but statistically insignificant, relationship for the office market of Berlin.[424]

4.1.4.3 Rent Review Provisions

In comparison with participants in the residential market, office tenants and landlords are experienced market participants. Therefore, in lease negotiations, they are interested not only in the initial level of contract rent but also in the level of effective rent.[425] In general terms, tenants (landlords) want to know how much rent they pay (receive) over the complete lease length. It is therefore argued that rent review provisions have a major

---

[420] Cf. Benjamin, J. D., et al. (1992b), p. 269

[421] Cf. Wheaton, W. C. /Torto, R. G. (1995), p. 7

[422] Cf. Gunnelin, A. /Söderberg, B. (2003), p. 254-255, Dunse, N. /Jones, C. (1998), p. 310

[423] Cf. Wheaton, W. C. /Torto, R. G. (1995), p. 7-9, Bond, S. A., et al. (2005), p. 13, Benjamin, J. D., et al. (1992b), p. 268-269

[424] Cf. Desyllas, J. (2000), p. 192-228

[425] Cf. Mills, E. S. (1992), p. 276

impact on the effective rent. For instance, some rent review provisions are based upon changes in the consumer price index (CPI). The risk of unexpected inflation is transferred to the tenant. Hence, the tenant should be charged a lower effective rent.[426] Different rent reviews exist: standard review with a rental underpinning clause, reviews with no underpinning clause, and rent review with 'cap and collar.' Some rent structures do not require reviews.[427] Furthermore, rent review provisions in office leases vary between countries. Although the importance of rent review provisions is generally accepted, most models that have been developed to quantify the effect of lease clauses remain of theoretical interest.[428]

Empirical investigations into the effect of frequency and basis of rent reviews have often been hampered by the lack of detailed and complete data (often because of confidentiality agreements). Again, some hedonic office rent studies attempt to control for rent review provisions by using the asking rent as a dependent variable.[429] Other researchers compute the present value of a lease by taking into account the rent provisions.[430] This undertaking, however, requires detailed data, and, in the case of CPI adjustments, an assumption about the expected inflation rate has to be made.

Englund, et al. (2004) include in their study about the Swedish office property market two dummy variables to control for the effect of different escalation clauses. Whereas the first variable represents leases with graduate rents, the second variable summarizes leases for which no specific information is available. However, both variables are statistically insignificant, which is partly explained by the fact that over 90 percent of the leases in the sample have inflation compensation only. In addition, the authors point out that most property owners use the standard contract provided by the Swedish Property Federation.[431]

Developing an effective rent index for the Chicago office market, *Webb /Fisher (1996)* include two variables measuring the effect of rent reviews in their hedonic model. One variable indicates the amount by which the lease payment is adjusted due to an increase in the CPI, and the second variable is an interaction variable calculated by multiplying

---

[426] Cf. Webb, B. R. /Fisher, J. D. (1996), p. 7, Gunnelin, A. /Söderberg, B. (2003), p. 246
[427] Cf. Robinson, J. (1999), p. 179-180
[428] Cf. Rowland, P. (2000), p. 177
[429] See Section 4.1.4.1
[430] Cf. Stanton, R. /Wallace, N. (2002), p. 1-27, Mills, E. S. (1992), p. 273-287
[431] Cf. Englund, P., et al. (2004), p. 183-215

the term of the lease by the CPI adjustment. The rationale for the interaction term is that the CPI adjustment should be more valuable to the owner when the lease term is longer. Although both variables show the expected relationship, they are statistically insignificant. The authors argue that the insignificance results from the economic environment of low inflation during the period under study.[432]

4.1.4.4 Options and Incentives

Besides the rent review provision, leases include many options. These options comprise clauses for canceling or renewing the lease, subletting the office space, downsizing, and expanding the office space. They often play a central role in lease negotiations, for they determine the amount of risk transferred to the other party, and, consequently, they also have value and may influence the level of rent.[433] As with rent review provisions, these options are important, and market participants are aware of their consequences over time. However, because their effects are hard to quantify, only a few studies have tried to explicitly do so.[434]

The results of a survey of office occupiers and agents indicate that the ability to take or to reduce space without moving is an important requirement for tenants when they are choosing an office location.[435] The importance of this option is further underscored if transaction costs are taken into account. If the tenant cannot expand within the current location, the tenant has to relocate, a process that has high transaction costs associated with it. These transaction costs include the time to search for a new location, the negotiation of a new contract, the disruption of business during the move, and the loss of the goodwill of the old location.[436]

Mooradian /Yang (2000) examine whether the subletting, cancelation, and downsizing clauses have an impact on the rent payable. Their sample consists of 311 leases that originated in September 2004 in the US. The different options are included as dummy variables in their regression analysis. Their empirical findings are that the tenants pay a

---

[432] Cf. Webb, B. R. /Fisher, J. D. (1996), p. 1-19
[433] Cf. Buetow, G. /Albert, J. (1998), p. 253, Posner, K. A. (1993), p. 47-48
[434] Cf. Wang, J. (2005), p. 32-35
[435] Cf. Leishman, C., et al. (2003), p. 51
[436] Cf. Posner, K. A. (1993), p. 49-52

significant premium for a downsizing lease provision, whereas the options for subletting or cancelation do not have any statistical significance.[437]

Instead of using dummy variables, *Bond, et al. (2005)* include a variable measuring the length of break for the lease. Their empirical results, which are surprising, demonstrate a statistically significant, negative relationship between the break variable and office rents. They presume that the value of this option decreases as the time to expiry increases.[438]

Closely linked with options is the issue of lease incentives. They become more and more frequent in oversupplied office markets and, in fact, often include the grant of options.[439] Broadly defined, "[...] lease incentives are concessions given to the tenants to entice them into signing new leases."[440] *Jefferies (1994)* lists the following types of incentives: abnormal rent-free periods, cash payments, rent subsidies, free hard or soft "fit outs" (tenant improvements), take-out existing space, payment of relocation costs, put options on additional space, caps in rental increases on review, and free naming rights. The range of different types demonstrates that lease incentives have an impact on managers, valuers, leasing agents, developers, financiers, lawyers, taxation offices, and landlords.[441] Landlords are affected first and foremost because lease incentives will decrease the effective income of the office building. From the enumeration of lease incentives it also becomes obvious that the majority of incentives are hard to quantify. In addition, as with options, they are often placed under nondisclosure, as "[...] landlords attempt to conceal the fall in the effective value of their rental income in order to protect expected capital values."[442] As a consequence, in hedonic office rent analysis, the impact of lease incentives on office rent remains uncontrolled. In lieu thereof, it is argued that asking rents should be employed as a dependent variable, as they implicitly control for lease incentives.

An exception is the study of *Stanton /Wallace (2002)*. In their regression analysis, they include a variable for tenant improvements. However, their empirical finding is that tenant improvements are significantly negatively correlated with realized rent. Nor-

---

[437] Cf. Mooradian, R. M. /Yang, S. X. (2000), p. 65-88
[438] Cf. Bond, S. A., et al. (2005), p. 1-27
[439] Cf. Wheaton, W. C. /Torto, R. G. (1995), p. 3, Jefferies, R. L. (1994), p. 21
[440] Rowland, P. (2000), p. 180
[441] Cf. Jefferies, R. L. (1994), p. 23-24
[442] Desyllas, J. (2000), p. 36

mally, the opposite impact would be expected. Unfortunately, a further interpretation is hampered by the fact that their regression analysis is based on leases of mixed property types (light industrial, suburban office, retail malls), and they do not formulate a separate regression equation for each property type.[443]

4.1.4.5 Type and Quality of the Tenant

As mentioned earlier, so-called clientele effects influence the term structure.[444] This idea suggests that the business environment, company size, and creditworthiness of the tenants - in other words, the quality of the tenant - might have an impact on the level of office rent. From a landlord's perspective, it makes sense to reduce the office rent for tenants with good credit standing, as their probability of default risk of tenants is generally lower than for other tenants. A good credit rating often goes hand in hand with the image and size of the company. Therefore, tenants with a good credit standing expect a discount because they create a positive externality for the landlord.[445]

In their research, *Benjamin, et al. (1992b)* explicitly test for the aforementioned hypothesis. Not only does their model include several dummy variables to measure the tenant's creditworthiness, but it also contains a variable measuring the amount of security deposit payable in advance. Based upon 320 rental contracts of Greensboro office buildings, their empirical findings are in line with the theory. Tenants with a good credit rating and tenants who renew their lease contract pay considerably less office rent than other tenants. In addition, the amount of security deposit paid in advance is significantly negatively correlated with the level of rent.[446] These findings are confirmed by another office property market analysis conducted at the same time by *Benjamin, et al. (1992a)*. Although this study has a different research focus, it confirms that creditworthiness and the amount of security deposit are significantly positively correlated to the level of office rent.[447]

Stanton /Wallace (2002) include in their regression model a dummy variable indicating if the tenant has an above-average investment bond rating. The regression coefficient shows a positive sign, which is surprising. This finding would indicate that creditworthy

---

[443] Cf. Stanton, R. /Wallace, N. (2002), p. 1-27

[444] See Section 4.1.4.1

[445] Cf. Benjamin, J. D., et al. (1992b), p. 259-272

[446] Cf. Ibid.p.

[447] Cf. Benjamin, J. D., et al. Ibid.p. 289-302

tenants pay higher rents than tenants with a moderate or low credit standing. However, as the regression coefficient is statistically insignificant and their sample consists of leases of different property types, this finding should be disregarded.[448]

Two analyses of the Swedish office property market by *Gunnelin /Söderberg (2003)* and *Englund, et al. (2004)* also include a dummy variable indicating whether the lease has been negotiated with a previous tenant or with a new tenant. The empirical findings show that old tenants pay between 4 and 10 percent less rent than new tenants.[449] These findings are intuitive, as the landlord is probably willing to extend the lease only if the tenant has proven to be trustworthy and reliable.

Contrary to the aforementioned findings, the results of a study by *Webb /Fisher (1996)* show that landlords receive less rent from newer tenants than from older tenants.[450] However, it should be kept in mind that the studies of *Gunnelin /Söderberg (2003)* and *Englund, et al. (2004)* use base rent as the dependent variable, whereas the study of *Webb /Fisher (1996)* uses effective rent, which corrects for incentives such as tenant improvements and rent-free periods.

Glascock, et al. (1993) deal with a different aspect. They examine whether partially owner-occupied office buildings rent for more than completely tenant-occupied office buildings. Based upon 127 leases originating between 1984 and 1990 for offices in Baton Rouge, their empirical results confirm a statistically significant, positive correlation between office rent and owner occupation.[451]

4.1.5 Market Situation and Bargaining Power

Different factors that might influence the level of office rents have been presented and discussed. As defined in chapter 2, these factors have been chosen on the assumption that they add and reduce the user's value of a leased office unit; therefore, they determine the level of office rent he is willing to pay. So far, the market situation in which the office lease contracts are negotiated has been ignored. Because the property market is inefficient,[452] there exist other factors determining office rents that are beyond the tenant's or landlord's influence (e.g., tenant and landlord psychology, agent behaviour,

[448] Cf. Stanton, R. /Wallace, N. (2002), p. 1-27

[449] Cf. Gunnelin, A. /Söderberg, B. (2003), p. 241-265

[450] Cf. Webb, B. R. /Fisher, J. D. (1996), p. 14, Englund, P., et al. (2004), p. 183-215

[451] Cf. Glascock, J. L., et al. (1993), p. 69-82

[452] See Section 3.4

and market liquidity). Unfortunately, as in many real estate areas, the research of the residential market is much more advanced than the research of the office market.[453] Therefore, only a few studies are presented.

Market liquidity is one factor that probably influences office prices. According to *Fisher, et al. (2004)*, market liquidity is "[...] the expected time required for a particular property to transact," or, more generally, "[...] market liquidity refers to the ease, or speed, at which properties transact."[454] Transaction frequency, which refers to the number of transactions that occur in a particular market during a certain time span, is a key indicator of market liquidity. It is often stated that transaction frequency changes from period to period, and in the period of high transaction frequency, landlords have less difficulty selling their assets at higher prices.[455] Although these contentions are applicable only to the asset prices and selling prices for commercial buildings, no evidence indicates that they cannot be applied to office rents as well.

In a property market study of different cities in the United Kingdom (UK), *Orr, et al. (2003)* examine the relationships between time on the market, asking office rent, and transacted office rent.[456] They define time on the market as the number of days between the date of the original listing with an agent and the contractual date of letting, which meets the aforementioned definition of market liquidity. They argue that time on the market is positively related to asking rent and to transacted rent. In other words, the longer the property unit is on the market, the higher is the level of rent. These hypotheses conflict with the aforementioned effect of market liquidity. However, it should be kept in mind that their hypotheses are derived from research studies of the residential market. Their empirical findings, however, could detect only a negative but insignificant relationship. In other words, the longer the office property is vacant, the lower the office rent. *Orr, et al. (2003)* attribute these insignificant results to the fact that landlords are more willing to offer incentives than to reduce the recorded transacted rent. Furthermore, they develop a model explaining the time on the market with location, building, and lease characteristics. However, the empirical results suggest that the marketing process for office property is more complicated, and, to explain it, other variables meas-

---

[453] Cf. Orr, A., et al. (2003), p. 490
[454] Fisher, J., et al. (2004), p. 241
[455] Cf. Haurin, D. (2003), p. 236-237, Fisher, J., et al. (2004), p. 241-242
[456] Their research is focused on the metropolitan areas of Aberdeen, Edinburgh, Glasgow and Stirling.

uring landlord's motivations, tenant characteristics, rental incentives, and search costs have to be included in the analysis.[457]

Webb /Fisher (1996) provide a further indication of the complexity of the marketing and negotiation process for office contracts. In their hedonic model, they include a dummy variable indicating whether an outside broker has represented the tenant during the lease contract negotiations. If the tenant has been represented by a broker, the regression analysis shows that the effective rent is lower.[458]

In a research study, *Colwell /Munneke (2006)* analyze the effects of bargaining power on the transaction prices of office properties. Using 477 observations to study the Illinois office property market, they discover that different types of buyers and sellers value attributes of office property differently and also have different bargaining strength. Although their research focuses on prices, the results probably hold true for office rents.[459]

Although it is beyond the scope of this research, other research studies contend that the size of the market and the number of participants have an influence on office rents. They assume that the smaller the market, the fewer participants who are active within this market. Therefore, the competitive pressures are weaker compared with those in larger markets. However, *D'Arcy, et al. (1997)* analyzed major European cities, and their empirical findings state that market size has no significant influence on office rents.[460]

---

[457] Cf. Orr, A., et al. (2003), p. 473-494

[458] Cf. Webb, B. R. /Fisher, J. D. (1996), p. 14

[459] Cf. Colwell, P. F. /Munneke, H. J. (2006), p. 197-213

[460] Cf. D'Arcy, E., et al. (1997), p. 297-308

4.2 German Office Property Market

In the previous section, research studies of office property markets of different countries were presented. These research studies sometimes provide counterintuitive and even contradictory results, which can often be traced back to the fact that they were undertaken in different office markets, at different time periods, and with different datasets. Therefore, it seems advisable to have a closer look at the German office property market and its lease structure.

4.2.1 City Profile of Major Office Property Markets

The German office property market is in many ways different from other property markets. In a central market, the majority of market actions take place within a city or region (e.g., Paris for France and London for the United Kingdom). However, in a dispersed market, several important office property markets exist. This results from the fact that Germany is a federal state, and each of the 16 'Länder' has its own miniature government, an elected assembly, a written constitution, and a constitutional court. Many different cities play an individual and distinctive role in the national economy. Different market behaviour, characteristics, and structures distinguish these dispersed office markets. The most important office property markets of Germany, namely, Berlin, Düsseldorf, Frankfurt, Hamburg, and Munich, are therefore discussed.[461]

4.2.1.1 Berlin

Berlin is the capital, and, with approximately 3.4 million inhabitants in 2006, it is Germany's largest city and the third most populous city in the European Union. As a matter of fact, it is one of the most influential centres in European politics, science, and culture. Although it is home to some prominent universities, sports events, and museums, and it serves as an international hub of continental transportation, the economy is still weak and underperforming as compared to those of other major metropolitan areas. In fact, Berlin's rate of unemployment is a very high of 20.1 percent in 2006. Among the fast-growing industry sectors are communications, life sciences, mobility, and services, including information and communication technologies, media and music, advertising and

[461] Cf. Maier, K. M. (1999), p. 57-58, Brühl, M. /Lizieri, C. (1994), p. 62-63, Ludwig, H. (2005), p. 11-12

design, biotechnology and environmental services, transportation, and medical engineering.[462]

The office locations are dispersed. Figure 16 shows that Berlin consists of two prime office locations, which are historically founded. One is the former western part of Berlin, while the other is around the German parliament and Potsdamer Platz. The large dispersion of office locations, as well as the high percentage of office buildings constructed before 1990, partly explains the big spread for office rents.[463]

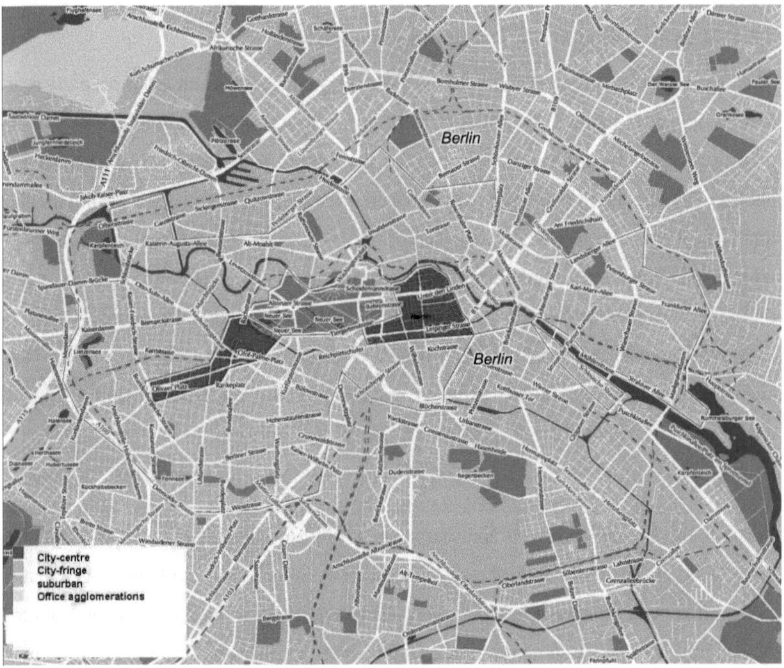

Figure 16: Office Locations in Berlin[464]

Although the real estate investment market is booming because of the increased interest of foreign investors and especially private equity funds, the office rental market is still in its recessionary stage, with extensive vacancy and decreasing office rents. In 2005

[462] Cf. Deka Bank (2007), w/o pages, CB Richard Ellis (2006a), w/o pages, Jones Lang LaSalle (2006a), w/o pages

[463] Bulwien Gesa AG reports that 62.62 percent of office stock has been completed before 1990..BulwienGesa (2008), w/o pages [Online Database]

[464] RIWIS (2007), w/o pages [Online Database]

governmental agencies were the main drivers of the rental market, whereas consultancies and other service companies drove the market in 2006. Although office rents are still under strain and the vacancy rate is still high, all major real estate consultancies and brokers confirm that they expect the office rental market to pick up soon.[465]

Berlin	German Real Estate Research Society (GIF)	BulwienGes a AG	CB Richard Ellis	Jones Lang LaSalle	ATIS*	Deutsche Immobilien Partner*	DTZ Zadelhoff Tie Leung*	IVG & Cushman Wakefield**
Office Stock in million sqm	17.8	14.21	17.44	16.61	18.36	n.a.	n.a.	n.a.
Vacant Office Space	1,650,000	1,650,000	1,691,800	1,655,100	1,543,000	1,740,000	1,666,000	n.a.
Vacancy Rate	9.30%	11.60%	9.70%	10.00%	8.40%	9.80%	9.60%	9.30%
Expected Total Completion for 20C	n.a.	n.a.	81,100	52,200	n.a.	n.a.	n.a.	n.a.
Expected Total Completion for 20C	n.a.	n.a.	147,300	55,400	n.a.	n.a.	n.a.	n.a.
Prime Rent per Month in EUR	20.50	20.50	21.00	20.50	20.50	20.00	23.00	20.50
Average Rent per Month in EUR	10.50	15.30	11.84	12.63	n.a.	15.00	n.a.	11.50

* End of June 2006 /** 3.Quarter 2006

Table 8: Berlin Office Property Market[466]

4.2.1.2 Düsseldorf

Düsseldorf lies in the federal state of North Rhine-Westphalia and is also its capital. Its estimated population is around 580,000 (Year 2006). It is, along with Cologne, the economic centre of western Germany. From an economic point of view, Düsseldorf is a stronghold of the German advertising and fashion industries, and has also become a top telecommunications centre in Germany.[467]

In Figure 17, the different office locations of Düsseldorf are presented. The Düsseldorf office market consists of several submarkets. While the prime and city-fringe office locations are in the city centre, several office agglomerations are also located within and outside of the city boundaries.

---

[465] Cf. ATIS Real (2006a), w/o pages, CB Richard Ellis (2007a), w/o pages, Deutsche Immobilien-Partner (2006), p. , DTZ Zadelhoff Tie Lung (2006b), w/o pages, Eberhard, A. (2007), p. , Jones Lang LaSalle (2007a), w/o pages

[466] Cf. ATIS Real (2006a), w/o pages, CB Richard Ellis (2007a), w/o pages, Deutsche Immobilien-Partner (2006), p. , DTZ Zadelhoff Tie Lung (2006b), w/o pages, Eberhard, A. (2007), p. , Jones Lang LaSalle (2007a), w/o pages

[467] Cf. Deka Bank (2007), w/o pages, DTZ Zadelhoff Tie Lung (2006a), w/o pages, Jones Lang LaSalle (2007b), w/o pages

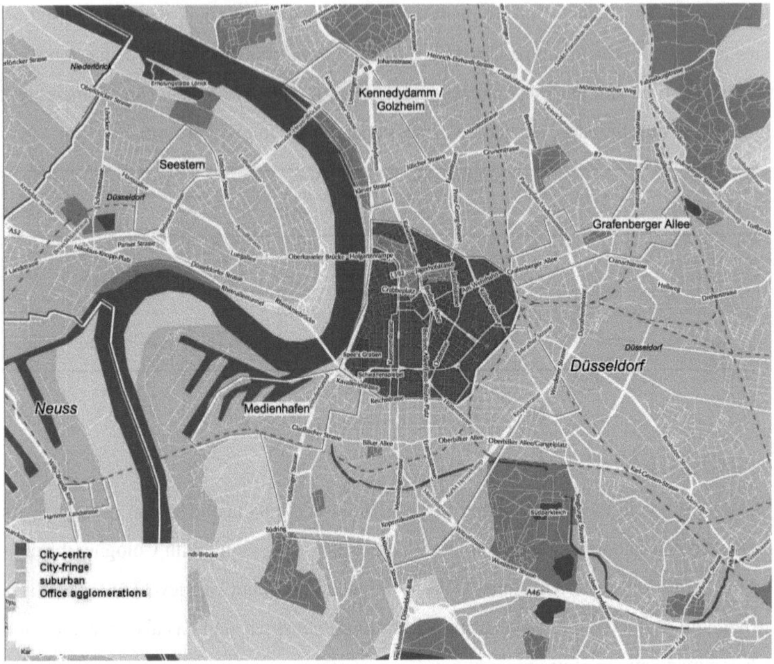

Figure 17: Office Locations in Düsseldorf[468]

The office market of Düsseldorf is relatively stable. The major demands for new office space arise from telecommunication companies. Because of the stable economic development and moderate construction activity, the vacancy rate has decreased, but it is still around 11 percent. Moreover, market participants noticed that the demand for high-quality office space especially increased in 2006.[469]

[468] RIWIS (2007), w/o pages [Online Database]

[469] Cf. AtisReal (2006), w/o pages, Deutsche Immobilien-Partner (2006), p. 1-12, DTZ Zadelhoff Tie Lung (2006a), w/o pages, Eberhard, A. (2007), p. 14-15, Gesellschaft für Immobilienwirtschaftliche Forschung (2007), p. 1-4, Jones Lang LaSalle (2007b), w/o pages

Düsseldorf	German Real Estate Research Society (GIF)	BulwienGesa AG	CB Richard Ellis	Jones Lang LaSalle	ATIS*	Deutsche Immobilien Partner*	DTZ Zadelhoff Tie Leung*	IVG & Cushman Wakefield**
Office Stock in million sqm	7.1	6.934	n.a.	8.45	n.a.	n.a.	n.a.	n.a.
Vacant Office Space	752,000	752,000	n.a.	1,035,100	736,000	932,000	940,000	n.a.
Vacancy Rate	10.70%	10.90%	n.a.	12.20%	n.a.	11.20%	12.30	11.60%
Expected Total Completion for 200	n.s	n.a.	n.a.	24,000	n.a.	n.a.	n.a.	n.a.
Expected Total Completion for 200	n.s	n.a.	n.a.	28,700	n.a.	n.a.	n.a.	n.a.
Prime Rent per Month in EUR	21.20	20.50	n.a.	22.00	21.50	20.50	20.70	21.00
Average Rent per Month in EUR	12.70	15.70	n.a.	12.34	11.80	15.50	n.a.	12.30

* End of June 2006 /** 3.Quarter 2006

Table 9: Düsseldorf Office Property Market[470]

4.2.1.3 Frankfurt

Frankfurt is the largest city in the German state of Hesse and the fifth largest city in Germany, after Berlin, Hamburg, Munich, and Cologne. Its estimated population is around 650,000 (Year 2006). The city is at the centre of the larger Frankfurt Rhine Main Area, which has a population of 5 million and is Germany's second largest metropolitan area. Frankfurt is especially well known as the transportation centre of Germany because of its airport, which is the largest in continental Europe. Frankfurt is the headquarters of the European Central Bank and the Frankfurt Stock Exchange, and is one of the three largest financial centres in Europe (the other two being London and Paris). Besides its importance as a financial centre, it is the headquarters of several international companies, and is home to chemical industries, advertising, software development companies, and call centres.[471]

Figure 18 shows the different office locations in Frankfurt. Major parts of the office stock are prime offices and are located within the city centre. It is also interesting to note that some decentralized office clusters exist.

---

[470] Cf. Deutsche Immobilien-Partner (2006), p. 1-12, AtisReal (2006), w/o pages, DTZ Zadelhoff Tie Lung (2006a), w/o pages, Eberhard, A. (2007), p. 14-15, Gesellschaft für Immobilienwirtschaftliche Forschung (2007), p. 1-4, Jones Lang LaSalle (2007b), w/o pages

[471] Cf. Deka Bank (2007), w/o pages, ATIS Real (2006a), w/o pages, CB Richard Ellis (2007b), w/o pages, DTZ Zadelhoff Tie Lung (2006b), w/o pages, Jones Lang LaSalle (2007c), w/o pages

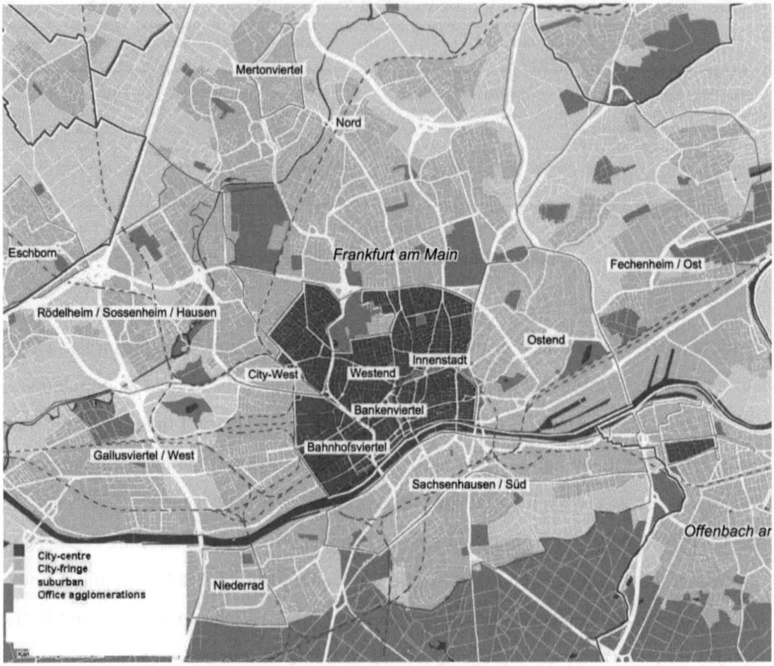

Figure 18: Office Locations in Frankfurt[472]

Finance companies still dominate the office property market in Frankfurt. In the past, many speculative developments took place, and, as a result, the vacancy rate has increased significantly. However, in 2006 only a small amount of speculative development was registered; therefore, real estate consultancies and agencies expect that the office market will remain stable. Nevertheless, they also observe that a high demand for high-quality office space exists, and that the demand for low- or average-quality office space is constantly decreasing.[473]

[472] RIWIS (2007), w/o pages [Online Database]

[473] Cf. ATIS Real (2006b), w/o pages, CB Richard Ellis (2007b), w/o pages, Deutsche Immobilien-Partner (2006), p. 1-12, DTZ Research (2005), w/o pages, Eberhard, A. (2007), p. 14-15, Gesellschaft für Immobilienwirtschaftliche Forschung (2007), p. 1-4, Jones Lang LaSalle (2007c), w/o pages

Frankfurt	German Real Estate Research Society (GIF)	BulwienGes a AG	CB Richard Ellis	Jones Lang LaSalle	ATIS*	Deutsche Immobilien Partner*	DTZ Zadelhoff Tie Leung*	IVG & Cushman Wakefield**
Office Stock in million sqm	12.1	9.77	11.99	11.64	13.41	n.a.	n.a.	n.a.
Vacant Office Space	2,020,000	1,780,000	1,297,000	1,889,700	2,254,000	2,130,000	2,131,000	n.a.
Vacancy Rate	16.80%	18.20%	10.80%	16.20%	16.80%	17.50%	17.60%	16.60%
Expected Total Completion for 20C	n.a.	n.a.	87,000	16,100	n.a.	n.a.	n.a.	n.a.
Expected Total Completion for 20C	n.a.	n.a.	99,000	54,400	n.a.	n.a.	n.a.	n.a.
Prime Rent per Month in EUR	34.60	32.00	34.50	35.00	34.00	32.00	33.00	34.00
Average Rent per Month in EUR	17.00	18.00	n.a.	18.23	n.a.	21.50	n.a.	13.00

* End of June 2006 /** 3.Quarter 2006

Table 10: Frankfurt Office Property Market[474]

4.2.1.4 Hamburg

Hamburg is the second largest city in Germany, with a population of 1.75 million in 2006. Because of its seaport, which is ranked ninth in the world, Hamburg's economy benefits from the growth of the world economy and trade flows, and is also partially independent from the developments of the German national economy. As a result, the rate of unemployment decreased and the number of employees subject to social insurance contribution increased. The mix of strong economic power, an excellent infrastructure, and a high quality of life makes Hamburg one of the most attractive and dynamic cities in Germany and Europe.[475]

Figure 19 presents the different office locations in Hamburg. While prime offices are in the city centre, the city-fringe offices are located around the prime offices. Unlike those in Düsseldorf, only a few office agglomerations have been developed in recent years.

---

[474] Cf. ATIS Real (2006b), w/o pages, CB Richard Ellis (2007b), w/o pages, Deutsche Immobilien-Partner (2006), p. 1-12, DTZ Research (2005), w/o pages, Eberhard, A. (2007), p. 14-15, Gesellschaft für Immobilienwirtschaftliche Forschung (2007), p. 1-4, Jones Lang LaSalle (2007c), w/o pages

[475] Cf. Deka Bank (2007), w/o pages, ATIS Real (2006c), w/o pages, CB Richard Ellis (2007c), w/o pages, DTZ Research (2006), w/o pages, Jones Lang LaSalle (2007d), w/o pages

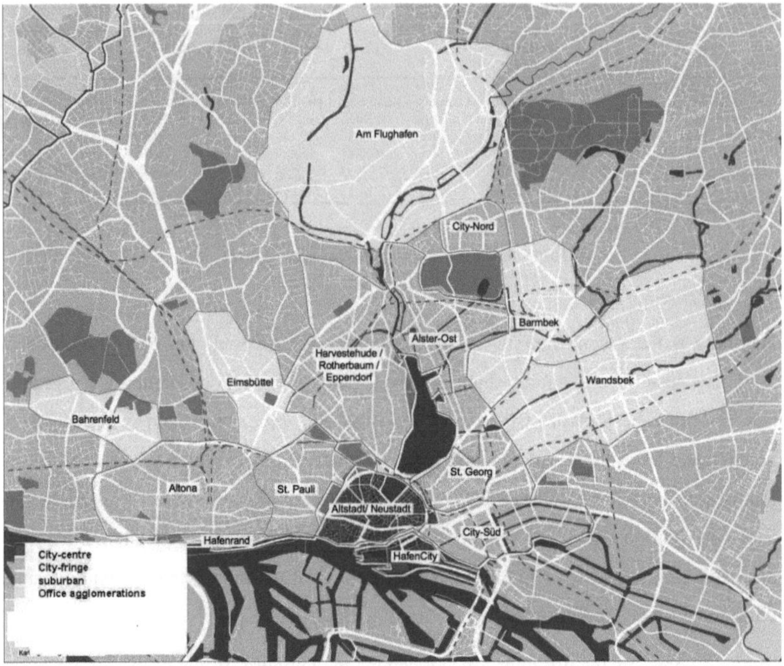

Figure 19: Office Locations in Hamburg[476]

Although many office property markets have been under considerable strain, Hamburg's office market remains stable and is experiencing a positive trend. The vacancy rate remains low, and rent levels have increased slightly as compared to levels in 2005. The major drivers for this positive development are service companies. Legal advisors, banks, financial services, and companies from the publishing, media, and advertising sectors have especially contributed to the positive development. However, real estate consultancies and agencies point out that the completion of new office space in the year 2008 will place significant pressure on the office rental market.[477]

---

[476] RIWIS (2007), w/o pages [Online Database]

[477] Cf. ATIS Real (2006c), w/o pages, CB Richard Ellis (2007c), w/o pages, Deutsche Immobilien-Partner (2006), p. 1-12, DTZ Zadelhoff Tie Lung (2006b), w/o pages, Eberhard, A. (2007), p. 14-15, Gesellschaft für Immobilienwirtschaftliche Forschung (2007), p. 1-4, Jones Lang LaSalle (2007d), w/o pages

Hamburg	German Real Estate Research Society (GIF)	BulwienGesa AG	CB Richard Ellis	Jones Lang LaSalle	ATIS*	Deutsche Immobilien Partner*	DTZ Zadelhoff Tie Leung*	IVG & Cushman Wakefield**
Office Stock in million sqm	13.00	10.47	13.03	13.71	13.06	n.a.	n.a.	n.a.
Vacant Office Space	1,030,000	1,030,000	961,000	1,066,900	901,000	985,000	1,000,000	n.a.
Vacancy Rate	7.90%	9.80%	7.40%	7.80%	6.90%	7.80%	7.60%	7.70%
Expected Total Completion for 20C	n.a.	n.a.	300,000	104,500	n.a.	n.a.	n.a.	n.a.
Expected Total Completion for 20C	n.a.	n.a.	175,000	130,800	n.a.	n.a.	n.a.	n.a.
Prime Rent per Month in EUR	21.50	21.00	23.00	22.00	23.50	21.25	22.00	21.00
Average Rent per Month in EUR	12.4	15.10	12.36	12.14	14.50	11.25	n.a.	12.50

* End of June 2006 /** 3.Quarter 2006

Table 11: Hamburg Office Property Market[478]

4.2.1.5 Munich

In 2006 the population of Munich amounts to 1.3 million. It is the third largest city in Germany and currently has the strongest economy of any German city. The reasons for this success are manifold: the geographical location of Munich, the above-average leisure facilities, and the enormous potential of a highly qualified workforce. Besides the fact that eight out of the 30 largest German companies have their headquarters in Munich, the city is also the centre for the German new economy in biotechnology, software, and other industries. The rate of unemployment is at a low of 8.8 percent (Year 2006), and purchasing power is the highest in Germany, which underpins the city's prosperity.[479]

Figure 20 presents the different office locations in Munich. Munich offices are located in a monocentric manner. The prime offices are in the city centre, and the other offices have settled around them. However, in the recent past some office agglomerations have been developed in different parts of the city.

---

[478] Cf. ATIS Real (2006c), w/o pages, CB Richard Ellis (2007c), w/o pages, Deutsche Immobilien-Partner (2006), p. 1-12, DTZ Zadelhoff Tie Lung (2006b), w/o pages, Eberhard, A. (2007), p. 14-15, Gesellschaft für Immobilienwirtschaftliche Forschung (2007), p. 1-4, Jones Lang LaSalle (2007d), w/o pages

[479] Cf. Deka Bank (2007), w/o pages, ATIS Real (2006d), w/o pages, CB Richard Ellis (2007d), w/o pages, DTZ Research (2006), w/o pages, Jones Lang LaSalle (2007e), w/o pages

Figure 20: Office Locations in Munich[480]

The office property market benefits from this economic situation. In comparison with 2005, the vacancy rate has decreased significantly, and an increase in office rents has been observed. Main drivers for the office rental markets are companies in the IT and communication sectors, other service companies, consultancies, and companies from the publishing, media, and advertising sectors. The office stock is decreasing slightly, and the confidence of market participants is increasing, as evidenced by the fact that speculative developments of office buildings have slowly started again.[481]

---

[480] RIWIS (2007), w/o pages [Online Database]

[481] Cf. ATIS Real (2006d), w/o pages, CB Richard Ellis (2007d), w/o pages, DTZ Zadelhoff Tie Lung (2006b), w/o pages, Eberhard, A. (2007), p. 14-15, Gesellschaft für Immobilienwirtschaftliche Forschung (2007), p. 1-4, Jones Lang LaSalle (2007e), w/o pages, Deutsche Immobilien-Partner (2006), p. 1-12

Munich	German Real Estate Research Society (GIF)	BulwienGesa AG	CB Richard Ellis	Jones Lang LaSalle	ATIS*	Deutsche Immobilien Partner*	DTZ Zadelhoff Tie Leung*	IVG & Cushman Wakefield**
Office Stock in million sqm	18.5	12.94	18.05	17.88	n.a.	n.a.	n.a.	n.a.
Vacant Office Space	1,621,000	985,000	1,395,000	1,675,100	1,564,000	1,700,000	1,720,000	n.a.
Vacancy Rate	12.90%	7.60%	7.70%	9.40%	n.a.	9.70%	9.80%	9.40%
Expected Total Completion for 20C	n.a.	n.a.	125,900	25,300	n.a.	n.a.	n.a.	n.a.
Expected Total Completion for 20C	n.a.	n.a.	226,700	157,000	n.a.	n.a.	n.a.	n.a.
Prime Rent per Month in EUR	30.00	28.00	30.50	28.50	28.50	28.50	29.50	29.00
Average Rent per Month in EUR	15.2	17.25	14.28	13.84	17.60	14.50	n.a.	14.50

* End of June 2006 /** 3.Quarter 2006

Table 12: Munich Office Property Market[482]

4.2.1.6 Comparison of Different Office Markets

The brief presentation of Berlin, Frankfurt, Hamburg, and Munich underpins the concept that Germany's office property markets are dispersed. Each city has different factors influencing its economy.[483] The growing business sectors, which require new office space, are also different across all cities,[484] and their needs and requirements for office space likely have to be analyzed separately.[485] However, to what extent the companies of different business sectors assign different value to office rent determinants remains uncertain.

Moreover, the office locations in each city are different and range from monocentric shapes (e.g. Munich) to polycentric, with several office submarkets (e.g., Düsseldorf). This observation further complicates the analysis of office markets on a nationwide level.

	Germany	Berlin	Düsseldorf	Frankfurt	Hamburg	Munich
Population in millions (Year 2006)	82,314,904	3,404,037	577,505	652,610	1,754,182	1,294,608
Unemployment Rate (Year 2006)	12.0%	20.1%	13.6%	12.6%	12.6%	8.8%
Gross Domestic Product per Employee in Euros (Year 2004)	56,967	51,678	64,921	81,329	75,277	71,843
Employees subject to social insurance contributions SVP (Year 2005)	26,178,266	1,013,758	335,361	460,363	738,493	665,407
Purchasing Power Index per Inhabitant (Year 2006)	100	94.0	120.0	111.3	108.5	134.5

Table 13: Comparison of General Economic Figures[486]

---

482 Cf. ATIS Real (2006d), w/o pages, CB Richard Ellis (2007d), w/o pages, DTZ Zadelhoff Tie Lung (2006b), w/o pages, Eberhard, A. (2007), p. 14-15, Gesellschaft für Immobilienwirtschaftliche Forschung (2007), p. 1-4, Jones Lang LaSalle (2007e), w/o pages, Deutsche Immobilien-Partner (2006), p. 1-12

483 See Table 13

484 See Table 14 and Table 15

485 Cf. Beidatsch, K. (2006), p. 62-63, Heyser, H. (2006), p. 105

486 Cf. CB Richard Ellis (2006a), w/o pages, CB Richard Ellis (2006b), w/o pages, CB Richard Ellis (2006c), w/o pages, CB Richard Ellis (2006d), w/o pages, Jones Lang LaSalle (2006a), w/o pages,

	Berlin	Düsseldorf	Frankfurt	Hamburg	Munich
Total Employees Subject to Social Insurance Contributions (SVP)	1,013,758	335,361	460,363	738,493	665,407
by Industry					
Agriculture, Forestry and Fishing	0.40%	0.20%	0.20%	0.40%	0.30%
Manufacturing	12.50%	16.00%	10.10%	15.20%	20.80%
Construction	4.90%	2.80%	2.80%	3.80%	2.60%
Wholesale and Retail Trade	12.50%	16.20%	9.70%	17.30%	12.50%
Hotels and Restaurants	4.40%	3.40%	3.90%	3.10%	3.90%
Transport, Storage and Communication	6.60%	7.10%	16.00%	9.90%	3.90%
Financial Services	3.30%	9.30%	15.30%	6.60%	8.70%
Real Estate, Renting and Business Activities	19.10%	21.70%	23.10%	20.70%	20.80%
Public Administration, Compulsory Social Security	9.10%	7.70%	4.10%	4.70%	5.60%
Education, Health and Social Work	19.10%	10.70%	9.70%	12.50%	13.40%
Other Activities	8.10%	4.90%	5.20%	5.80%	7.50%

Table 14: Employees Subject to Social Insurance Contributions (SVP) by Industry[487]

	Berlin	Düsseldorf	Frankfurt	Hamburg	Munich
Total	567,491	213,999	294,766	440,216	429,995
thereof SVP-office employed	421,604	174,388	252,202	350,322	346,677
by occupation					
managerial occupations	7%	6%	6%	6%	7%
administrative occupations	49%	45%	40%	45%	39%
finance occupations	7%	13%	19%	11%	12%
technical occupations	17%	14%	16%	16%	20%
consulting services	10%	16%	14%	13%	16%
merchants	2%	3%	2%	3%	2%

Table 15: Office Employment by Occupation[488]

In Figure 21 the office rents of different German cities are displayed for the third quarter of 2006. This 'real estate clock,' published by Jones Lang LaSalle, classifies the regional office market in the stages of the real estate cycle. The first quadrant (North-East) stands for a rapid rent decrease, the second quadrant (South-East) for a slowed rent decrease, the third quadrant (South-West) for a rapid rent increase, and the fourth quadrant (North-West) for a slowed rent increase. Although it might be argued that the comparison of real estate rental markets to a clock is inappropriate,[489] the analogy points out that the different regional office markets are not in the same stage of the real estate cycle, and therefore the regional office markets cannot be compared directly with each other.[490] Although this real estate clock is widely used in real estate practice, it must be kept in mind that the assessment and development of this real estate clock is based on the perceptions of real estate agents and consultants.[491] Therefore, some doubts exist as

Jones Lang LaSalle (2006b), w/o pages, Jones Lang LaSalle (2006c), w/o pages, Jones Lang LaSalle (2006d), w/o pages

487 RIWIS (2007), w/o pages [Online Database]

488 Ibid., w/o pages [Online Database]

489 In the author's opinion, the denotation of ‚real estate clock' is inappropriate because it assumes that each office property market runs through each real estate cycle stages with a constant speed.

490 Cf. Heyser, H. (2006), p. 105

491 Cf. Ibid.p. 84

to whether it is appropriate to deduct from the real estate clock the contention that German office markets should be analyzed separately.

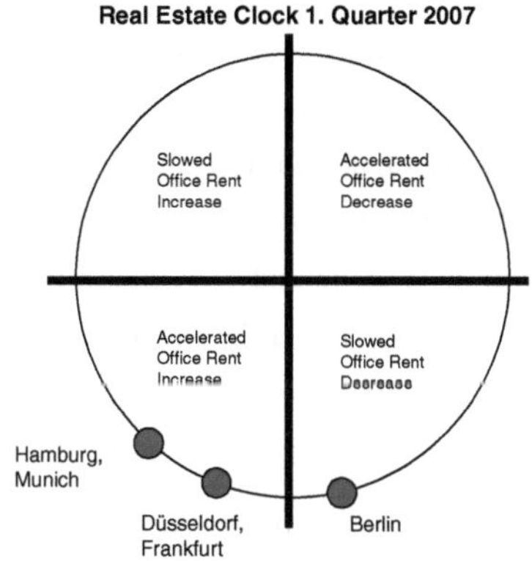

Figure 21: Office Rents in Germany[492]

4.2.2 Office Market Data and Research Situation

In the previous section, key data of the office rental markets in Berlin, Düsseldorf, Frankfurt, Hamburg, and Munich are depicted.[493] The data have been summarized from various market reports of international real estate consultancies. However, the important differences between the reported data are ostensible. In addition, many market reports apply different definitions and measurements of rent, office stock, vacancy rate, and so forth. Both problems have been recognized for a long time. The German Society of Property Researchers (gif) made ambitious efforts and motivated market participants to harmonize and unify the key data. As a result, gif published an office market report that summarizes the transaction volume, the average rental prices per EUR/sqm/month, and vacancy rates.[494] Nevertheless, the discrepancies and the problems of inaccurate market data are still prevalent.[495]

In addition, although the market participants, such as developers, city planners, lease agents, investors, and bankers, have a fundamental interest in accurate data, the property data situation is still underdeveloped in comparison with the UK or the US. For in-

[492] Adapted from Jones Lang LaSalle (2007b), w/o pages
[493] See Table 8 to Table 12
[494] Cf. Gesellschaft für Immobilienwirtschaftliche Forschung (2007), p. 1-4
[495] Cf. Heyser, H. (2006), p. 88-90, Flüshöh, C. /Stottrop, D. (2005), p. 189-190, Degener, A. (2005), p. 8.

stance, in Germany, all figures published for the office stock of different cities are only estimates.[496] *Flüshöh /Stottrop (2005)* examined the office property market of Düsseldorf and made a complete inventory count of the office stock. Their methdology comprised three steps. First, they identified all possible office building in Düsseldorf with the help of the yellow pages. Second, they verified with on-site inspections whether an office building was present. Third, they measured the building area with digital cadastral maps.[497] Afterward, they compared their results with other market reports and found inexplicable differences of up to 29 percent.[498] Although their methodology has some limitations (e.g. only gross building area can be reported), their work represents the first complete inventory count of the office stock of a German city. It is more accurate and consistent with scientific methodologies than most other published estimates.

Further confusion regarding office stock figures results in the fact that it is not always comprehensible which city boundaries the published office stock figures are based on.[499]

Another problem that aggravates office property market research is the fact that many lease contracts are not published because of data protection reasons. It must be kept in mind, that unlike other countries, Germany does not have a central government agency that collects all relevant information on office lease contracts.[500]

Real estate research in Germany has experienced tremendous development in the recent past. Initially, real estate research departments were mainly "one-man-shows" established by banks and finance companies. Now, however, they can be found in most important real estate companies. These research departments have employees with different academic backgrounds, from geography to business administration to economics, and their working methods changed from standard office market analysis to the use of econometric models.[501]

As indicated by the aforementioned examples, it is important to note that, if German office property markets are examined, one cannot use the same high-quality method and

---

[496] Cf. Rohmert, W. (2002), p. 5, Flüshöh, C. /Stottrop, D. (2005), p. 1

[497] Cf. Flüshöh, C. /Stottrop, D. (2005), p. 130-131

[498] Cf. Ibid.p. 189-190

[499] Cf. Deutsche Gesellschaft für Immobilienfonds (2008), w/o pages, Flüshöh, C. /Stottrop, D. (2005), p. 189

[500] Cf. Hoffmann, J. /Lorenz, A. (2006), p. 1

[501] Cf. Beyerle, T. (2006b), p. 1-12

proficiency used in other research areas (e.g., finance) because of the lack of accurate data, the lack of a government agency to collect relevant data, and the protection of data privacy.

4.2.3 Legal and Economic Foundation of German Office Leases

Significant differences exist between the office lease structures that govern the various property markets around the world.[502] After the 'Schuldrechtsreform,' reform of law of obligations, the most important laws governing German office leases can be found in the Bürgerliches Gesetzbuch (BGB), the Civil Code of Germany. Here, the main articles for office leases are the general provision for tenancies BGB §§535 to 548 and the tenancies for other objects BGB §§578 to 580a. Moreover, it is important to note that buildings are treated as essential components of land under German law and therefore cannot be dealt with separately.[503]

4.2.3.1 Grant of Lease and Lease Length

For office leases (longer than one year) it is strongly recommended that they are in writing to be valid.[504] Many leases are evidenced by detailed written agreements prepared by agents and lawyers. Without these detailed agreements, the Civil Code, which tends to favour the tenant, would apply.[505]

The *typical lease length* is usually five years. For whole buildings under single lettings, the length is five to ten years.[506] Most five-year leases contain an option for the tenant to renew for an additional five years. Otherwise, there are no legal restrictions for the length of an office lease unless a lease length of over 30 years has been agreed upon. For leases longer than 30 years, the Civil Code gives both landlord and tenant the right to terminate the lease within the legal period of notice.[507]

---

[502] Cf. Baum, A. /Turner, N. (2004), p. 215, Turner, N. /Thomas, M. (2001), p. 182
[503] Cf. Royal Institution of Chartered Surveyors /Centre for European Property Research p. 28
[504] Cf. Lindner-Figura, J., et al. (2005), p. 152
[505] Cf. Royal Institution of Chartered Surveyors /Centre for European Property Research p. 25
[506] Cf. Baum, A. /Turner, N. (2004), p. 216
[507] Cf. Lindner-Figura, J., et al. (2005), p. 269-270

4.2.3.2 Rent Revisions

Rent revisions are normally designed in advance to avoid recourse to arbitration, which can be time consuming and unpredictable in its results.[508] Different rent provisions exist: step-up clause, escalation clause, and arbitration.

The office lease contains a *step-up rent clause* if the parties define and agree to in advance the amount and the exact point of time when the rent will increase. Thus, it is also possible to define the rent increase as a percentage change of the base rent rather than as a fixed amount. Moreover, a step-up clause can also contain an escalation clause.[509]

The *escalation clause* is another provision for rental change and includes different versions. The purpose of an escalation clause is to keep the equivalent ratio between landlord benefits and tenant benefits consistent.[510] Therefore, in contrast to UK office leases, upwards-only escalation clauses are not possible and, if agreed to, are void by law. As *Turner /Thomas (2001)* point out, "[…] the landlord does not enjoy the general comfort that rents will not fall."[511] If a rent increase is triggered automatically, then a 'true' escalation clause is on hand. Otherwise, if a rent change must be triggered by the action of the tenant or landlord, then a 'false' escalation clause is on hand. Strictly speaking, 'true' escalation clauses have to be approved by a government authority called the Bundesamt für Wirtschaft und Ausfuhrkontrolle (BAFA). However, the approval is mainly feigned if the rent change in the escalation clause is triggered by an agreed fluctuation of consumer price index or cost-of-living index provided by the German or European federal statistics office, or by the fluctuation of an index measuring the average prices of the services or products that the tenant generates. Furthermore, the landlord gives up the right to duly terminate the contract within a period of ten years. Clauses that lead to above-average rent increases and below-average rent decreases are void by law.[512]

Finally, provisions for rental change can also be determined by *arbitration*. Germany does not possess an exact counterpart to the UK's professional valuers. The arbiter has to be selected by both parties and is normally provided by the local Chamber of Com-

---

508 Cf. Royal Institution of Chartered Surveyors /Centre for European Property Research p. 26

509 Cf. Lindner-Figura, J., et al. (2005), p. 302-303

510 Cf. Ibid., p. 303

511 Turner, N. /Thomas, M. (2001), p. 183

512 Cf. Lindner-Figura, J., et al. (2005), p. 303-311

merce. Although many office leases with an arbitration clause define the range and benchmark for the rent review, arbitration clauses are still time consuming and, to a certain degree, unpredictable. Therefore, arbitration clauses are generally avoided.[513]

4.2.3.3 Maintenance, Repair and Additional Expenses

In Germany, as opposed to the UK or the US, triple-net, or 'clear,' leases—in which the tenant pays for the rent, taxes, insurance, and repair costs—are virtually unknown. Normally, the landlord is responsible for structural and major repairs (in German, Dach und Fach), and the tenant assumes the costs for internal repairs and decoration. Because the landlord's costs for structural and major repairs are sometimes substantial, some landlords adopt the strategy of decreasing the contractual rent by simultaneously adding a clause whereby the tenant participates at least partially in the payment of repair and maintenance costs.[514]

The topic of additional and operating expenses is important and has to be handled with reasonable care because additional expenses can add up to 20 percent of the total office expenses.[515] Additional expenses (in German, Nebenkosten) comprise all costs that are chargeable to the tenant. The umbrella term also refers to operating expenses (in German, Betriebskosten), administration charges, maintenance costs, and repair costs. Although no distinction between the terms *additional expenses* and *operating expenses* is made in some office leases, it has to be pointed out that operating expenses are defined by law and do not include any administration charges, maintenance costs, or repair costs. Thus, operating expenses are costs that occur regularly and result from the ownership or use of the property and its buildings. Although German legislation assumes that these additional expenses are the landlord's responsibility, in practice, the tenant often pays the additional expenses. Consequently, different definitions of contract rent exist. If the tenant is charged a rent that does not distinguish between rent and additional expenses, then an inclusive rent (in German, Inklusivmiete) has been agreed upon. If the tenant is charged rent and expenses for heating and hot water but not any other expenses separately, then a gross rent (in German, Bruttokaltmiete) has been agreed upon. If the lease contract specifies in detail which type of additional expenses is chargeable to the

[513] Cf. Ibid., p. 311-312, Royal Institution of Chartered Surveyors /Centre for European Property Research p. 26-27

[514] Cf. Royal Institution of Chartered Surveyors /Centre for European Property Research p. 27

[515] Cf. Diehl, B. (2006), p. 40

tenant, then it is a partial inclusive rent (in German, Teilinklusivmiete). Finally, if the tenant has to pay for the rent, heating, and hot water expenses, and partially to the reversible other additional expenses, then a net rent (in German, Nettokaltmiete) has been agreed upon. In the recent past, most contracts have had a net rent basis.[516]

4.2.3.4 Value-Added Taxes

In German tax law, revenues of land and buildings are exempted from value-added tax (VAT). However, the landlord has the option to waive this tax exemption and to charge VAT to the tenant separately. However, he is allowed to do so only if the tenant carries on a business subject to VAT. For instance, banks, insurance, medical practices, and government authorities are exempted from VAT. The landlord's advantage in exercising this option is that he is allowed to reclaim all VAT for development and construction of the office building. The tenant benefits from this undertaking as well. He is allowed to offset the VAT on rent as tax on input. The election of this option is valid only for a period of 10 years, which commences on the date that the option tax is exercised.[517]

This issue is important for two reasons. First, if a new tenant who carries a business with nondeductible input on VAT moves into the office building, then the current landlord has to repay the VAT he reclaimed during development. This rule applies even if the office building has been sold during the 10-year period. Second, in recessionary office markets with high vacancy and low rent levels, many landlords forget to ask the prospective tenant whether his business is subject to VAT. As a result, the landlord has to pay the VAT out of the agreed contractual rent.[518]

4.2.3.5 Rental Area Definitions

One major problem in analyzing office market and German office leases stems from the fact that the parties do not specify in the lease contract which definition of rental area they have in mind.[519] So far, no legal definition of rental area for office space has been provided, which is a common source of legal disputes.[520] Furthermore, as mentioned

---

[516] Cf. Lindner-Figura, J., et al. (2005), p. 333-339

[517] Cf. Ibid., p. 296-301, Royal Institution of Chartered Surveyors /Centre for European Property Research p. 31

[518] Cf. Lindner-Figura, J., et al. (2005), p. 296-301

[519] Cf. Heyser, H. (2006), p. 74

[520] Cf. Lovells (2006), p. 14

earlier, it makes real estate research more difficult.[521] Currently, two widely accepted standard guidelines exist. One standard is set by the German Society of Property Researchers. Although its primary purpose it is not the definition of rental areas, the second standard referred to in lease contracts is set by the Deutsches Institut für Normung e.V. (DIN).[522] However, these guidelines offer multiple definitions of rental area. The main difference between the guidelines is that the gif guideline differentiates between fully lettable and partly lettable circulation space. As a result the rental size can vary by 10 percent.[523] From the following figure it becomes evident that depending on the choice of rental area definition, the office rent per square metre can differ significantly.[524]

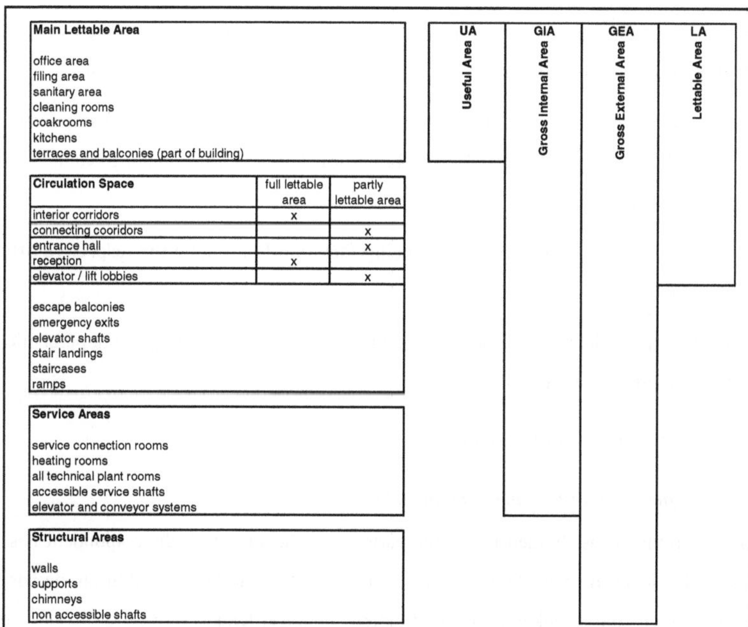

Figure 22: Lettable Area of Office Space[525]

[521] See Section 4.2.2

[522] The first edition of the DIN has been published in 1934. It is mainly a technical standard and its main purpose is to provide area definitions for the calculation of construction costs. Cf. Flüshöh, C. /Stottrop, D. (2005), p. 47-48

[523] Cf. Heyser, H. (2006), p. 107

[524] See Figure 22

[525] Adapted from Schulte, K.-W., et al. (2005a), p. 729

4.3 Survey among German Real Estate Professionals

Section 4.1 demonstrated that many different location, building, and lease factors have an impact on office rents, and the degree of their impact varies between office markets and considered time periods. Section 4.2 gave strong indications that this is also the case for the German office property market. The German office property market is dispersed, and the German lease structures and legal framework differ from the UK and the US, where the majority of office market research has been undertaken. In Germany, only limited research has been done to date. Therefore, to identify the potential factors influencing the level of office rents in Germany, a survey of German real estate professionals has been conducted.[526]

The nature of this survey is explorative. Consequently, no specific hypotheses are formulated or tested. Instead, this research tries to answer the following questions:

- What are the influencing factors determining office rents in the major German office property markets (Berlin, Frankfurt, Düsseldorf, Hamburg, Munich, and Stuttgart)?
- Do the evaluations of the influencing factors differ among the respective office markets?
- Do the evaluations of the influencing factors differ according to the perceptions of market participants?

4.3.1 Methodology and Statistical Tests

4.3.1.1 Questionnaire Content and Structure

The questionnaire is divided into three parts.[527] In the first part, the respondent has to classify his level of expertise in the different real estate markets. In addition, he has to specify which role he takes on in the market (landlord, tenant, broker, or service provider) and has to choose the office market (Berlin, Düsseldorf, Frankfurt, Hamburg, Munich, or Stuttgart) that he knows best. All subsequent questions are answered in regard to the selected office market. In the last part of the questionnaire, the participant is asked to specify his company's activities and the number of years of his professional

[526] The survey results have been partially presented at the 13th European Real Estate Society Conference in Weimar, Germany. See Kempf, S. (2006), p. 1-48.

[527] See Appendix A.2.2

experience. While the first and last parts contain auxiliary questions to classify and analyze the participants' answers, the second part constitutes the core of the study and is divided into six subsections: location factors (2.1), building factors (2.2), equipment and layout factors of an office unit (2.3), and lease factors (2.4). Each subsection can be seen as a main category in which a number of different attributes are summarized. For each attribute the respondent has to evaluate, on the one hand, whether the attribute increases or decreases the net office rent and, on the other hand, the degree of influence of the attribute. In subsection (2.5), the participants are asked to evaluate the importance of macroeconomic attributes in the negotiation process of office rents.[528]

All attributes have been derived from international literature research[529] and from several expert interviews with German real estate professionals. The interview partners work in different regional real estate markets and in different market functions.[530] This undertaking has been necessary to ensure that all different perspectives of influencing factors determining office rents have been considered. In a manner similar to the hygiene factors of Frederik Herzberg's theory, some attributes have to be formulated in a positive and negative way.[531] The reason is that these attributes have a peculiar characteristic when being evaluated by the tenant: If these attributes are not met or are only partly met, then the tenant evaluates them with a discount. But if they are met, they do not necessarily lead to the payment of a premium because they are considered to be "standard." For instance, a high emission of traffic noise and pollution causes the tenant to ask for a discount on the payable rent. However, he is not willing to pay a premium if the office building is located in an area with little emission of traffic noise and pollution. Moreover, as indicated in the international literary review, many attributes attempt to capture the effect of soft factors and serve as proxies. As a result, the length of the questionnaire is quite extensive and includes more than 160 attributes.[532] Finally, in the last subsection (2.6), the participant is asked to evaluate and to rank the different categories.[533]

---

[528] Cf. Kempf, S. (2006), p. 3-4
[529] See Section 4.1 and 4.2
[530] See Appendix A.2.1
[531] Cf. Thommen, J.-P. /Achleitner, A.-K. (1998), p. 628-629
[532] See Appendix A.2.2
[533] Cf. Kempf, S. (2006), p. 4

4.3.1.2 *Questionnaire Design*

With a few exceptions, the questionnaire contains only closed-ended questions to reduce the answering time and—more important—to conduct a quantitative statistical analysis. Bipolar, 9-step answering scales have been used for parts 2.1 to 2.4 of the questionnaire, with graphical support.

	Premium on Net Office Rent				no influence	Discount on Net Office Rent			
	very high	high	medium	small		small	medium	high	very high
	++++	+++	++	+	0	-	--	---	----
Proximity to the Airport	☐	☐	☐	☐	☐	☐	☐	☐	☐
...	☐	☐	☐	☐	☐	☐	☐	☐	☐

Figure 23: Example of a Survey Question

A score of +4 signifies that the attribute leads to a very high increase of the payable office rent. A score of -4 signifies that the attribute leads to a very high decrease of the payable office rent. A score of 0 signifies that the attribute has no influence at all. Beforehand, a definition of office net rent has been given to provide a common basis for the evaluation. In Germany, net office rent is defined as the payable rent excluding all additional costs (e.g., heating, water, and security).[534]

For part 2.5 (macroeconomic factors), the scale has been changed to a 4-step scale, as these questions do not aim to identify the influencing factors (increase or decrease) on office rents but rather to identify their general importance in rent negotiations. In part 2.6, a 6-step scale is used to measure the importance of the main categories (location characteristics, physical characteristics of an office building, physical characteristics of an office unit, lease characteristics, and macroeconomic factors). Furthermore, in a separate question, the participant is asked to rank the categories according to their importance, with the rank of 1 indicating the most important category and 5, the least important category.

The order of the variables has been chosen in such a way so as to avoid a one-way positive or negative attitude of answering.[535] In addition, the questionnaire contains several control variables. The design and content of the questionnaire has been pretested.

---

[534] See Section 4.2.3.3

[535] Cf. Mayer, H. (2004), p. 57-132

4.3.1.3 Evaluation and Statistical Tests

The primary goal of this survey is to identify the influencing factors determining the level of office rents in Germany. To that end, a simple comparison of means and standard deviations of the various attributes is performed. The scores are categorized as follows:

- very high premium (discount) on office rent: mean score >=3.5 (<= -3.5)
- high premium (discount) on office rent: mean score >= 2.5 (<= -2.5)
- medium premium (discount) on office rent: mean score >= 1.5 (<= -1.5)
- low premium (discount) on office rent: mean score < 1.5 (<= -1.5)

For the second and third research questions, a one-way univariate analysis is conducted.[536] [537] In both cases, the dependent variables are the attributes listed in the questionnaire from subsections 2.1 to 2.6. To help researchers detect regional differences in the evaluations, the specification of the respective office market (question 1.2 of the survey) serves as an independent variable. To help researchers find differences in perceptions of market participants, question 1.3 is the independent variable.

The null hypothesis of the univariate analysis is that the attributes are independent from different regional office markets (Berlin, Düsseldorf, Frankfurt, or Hamburg)[538] and also independent from the role of the market participant (landlord, tenant, broker, or service provider). The hypothesis is tested using a Fisher-test at a 95% significance level. In addition, a significance test of Brown-Forsythe and Welch are used. An important assumption in univariate analysis is that the residuals between the groups are homogeneous. Moreover, only those attributes that meet this assumption are included in the analyses. The assumption has been tested using Levene's test of homogeneity. If a difference for a specific attribute exists, then a post hoc test by Turkey is undertaken to identify the office markets or market participants between which the difference is significant.[539]

---

[536] See Section 4.3.2.2 and 4.3.2.3

[537] See Appendix A.2.3 for detailed statistics. The statistics were calculated using Statistical Package for Social Scientists (SPSS).

[538] The cities Munich and Stuttgart are dropped out due the small response rate. See Section 4.3.1.4

[539] Cf. Backhaus, K., et al. (2003), p. 119-154, Rudolf, M. /Müller, J. (2004), p. 77-86, Bortz, J. (1999), p. 237-276

4.3.1.4 Sample Selection and Response Rate

The questionnaire was sent via email to all alumni members of immoebs e.V. - the post-graduate program of the **ebs** REAL ESTATE ACADEMY - in April and May 2006. This sample was chosen for the following reasons: First, this alumni network is considered "[...] the biggest profession-orientated network [...]" of the German real estate sector.[540] It has more than 1,700 members organized into eight regional research groups. Second, the regional organization is similar to the selected metropolitan areas of the questionnaire. The regions are Berlin, North (the region around Hamburg), Munich, Rhein-Main (the region around Frankfurt), Rhein-Ruhr (the region around Essen, Düsseldorf, and Cologne), Stuttgart, Nuremberg, and Austria. Third, the members of *immo*ebs work in different fields, which perfectly suits the multidisciplinary approach of the questionnaire. However, it should be kept in mind that not all members work in the office sector. Unfortunately, it was not possible to draw a sample of members who work only in the office sector. As a consequence, the questionnaire had to be sent to all members. This undertaking has a direct effect on the response rate of the survey.

The questionnaire was sent to 1,732 real estate professionals. To date, 102 questionnaires have been sent back, a response rate of 5.9%. Figure 24 shows the distribution of the office markets on which the respondents chose to focus their evaluations. Munich and Stuttgart have not been taken into consideration because fewer than 10 responses were obtained. Furthermore, because some respondents did not answer all of the questions, the number of questionnaires (N) that entered the different analyses varies.

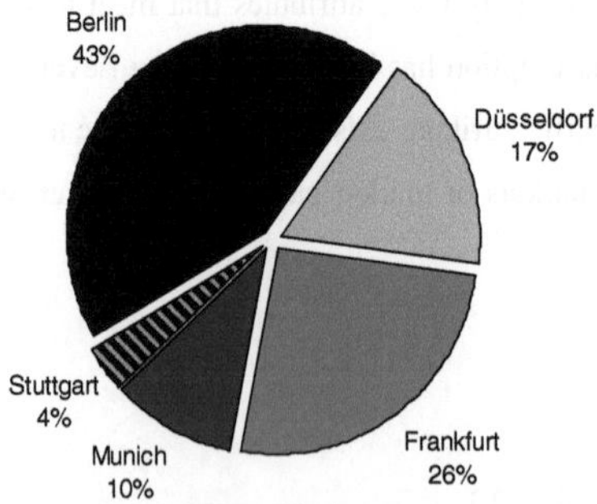

Figure 24: Regional Distribution of Respondents

540 Cf. FAZ (2001), p. 55

Figure 25 further reveals which roles the respondents play in the office market. The majority of the respondents act as landlords (43.0%), followed by service providers (38.7%) and brokers (10.8%). The number of brokers is small because the public image of brokers in Germany is not highly appreciated. Therefore, many brokers consider themselves consultants or service providers, although they receive a commission.[541] Unfortunately, only a small number of the respondents (7.5%) are tenants. However, this is not surprising and is due to the selected sample. Most non-property companies have not yet recognized that real estate is a major asset and therefore they do not send their employees to postgraduate real estate educational programs.

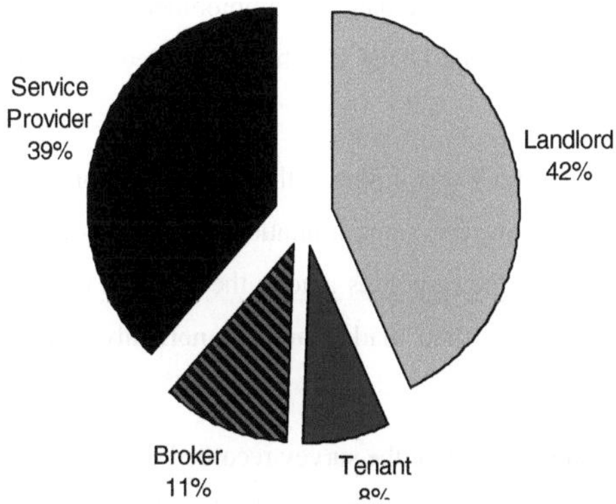

Figure 25: Distribution of Respondents' Market Role

4.3.1.5 Limitations

As with many quantitative surveys conducted by questionnaires, the limitations of this research and therefore the general application of its results are directly connected to the quality of the sample selection and its response rate. Two questions have to be asked before any general application can take place:

1. Is the selected sample representative of the population—in this case, of all participants in the German real estate office markets?
2. Is the response rate sufficient such that a meaningful statistical analysis and meaningful results can be drawn?

---

[541] Cf. Flüshöh, C. /Stottrop, D. (2005), p. 74

First, it can be ensured that the selected sample is representative of the real estate office market because the members are experts in different regional markets and - even more important - play different roles in these markets. The representativeness is constraint as the regional distribution of respondents does not necessarily reflect the importance of the regional office markets. For instance, while the majority of respondents are active in Berlin's real estate market, it is argued that Frankfurt's office market has a greater importance for the German real estate market as well as the German economy. Regarding the respondents' market role it must be kept in mind that the German real estate market is fragmented. Most real estate organizations represent a specific occupational group. For instance, brokers are mainly organized in the IVD (Immobilienverband Deutschland), valuers in the BIIS (Bundesverband der Immobilien-Investment Sachverständigen), and facility managers in the DDIV (Dachverband Deutscher Immobilienverwalter).

Second, the response rate of 5.9% is in line with other surveys and should yield generally applicable results.[542] However, some limitations arise when it comes down to the univariate analysis. Because the responses among the different regional office markets and participants' role in the office market are not normally distributed, the results should be treated with caution.[543]

Moreover, it must be pointed out that the survey recorded the opinion of market participants at a specific time during the real estate cycle. To what extent the empirical findings hold true for other time periods and are valid for other stages in the real estate cycle remains unanswered.[544]

542 Cf. Alreck, P. /Settle, R. (1985), p. unknown in Redman, A. L., et al. (2002), p. 170
543 Cf. Kempf, S. (2006), p. 19-20
544 Cf. Ibid., p. 20

4.3.2 Empirical Results

4.3.2.1 Office Rent Determinants across German Metropolitan Areas

4.3.2.1.1 Location Factors

The following figure shows the results for the location attributes.[545] According to the survey, the availability of parking and proximity to public transportation lead to high premiums on office rents, whereas other attributes measuring the infrastructural quality of office location (proximity to the airport, train station, or highway) have only a medium impact on office rents.

Attributes determining the quality of an office location for employees, namely, proximity to shops, hotels, and restaurants, lead to only a medium premium on office rents. Attributes determining the quality for employers (proximity to companies of the same sector and proximity to companies) have only a minor positive impact, according to the survey's respondents.

The image and reputation of the business environment where the office is located have a great influence on office rent. This observation supports the assumption that the image of an office's location influences the reputation of the company itself. Tenants are therefore willing to pay a higher rent.[546] Likewise, it is important that the office building have good visibility. The attributes 'high/low emissions of traffic pollution and noise' can be considered hygiene factors. The mean score of high emissions (-1.65) exceeds the mean score of low emissions (1.00).

The analysis of the location factors shows that soft factors (e.g., image of the surroundings) are as important as hard factors (e.g., availability of parking space, proximity to public transportation). The question of how soft factors can be measured and influenced remains unanswered.

---

[545] See Figure 26

[546] See Section 4.1.1.3

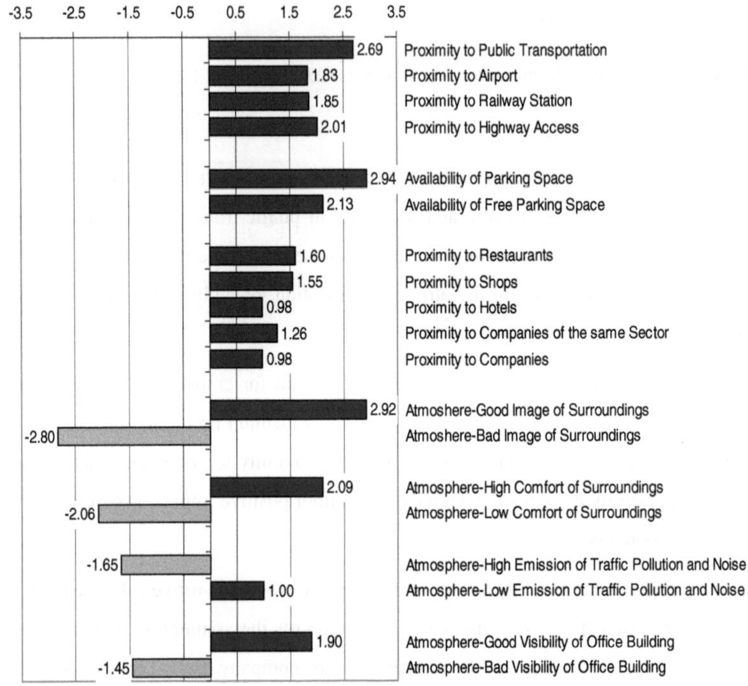

Figure 26: Importance of Location Factors (N=96)

4.3.2.1.2 Building Factors

In the following figure, the impact of building attributes on office rents is depicted.[547] Of the easily quantifiable hard factors, the attributes measuring the year of construction or renovation of the office building have the greatest impact. According to the opinion of real estate professionals, rents for office buildings constructed before 1996 account for a medium discount. No influence on the level of office rent is reported for buildings constructed between 1996 and 2000. Instead, landlords of buildings constructed between 2001 and 2005 can charge a medium premium. For office developments completed in 2006, landlords can even expect a high premium. These findings are in line

[547] See Figure 27

with earlier studies and confirm the contention that building age is a major determinant of the office building's quality.[548]

Nevertheless, attributes measuring soft factors, namely, architectural quality and prestige, also have a great influence on office rents. Again, the question of how these soft factors can be operationalized arises, as these factors embrace a multitude of subjective attitudes.[549]

In addition, many attributes measuring the fit-out and building quality, namely, climate control, IT-infrastructure, emergency power systems, and security systems, have only a minor impact on office rents. The low mean scores for these attributes suggest that tenants expect an office building to have these attributes. Further support for this contention is reported by the fact that the opposite attributes (control variables of these attributes) received higher negative mean scores (e.g., no climate control and no IT-infrastructure).

Many lease contracts do not specify the rental area definition in use, even though unclear definitions often lead to legal disputes.[550] However, it is not surprising, as even market professionals ignore the impact of different rental area definitions.

Finally, ecological aspects have almost no effect on office rents. In contrast to that finding, the attribute 'economic energy consumption' leads to a medium increase in office rents. Obviously, tenants are aware of the fact that energy costs should not be neglected, but they are indifferent to the source of the reduced energy consumption of the building. Office occupiers are not aware of the advantages, other than lower energy consumption, generated by green buildings.[551]

---

548 See Section 4.1.2.1
549 See Section 4.1.2.2
550 See Section 4.2.3.5
551 See Section 4.1.2.3

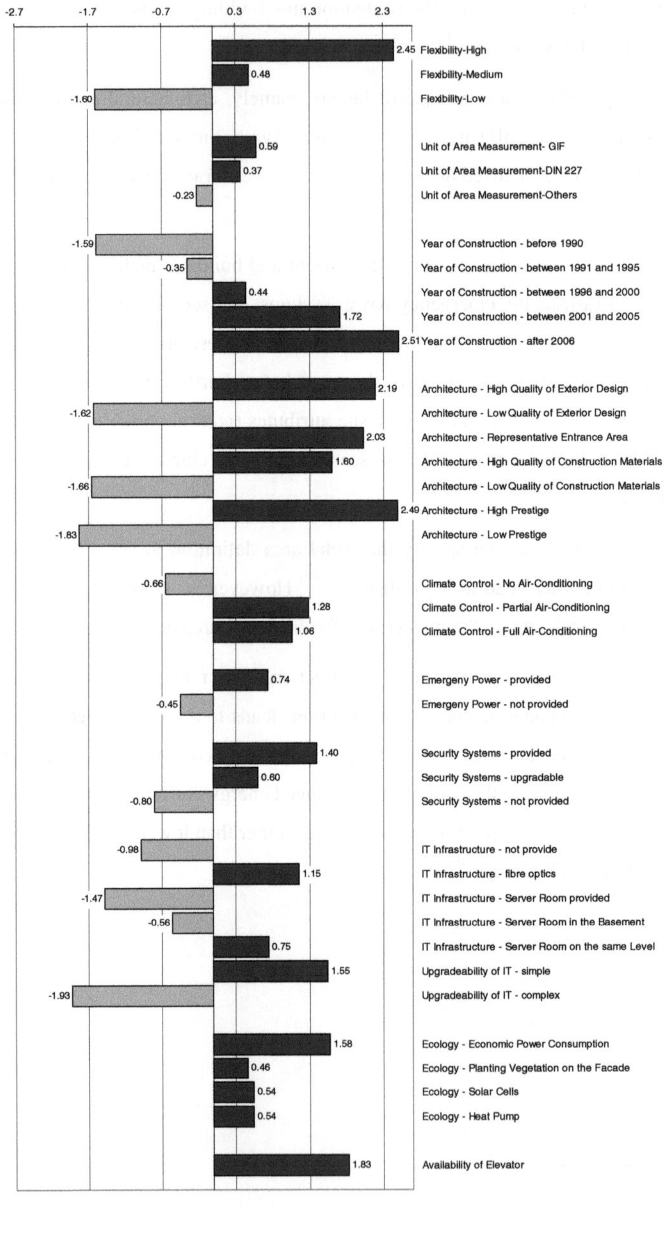

Figure 27: Importance of Building Factors (N=96)

4.3.2.1.3 Equipment and Layout Factors of an Office Unit

In Figure 28, the means of the attributes describing the office unit are shown. Of the various types of layout, only 'combined office' (in German: Kombibüro) leads to a premium on office rents. All other types of layout either have no influence or lead to a discount. Real estate professionals recognize the layout of 'combined office' as the most advantageous.[552] Moreover, office occupiers and their corporate real estate strategies perceive the need for flexible space.[553]

The flooring material of the office floor, which is often used as proxy for representativeness, has no influence, nor does the preference for the different types of regulation of air conditioning (for the room or for each individual workplace). However, the time on the market of the office unit plays an important role. If the time on the market is greater than nine months, then tenants expect a medium discount on the level of office rent. This observation is explainable because, for each month that the office unit remains vacant, the landlord loses money as well as bargaining power.[554]

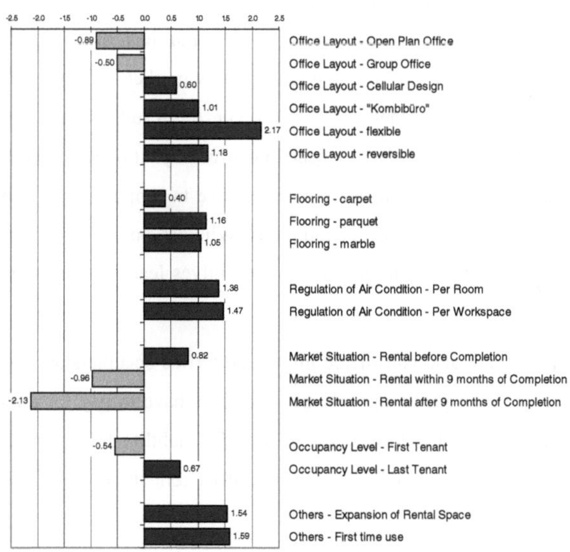

Figure 28: Importance of Equipment and Layout Factors of an Office Unit (N=96)

---

552 Cf. Hahr, H. (2006), p. 87-90

553 Cf. Leishman, C., et al. (2003), p. 52

554 See Section 4.1.5

4.3.2.1.4 Lease Factors

In the following figure,[555] two important findings of international real estate research are underpinned. The first confirmation is that the longer the lease length is, the higher the discount will be. This finding supports the contention that the landlord is willing to agree on a discount for long-term leases to save transaction costs.[556] Because a lease length of five years has no influence on rent, it can be derived that this lease length is currently standard in the market.[557] Leases that run shorter than five years are expected to receive a premium. Nevertheless, it should be remarked that this result also could be attributed to the fact that, when the survey was conducted, most office rental markets were in a downturn.[558] [559]The second confirmation is that, because of economies-of-scale effects, the larger the rental space is, the higher the discount on the level of rent will be.[560] A brief comparison of the means reveals that those office units between 500 and 1,000 sqm are currently considered standard. Larger office units receive a discount; smaller ones, a premium.

Landlords who have high cash flow constraints (mortgage payments) are motivated to let properties more quickly, but they prefer to offer nonfinancial incentives rather than discount the agreed rent. Therefore, in a recessionary market, it is expected that options and incentives play an important role.[561] However, the results demonstrate that all different kinds of options have only a marginal positive impact on rent. These findings can be interpreted in two ways. Either the options have no importance for the tenants, or they are already standard in lease negotiations. Whereas options have a negligible impact on the level of office rent, all kinds of incentives lead to a medium premium on office rents.

Additional charges are also considered important. Office occupiers are aware that landlords can increase their profit significantly if tenants have to pay for maintenance and structural repairs. If the landlord wants to limit his liability for structural repairs and management, he is expected to decrease the net office rent significantly.

---

555 See Figure 29
556 See Section 4.1.4.1
557 See Section 4.2.3.1
558 See Appendix A.2.3
559 Cf. Thomas Daily (2007), w/o pages [Online Database]
560 See Section 4.1.4.2
561 See Section 4.1.4.4

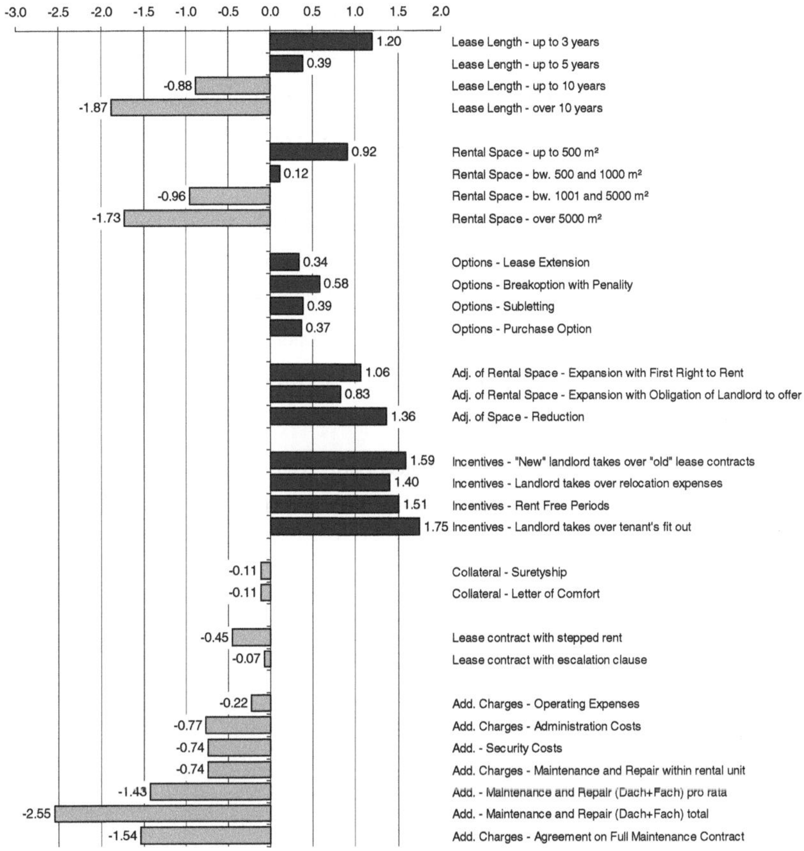

Figure 29: Importance of Lease Factors I

The questionnaire also included attributes that are supposed to measure the default risk of tenants and the quality of the tenant.[562] The findings are surprising because no attribute has any significant impact on rent. In other words, neither the legal form of the tenant nor the company's country of origin has an impact on the level of rent. A difference regarding the legal form was expected because the owners of partnership companies are liable with their personal wealth.

[562] See Figure 30

In addition, the results of this survey demonstrate that collaterals have no influence on the level of rent. One explanation is that both attributes are common in lease negotiations in Germany. Furthermore, the sector of business in which the tenant is active and the location of the tenant's headquarters are irrelevant for the level of office rent, according to the survey's respondents.

Another surprising finding is that it does not matter if the tenant's business can charge VAT (value-added tax). It was expected that, if a tenant did not fulfill this requirement (e.g., banks), landlords would automatically ask for a premium.[563] However, the fact that these attributes have no influence on rent does not necessarily mean that the market participants are not aware of their importance. Rather, it indicates that landlords cannot be choosy when it comes to finding new tenants.

Finally, all additional services do not necessarily lead to higher office rents, according to the survey's respondents. This finding thwarts a landlord's plan of increasing the office rent by offering additional services.

---

[563] See Section 4.2.3.4

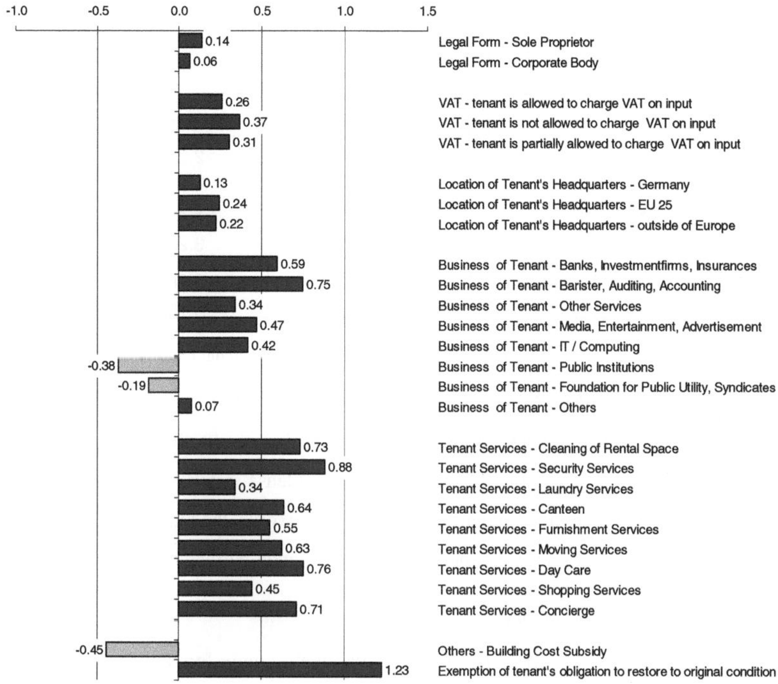

Figure 30: Importance of Lease Factors II

4.3.2.1.5 Ranking of Factors

At the end of the survey, respondents were asked to rank the importance of location, building, equipment and layout, lease, and macroeconomic factors. The ranking asked two different questions with an inverse scaling. First, the respondent had to decide the importance of each factor separately on a 5-step scale (score 5 = very important, 1 = unimportant). Second, the respondent was asked to arrange the factors in order according to their impact on office rents (1 = highest rank; 5 = lowest rank). The results are reported in the following table.[564]

From both figures it can be derived that the old proverb "location, location, location" still holds true. This result is in line with a survey conducted by Pfnür and Armonat in 2001. They analyzed the success factors for real estate investments among institutional

[564] See Table 16

investors. The overwhelming majority of the participants acknowledged that location factors are the main decision factor for success.[565]

	Importance of Factors		Ranking of Factors	
	Mean Score*	Ranking	Mean Score**	Ranking
Location Factors	4.084	1	2.215	1
Lease Factors	3.705	2	2.902	2
Building Factors	3.684	3	3.011	3
Equipment and Layout Factors	3.674	4	3.204	4
Macroeconomic Factors	3.358	5	3.587	5
	* 5 = very important; 1 = unimportant		** 1 = Highest Rank; 5 = Lowest Rank	

Table 16: Importance and Ranking of Influencing Factors

4.3.2.2 Regional Differences in Office Rent Determinants

The statistical analysis reveals only a few interesting results for the second research question. With the exception of some location and lease factors, the majority of attributes do not show any regional differences. In other words, the majority of attributes are valued similarly across the metropolitan areas by market participants.[566]

4.3.2.2.1 Location Factors

Of the attributes measuring the infrastructural quality, only 'proximity to public transport' and 'proximity to railway station' meet the statistical tests.[567] They indicate that, for the office market in Düsseldorf, the proximity to public transportation is not as important as for Berlin, Frankfurt, and Hamburg. The same observation can be made for the attribute 'proximity to railway station'. Among the attributes measuring the influence of different amenities on office rents, only the attribute 'proximity of restaurants' is statistically significant. While this attribute leads to a medium premium in Berlin and Hamburg, it leads to only a small premium in Düsseldorf and Frankfurt. Finally, only the attribute 'high emission of traffic noise and pollution' passes the statistical tests. This attribute leads to a medium discount in Hamburg, but it has almost no influence in Düsseldorf.[568]

---

[565] Cf. Pfnür, A. /Armonat, S. (2001), p. 39-42

[566] Cf. Kempf, S. (2006), p. 17-18

[567] See Appendix A.2.4.2.1

[568] Cf. Kempf, S. (2006), p. 17

4.3.2.2.2 *Lease Factors*

The attribute 'lease length of 10 years' proves to be statistically significant. The statistical analysis demonstrates that there are significant regional differences between Frankfurt and Düsseldorf.[569] In Düsseldorf, leases with a length of 10 years get a medium discount, whereas this discount is almost negligible in Frankfurt. This finding suggests that the competition for the rental market is fiercer in Düsseldorf than in Frankfurt and that a lease length of 10 years is the current standard of the market in Frankfurt.[570] Further evidence for this assumption is revealed when 'lease contract under 500 sqm' and 'lease contract between 500 and 1000 sqm' are analyzed. Both attributes meet the necessary statistical requirements. The statistical tests reveal that, for these leases, a small premium has to be paid in Frankfurt; in Hamburg and Düsseldorf, a discount is already given for leases between 500 sqm and 1000 sqm. In addition, a break option with penalty has no influence on office rents in Hamburg and Düsseldorf, whereas a small premium has to be paid in Frankfurt.[571]

4.3.2.3 *Differences in Market Participants' Perceptions of Office Rent Determinants*

The statistical tests analyzing whether market participants value office rent determinants differently report only a few differences. In most cases, market participants value similarly the office rent determinants.

4.3.2.3.1 *Building Factors and Equipment/Layout Factors*

The statistical analysis reveals that the attribute 'no air conditioning' is evaluated differently. Whereas brokers and service providers are of the opinion that the absence of air conditioning leads to a small discount on office rents, landlords indicate that this attribute has almost no influence at all.[572] It is surprising that the difference in means of landlord and tenant is smaller than that between landlord and broker or service provider. Similar results are obtained for the attribute 'parquet.' Landlords evaluate this attribute with a small to medium premium on office rent; brokers assess almost no influence.[573]

---

[569] See Appendix A.2.4.2.2
[570] Cf. Hermann, A. (2005), p. 48
[571] Cf. Kempf, S. (2006), p. 17-18
[572] See Appendix A.2.4.3.1
[573] See Appendix A.2.4.3.2

Again, the perception of tenant and landlord, as measured by the difference in means, is closer than that of landlord and broker.[574]

4.3.2.3.2 Lease Factors

The statistical analysis shows that important differences concerning lease characteristics exist among the market players.[575] Whereas the brokers argue that the attribute 'office unit between 1,001 and 5,000 sqm' leads to a medium discount, landlords assess only a small discount or no discount at all.[576]

Landlords and tenants have opposing perceptions of collaterals. Tenants suggest that a letter of comfort should decrease the office rent; landlords assign no influence to this attribute. This finding conflicts with previous international empirical research suggesting that collaterals reduce landlord uncertainty and that landlords are therefore willing to offer rental discounts.[577] In Germany, however, de facto a letter of comfort does not protect sufficiently a landlord from the tenant's default risk in contrast to a suretyship.[578]

Similar differences in perceptions exist for the attributes 'additional charges – administration costs' and 'additional charges – object surveillance cost.' In both cases, tenants think that their taking over these additional costs should result in a small to medium discount of the net office rent. These findings are a strong indication that tenants become aware of the cost significance of additional charges. Landlords, however, assess these attributes as having no influence at all.[579]

Finally, statistically significant differences in perception exist for the attribute 'lease contract with stepped rent.' For the tenants, this attribute should lead to a medium discount. Brokers, however, value this attribute as standard and therefore see it as having no influence at all.[580]

---

574 Cf. Kempf, S. (2006), p. 18
575 See Appendix A.2.4.3.3
576 Cf. Kempf, S. (2006), p. 18-19
577 See Section 4.1.4.5
578 Cf. Lindner-Figura, J., et al. (2005), p. 409-410
579 Cf. Kempf, S. (2006), p. 19
580 Cf. Ibid., p.

4.4 Implications for the Development of Hedonic Office Rent Indices

The survey is only explorative in its nature. However, when its findings are combined with the findings of the literature review and the analysis of the German office market, some important implications for the development of hedonic office rent indices for German metropolitan areas are derived.

4.4.1 Selection of Variables

The location variables play an important role in location decisions and therefore in the determination of the level of office rents. The survey of German real estate professionals is in line with the literature review and suggests that hard factors, such as the accessibility to public transportation and parking space, as well as soft factors measuring the quality and the representativeness of the surroundings should be included in the hedonic model. Whereas some hard factors might be operationalized with dummy variables or through Euclidean distance measures, soft factors are hard to delineate and to quantify. Furthermore, it is difficult to account for all relevant location characteristics. Research for housing markets and residential prices has encountered the same problem and put forward spatial autoregression as a solution.[581] Spatial autoregression is a statistical technique, and it assumes that any information not captured by the normal regression model can be found in the residual of the regression equation. Spatial autoregression "[...] uses this information contained in the spatial residual and improves the accuracy of predictions made from multiple regression models."[582] For office rent indices to be developed using spatial autoregression analysis, it is essential that the sample data be stored within a geographic information system (GIS) with precise coordinates. In addition, one has to be aware of the fact that GIS-coded office lease contracts are confidential and are probably unavailable due to data security reasons.

Although location factors are considered important, the survey reveals that the majority of building factors and equipment and layout factors are negligible. In particular, the finding that the features of climate control, security systems, IT-infrastructure, environmental aspects, and office layouts have only a small impact on the level of office rents makes a lower demand on data availability. However, the international literature

[581] Cf. Des Rosiers, F., et al. (2000), p. 291-294, Pavlov, A. D. (2000), p. 249-283, Clapp, J. M. (2004), p. 127-160, Brasington, D. M. /Hite, D. (2005), p. 57-82

[582] Dubin, R., et al. (1999), p. 80

review partly challenges this perception.[583] The survey also points out that tenants appreciate soft factors, such as prestige and the quality of the architecture. However, some proxies suggested by the international literature review have been included in the survey and have not been considered as important. Therefore, the quantification of soft factors remains a challenge, and other proxies have to be found.

Not surprisingly, the survey results, in line with the literature review, demonstrate that lease factors become increasingly important for office occupiers. Lease lengths and the size of the rental area are important variables that have to be included in the hedonic model. Attributes measuring options and the quality of the tenant are not seen as influential; therefore, this finding makes lower demands on lease contract data. Moreover, according to the survey and the literature review, incentives have a high impact on the level of office rents, especially in recessionary rental markets. However, from the perspective of data availability, it will be difficult to deal with incentives.

4.4.2 Location Delimitation of German Office Markets

Most research studies on office rent determinants have been undertaken on a regional or city-specific level. A descriptive analysis of the German office markets indicates that the pattern of demands is different across the major office cities. This indication provides evidence that each office market has to be analyzed separately. However, some counterevidence is provided by the survey of German real estate professionals. The empirical analysis did not detect any major, statistically significant differences in the valuation of influencing factors between the regional office markets.[584] Hence, it can be concluded that it is not essential to model each regional office property market separately.

The issue of developing hedonic office rent indices is heavily dependent on the data availability in terms of sample size (e.g., number of leases) and number of independent variables. As already stated, the issue of data availability is, for the most part, not in the hands of the researcher. In addition, the question of whether all independent variables are valued differently across office markets and affected by the different regional demand patterns needs to be addressed. For instance, it could be argued that some building factors as well as equipment and layout factors have to meet the specific needs of the

[583] See Section 4.1.2.4
[584] See Section 4.3.2.2

tenant's business activities, whereas other factors are valued with the same importance no matter what the tenant's business area.

4.5 Chapter Summary

In this chapter the goal has been to examine which influencing factors might determine the level of office rent (Objective I).[585] The key findings are summarized as follows:

- The international literature review covered research studies that employ a quantitative, qualitative, and econometric approach. These studies have been undertaken for various office markets during different time periods. The literature review reveals that many different influencing factors have an impact on office rents. These factors are broadly categorized as location, building, equipment and layout, and lease factors.
- The international literature review further reveals that the operationalization of these factors has been undertaken differently. In other words, different studies attempt to quantify the same factor by different measures. Some empirical findings are counterintuitive and sometimes even contradictory to the theoretical expectations.
- The use of different measurements for the investigation of the same factor is not solely responsible for these counterintuitive findings. Rather, it is argued that the impact of the influencing factors varies between stages of the real estate cycle and between office markets because of their individual economic structures and legal environments. Therefore, a descriptive analysis of the office property markets of the major German metropolitan areas has been suggested.
- The description and analysis of Germany's office property markets demonstrate that the German office market is dispersed and that different regional office markets exist. Because each regional office market has different economic forces and is perceived by market participants to be in different stages of the real estate cycle, each office property market should be analyzed separately.
- The descriptive analysis also reveals that the research on office property markets in Germany is still underdeveloped in comparison with more mature markets,

[585] See Section 1.2

such as the UK and the US. In addition, the legal and economic foundation of German leases differs significantly from that of the UK and the US, where most hedonic office rent studies have been undertaken. These observations serve as an impetus for researchers to conduct additional surveys.

- Based on the findings of the literature review and the description of the German office property market, a survey of German real estate professionals was conducted to get an idea of what the influencing factors determining the level of office rents in Germany are.
- The survey's findings highlighted the importance of location and lease factors. Moreover, the contention that market participants place different values on office rent determinants for each regional market as a result of different demand patterns and economic forces could not be reinforced.
- Finally, based on the findings of the international literature review, the descriptive analysis of the German office market, and the survey of German real estate professionals, implications for the development of hedonic office rent indices are derived. On the one hand, variables having to do with location and lease characteristics should be selected. On the other hand, the possibility of modeling individual submarkets depends on data availability.

5 Hedonic Analysis of German Office Rents

This chapter presents the main empirical analysis and the nucleus of this thesis. Following a brief description of the data provider and database structure, an univariate analysis is presented, shedding light on the characteristics and problems of the employed variables. Thereafter, the most important steps undertaken in the data-mining process are explained. In particular, the problems of missing values and the strategies for solving this issue are explained in detail. Because the choice of the hedonic function is an empirical rather than a theoretical question, the second part of this chapter involves the analysis and interpretation of different hedonic functions.

5.1 Data Source

5.1.1 Data Provider and Representativeness of Lease Contract Data

The dataset used in this study is based on information stored in the Rental Database[586] of IPD Germany, formerly named the Deutsche Immobilien Datenbank GmbH (DID).[587] In 2003 the DID introduced the Rental Database, a database that stores the lease contracts of different property types and companies.

The lease contract data are supplied by the companies' databases, and, after plausibility and accuracy checks by the IPD, the data are stored in the database. It must be pointed out that the majority of lease data are transferred from Entreprise Resource Planning (ERP) systems such as Oracle or SAP, which provide the basis for all companies' financial statements. Therefore, the high quality of the data can be assumed. The companies delivering the lease contract data are mainly institutional investors, real estate brokerage firms, non-property companies, asset management and real estate research companies. The following table displays the companies:

---

586 In German: Vermietungdatenbank (VMDB)

587 IPD is an independent research company and publishes Germany's performance index based upon appraisals of commercial real estate held in portfolios of professional investors.

AENGEVELT Immobilien GmbH & Co. KG	HANSAINVEST Hanseatische Investment GmbH
Allianz Immobilien GmbH	HIH Hamburgische Immobilien Handlung GmbH
AMB Generali Immobilien GmbH	iii Investments
ampegaGerling Investment GmbH	IVG Immobilien AG
apollo real estate AG Co. & KG	Kapitalanlagegesellschaft mbH
AXA Real Estate Managers Deutschland GmbH	MEAG Munich ERGO AssetManagement GmbH
BASF Pensionskasse	R + V Allgemeine Versicherung AG
Bayerische Versorgungskasse	REDEVCO Services Deutschland GmbH
Commerz Grundbesitz Investmentgesellschaft mbH	Rodamco Europe
Credit Suisse Asset Management Immobilien	SEB Immobilien-Investment GmbH
RREEF Investment GmbH	CORPUS SIREO Asset Management GmbH
DEFO Deutsche Fonds für Immobilienvermögen GmbH	Union Investment Real Estate AG
DEGI Deutsche Fonds für Immobilienfonds mbH	Vivico Real Estate GmbH
Deka Immobilien Investment GmbH	WestInvest Gesellschaft für Immobilienfonds mbH
DG Anlage Gesellschaft mbH	Zurich Group Invest Europe GmbH
HALVERTON REAL ESTATE INVESTMENT MANAGEMENT Ltd.	

Table 17: Customer/Data Provider of IPD Rental Database

An important issue that directly affects the quality of any index construction is the quality and representativeness of the data. For instance, *Gatzlaff /Geltner (1998)* argue that the NCREIF Property Index is biased because the properties held by the NCREIF members "[...] tend to be confined to the largest and highest quality commercial buildings in prime locations."[588] They further argue that commercial properties that cannot be categorized as being of "institutional quality" perform differently throughout the real estate cycles.[589] In the case of the IPD Rental Database, one has to admit that many of the companies providing lease contract data have backgrounds in institutional investing. However, the quality and representativeness should be evaluated in comparison with other hedonic office rent studies from the perspective of what is actually possible.[590] A major advantage of the IPD Rental Database is that the lease contract data is retrieved from ERP systems which ensures a high quality and objectiveness of the data. While many hedonic studies use data solely from a real estate brokerage firm, real estate brokerages firms as well as institutional investors provide data directly to the IPD Rental Database. Moreover, Germany, unlike other countries, does not have a government agency to collect all the lease contracts of commercial properties.[591]

[588] Gatzlaff, D. /Geltner, D. (1998), p. 3
[589] Cf. Ibid.p. 2-3
[590] Cf. Hulten, C. R. (2003), p. 10
[591] See Section 4.2.2

5.1.2 Representativeness of Lease Contract Data (Initial Dataset)

In Table 18, a comparison of the rental space transaction volume published by the German Society of Property Researchers (gif) and the IPD Rental Database is made. Unfortunately, the gif's office market report does not present figures from before 2000. For 2006, only a restricted comparison is possible because, at the time of the data collection, the IPD Rental Database contained leases only up to June 2006. The comparison reveals that, although the IPD Rental Database exceeds significantly the total rental space published by the gif for some cities (Frankfurt and Berlin) and years, it is understated for other cities (Hamburg, Stuttgart, and Munich). The differences result from the fact that the IPD Rental Database also records leases that have been renegotiated, leases that have been negotiated without the support of real estate lease agents and leases where the lettable office space is less than 500 sqm.[592] Although some differences exist, one can assume that the IPD Rental Database covers the office rental market well.

Total Rental Space in m²		2000	2001	2002	2003	2004	2005	2006*	Total
Berlin	*gif*	*515,000*	*430,000*	*430,000*	*370,000*	*395,000*	*485,000*	*620,000*	***3,245,000***
	Rental Database	98,747	132,051	96,648	350,430	670,117	504,954	123,090	**2,176,538**
	Market Coverage	*19.17%*	*30.71%*	*22.48%*	*94.71%*	*169.65%*	*104.11%*	*19.85%*	*67.07%*
Düsseldorf	*gif*	*335,000*	*401,000*	*336,500*	*253,000*	*258,000*	*267,142*	*322,400*	***2,173,042***
	Rental Database	117,264	124,854	244,038	178,030	244,701	224,427	65,820	**1,470,363**
	Market Coverage	*35.00%*	*31.14%*	*72.52%*	*70.37%*	*94.85%*	*84.01%*	*20.42%*	*67.66%*
Frankfurt am Main	*gif*	*800,000*	*610,000*	*460,000*	*510,000*	*344,000*	*485,000*	*515,000*	***3,724,000***
	Rental Database	248,634	505,755	363,770	736,625	713,993	663,343	116,645	**4,013,622**
	Market Coverage	*31.08%*	*82.91%*	*79.08%*	*144.44%*	*207.56%*	*136.77%*	*22.65%*	*107.78%*
Hamburg	*gif*	*52,000*	*410,000*	*320,000*	*300,000*	*449,000*	*428,000*	*480,000*	***2,439,000***
	Rental Database	118,290	217,798	128,643	187,158	285,541	122,291	58,982	**1,475,202**
	Market Coverage	*227.48%*	*53.12%*	*40.20%*	*62.39%*	*63.59%*	*28.57%*	*12.29%*	*60.48%*
Köln	*gif*					*190,000*	*235,000*	*300,000*	***725,000***
	Rental Database	31,562	53,375	49,947	38,678	193,711	41,202	15,362	**575,066**
	Market Coverage					*101.95%*	*17.53%*	*5.12%*	
Munich	*gif*	*1,045,000*	*883,000*	*506,000*	*500,000*	*505,000*	*581,000*	*654,000*	***4,674,000***
	Rental Database	77,496	154,768	129.611	254.285	215.885	173.389	71.885	**1.233.721**
	Market Coverage	*7.42%*	*17.53%*	*25.61%*	*50.86%*	*42.75%*	*29.84%*	*10.99%*	*26.40%*
Stuttgart	*gif*	*240,000*	*179,500*	*127,000*	*149,000*	*152,000*	*145,000*	*141,700*	***1,134,200***
	Rental Database	29,629	15,000	54,217	86,989	72,432	59,518	3,106	**449,283**
	Market Coverage	*12.35%*	*8.36%*	*42.69%*	*58.38%*	*47.65%*	*41.05%*	*2.19%*	*39.61%*
Total	*gif*	*2,987,000*	*2,913,500*	*2,179,500*	*2,082,000*	*2,293,000*	*2,626,142*	*3,033,100*	***18,114,242***
	Rental Database	**1,335,612**	**1,600,865**	**1,599,760**	**2,668,582**	**5,670,710**	**2,572,077**	**766,809**	**19,267,507**
	Market Coverage	*44.71%*	*54.95%*	*73.40%*	*128.17%*	*247.31%*	*97.94%*	*25.28%*	*106.37%*

*Includes only leases till June 2006

Table 18: Comparison of Transaction Volume[593]

The data covers a time span from 1997 to 2006, and the working data set contains 22,005 office lease contracts from throughout Germany. As mentioned earlier, only leases up to June 2006 have been collected. These leases are based on 4,718 different buildings.[594] For the period 1997 to 2000, the leases for fewer than 200 office buildings

[592] See Section 6.1.3 for a description how the German Society of Property Researchers derives its yearly office figures.

[593] Cf. Gesellschaft für Immobilienwirtschaftliche Forschung (2007), p. 2

[594] See Table 19

have been collected. Starting from the year 2001, the leases are based on more than 200 office buildings, with the peak in the year 2004, with 1614 office buildings.

	No. of Buildings
1997	36
1998	49
1999	101
2000	145
2001	236
2002	324
2003	645
2004	1614
2005	1111
2006*	457
Total	**4718**

*Includes only leases till June 2006

Table 19: Number of Buildings

Table 20 reports the distribution of the 22,005 leases across cities and years. Although for the period 1997 to 1999 the working datasets contain fewer than 2,000 leases per year, all subsequent periods have more than 2,000. Moreover, the percentage of leases in the major office markets increases steadily.

	Cities									
	Berlin	Düsseldorf	Frankfurt am Main	Hamburg	Köln	Leipzig	Munich	Stuttgart	Others	Total
	Count	Count	Count	Count	Count	Count	Count	Count	Count	Count
1997	85	78	174	127	36	4	62	19	430	**1,015**
1998	113	96	231	172	61	12	77	42	462	**1,266**
1999	135	198	267	213	93	26	140	54	650	**1,776**
2000	176	174	257	230	109	49	150	57	871	**2,073**
2001	187	278	366	314	79	18	216	29	951	**2,438**
2002	165	205	404	230	63	9	181	50	776	**2,083**
2003	340	158	442	256	67	29	267	67	1,002	**2,628**
2004	611	225	536	449	174	72	271	61	2,382	**4,781**
2005	479	279	469	202	122	128	246	45	980	**2,950**
2006*	155	116	148	104	40	38	75	4	315	**995**
Total	**2,446**	**1,807**	**3,294**	**2,297**	**844**	**385**	**1,685**	**428**	**8,819**	**22,005**

*Includes only leases till June 2006

Table 20: Distribution of Number of Leases across Cities and Years

5.1.3 Database Structure

The IPD Rental Database is structured in four clusters. The first cluster holds information about the companies providing the data (e.g., owner or brokerage firm). The second cluster stores detailed information about the properties themselves. The third cluster displays information about the lease contract, and the fourth cluster provides information about the latest valuation.

General Information	**Unit**
Customer Type	Unit Floor Area
Effective Date	Number of Parking Units
	Unit Use Type
	Owner Occupied
Property	Indexed Rents
Street & House Number	Indexed Rents Frequency of Change
City	Storey
ZIP Code	Area Definition
Predominant Use	Parking Area
Property Type	Office Design
Economic Date of Construction	Emergency Power Supply
Historical Date of Construction	Network Infrastructure
Building Area	Network Infrastructure Upgrade Option
Building Area Defintion	Air Conditioning
Number of Storeys	Vacant from
Remaining Useful Life	Vacant until
Total Useful Life	Vacancy Reason
Ownership Share	Agency
Project Development	Legal Person
Projected Date of Completion	Industry
Office Design	Role
Emergency Power Supply	Collective Contract
Network Infrastructure	Subletting Allowed
Network Infrastructure Uprade Option	Contract Start Date
Air Conditioning	Contract End Date
Office Services	Extension Option
	Extension Option Period
	Contractual Extension
Valuation	Contractual Extension Period
Valuation	Tenant Option to Break
Total Floor Area	Landlord Option to Break
	Contract Type
	VAT
	Rental Income Type and Amount
	Letting Marketing Cost Type
	Letting Marketing Cost Value Type
	Letting Marketing Cost Payment due

Table 21: IPD Rental Database Structure

From Table 21 it can be seen that the database structure is quite extensive and provides opportunities for more in-depth analysis. For some data arrays only a predefined set of values can be chosen, which significantly reduces the possibility for errors. An important issue is that the database differentiates obligatory and optional data arrays. As a consequence, the lease contract data details are seldom entered in full. Another notable issue is that the number 0 is a valid data; in other databases, it is interpreted as a missing value. Nevertheless, in terms of the number of lease contracts and the number of variables for the empirical analysis, it still outperforms many hedonic office rent studies published to date.[595]

[595] See Appendix A.1

5.2 Step 1A: Data Mining

The IPD Rental Database conducts some plausibility checks before the data are accepted and finally stored. Nevertheless, before a hedonic analysis is conducted, the dataset's variables have to be selected, checked, and eventually transformed. It is important to note that transformations have been undertaken only if they are considered necessary from a statistical point of view or if the variable has some unrealistic values that could be attributed to typing errors. That excludes any procedures such as case deletion due to statistical outliers. Thereafter, the descriptive statistics of the variables on a city level are presented. An overview of the complete data-mining proceedings is presented in the following graph.[596]

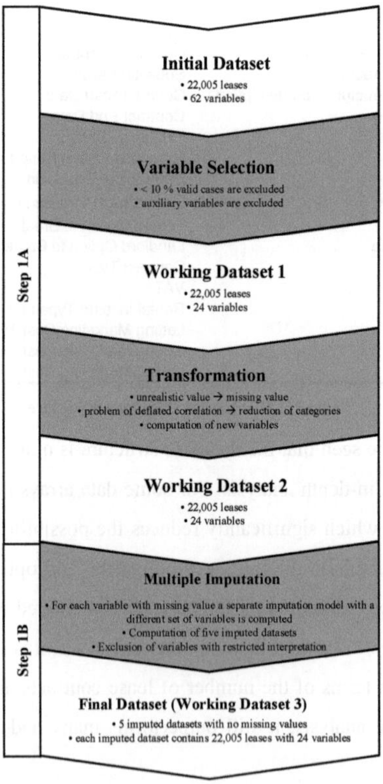

Figure 31: Overview of Data Mining Proceedings

---

[596] See Figure 31

5.2.1 Variable Selection (Initial Dataset to Working Dataset 1)

The variables entered into the empirical analysis are presented in the following table.[597] In comparison with the variables offered by the IPD Rental Database's structure,[598] many variables could not be used because the number of valid cases was below 10 percent. In addition, some variables could not be entered into the analysis because of data security reasons. These confidentiality agreements with the IPD Rental Database's clients also explain why all lease data have been made anonymous at the city level. Consequently, spatial statistic analysis could not be undertaken.[599] In addition, all tenant characteristics, namely, legal person and industry, have been made anonymous.

Location Variables	**Lease Factors**
City	Rental Income Type and Amount
	Rental Area
Building Variables	Rental Area Definition
Economic Date of Construction	Rent-free Months
Building Area	Indexed Rents
Building Area Definition	Indexed Rents Frequency of Change
Number of Stories	Collective Contract
	Subletting Allowed
Tenant Variables	Owner Occupied
Value-Added Tax (VAT)	Contract Start Date
	Contract End Date
	Extension Option
	Extension Option Period
	Contractual Extension
	Contractual Extension Period
	Tenant Option to Break
	Landlord Option to Break
	Contract Type

Table 22: Working Dataset 1

5.2.2 Plausibility Checks and Data Transformation (Working Dataset 1 to Working Dataset 2)

After the variables have been selected, it is important to check them for any unrealistic values. Furthermore, where it is necessary and useful, new variables are computed.

The measurement unit for the variable *'contract rent'* is EUR per square meter per month (EUR/sqm/month) and is computed by dividing the rental amount by the rental

---

[597] See Table 22
[598] See Table 21
[599] See Section 4.4

area. Although the variable spread is extremely wide, ranging from 1.00 to 56.00 EUR/sqm/month, it is still realistic. Therefore, no further transformations are undertaken.[600] Unfortunately, most leases do not specify which rental area definition is used. The missing definition of the rental area is a major drawback because it renders the dependent variable inaccurate. However, even if all office leases specify a rental area definition, most contract parties reach individual agreements.[601] As a consequence, this imprecision is beyond the reach of the researcher, and any transformation would do more harm than good.

The importance of the year of construction as a measurement of building quality has been explained earlier.[602] The difference between the year of construction and the contract date permits one to calculate the age of the building, which is a proxy for the quality of the building. The IPD Rental Database has two arrays: *'historic date of construction'* and *'adjusted year of construction.'* Whereas the historic date of construction is entered directly, the adjusted year of construction is computed by the two auxiliary variables *'remaining useful life'* and *'total useful life'* with the following formula:

$$\textit{adjusted year of construction} = \textit{data entry date} + \textit{remaining useful life} - \textit{total useful life}$$

Equation 5-1

The auxiliary variable 'remaining useful life' would serve perfectly as proxy for building quality, as it accounts for any modernisation or refurbishment of the office building. Unfortunately, this variable cannot be extracted directly from the IPD Rental Database. Therefore, an alternative methodology to derive the building age has been adopted. More valid cases were available for the variable 'adjusted year of construction.' The variable 'historic date of construction' has been dropped from the analysis. Besides, both variables are highly correlated and would probably cause multicollinearity problems.[603] A closer inspection of the variable 'adjusted year of construction' revealed that some cases took unrealistic values. Therefore, only cases in which the adjusted year of

---

[600] The variable *'contract rent'* does not undergo any adjustment for inflation which would require making an assumption about the appropriate measure of inflation as well as the inflation rate itself. In addition, the aim of the hedonic office rent indices is to represent an market as well as economic indicator (See Section 1.4)

[601] Cf. Heyser, H. (2006), p. 76-77

[602] See Section 4.1.2.1

[603] In Section 5.3.4.2, however, the variable is used for the computation of the imputation model.

construction is in the range of 1950 to 2006 entered the analysis.[604] In total, 906 cases have been set as missing.

However, the variable 'adjusted year of construction' is, as a measurement of building quality, not as useful as the variable age because the adjusted year of construction does not take any dimension of time when the contract started. Therefore, the variable *'age1'* has been computed by taking the difference between the contract start date and the adjusted year of construction. Some cases take negative values, which is unlikely. Therefore, these cases (=326) are set as missing.

Another important variable is *'building area,'* which is a measurement for the representativeness of an office building. As a building of 0 sqm does not make any sense, all cases with a zero are set as missing values. In total, 5,573 cases are affected. Although there are still some extremely low values for building area (less than 1 percent of all cases have a building area smaller than 485 sqm), no further transformations are undertaken, as no cutoff point is suggested in real estate literature.

Similar to building area, the variable *'number of storeys'* is a measurement for the representativeness of an office building. An inspection of the values' range showed that a few cases had extremely high and unrealistic values. Hence, all cases (=52) that took numbers higher than 56 are set as missing values.[605]

To what percentage a change[606] in the relative index[607] is passed through to the tenant is measured by the variable *'rent index pass through.'* A closer inspection of this variable, however, revealed that, in the majority of cases, a change in the relative index is passing through at a 100 percent.[608] Therefore, it seemed advisable to reduce the variable's scale to a binary dummy variable. Further discussion with the IPD Rental Database managers

[604] The year 1950 was chosen as cut-off data as this year is often associated with the start of the post-war period and is used as cut-off date in other studies. Cf. Dunse, N. /Jones, C. (1998), p. 305, Dunse, N. /Jones, C. (2002), p. 166, Rohmert, W. (2007), p. 24-25

[605] The cut-off point was chosen due to the fact that in 2006, the highest German office building in Germany was the Commerzbank Tower in Frankfurt. This skyscraper has 56 floors. www.emporis.com (2008), w/o pages [Online Database]

[606] See Section 4.2.3.2. The lease contract must allow that the rent is adapted if the relative index increases or decreases. An upwards-only clause in a lease contract is prohibited in German law. Cf. Lindner-Figura, J., et al. (2005), p. 303-308.

[607] Mostly the consumer price index (CPI) is used. Cf. Ibid., p. 303-307.

[608] Cf. Deutscher Immobiliendatenbank (2006), w/o pages.

and plausibility checks revealed that cases that did not contain any value should be interpreted not as missing but as 0.

The variable *'rent index adaptation frequency'* shows at what interval (measured in months) the rent is adapted. An inspection of this variable showed that a majority of cases either take the value of 1, 2, or 12. In other words, the range of responses is restricted. Therefore, to avoid the problem of deflated correlation,[609] the variable has been transformed from a metric variable to a variable with the following categories: category 0, in which no such clause has been explicitly specified; category 1, in which the rent is adapted every month; category 2, in which the rent is adapted every 2 months; category 3, in which the rent is adapted every 3 to 12 months; and category 4, in which the rent is adapted after 12 months. Further discussion with the IPD Rental Database managers and plausibility checks revealed that cases that did not contain any value should be interpreted not as missing but as 0.

The literature review and the survey revealed that the variable *'lease length'* is of utmost importance and has a significant influence on the rent level. The variable is computed by taking the difference of the contract end date and the contract start date. A closer look identified some cases with a lease length of over 30 years. As leases after 30 years are due notice,[610] these cases (=13) are set as missing. Closely related to the variable 'lease length' is the variable '*indefinite lease length,*' which covers all leases for which no contract end had been agreed upon. So that as many complete cases as possible could be obtained, both variables were combined and a new variable with the following categories was computed: category 1 for a lease length of up to 12 months, category 2 for leases between 13 and 36 months, category 3 for leases between 37 and 60 months, category 4 for leases between 61 and 120 months, category 5 for leases longer than 120 months, and category 6 for leases with indefinite lease end. The categories' limits have been chosen in accordance with the survey's question.[611] This undertaking allows a new variable to be obtained, with 22,005 observations.

The variable *'extension option period'* defines how long the lease can be extended for. It is closely linked to the variable '*extension option,*' which defines whether the lease can be extended once, several times, or not at all. Both variables have to be interpreted

[609] Cf. Tabachnick, B. G. /Fidell, L. S. (2006), p. 61-62

[610] See Section 4.2.3.1

[611] See Appendix A.2

as a right for the tenant and a risk for the landlord. If the variable 'extension option' has the value of 0, then the value of the variable 'extension option period' is, logically, also 0.[612] Neither variable contains missing values.

The variable *'contract extension period'* defines how long the lease is automatically extended for if the tenant does not give notice. It is closely linked to the variable '*contract extension*,' which defines whether the lease extends itself once, several times, or not at all. The interpretation of these variables is more difficult and probably depends on which stage of the real estate cycle it is exercised in. If the variable 'contract extension' has a value of 0, then the value of the variable 'contract extension period' is, logically, also 0.[613] Neither variable contains missing values.

Because the survey indicated that the level of rent diminishes with the size of the rental area, the variable *'rental area'* is of great importance. The inspection of the variable showed extremely low and unrealistic values. In fact, less than 4.0 percent of all cases have a rental area smaller than 35.00 sqm. An explanation is that in addition to a lease agreement for the office areas the contract parties conclude a separate lease agreement for storage areas (e.g. archives). However, no cutoff point is suggested in real estate literature and no transformation has taken place. In addition, the underlying rental area definition is not specified.

The significance of lease incentives (e.g., rent-free months) has been highlighted throughout the thesis. Although the IPD Rental Database's structure has different arrays to include lease incentives, only the variable *'rent free months'* is obligatory and therefore has no missing values. A closer inspection of the variable revealed that, in the majority of cases, no rent-free months have been granted to the tenant. Hence, to avoid the possibility of deflated correlation, the scale of this variable is reduced to a binary dummy variable with the value of 0 if no rent-free months have been granted and the value of 1 if rent-free months have been granted.

The variables *'collective contract' (in German: Generalmietvertrag), 'subletting allowed,' 'tenant break option,'* and *'landlord break option'* have not undergone any transformations. The variables 'tenant break option' and 'landlord break option' are computed as binary dummy variables. The IPD Rental Database allows entering only a

---

612 Cf. Vermietungsdatenbank (2003), p. 26-27

613 Cf. Ibid., p. 27-28

precise date when these options can be exercised. Further discussion with the IPD Rental Database managers and plausibility checks confirmed that, in cases where no tenant or landlord break option date has been entered, break options were not agreed upon. Therefore, to increase the number of valid observations, these binary dummy variables have been introduced with the value of 0 if no break option date has been specified and the value of 1 if a break option date has been entered.

The variables *'value added tax'* and *'owner occupied'* have not undergone any transformations.

The variable *'cities'* has been reduced. Instead of 156 categories (one category for each city), a new variable has been computed with eight categories: category 1 stands for all lease contracts in Berlin, category 2 for Düsseldorf, category 3 for Frankfurt, category 4 for Hamburg, category 5 for Cologne, category 6 for Munich, category 7 for others, and category 8 for Stuttgart. These cities represent the major office centers in Germany.[614] Moreover, the city boundaries are defined according to the political limits.

Two categorical variables, namely, *'building area definition'* and *'rental area definition,'* have no missing values and remain untransformed.

The variable *'contract type'* has been reduced from seven categories to six categories because one category contained only four observations. The categories are as follows: category 0 for all leases with no specifications, category 1 for contracts that have an indexation clause to the CPI or turnover of the company, category 2 for step-up leases, category 3 for step-up leases indexed to the CPI, category 4 for leases indexed to the CPI and turnover of the company, category 5 for leases with free adaptation, and category 6 for leases with no adaptation.

Table 23 gives an overview of the variables, their transformations, and the number of valid cases before and after the transformations.

---

[614] See Table 20

Description	Measurement	Scale	Transformation / Restrictions	New Variable Name	Scale	Number of Valid Cases before transformation	Number of Valid Cases after transformation
Contract Rent	in €/m²/month		only positive values	-	-	21,853	21,853
age of the buidling	years	metric	only positive values	age1	metric	17,999	17,673
Economic Year of Construction	year	metric	between 1950 and 2006	X04A	metric	18,905	17,999
Building Area	m²	metric	greater 0 m²	X06A	metric	22,005	16,432
Number of Storeys	storey	metric	between 0 and 80	X08B	metric	7,078	7,026
Rent Index Pass Through	percentage	metric	**1.**transformation to dummy variable, as majority of observations is close to 1 **2.**After discussion with Rental Dabase responsibles and plausibility checks all missing values defined as 0	D_X12	metric / dummy variable	9,507	22,005
Rent Index Adaptation Frequency	months	metric	**1.**transformation to categorical variable, as majority of cases take either the value of 1,2 or 12 **2.**After discussion with Rental Database responsibles and plausibility checks all missing values defined as 0	C_X14	categorical	9,516	22,005
Lease Length	months	metric	**1.**greater than 360 months (30 years) are defined as missing **2.**transformed to categorical variable in combination with d_x20	C_X19	categorical	15,741	22,001
Extension Option Period	months	metric	all cases with missing are set to 0 (see c_x21)	X22A	metric	4,272	22,005
Contractual Extension Option Period	months	metric	all cases with missing are set to 0 (see c_x21)	X24A	metric	3,212	22,005
Rental Area	m²	metric	---	---	metric	---	22,005
Rentfree monts	months	metric	transformed to dummy variable, as majority of observations take the value of 0	D_X35	metric / dummy variable	22,005	22,005
Collective Contract	0;1	metric / dummy variable	---	---	---	---	8,084
Subletting Allowed	0;1	metric / dummy variable	---	---	---	---	5,483
Undefinite Lease Length	0;1	metric / dummy variable	---	see C_X19	---	---	6,264
Tenant Break Option	0;1	metric / dummy variable	---	---	---	---	22,005
Landlord Break Option	0;1	metric / dummy variable	---	---	---	---	22,005
Value Added Tax	0;1	metric / dummy variable	---	---	---	---	9,570
Owner Occupied	0;1	metric / dummy variable	---	---	---	---	22,005
Cities	156 factors	categorical	Reduction to 8 cities (categories) according to observation frequency	C_X07	categorical	22,005	22,005
Building Area Definition	6 categories	categorical				22,005	22,005
Rental Area Definition	6 categories	categorical				22,005	22,005
Extension Option	3 categories	categorical	---	---	---	22,005	22,005
Contract Extension Option	3 categories	categorical	---	---	---	22,005	22,005
Contract Type	7 categories	categorical	Reduction to 6 categories	C_X29A	categorical	22,005	22,005
Contract Begin Year		string	---	---	---	---	---

Table 23: Transformation 2 (Working Dataset 1 to Working Dataset 2)

A more in-depth analysis of the working data revealed that two categorical variables, namely, 'building area definition' and 'rental area definition,' as well as the dummy variable 'rent index pass through,' had to be dropped out of the hedonic analysis, although their effects on the level of office rents are of scientific and practical interest.

The two categorical variables could not be interpreted because of the ambiguity of their categories; therefore, they are excluded from the analysis. Both variables have the same categories, namely, category 0 for all leases in which the area definition is unknown or inconsistent, category 1 for all leases with the area definition of the German Society of Property Researchers (gif), category 2 for all leases with the gross external area, category 3 for all leases with net external area, category 4 for all leases with an area definition DIN 283, and category 5 for all leases with any other area definition. Category 0 is problematic because the majority of cases within the datasets take the value of category 0.[615] As mentioned earlier, the majority of German leases use the area definition of category 1, 2, or 3.[616] Therefore, it can be assumed that most of the leases that take the value of category 0 should actually take the value of category 1, 2, or 3. Because a later interpretation of these regression coefficients will be very restricted, these variables are left out of the hedonic model.

The rationale to leave out the variable 'rent index pass through' is that, when this variable takes the value of 0, the categorical variable 'rent index adaptation frequency' logically takes the value of 0 as well. Therefore, if both variables are included in the regression equation, the problem of multicollinearity will arise.[617]

Although these variables are not interpreted, they are used at a later stage for the computation of multiple imputed datasets.[618] The following table depicts the working dataset used for interpretations.

---

[615] See Appendix A.3.1

[616] See Section 4.2.3.5

[617] See Section 5.4.1.4.4

[618] See Section 5.2.2.

Variables*	Description	Measure-ment	Scale	N	Missing Values
RENT	Contract Rent	in €/m²/month		21,853	0.69%
age1	Building age	years	metric	17,673	19.69%
X06A	Building Area	m²	metric	16,432	25.33%
X08B	Number of Storeys	storey	metric	7,026	68.07%
X22A	Extension Option Period	months	metric	22,005	0.00%
X24A	Contractual Extension Option Period	months	metric	22,005	0.00%
X31	Rental Area	m²	metric	22,005	0.00%
D_X17	Collective Contract	0;1	metric / dummy variable	8,084	63.26%
D_X18	Subletting Allowed	0;1	metric / dummy variable	5,483	75.08%
D_X25	Tenant Break Option	0;1	metric / dummy variable	22,005	0.00%
D_X27	Landlord Break Option	0;1	metric / dummy variable	22,005	0.00%
D_X30	Value Added Tax	0;1	metric / dummy variable	9,570	56.51%
D_X32	Owner Occupied	0;1	metric / dummy variable	22,005	0.00%
D_X05	Rentfree Months	0;1	metric / dummy variable	22,005	0.00%
C_X01	Cities	8 categories	categorical	22,005	0.00%
C_X14	Rent Index Adaption Frequency	5 categories	categorical	22,005	0.00%
C_X19	Lease Length	6 categories	categorical	22,005	0.00%
C_X21	Extension Option	3 categories	categorical	22,005	0.00%
C_X23	Contract Extension Option	3 categories	categorical	22,005	0.00%
C_X29A	Contract Type	6 categores	categorical	22,005	0.00%
B_YEAR	Contract Begin Year		string		

*Variables after Checking for Outliers

Table 24: Working Dataset 2

5.2.3 Descriptive Statistics of Working Dataset 2

In this section, the distribution of the lease characteristics across German cities is detailed and summarized in the following tables.[619] The distribution of the rent index adaptation frequency shows that, for the majority of leases across all cities, no specific adaptation frequency has been specified. In particular, no specification applies in over 65 percent of the leases in Frankfurt, Berlin, and Leipzig. Moreover, if a rent index adaptation has been specified, it occurs mostly within 12 months.

The distribution of lease length is relatively homogenous across the cities, with the exception of Leipzig. Otherwise, most leases run between 37 and 60 months or 61 and 120 months, or the duration has not been specified. No significant differences exist between the cities regarding the extension option and contract extension option. In the majority of leases, no such options have been agreed upon.

In the majority of leases, landlord and tenant have the possibility of terminating the lease prematurely (break option). The highest percentage is recorded in Berlin, Leipzig,

[619] See Table 25 and Table 26

and Frankfurt. In addition, the number of leases with a tenant-only break option is small.

Further regional differences exist in terms of the contract type. Whereas a free adaptation to rent adjustments (rent indexation) is negotiated for over 50 percent of the leases in Berlin and Leipzig, this contract type can be found in less than 25 percent of all leases in all other cities, with the exception of Frankfurt.

For the lease characteristics 'collective contract,' 'subletting allowed,' and 'value added tax,' a high percentage of missing data is observed, which will be discussed in the following sections.[620] The lease characteristics *'owner occupied'* and *'rent free months'* present a relatively homogeneous picture across the office markets of the data sample at hand.

The descriptive statistics of *building age* across German cities show some regional differences, specifically between cities in East Germany and West Germany. After the reunification, many new office buildings in Berlin and Leipzig were constructed and old offices completely refurbished, which explains why offices in these cities are, on average, newer than in other cities.[621]

Frankfurt has the highest average in terms of building area, followed by Berlin and Munich. Frankfurt also has the highest average in building height (measured in number of storeys). The highest office building is located in Frankfurt and has 25 storeys.

Some interesting observations are made regarding the variables *'extension option periods'* and *'contractual extension periods.'* The lowest average of extension option periods, with a value of 42 months, is found in Cologne, and the highest average, with a value of 54 months, is found in Frankfurt. In contrast, the average of contractual extension periods is lower. While the lowest average, with a value of 11 months, is in Leipzig, the highest average, with a value of 29 months, is located in one of the "other" cities.

Finally, the distribution of rental area shows that Frankfurt has the highest average, with a value of 1,218 sqm; the lowest average, with a value of 681 sqm, is in Cologne. The absolute highest rental area is found in Frankfurt, which is understandable and expected.

---

620 See Section 5.3

621 Cf. Desyllas, J. (2000), p. 198-199

		Berlin	Düsseldorf	Frankfurt	Hambur	Cologne	Leipzig	Munich	Others	Stuttgart	
Rent Index Adaption Frequency (C_X14)	no adaptation specified	1,925	792	2,198	1,075	460	322	929	4,658	200	12,559
	every month	24	226	154	151	64	14	136	510	42	1,321
	every two month	44	13	34	44	4	14	45	922	27	1,147
	between 3 and 12 months	406	674	804	792	236	30	484	2,347	132	5,905
	after 12 months	47	102	104	235	80	5	91	382	27	1,073
	Total	2,446	1,807	3,294	2,297	844	385	1,685	8,819	428	22,005
Lease Length (C_X19)	up to 12 months	55	50	69	103	43	33	59	335	9	756
	between 13 and 36 months	234	224	266	291	98	130	149	1,217	46	2,655
	between 37 and 60 months	566	468	779	776	245	101	501	2,229	123	5,788
	between 61 and 120 months	311	501	925	620	153	27	481	2,229	127	5,374
	longer than 120 months	71	82	297	103	33	5	110	441	13	1,155
	indefinite lease length	1,209	482	958	404	272	89	385	2,368	110	6,277
	Total	2,446	1,807	3,294	2,297	844	385	1,685	8,819	428	22,005
Extension Option (C_X21)	no extension	2,123	1,409	2,728	1,783	700	362	1,331	6,972	351	17,759
	extended once	208	255	349	307	97	12	246	765	26	2,265
	extended several times	115	143	217	207	47	11	108	1,082	51	1,981
	Total	2,446	1,807	3,294	2,297	844	385	1,685	8,819	428	22,005
Contract Extension Option (C_X23)	no contract extension	2,250	1,530	2,961	1,919	674	338	1,493	7,149	336	18,650
	once	18	12	50	27	5	1	25	87	0	225
	automatically several times	178	265	283	351	165	46	167	1,583	92	3,130
	Total	2,446	1,807	3,294	2,297	844	385	1,685	8,819	428	22,005
Break Options (C_X2527)*	None	587	575	991	1,013	364	106	661	2,558	208	7,062
	Tenant only	4	23	10	11	1	0	8	26	0	84
	Landlord only	162	399	329	308	64	35	177	1,049	55	2,579
	Both	1,693	810	1,963	967	415	244	839	5,194	165	12,290
	Total	2,446	1,807	3,294	2,297	844	385	1,685	8,819	428	22,005
Contract Type (C_X29A)	no specifications	7	4	13	21	5	0	3	77	3	133
	indexation clause to the CPI or turnover	581	1,005	1,112	1,207	398	75	808	4,306	231	9,723
	step-up leases	252	100	171	135	98	7	80	578	11	1,432
	indexed to the CPI	40	58	94	166	19	0	82	249	3	711
	free adaptation	1,227	364	1,427	265	183	233	332	2,251	67	6,349
	leases with no adaptation	339	276	477	503	141	70	380	1,358	113	3,657
	Total	2,446	1,807	3,294	2,297	844	385	1,685	8,819	428	22,005
Collective Contract (D_X17)	Missing Values	1,994	1,172	2,723	1,480	471	283	1,014	4,528	256	13,921
	0	265	290	175	297	189	46	256	3,015	95	4,628
	1	187	345	396	520	184	56	415	1,276	77	3,456
	Total	2,446	1,807	3,294	2,297	844	385	1,685	8,819	428	22,005
Subletting Allowed (D_X18)	Missing Values	2,145	1,434	2,911	1,878	669	303	1,416	5,456	310	16,522
	0	221	166	168	221	140	49	160	2,762	81	3,968
	1	80	207	215	198	35	33	109	601	37	1,515
	Total	2,446	1,807	3,294	2,297	844	385	1,685	8,819	428	22,005
Value Added Tax (D_x30)	Missing Values	958	1,124	2,160	1,577	495	108	1,127	4,616	270	12,435
	0	474	170	698	135	80	171	159	818	47	2,752
	1	1,014	513	436	585	269	106	399	3,385	111	6,818
	Total	2,446	1,807	3,294	2,297	844	385	1,685	8,819	428	22,005
Owner Occupied (D_X32)	0	2,086	1,692	3,255	2,244	776	375	1,546	8,602	394	20,970
	1	360	115	39	53	68	10	139	217	34	1,035
	Total	2,446	1,807	3,294	2,297	844	385	1,685	8,819	428	22,005
Rentfree Months (D_X35)	0	2,221	1,501	2,933	1,992	723	353	1,421	7,775	354	19,273
	1	225	306	361	305	121	32	264	1,044	74	2,732
	Total	2,446	1,807	3,294	2,297	844	385	1,685	8,819	428	22,005

*Based on D_X25 and D_X27

Table 25: Descriptive Statistics of Working Dataset 2 (Dummy and Categorical Variables)

		Building Age	Building Area	Building Height	Extension Option Period	Contractual Extension Period	Rental Area
Berlin	Minimum	0.00	116.00	0.00	0	0	6
	Mean	8.12	16,026.50	6.24	48	17	890
	Maximum	55.00	71,969.00	14.00	180	120	34,088
Düsseldorf	Minimum	0.00	200.00	0.00	0	0	2
	Mean	16.17	14,547.72	6.73	59	12	814
	Maximum	55.00	89,760.00	11.00	180	60	28,995
Frankfurt am Main	Minimum	0.00	146.00	0.00	0	0	1
	Mean	12.77	18,399.36	8.47	54	28	1,218
	Maximum	53.00	87,719.00	25.00	120	120	88,167
Hamburg	Minimum	0.00	150.00	0.00	0	0	3
	Mean	14.97	12,663.80	6.62	48	17	642
	Maximum	56.00	49,150.00	17.00	120	60	57,604
Cologne	Minimum	0.00	194.00	0.00	0	0	7
	Mean	21.39	6,470.70	4.88	42	16	681
	Maximum	54.00	58,320.00	20.00	139	72	19,079
Leipzig	Minimum	0.00	865.00	0.00	0	0	7
	Mean	6.35	13,837.53	5.33	38	11	505
	Maximum	40.00	56,393.00	10.00	60	60	12,276
Munich	Minimum	0.00	126.00	0.00	0	0	3
	Mean	13.90	15,774.33	6.27	47	23	732
	Maximum	56.00	54,399.00	17.00	120	60	40,017
Stuttgart	Minimum	0.00	105.00	0.00	0	0	5
	Mean	13.31	9,095.47	4.70	47	26	1,050
	Maximum	52.00	54,945.00	7.00	60	60	20,920
Others	Minimum	0.00	100.00	0.00	0	0	1
	Mean	15.46	9,083.30	4.10	49	29	871
	Maximum	56.00	292,266.00	18.00	173	146	80,989
Total	*Minimum*	*0.00*	*100.00*	*0.00*	*0*	*0*	*1*
	Mean	*14.62*	*11,886.20*	*5.18*	*50*	*24*	*876*
	Maximum	*56.00*	*292,266.00*	*25.00*	*180*	*146*	*88,167*

Table 26: Descriptive Statistics of Working Dataset 2 (Continuous Variables)

5.3 Step 1B: Data Mining - Missing Value Analysis

In data analysis, missing values is one of the most pervasive and difficult problems to handle.[622] As one can see from Table 24, the problem of missing values also occurs in the working dataset. Although the problem of missing values has been acknowledged in many research fields, it is rarely mentioned in economics, finance, and real estate research. For instance, in a literature research of five major journals of banking and finance, *Kofman /Sharpe (2003)* identify only 27% of empirical studies (257 articles) in which the problem of missing values has been recognized explicitly.[623] As real estate research is known for data scarcity, it can be assumed that the problem of missing val-

622 Cf. Tabachnick, B. G. /Fidell, L. S. (2006), p. 62

623 Cf. Kofman, P. /Sharpe, I. G. (2003), p. 220

ues is present but ignored. However, in the following sections, the type of missingness, the problem, and the strategies of handling incomplete datasets are discussed in detail. Thereafter, different strategies are adopted and compared to obtain a complete dataset, which will enter the regressions analysis.

5.3.1 Types of Missingness

To get an insight into the consequences of missing values and their potential solutions for statistical analysis, one must understand the pattern of missing data or, more precisely, "[...] the pattern of missing data is more important than the amount missing."[624] Three types of missingness are characterized and distinguished by whether the occurrence of missing data is completely independent from the dataset or any other source, internal or external to the dataset. In more technical terms, these types of missingness are as follows: missing completely at random (MCAR), missing at random (MAR), and missing not at random (MNAR).[625]

5.3.1.1 Missing Completely at Random (MCAR)

The first type of missingness is referred to as missing completely at random (MCAR) and relates to the missing values that occur purely by chance. In more technical terms, missing values are MCAR if the probability of a missing value is independent of all the measured and unmeasured characteristics. In a generic notation, Y_{com} stands for the complete dataset, Y_{obs} for the observed part, and Y_{mis} for the missing part of the complete dataset. In other terms, $Y_{com} = (Y_{obs}, Y_{mis})$. R is referred to as the missingness and P as the probability. Therefore, the MCAR is denoted as

$$P(R/ Y_{com}) = P(R).$$ [626]

Equation 5-2

However, as *Davey, et al. (2000)* point out, the assumption that data are MCAR is typically unrealistic.[627]

---

[624] Tabachnick, B. G. /Fidell, L. S. (2006), p. 62

[625] Cf. Donders, R., et al. (2006), p. 1087-1088, Sinharay, S., et al. (2001), p. 318, Tabachnick, B. G. /Fidell, L. S. (2006), p. 62-63, Kofman, P. /Sharpe, I. G. (2003), p. 223-225, Demirtas, H. /Schafer, J. L. (2003), p. 2554

[626] Cf. Schafer, J. L. /Graham, J. M. (2002), p. 151, Sinharay, S., et al. (2001), p. 318, Davey, A., et al. (2000), p. 501-502

[627] Cf. Ibrahim, J., et al. (2005), p. 333, Davey, A., et al. (2000), p. 502

5.3.1.2 Missing at Random (MAR)

The second type of missingness is referred to as missing at random (MAR) if the missingness does not depend on the missing values. However, missingness can depend on the other observed characteristics. The assumption of MAR is valid if

$$P(R/ Y_{com}) = P(R/ Y_{obs}).$$

Equation 5-3

Again, in more technical terms, MAR allows the probability of missingness to depend on observed data but not on missing data.[628]

5.3.1.3 Missing not at Random (MNAR)

If the assumption of MAR is violated, then the incomplete dataset is said to be missing not at random (MNAR), meaning there is no ignorable missing data. In other words, the missingness is related to the value that would have been observed.[629]

It is important to recognize that the relationships between the data and the missingness are statistical and causal. Following the explanations of *Schafer /Graham (2002)*, it is assumed that all reasons why data are missing can be combined into a set of variables, denoted as *Z*. Of course, it is unrealistic to assume that these causes of missingness are present, but some of them by omission induce relationships between *X*, *Y* or *R*, where X represents the variables that are known for all cases, Y represents a variable that is missing for some cases, and R represents the missingness. As can be seen in Figure 32, the assumption of MCAR is then fulfilled if the causes of missingness are completely contained within the unrelated part Z, while MAR allows some causes to be related to X, and MNAR is present if some cases are residually related to Y after relationships between X and R are taken into account.[630]

[628] Cf. Ibrahim, J., et al. (2005), p. 333, Tabachnick, B. G. /Fidell, L. S. (2006), p. 62-63, Sinharay, S., et al. (2001), p. 318, Schafer, J. L. /Graham, J. M. (2002), p. 151, Kofman, P. /Sharpe, I. G. (2003), p. 223-225

[629] Cf. Tabachnick, B. G. /Fidell, L. S. (2006), p. 62-63, Sinharay, S., et al. (2001), p. 318, Schafer, J. L. /Graham, J. M. (2002), p. 151, Kofman, P. /Sharpe, I. G. (2003), p. 223-225

[630] Cf. Schafer, J. L. /Graham, J. M. (2002), p. 152

Figure 32: Graphical Presentation of MCAR, MAR and MNAR[631]

5.3.1.4 Plausibility of MAR

Many strategies for handling missing data require that the incomplete dataset be MAR. Therefore, it seems advisable to test whether the working dataset of this thesis is MAR. Unfortunately, "[…] when missingness is beyond the researcher's control there is no way to test whether MAR holds in the data set."[632] Therefore, MAR remains an assumption, except in certain settings where the missingness is planned. Recent research, however, shows that, even if the dataset does not hold the assumption of MAR, the standard errors and estimates are only slightly biased.[633]

5.3.2 Strategies for Handling Missing Data

In literature, different strategies for handling missing data are discussed. While some strategies are popular due to their simplicity, other strategies involve considerable preparatory work but are considered more accurate. In the following section, only the main strategies and their disadvantages are briefly presented.

5.3.2.1 Case Deletion

One classical procedure for handling missing data is to discard units whose information is incomplete. Case deletion summarizes methods known as listwise deletion (LD) or complete case analysis (CCA) and available case analysis (AC). Case deletion is often set as a default by many statistical software programmes. Whereas LD and CCA focus attention on units that have observed values for all variables under consideration, AC uses different sets of sample units for different parameters.[634]

---

631 Ibid.p.

632 Ibid.p.

633 Cf. Schafer, J. L. /Olsen, M. K. (1998), p. 552-553, Schafer, J. L. /Graham, J. M. (2002), p. 152

634 Cf. Tabachnick, B. G. /Fidell, L. S. (2006), p. 63-66, Schafer, J. L. /Graham, J. M. (2002), p. 155-156

Although case deletion seems appropriate for handling missing data, it has several theoretical and practical limitations. From a theoretical point of view, the dataset must hold the MCAR assumption for case deletion to be conducted. If this is not the case, then the results probably will be biased, as the reduced (but now complete) sample is unrepresentative of the full sample. In addition, if the AC method is chosen, it is difficult to compute standard errors or other measures of uncertainty, as the parameters are computed from different sets of units. From a practical point of view, case deletion is unfavourable for multivariate regression analysis because the size of the dataset (number of observations) is artificially reduced. As a consequence, the researcher must decide between two options. The first option is to perform a regression analysis with few variables. The second option for many cases is to perform a regression analysis with many variables but few observations. Both options are unsatisfactory.[635]

5.3.2.2 Mean Substitution

Mean substitution is also a popular method. In this method, the missing values are replaced by the mean of the available data. One advantage of the mean substitution method is that the mean for the distribution remains unchanged; thus, the researcher does not have to guess. The main disadvantage of this method is that the variance of a variable is reduced artificially, as the "replaced value" is closer to the mean than to the missing value it replaces. Furthermore, other aspects, such as variance, quantiles, and confidence intervals, are altered as well.[636] As *Schafer /Graham (2002)* demonstrate, a large sample 95% confidence interval for the population mean

$$\bar{y} \pm 1.96\sqrt{\frac{S^2}{N}}$$

Equation 5-4

is narrowed by both the reduced variance S^2 and by the overstatement of N. In addition, as a consequence of the reduced variance, the correlation with other variables is reduced. The extent of loss in variance mainly depends on the amount of missing data.[637]

[635] Cf. Tabachnick, B. G. /Fidell, L. S. (2006), p. 63-66, Schafer, J. L. /Graham, J. M. (2002), p. 155-156
[636] Cf. Tabachnick, B. G. /Fidell, L. S. (2006), p. 67
[637] Cf. Schafer, J. L. /Graham, J. M. (2002), p. 158-159

5.3.2.3 Regression

The regression method is another method for estimating and replacing missing values. The variable with the missing value is used as a dependent variable, while the other variables are used as independent variables. Hence, a regression equation can be formulated based upon cases with complete data. Although the regression method is viewed as more objective than the mean substitution method, it has some important disadvantages. First, as a result of the regression, the replaced values fit together better than they should. Second, the variance is reduced, as the replaced values are too close to the mean. Third, the application of the regression method implies that the dataset contains good independent variables. Otherwise, the estimate of the regression is similar to inserting the mean.[638]

5.3.2.4 Expectation Maximization

An alternative is provided by the expectation maximization method (EM). The distribution of the incompletely observed data Y_{com} is split into an observed data distribution Y_{obs} and an incomplete data distribution Y_{mis},

$$f(Y|\theta) = f(Y_{obs}|\theta) f(Y_{mis}|Y_{obs},\theta)$$

Equation 5-5

The data likelihood for the parameters of interest can be expressed as

$$L(\theta|Y) = L(\theta|Y_{obs}) + \ln f(Y_{mis}|Y_{obs},\theta) + \varepsilon$$

Equation 5-6

where ε is a constant. The second term on the right-hand side of Equation 5-6 is a predictive distribution of the incomplete data, given the observed data and the parameters. Logically, as the missing values are not observed, this term cannot be computed. Therefore, θ is replaced with $\theta^{(i)}$, which for i=0 is an initial estimate of the unknown parameters. The first step (expectation) finds the conditional expectation of the missing data $Y^{(1)}_{mis}$, given the initial estimate of the parameters $\theta^{(0)}$ and the observed data Y_{obs}. The second step (maximization) performs maximum likelihood estimation as though the missing data had been filled in $Y^{(1)}$ to calculate the unknown parameters $\theta^{(1)}$. These

---

[638] Cf. Durrant, G. B. (2005), p. 6, Tabachnick, B. G. /Fidell, L. S. (2006), p. 68

steps are performed (where $\theta^{(1)}$ is the new parameter estimate to find updated expected values for the missing values $Y^{(2)}_{mis}$) until convergence is achieved ($\theta^{(i)} = \theta^{(i-1)}$).[639]

Beyond the fact that the EM method has proven to be very useful, it is associated with a "[…] fundamental shift in the way statisticians viewed missing data."[640] Instead of seeing missing data as a problem to solve, either by case deletion of imputation, statisticians interpret missing values as a "[…] source of variability to be averaged over".[641] Nevertheless, the EM method carries the main disadvantage that the EM-imputed dataset is biased because no error is added to the imputed dataset. Thus, the interpretation becomes difficult, as the dataset has inappropriate standard errors.[642]

5.3.2.5 *Multiple Imputation*

The multiple imputation (MI), first proposed by Rubin (1987), involves creating multiple "complete" datasets by filling in values for the missing data. Each imputed (or filled-in) dataset is analyzed as if it were a complete dataset. The inferences from the imputed datasets are then combined into one result by averaging over the imputed datasets.[643] In detail, three steps are involved: imputation step, "complete data" analysis step, and combination step.

Imputation step: In MI, a dataset is composed of the observed values and multiple imputed values for the missing values generated using a special procedure (algorithm). This procedure is undertaken *m* times, with each dataset having the observed values and different imputations for the missing values, yielding *m* complete datasets. The variation among the *m* imputations reflects the uncertainty with which the missing values can be predicted from the observed values.[644]

---

[639] Cf. Zhang, P. (2001), p. 21-25, Tabachnick, B. G. /Fidell, L. S. (2006), p. 68, Kofman, P. /Sharpe, I. G. (2003), p. 226-227, Schafer, J. L. /Graham, J. M. (2002), p. 162-163

[640] Schafer, J. L. /Olsen, M. K. (1998), p. 546-547

[641] Ibid.p. 546

[642] Cf. Tabachnick, B. G. /Fidell, L. S. (2006), p. 68

[643] Cf. Sartori, N., et al. (2005), p. 940-942, Ibrahim, J., et al. (2005), p. 333

[644] Cf. Sinharay, S., et al. (2001), p. 320, Schafer, J. L. /Olsen, M. K. (1998), p. 547, Schafer, J. L. /Graham, J. M. (2002), p. 165, Horton, N. J. /Lipsitz, S. R. (2001), p. 245-246

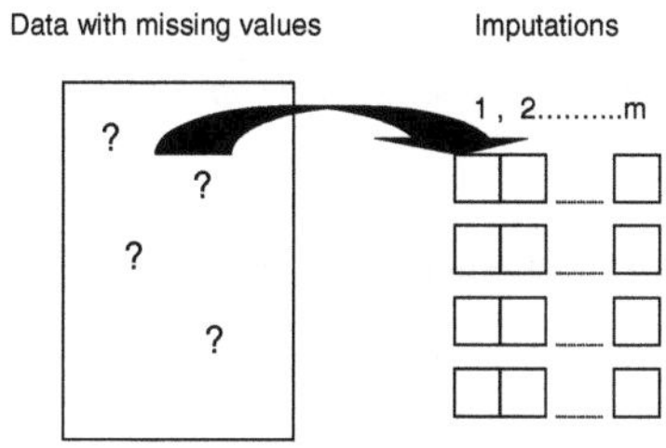

Figure 33: Schematic Representation of Multiple Imputations[645]

For the imputation step to be performed, assumptions about the missingness and decisions about the procedure for replacing the missing values have to be made. The assumptions and decisions have to be made with caution, as they determine the overall quality of the MI and, as a consequence, of the statistical analysis.[646]

MI, like many other strategies handling missing data, assumes that the data is MAR. This assumption permits the generation of imputations $(Y^{(1)}, Y^{(2)} \dots Y^{(m)})$ from the distribution $f(Y_{mis}|Y_{obs})$ because, after conditioning on Y_{obs}, missingness is assumed to be due to chance.[647] However, simulation analysis has demonstrated that "[...] in many realistic scenarios, multiple imputations may tend to be more robust to departures from the data model than parameter simulations."[648]

Furthermore, an imputation model has to be chosen. A number of different models have been developed (e.g., regression model, predictive mean matching, propensity score method, and Markov Chain Monte Carlo).

"Complete data" analysis step: After the imputation step *m*, apparently complete datasets exist. The analysis of interest is performed for each of the m datasets, storing the parameter estimates and standard errors.[649]

Combination step: The parameter estimates and the standard errors are combined using simple rules to produce overall estimates and standard errors that reflect the missing values uncertainty.[650]

The estimated quantities (regression coefficients, estimates, or means) from the *m* imputations are combined using the *Schafer /Graham (2002)* notation with the following formulas:[651]

Consider a quantity $\hat{Q}$ with an estimated variance U. After analysis of the m datasets, there are now m estimates of $\hat{Q}$ and U. A combined estimate is

$$\overline{Q} = \frac{1}{m}\sum_{i=1}^{m}\hat{Q}_i$$

Equation 5-7

There are two components to the variability of Q. The within-imputation variance,

$$\overline{U} = \frac{1}{m}\sum_{i=1}^{m}\hat{U}_i$$

Equation 5-8

And the between-imputation variance,

$$B = \frac{1}{m-1}\sum_{i=1}^{m}(\hat{Q}_i - \overline{Q})^2$$

Equation 5-9

T is the total variance, which is the sum of B and U corrected for m being finite by the term $\frac{m+1}{m}$.

$$T = \overline{U} + \frac{m+1}{m}B$$

Equation 5-10

645 Schafer, J. L. /Olsen, M. K. (1998), p. 547

646 Cf. Schafer, J. L. (1999), p. 3, Horton, N. J. /Lipsitz, S. R. (2001), p. 253

647 Cf. Sinharay, S., et al. (2001), p. 321, Horton, N. J. /Lipsitz, S. R. (2001), p. 245

648 Schafer, J. L. (1997), p. 136 quoted after Fichman, M. /Cummings, J. N. (2003), p. 289

649 Cf. Sinharay, S., et al. (2001), p. 320, Schafer, J. L. /Olsen, M. K. (1998), p. 547, Schafer, J. L. /Graham, J. M. (2002), p. 165, Horton, N. J. /Lipsitz, S. R. (2001), p. 245-246

650 Cf. Sinharay, S., et al. (2001), p. 320, Schafer, J. L. /Olsen, M. K. (1998), p. 547, Schafer, J. L. /Graham, J. M. (2002), p. 165, Horton, N. J. /Lipsitz, S. R. (2001), p. 245-246

651 Cf. Schafer, J. L. /Graham, J. M. (2002), p. p.165-166

Confidence intervals are calculated as

$$\overline{Q} \pm t_{df}\sqrt{T}$$

Equation 5-11

Where the *t* distribution degrees of freedom *df* are calculated as

$$df = (m-1)\left(1+\frac{1}{r^2}\right)$$

Equation 5-12

with

$$r = \left(1+\frac{1}{m}\right)\frac{B}{\overline{U}}$$

Equation 5-13

which indicates the relative increase in variance due to nonresponse.

The fraction of information about $\overline{Q}$ missing due to nonresponse is

$$\gamma = \frac{r+\frac{2}{df+3}}{r+1}$$

Equation 5-14

Moreover, r and γ can be used as diagnostic statistics to analyse the impact of missing data on estimates of $\overline{Q}$.

The previously discussed methods for handling missing data are seen as single imputation methods, and they carry one inherent flaw. In contrast with multiple imputation methods, single imputation methods tend to underestimate the standard errors; hence, they overestimate the level of precision. In other words, the Type I error rate[652] for any hypothesis test would be higher than the intended rate. As a consequence, single imputation methods give the researcher more apparent power than the data actually justify. Therefore, the main advantage of MI is that the combined results are accurately corrected for the uncertainty introduced through the imputation process because the total variability in parameter estimates is decomposed into within-imputation variability and

[652] Type I error occurs when the null hypothesis is rejected although the true value of the outcome variable confirms the null hypothesis. Kemp, S. M. /Kemp, S. (2004), p. 229

between-imputation variability. In addition, MI is considered particularly useful when a series of analyses and the data analysis plan are uncertain and open-ended.[653]

5.3.3 Missing Value Analysis

Before a decision as to which strategy to use to handle the missing value problem is made, it is important to investigate the pattern of missingness in the dataset.

Univariate Statistics

	N	Mean	Std. Deviation	Missing		No. of Extremes[a]	
				Count	Percent	Low	High
RENT	21853	12.0073	6.20553	152	.7	0	916
AGE1	17673	14.6228	13.41581	4332	19.7	0	1017
M_X04A	17999	1987.5068	13.37119	4006	18.2	1021	0
M_X06A	16432	11886.20	12804.86496	5573	25.3	0	726
M_X08B	7026	5.1773	3.51414	14979	68.1	0	244
M_X22A	22005	9.6622	22.40212	0	.0	0	2925
M_X24A	22005	3.5603	12.39098	0	.0	0	882
M_X31	22005	875.60	2487.119	0	.0	0	498
D_X12	22005	.4242	.49424	0	.0	0	0
D_X17	8084	.43	.495	13921	63.3	0	0
D_X18	5483	.28	.447	16522	75.1	0	0
D_X25	22005	.56	.496	0	.0	0	0
D_X27	22005	.68	.468	0	.0	0	0
D_X30	9570	.71	.453	12435	56.5	0	0
D_X32	22005	.05	.212	0	.0	0	1035
D_X35	22005	.1242	.32976	0	.0	0	2732
C_X07	22005			0	.0		
C_X14	22005			0	.0		
C_X15	22005			0	.0		
C_X19	22005			0	.0		
C_X21	22005			0	.0		
C_X23	22005			0	.0		
C_X29A	22005			0	.0		

a. Number of cases outside the range (Mean - 2*SD, Mean + 2*SD).

Table 27: Univariate Statistics

[653] Cf. Davey, A., et al. (2000), p. 503, Sinharay, S., et al. (2001), p. 320, Fichman, M. /Cummings, J. N. (2003), p. 289, Acock, A. C. (2005), p. 1019

In Table 27, it is depicted that the percentage of missingness is extremely high (> 50 percent) for some variables:

- Number of Storeys (m_x08b)
- Collective Contract (d_x17)
- Subletting Allowed (d_x18)
- Value Added Tax (d_x30)

Other variables have up to 25 percent of observations missing:

- Building Age (age1)
- Adjusted Year of Construction (m_x04a)
- Building Area (m_x06a)

The dependent variable rent has an insignificant percentage of missing observations (0.7 percent). Moreover, only metric variables (with dummy variables as a special case of metric variables) are affected by missingness.

In the previous section, it was pointed out that in most cases it is impossible to test whether the assumption of MAR holds true for a dataset.[654] *Tabachnick /Fidell (2006)* argue that the MCAR assumption can be inferred at least by Little's MCAR test. According to their procedure, the EM correlations with missing values filled in using the EM method are computed, and Little's MCAR test is reported.[655] From the significance test's result, it is inferred that the dataset diverges significantly from randomness.[656]

The Separate Variance t-Test offers further evidence that the MCAR assumption for the working dataset is invalid.[657] For the majority of variables, the Separate Variance t Test shows a systematic relationship between the missingness on a variable (with missing values) and any of the other variables.[658]

---

[654] One exception is if the missingness of a dataset is planned (Cf. Schafer, J. L. /Graham, J. M. (2002), p. 152)

[655] Cf. Tabachnick, B. G. /Fidell, L. S. (2006), p. 63

[656] See Appendix A.4.1

[657] Separate Variance t-Test indicates whether the missingness is predictable from variables (other than the dependent variable). Cf. Tabachnick, B. G. /Fidell, L. S. (2006), p. 63

[658] See Appendix A.4.2

The high percentage of missing observations and the fact that the dataset does not hold the MCAR assumption imply that the unique use of case deletion, mean substitution, EM method, or any other single imputation method is not recommended.

5.3.4 Adopted Strategies for Handling Missing Data

The missing value analysis has given strong indication that single imputations would lead to suboptimal results and complicate the results of the statistical analysis. However, for the scope of this research, the complete case analysis, the mean substitution, and the multiple imputation methods are adopted as strategies for handling the missingness. The focus, however, is on the multiple imputation method (MI). The main reasons for following several strategies is to demonstrate that MI is superior to other strategies and that simple imputations can lead to misleading results.

Most imputation models of MI advise that the data be multivariate normal. Therefore, in the first step, the distributions of the variables are inspected and transformed accordingly. Second, the descriptive statistics of the variables of the complete case analysis and mean substitution are presented. Then the MI is performed. Because further analyses are based upon the multiple imputed datasets, the chosen imputation model is discussed in detail. Finally, the different strategies are compared and evaluated by univariate and bivariate statistics.

5.3.4.1 Data Transformation

For the computation of multiple imputed datasets, it is recommended that the original dataset be multivariate normal.[659] The distribution of each metric variable is checked for normality using statistical and graphical methods. Dummy variables are not transformed. The principal components of normality are skewness and kurtosis. Skewness deals with the symmetry of the distribution, and kurtosis deals with the peakedness. When the distribution is normal, the values of skewness and kurtosis are 0.[660] The starting point of the transformations is the observed cases (complete case analysis).

---

[659] Cf. Schafer, J. L. (1999), p. 6, Sinharay, S., et al. (2001), p. 321, Fichman, M. /Cummings, J. N. (2003), p. 292

[660] Cf. Tabachnick, B. G. /Fidell, L. S. (2006), p. 79-83

	Contract Rent	AGE1	M_X04A	M_X05A	M_X06A	M_X08B	M_X22A	M_X24A	M_X31
N Valid	21,853	17,673	17,999	9,398	16,432	7,026	22,005	22,005	22,005
Missing	152	4,332	4,006	12,607	5,573	14,979	0	0	0
Mean	12.01	14.62	1,987.51	1,978.46	11,886.20	5.18	9.66	3.56	875.60
Std. Error of	0.04	0.10	0.10	0.27	99.89	0.04	0.15	0.08	16.77
Median	11.05	10.00	1,992.00	1,987.00	7,805.00	5.00	0.00	0.00	331.00
Mode	10.00	0.00	1,993.00	1,993.00	48,025.00	5.00	0.00	0.00	200.00
Std. Deviation	6.21	13.42	13.37	25.85	12,804.86	3.51	22.40	12.39	2,487.12
Variance	38.51	179.98	178.79	668.17	163,964,566.53	12.35	501.85	153.54	6,185,762.80
Skewness	2.18	0.99	-0.97	-2.03	3.81	1.45	2.30	4.44	13.19
Std. Error of	0.02	0.02	0.02	0.03	0.02	0.03	0.02	0.02	0.02
Kurtosis	8.30	0.10	0.11	6.51	46.91	5.16	4.90	21.62	285.56
Std. Error of	0.03	0.04	0.04	0.05	0.04	0.06	0.03	0.03	0.03
Range	59.29	56.00	56.00	356.00	292,166.00	27.00	180.00	146.00	88,166.00
Minimum	0.06	0.00	1,950.00	1,650.00	100.00	0.00	0.00	0.00	1.00
Maximum	59.35	56.00	2,006.00	2,006.00	292,266.00	27.00	180.00	146.00	88,167.00
Degree of Skewness	moderate	small	small	moderate	moderate	moderate	moderate	substantial	substantial

Table 28: Univariate Statistics - Checking for Normality (before Transformation)

In Table 28 the skewness and kurtosis for the metric variables are presented. Except for the variables 'building age / age1' and 'adjusted year of construction / M_X04A,' the skewness and kurtosis of all variables clearly deviate from 0. The individual frequency curves provide further evidence that the metric variables are not normally distributed.[661] As a consequence, all variables are transformed by their logarithm.[662] The choice of logarithm for all variables is justified because the influence of potential outliers is reduced and it is easier to interpret in comparison with other transformations.[663]

	RENT_LG	LG_AGE1	LG_X04A	LG_X05A	LG_X06A	LG_X08B	LG_X22A	LG_X24A	LG_X31
N Valid	21,853	17,673	17,999	9,398	16,432	7,026	22,005	22,005	22,005
Missing	152	4,332	4,006	12,607	5,573	14,979	0	0	0
Mean	1.029	0.981	1.181	1.299	3.857	0.707	0.312	0.172	2.531
Std. Error of Mean	0.001	0.004	0.002	0.004	0.004	0.004	0.004	0.003	0.004
Median	1.043	1.041	1.176	1.301	3.892	0.778	0.000	0.000	2.520
Mode	1.000	0.000	1.146	1.146	4.681	0.778	0.000	0.000	2.301
Std. Deviation	0.212	0.489	0.324	0.378	0.467	0.302	0.657	0.461	0.564
Variance	0.045	0.240	0.105	0.143	0.218	0.091	0.431	0.212	0.319
Skewness	-0.492	-0.585	-0.337	-0.048	-0.369	-1.061	1.701	2.500	0.045
Std. Error of	0.017	0.018	0.018	0.025	0.019	0.029	0.017	0.017	0.017
Kurtosis	3.096	-0.595	-0.377	-0.571	0.013	0.847	1.014	4.831	0.885
Std. Error of	0.033	0.037	0.037	0.051	0.038	0.058	0.033	0.033	0.033
Range	2.995	1.756	1.756	2.553	3.466	1.447	2.258	2.167	4.945
Minimum	-1.222	0.000	0.000	0.000	2.000	0.000	0.000	0.000	0.000
Maximum	1.773	1.756	1.756	2.553	5.466	1.447	2.258	2.167	4.945
Degree of Skewness	small	small	small	none	small	moderate	moderate	moderate	none
Transformation	LOG(X)	LOG(X+1)	LOG(1+MAX(X)-X)	LOG(1+MAX(X)-X)	LOG(X)	LOG(X+1)	LOG(X+1)	LOG(X+1)	LOG(X)

Table 29: Univariate Statistics –Checking for Normality (after Transformation)

After transformation, the univariate statistical analysis is run again.[664] It can be derived from the statistical figures and from the graphs that the transformations significantly

---

[661] See Appendix A.4.3

[662] Variables with negative skewness were reflected first and variables with 0 as minimum are added 1 in order to compute their logarithm.

[663] Cf. Tabachnick, B. G. /Fidell, L. S. (2006), p. 86-88

[664] See Table 29 and Appendix A.4.4

improved the distributions of the variables. However, the variables 'extension option period/LG_X22A' and 'contract extension/LG_X24A' are still skewed.

5.3.4.2 *Multiple Imputation (Working Dataset 2 to Final Working Dataset)*

5.3.4.2.1 *Choice of Statistical Package and Imputation Algorithm*

The quality of multiple imputed datasets depends to a great extent on the choice of the appropriate imputation algorithm. In this thesis, the imputation algorithm of the package MICE (Multiple Imputation with Chained Equations) implemented in the statistical programme R is used. MICE was chosen as the statistical package because it received favorable reviews.[665] Furthermore, it is a free and flexible programme. This flexibility is achieved by using an algorithm based on Gibbs sampling and has been validated by *Brand (1999)*.[666] This algorithm imputes each variable of the dataset in an iterative way, variable by variable. Therefore, it is possible to build a different imputation model with different assumptions for each variable and to impute variables with mixed measurement levels (metric or categorical). These features constitute an important advantage over other statistical programmes (e.g., SOLAS[667] and NORM[668]). Their algorithms always use the same set of variables (so-called predictor variables and donors) for each imputed variable, and, as a result, memory problems or ill-conditioning problems (e.g., multicollinearity) may occur.[669]

Gibbs sampling is a computational algorithm and belongs to the Markov Chain Monte Carlo (MCMC) techniques. This algorithm will not be explained through mathematical formulas. Instead, the basic explanation of *Schafer (2001)* is followed.[670] A more detailed and mathematical explanation is given by *Schafer /Yucel (2002)*.[671]

The following unknown components are assumed: the missing values in $y_1, y_2, \ldots y_N$, the random effects $b_1, b_2, \ldots b_N$, the fixed effects, and the covariances' matrices $\sum$ and Ψ. The principal aim is to impute the missing values $y_1, y_2, \ldots y_N$; all other unknown quantities

---

[665] Cf. Horton, N. J. /Lipsitz, S. R. (2001), p. 248-256

[666] Cf. Brand, J. (1999), p. cited in Oudshoorn, C. G. M., et al. (1999), p. 10

[667] SOLAS is a commercial software designed specifically for the analysis of datasets with missing observations (www.statsol.ie/solas/solas.htm).

[668] NORM is free standalone statistical software for handling missing observations programmed by Joseph. L. Schaefer (http://www.stat.psu.edu/~jls/misoftwa.html#top)

[669] Cf. Oudshoorn, C. G. M., et al. (1999), p. 7-8

[670] Cf. Schafer, J. L. (2001), p. 17-19

[671] Cf. Schafer, J. L. /Yucel, R. M. (2002), p. 426-427

are more of an annoyance. Nevertheless, the uncertainty in these other quantities and how it contributes to missing data uncertainty are important for imputing the missing values correctly. These unknown quantities are obtained through a 3-step cycle simulation. First, random values of $b_1, b_2, \dots b_N$ are drawn based upon plausible assumed values for the missing data and the parameters Ψ, $\sum$, and β (step1). In step 2, new random values of the unknown parameters Ψ, $\sum$, and β are drawn based on the assumed values for the missing data and the values of $b_1, b_2, \dots b_N$ obtained in step 1. In step 3, new random values for the missing data are drawn given the values of $b_1, b_2, \dots b_N$ obtained in step 1 and the parameters Ψ, $\sum$, and β obtained in step 2. Finally, the parameters and missing data from step 2 and 3 become the assumed values in step 1 at the start of the next cycle. When these steps are repeated, a Markov chain, which is defined as a sequence in which the distribution of the unknown quantities at any cycle depends on their simulated values in the previous cycle, is obtained. With each new cycle, the relationship to the state of cycle 1 (original state) weakens. After several cycles, the resulting state becomes independent from the original state, and so-called convergence is achieved. To get *m* complete datasets, the Gibbs sampling algorithm is run until the simulated values achieve convergence. These values are then used for the first imputed dataset. The second imputed dataset is obtained by returning to the original dataset and running the Gibbs sampling algorithm with a new random-number generator seed, and so forth.[672]

5.3.4.2.2 Choice of Predictors

In order to avoid memory and ill-conditioning problems, it is necessary to build a different imputation model for each variable. For each incomplete variable, a separate imputation with a set of predictor variables is used. The imputation model consists of a set of predictor variables, called donors, and a statistical model that characterizes the relationship between the imputed variable and its donors. However, special care has to be taken in the selection of predictors. In this thesis, the approach presented by *Oudshoorn, et al. (1999)* is followed.[673]

Oudshoorn, et al. (1999) recommend a 4-step strategy for the selection of the predictors. First, all variables that appear in the complete-data model have to be included so that the variables are not biased toward 0. Second, all variables that appear in the re-

---

[672] Cf. Schafer, J. L. (2001), p. 17-19
[673] Cf. Oudshoorn, C. G. M., et al. (1999), p. 7

sponse model have to be included. Third, all variables that explain a considerable amount of the variance of the target variable should be added. Fourth, all variables whose missingness within the subgroup of incomplete cases exceeds a certain level are dropped out. Indicators are the percentage of usable cases and the percentage of relevant cases. The percentage of usable cases stands for the percentage of cases in the data matrix that has missing values for the imputed, but not for the donor, variable. The percentage of relevant cases is the percentage of cases in which both the imputed variable and the donor variable are observed. In step 1, the choice of predictors is based on theory. For step 2 and step 3, the correlations have to be calculated.[674] For continuous or dummy variables, then, the Pearson correlation is computed, and for categorical variables, the analysis of variance (ANOVA) is used to analyze the dependency between the predictor and the imputed variable. If the donors have missing data themselves, these steps have to be repeated accordingly for the donors.[675] In addition, *Allison (2000)* states that it is important to use the dependent variable in the imputation models.[676]

After the predictors have been identified and the imputation model for each variable has been built,[677] five imputed datasets with 20 iterations each are generated. Twenty iterations are chosen to ensure the convergence of the imputed variables.[678]

5.3.4.3 Comparison and Evaluation of Adopted Strategies

For investigating the quality of the five imputed datasets, their univariate statistics are compared with the complete case analysis and mean substitutions. Furthermore, the correlations of the imputed variables (of each dataset) and the correlations of the complete case and mean substitution analysis are compared. However, these comparisons give only an idea of the quality. As *Oudshoorn, et al. (1999)* point out, "[...] only artificially made data with missing data where the real values are of missing entries are known, one can check by statistical methods whether the imputed values are [...] drawn from the correct posterior predictive distribution."[679]

---

[674] In order to increase the quality of the imputation model, all variables have been considered. That includes also variables (X04A, X05A, D_X12, C_X07, C_X15) which will not appear in the final models.

[675] Cf. Oudshoorn, C. G. M., et al. (1999), p. 10-11

[676] Cf. Allison, P. D. (2000), p. 301-309

[677] See Appendix A.5

[678] Cf. Oudshoorn, C. G. M., et al. (1999), p. 17

[679] Ibid.p. 19

5.3.4.3.1 Univariate Statistics: Complete Case Analysis; Mean Substitution and Multiple Imputation

In the following tables, the univariate statistics of the complete case analysis, mean substitution, and imputed data are presented.[680] In the majority of cases, the imputed datasets are closer in terms of descriptive statistics (standard deviations, skewness and kurtosis) to the complete case datasets. Specifically, the standard deviations from the imputed variables are not reduced, as with the mean substitution. Another observation is that the metric variables are better estimated (in terms of being closer to the complete case variables) than the dummy variables.

MI01			Skewness			Kurtosis			Standard Deviation		
Variables	N	Per-centage Missing	Complete Case Analysis	Mean Sub-stitution	Multiple Imputation	Complete Case Analysis	Mean Sub-stitution	Multiple Imputation	Complete Case Analysis	Mean Sub-stitution	Multiple Imputation
Rent_LG	21853	0.69%	-0.49190	-0.49361	-0.49109	3.09641	3.13881	3.09053	0.21228	0.21154	0.21224
LG_AGE1	17673	19.69%	-0.58485	-0.65270	-0.553053	-0.595078	-0.00497	-0.644477	0.48949	0.43867	0.491397
LG_X04A	17999	18.20%	-0.33655	-0.37212	-0.30909	-0.37693	0.20692	-0.41817	0.32413	0.29314	0.32938
LG_X05A	9398	57.29%	-0.04771	-0.07299	-0.05248	-0.57114	2.68717	-0.58128	0.37768	0.24681	0.37509
LG_X06A	16432	25.33%	-0.36886	-0.42684	-0.40718	0.01305	1.03496	0.06827	0.46657	0.40318	0.46071
LG_X08B	7026	68.07%	-1.06149	-1.87828	-1.41959	0.84740	9.04757	3.27050	0.30164	0.17043	0.25253
D_X17	8084	63.26%	0.29311	0.48353	0.10183	-1.91456	-0.04393	-1.98972	0.49475	0.29986	0.49936
D_X18	5483	75.08%	1.00075	2.00441	1.81690	-0.99887	5.03184	1.30118	0.44721	0.22322	0.37009
D_X30	9570	56.51%	-0.93882	-1.42347	-0.52035	-1.11885	1.32594	-1.72932	0.45265	0.29850	0.48390

Table 30: Univariate Statistic (Imputed Dataset 1)

MI02			Skewness			Kurtosis			Standard Deviation		
Variables	N	Per-centage Missing	Complete Case Analysis	Mean Sub-stitution	Multiple Imputation	Complete Case Analysis	Mean Sub stitution	Multiple Imputation	Complete Case Analysis	Mean Sub-stitution	Multiple Imputation
Rent_LG	21853	0.69%	-0.49190	-0.49361	-0.49066	3.09641	3.13881	3.08693	0.21228	0.21154	0.21217
LG_AGE1	17673	19.69%	-0.58485	-0.65270	-0.551314	-0.595078	-0.00497	-0.618066	0.48949	0.43867	0.492225
LG_X04A	17999	18.20%	-0.33655	-0.37212	-0.31615	-0.37693	0.20692	-0.40802	0.32413	0.29314	0.32843
LG_X05A	9398	57.29%	-0.04771	-0.07299	-0.06433	-0.57114	2.68717	-0.56660	0.37768	0.24681	0.37345
LG_X06A	16432	25.33%	-0.36886	-0.42684	-0.39757	0.01305	1.03496	0.03808	0.46657	0.40318	0.46031
LG_X08B	7026	68.07%	-1.06149	-1.87828	-1.417429	0.84740	9.04757	3.28822	0.30164	0.17043	0.25413
D_X17	8084	63.26%	0.29311	0.48353	0.07922	-1.91456	-0.04393	-1.99382	0.49475	0.29986	0.49962
D_X18	5483	75.08%	1.00075	2.00441	1.83950	-0.99887	5.03184	1.38384	0.44721	0.22322	0.36801
D_X30	9570	56.51%	-0.93882	-1.42347	-0.50315	-1.11885	1.32594	-1.74692	0.45265	0.29850	0.48490

Table 31: Univariate Statistic (Imputed Dataset 2)

[680] Cf. Table 30 to Table 34

MI03			Skewness			Kurtosis			Standard Deviation		
Variables	N	Per-centage Missing	Complete Case Analysis	Mean Sub-stitution	Multiple Imputation	Complete Case Analysis	Mean Sub-stitution	Multiple Imputation	Complete Case Analysis	Mean Sub-stitution	Multiple Imputation
Rent_LG	21853	0.69%	-0.49190	-0.49361	-0.48672	3.09641	3.13881	3.08798	0.21228	0.21154	0.21221
LG_AGE1	17673	19.69%	-0.58485	-0.65270	-0.561719	-0.595078	-0.00497	-0.633603	0.48949	0.43867	0.490813
LG_X04A	17999	18.20%	-0.33655	-0.37212	-0.31121	-0.37693	0.20692	-0.41749	0.32413	0.29314	0.32846
LG_X05A	9398	57.29%	-0.04771	-0.07299	-0.07285	-0.57114	2.68717	-0.55035	0.37768	0.24681	0.37525
LG_X06A	16432	25.33%	-0.36886	-0.42684	-0.41703	0.01305	1.03496	0.04055	0.46657	0.40318	0.46236
LG_X08B	7026	68.07%	-1.06149	-1.87828	-1.344549	0.84740	9.04757	2.99232	0.30164	0.17043	0.26001
D_X17	8084	63.26%	0.29311	0.48353	0.07867	-1.91456	-0.04393	-1.99390	0.49475	0.29986	0.49963
D_X18	5483	75.08%	1.00075	2.00441	1.91693	-0.99887	5.03184	1.67469	0.44721	0.22322	0.36097
D_X30	9570	56.51%	-0.93882	-1.42347	-0.54836	-1.11885	1.32594	-1.69937	0.45265	0.29850	0.48221

Table 32: Univariate Statistic (Imputed Dataset 3)

MI04			Skewness			Kurtosis			Standard Deviation		
Variables	N	Per-centage Missing	Complete Case Analysis	Mean Sub-stitution	Multiple Imputation	Complete Case Analysis	Mean Sub-stitution	Multiple Imputation	Complete Case Analysis	Mean Sub-stitution	Multiple Imputation
Rent_LG	21853	0.69%	-0.49190	-0.49361	-0.48605	3.09641	3.13881	3.07826	0.21228	0.21154	0.21238
LG_AGE1	17673	19.69%	-0.58485	-0.65270	-0.55565	-0.59508	-0.00497	-0.63415	0.48949	0.43867	0.49044
LG_X04A	17999	18.20%	-0.33655	-0.37212	-0.30810	-0.37693	0.20692	-0.41341	0.32413	0.29314	0.32774
LG_X05A	9398	57.29%	-0.04771	-0.07299	-0.10036	-0.57114	2.68717	-0.58819	0.37768	0.24681	0.37676
LG_X06A	16432	25.33%	-0.36886	-0.42684	-0.40513	0.01305	1.03496	0.05777	0.46657	0.40318	0.46157
LG_X08B	7026	68.07%	-1.06149	-1.87828	-1.32828	0.84740	9.04757	3.23401	0.30164	0.17043	0.25345
D_X17	8084	63.26%	0.29311	0.48353	0.08086	-1.91456	-0.04393	-1.99355	0.49475	0.29986	0.49960
D_X18	5483	75.08%	1.00075	2.00441	1.88825	-0.99887	5.03184	1.56557	0.44721	0.22322	0.36356
D_X30	9570	56.51%	-0.93882	-1.42347	-0.54452	-1.11885	1.32594	-1.70358	0.45265	0.29850	0.48245

Table 33: Univariate Statistic (Imputed Dataset 4)

MI05			Skewness			Kurtosis			Standard Deviation		
Variables	N	Per-centage Missing	Complete Case Analysis	Mean Sub-stitution	Multiple Imputation	Complete Case Analysis	Mean Sub-stitution	Multiple Imputation	Complete Case Analysis	Mean Sub-stitution	Multiple Imputation
Rent_LG	21853	0.69%	-0.49190	-0.49361	-0.48989	3.09641	3.13881	3.08627	0.21228	0.21154	0.21212
LG_AGE1	17673	19.69%	-0.58485	-0.65270	-0.57299	-0.59508	-0.00497	-0.61181	0.48949	0.43867	0.48994
LG_X04A	17999	18.20%	-0.33655	-0.37212	-0.31173	-0.37693	0.20692	-0.40821	0.32413	0.29314	0.32930
LG_X05A	9398	57.29%	-0.04771	-0.07299	-0.05649	-0.57114	2.68717	-0.52218	0.37768	0.24681	0.37197
LG_X06A	16432	25.33%	-0.36886	-0.42684	-0.42183	0.01305	1.03496	0.07727	0.46657	0.40318	0.45889
LG_X08B	7026	68.07%	-1.06149	-1.87828	-1.380507	0.84740	9.04757	3.39276	0.30164	0.17043	0.25269
D_X17	8084	63.26%	0.29311	0.48353	0.12228	-1.91456	-0.04393	-1.98514	0.49475	0.29986	0.49908
D_X18	5483	75.08%	1.00075	2.00441	1.84865	-0.99887	5.03184	1.41758	0.44721	0.22322	0.36717
D_X30	9570	56.51%	-0.93882	-1.42347	-0.57833	-1.11885	1.32594	-1.66561	0.45265	0.29850	0.48033

Table 34: Univariate Statistic (Imputed Dataset 5)

5.3.4.3.2 Bivariate Statistics: Complete Case Analysis, Mean Substitution and Multiple Imputation

In addition to the univariate statistics, the correlations with the dependent variable (RENT_LG) have been analysed and compared with the various imputed datasets. Again, in comparison with the mean substitution dataset, the metric variables of the imputed datasets are closer to the complete case dataset, in contrast to the dummy variables (D_X17 and D_X18). As a consequence, it has to be kept in mind that these dummy variables have to be interpreted carefully.

Correlation with RENT_LG

	CCA	Mean Substitution	MI01	MI02	MI03	MI04	MI05
RENT_LG	1	1	1	1	1	1	1
LG_AGE1	-0.28	-0.25	-0.26	-0.27	-0.27	-0.27	-0.27
LG_X04A	-0.26	-0.23	-0.24	-0.25	-0.24	-0.25	-0.24
LG_X05A	-0.23	-0.16	-0.17	-0.18	-0.16	-0.17	-0.18
LG_X06A	0.26	0.23	0.27	0.27	0.27	0.27	0.26
LG_X08B	0.18	0.10	0.15	0.17	0.15	0.16	0.15
LG_X22A	0.00	0.00	0.01	0.00	0.00	0.01	0.00
LG_X24A	-0.10	-0.10	-0.10	-0.10	-0.10	-0.10	-0.10
LG_X31	0.19	0.19	0.19	0.19	0.19	0.19	0.19
D_X12	0.04	0.04	0.04	0.04	0.04	0.04	0.04
D_X17	0.24	0.15	0.08	0.08	0.10	0.08	0.08
D_X18	0.35	0.19	0.07	0.08	0.09	0.08	0.08
D_X25	-0.05	-0.05	-0.05	-0.06	-0.06	-0.06	-0.06
D_X27	0.02	0.02	0.02	0.02	0.02	0.02	0.02
D_X30	-0.06	-0.04	-0.06	-0.04	-0.07	-0.05	-0.05
D_X32	0.01	0.01	0.01	0.01	0.01	0.01	0.01
D_X35	0.03	0.03	0.03	0.03	0.03	0.03	0.03

Table 35: Comparison of bivariate Correlations[681]

The comparison of the univariate and bivariate statistics clearly favours the multiple imputed datasets. Furthermore, they do not have the disadvantages of the single imputation methods. Therefore, the multiple imputed datasets will be employed for further statistical analysis.

---

681 The gray shaded cells indicate the variables which had missing values.

5.4 Step 2: Hedonic Function

This section presents the estimate stage of the hedonic analysis.[682] Based upon the international literature review and the survey of German real estate professionals, the hypotheses for the different variables are formulated, the econometric models defined, and the statistical tests explained. Thereafter, the best functional form is derived, and then the empirical findings and statistical results of the nationwide time dummy variable model, the nationwide characteristic price index model, and the city-specific time dummy variable models are presented. Finally, the lessons learned for the development of the office indices are derived.

5.4.1 Hypotheses, Econometric Models and Statistical Tests

5.4.1.1 Hypotheses

The dependent variable is contract rent (denoted as *RENT*). Contract rent has the advantage and has been chosen over other definitions of rent because the impact on office rents of all influencing factors can be monitored. As mentioned earlier, asking rent, consideration rent, and effective rent already, to some extent, control for some influencing factors.[683] The following table gives an overview of the hypotheses.[684]

---

[682] See Section 2.1

[683] See Sections 3.2.1 and 4.1

[684] See Table 36

	Correlation Complete Case Analysis (CCA)	Hypothesised Relationship	Strength of Relationship
Rent Index Adaption Frequency			
no adaptation (reference point)	0	0	0
every month	positive	negative	-----
every two month	negative	negative	---
within 12 months	positive	negative	--
after 12 months	negative	negative	-
Lease Length			
shorter than 13 months (reference point)	0	0	0
between 13 and 36 months	positive	negative	-
between 37 and 60 months	positive	positive	--
between 61 and 120 months	positive	neutral	---
longer than 120 months	positive	negative	----
indefinite lease length	positive	unknown	explorative
Extension Option			
no extension (reference point)	0	0	0
extended once	positive	positive	+
extended several times	negative	positive	++
Contract Extension Option			
no extension (reference point)	0	0	0
automatically once	positive	unknown	explorative
automatically several times	negative	unknown	explorative
Break Options			
no break option (reference point)	0	0	0
Tenant only	positive	positive	+
Landlord only	positive	negative	-
Both	negative	unknown	explorative
Contract Type			
no specification	0	0	0
indexation clause to the CPI or turnover	positive	unknown	explorative
step-up leases	positive	unknown	explorative
step-up leases indexed to the CPI	positive	unknown	explorative
free adaptation	positive	unknown	explorative
leases with no adaptation	positive	positive	+
Dummy Variables			
Collective Contract	positive	negative	-
Subletting Allowed	positive	positive	+
Value Added Tax	negative	negative	-
Owner Occupied	positive	positive	+
Rentfree Months	positive	positive	+
Continuous Variables			
Building Age	negative	negative	-
Building Area	positive	positive	+
Building Height	positive	positive	+
Extension Option Period	positive	positive	+
Contract Extension Option Period	negative	unknown	explorative
Rental Area	positive	negative	-

Table 36: Summary of Hypotheses

Moreover, the table presents the relationship between the dependent variable and the independent variables based on the observed dataset (respectively bivariate correlations).[685] The hypotheses are strictly derived from the international literature review and the survey. If the bi-variety correlation points to a different relationship, that is indicated, but the hypotheses do not change. It is important to note that the hypotheses are formulated as if each lease clause were negotiated separately. However, in practice, leases are negotiated as a package of terms.[686] As the dataset does not keep record of all lease clauses, it is possible that the effect of an unobserved variable coincides with the effect of an observed variable, leading to an unexpected result (effect) of the observed variable.[687]

The variable '*age1*' is supposed to capture the building quality. A negative relationship between *age1* and contract rent is assumed. In other words, the older the office building, the lower the rent. Moreover, because some researchers argue that old offices develop prestige and status,[688] the square of age1 (denoted as *age2*) is computed and included in the analysis in order to capture the effect of representativeness of the location.[689]

The building area (denoted as *X06A*) is assumed to capture the representativeness of an office building. Therefore, a positive relationship between building area and rent is expected.[690]

Similarly, the number of storeys (denoted as *X08B*) is positively correlated to the contract rent. This variable is included to capture the representativeness of the office building itself and of the office building location.[691]

Based upon the survey's finding,[692] it is assumed that the rental area (denoted as *X31*) has a negative relationship with rent. The larger the rented office unit, the lower the rent. The hypothesis is based on the observation that rent decreases as the size of the rental area increases because of economies-of-scales and bargaining power.[693]

---

[685] See Table 24

[686] Cf. Rowland, P. (2000), p. 183

[687] Cf. Hulten, C. R. (2003), p. 10

[688] See Section 4.1.2.1

[689] However, this variable age2 is only computed for the linear and semi-log model. In double-log model it causes the regression equation to produce a singular matrix.

[690] See Section 4.1.2.2

[691] See Section 4.1.2.2

[692] See Section 4.3.2.1.4

[693] See Section 4.1.4.2

The variable 'extension option period' (denoted as *X22A*) is expected to be positively correlated with rent. It represents the unilateral right of the tenant to extend the contract and therefore shifts the risk from the tenant to the landlord. However, because of the survey's finding that options do not have a large impact on office rent, only a weak relationship is expected.[694] In a similar manner, it is expected that the categorical variable 'extension option' (denoted as *C_X21*) will show a positive but probably negligible relationship with rent. The bivariate correlation, however, will show a negative relationship if the lease can be extended several times.

No specific hypothesis is expressed regarding the relationship between rent and the variables 'contract extension option period' (denoted as *X24A*) and 'contract extension option' (denoted as *C_X23*).

The categorical variable 'break options' (denoted as C_X2527)[695] represents the different break options of the lease contract. It is assumed that, if the tenant alone has the possibility to terminate the lease (category 1), a positive relationship is expected with rent as it shifts the risk toward the landlord. Logically, if only the landlord has the right to terminate prematurely the lease (category 2), a negative relationship with rent is expected. However, it must be remarked that the bivariate correlation indicates a positive relationship, which is surprising. No hypothesis is formulated in the event that tenant and landlord have a break option (category 3).

Although in theory rent escalation clauses in Germany are supposed to keep the equivalent ratio between landlord and tenant constant,[696] in practice, they shift the risk from the landlord to the tenant. In general, the rent index pass through is based upon a change in the CPI. In the recent past (1991 to 2008), however, the CPI always increased, indicating an inflation of prices.[697] Therefore, it is expected that the categorical variable 'rent index adaptation frequency' (denoted as *C_X14*) will be negatively related to the level of rent. This implies that the more frequently the rent is adapted, the lower the initial rent. The bivariate correlation, however, shows that the relationship is not as monotonous as expected.

---

[694] See Section 4.3.2.1.4

[695] The variable C_X2527 combines the variable D_X25 and D_X27.

[696] See Section 4.2.3.2

[697] Cf. Federal Statistical Bureau of Germany (2008), w/o pages [Online Database]

Closely linked to the variables 'rent index pass through' and 'rent index adaptation frequency' is the categorical variable 'contract type' (denoted as *C_X29A*). Here, only a hypothesis for one category is formulated. It is expected that leases with no adaptation clause (category 6) will be positively related to office rent, as the landlord bears the risk of price inflation. How the other categories with different rent review clauses are related to rent has to be answered empirically and is therefore of an explorative nature.

The dummy variable 'collective contract' (denoted as *D_X17*) is assumed to have a negative relationship with rent, although the bivariate correlation shows a positive relationship. A collective lease contract specifies that the complete office building be rented to a tenant who in turn sublets it to other tenants. The risk of subletting is therefore shifted to the tenants. Collective lease contracts are often signed before the development takes place and often play an important role in securing the project funding.[698]

The dummy variable 'subletting allowed' (denoted as *D_X18*) shifts the risk toward the landlord, as he has only limited control of the subtenants. Because this lease option clearly favours the tenant, it is expected to have a positive relationship with office rents. However, according to the findings from the survey of German real estate professionals, the impact of the subletting option is probably only marginal.[699]

The dataset also contains two measures for quality and type of the tenant. First, the dummy variable 'value added tax' (denoted as *D_X30*) shows whether the tenant carries on a business subject to VAT. If the tenant does so, then the office rents should be lower for office buildings which have been constructed or refurbished within a 10-year period.[700] In other words, a negative relationship with rent is expected. However, the impact on rent is probably only marginal in regard to the fact that the dataset contains many office building which are older than 10 years and,[701] to the finding from the survey of German real estate professionals.[702] Second, in line with the literature review, it is expected that the dummy variable 'owner occupied' (denoted as *D_X32*) will be positively correlated with rent.[703]

---

698 Cf. Brade, K., et al. (2005), p. 768
699 See Section 4.3.2.1.4
700 See Section 4.2.3.4
701 See Table 26
702 See Section 4.3.2.1.4
703 See Section 4.1.4.5

The international literature review and the survey reveal that the lease length is an important influencing factor on the level of office rent.[704] In this analysis, lease length is measured with a variable (denoted as *C_X19*) containing six different categories. It is assumed that leases between 61 and 120 months (category 4) are the current market standard and have no influence on the level of rent. Leases that are shorter (category 1 to category 3) will show a positive relationship, and leases that are longer will show a negative relationship with rent (categories 5 and 6).

In line with the literature review and the survey's findings, the dummy variable 'rent-free months' (denoted as *D_X35*) is expected to be positively correlated with rent.[705]

5.4.1.2 Econometric Models

For the development of hedonic models, three important decisions have to be made. The first decision concerns which functional form to choose; the second decision, how to model the different geographic regions; and the third decision, how to include the dimension of time in the hedonic model.[706]

Section 2.1.4 has provided some answers regarding the first decision. Because the choice of the functional form is an empirical question rather than a theoretical one, it would be preferable to test all different functional forms. Box-Cox and semi- or nonparametric models are not the focus of the analysis because, so far, no statistical procedures have been discussed to combine nonparametric models on multiple imputed datasets. The regression equations are therefore tested with linear, semilog, and double-log functional forms.[707]

Data availability and theoretical considerations heavily influence the second and third decisions. Geographical regions could be captured with dummy variables in the regression equation *(nation-wide models)*, or a separate regression equation for each city could be formulated *(city-specific models)*. Concerning the third decision, different index construction methodologies, their advantages, and their disadvantages have been presented in section 2.2, namely, the time dummy variable method (TDV), the adjacent period dummy variable method, and the characteristic price index method (CPI). In this

---

[704] See Sections 4.1.4.1, 4.2.3.1 and 4.3.2.1.4

[705] See Sections 4.1.4.4 and 4.3.2.1.4

[706] Cf. Aizcorbe, A. /Aten, B. (2004), p. 2-5, Hill, R. J. /Melser, D. (2007), p. 5-10

[707] See Interview/Email Prof. van Buuren

thesis the time dummy variable and the characteristic price index method are examined. In total, four different types of models could be computed:

- Nationwide Time Dummy Variable Model
- Nationwide Characteristic Price Index Model
- City-specific Time Dummy Variable Model
- City-specific Characteristic Price Index Model

Each model is based on a different set of assumptions. The nationwide time dummy variable model assumes that the influence of the independent variables is constant between the years 1997 and 2006 and across the cities. The nationwide characteristic price index model relaxes the first assumption. Hence, the influence of the independent variables is allowed to vary between time periods. The city-specific time dummy variable model relaxes the second assumption so that the influence of the independent variables is constant between time periods. Finally, the city-specific characteristic price index model relaxes both assumptions.[708]

		Based on Assumption I: Independent Variables are constant over time	
		Yes	No
Based on Assumpption II: Independent Variables are constant across cities	Yes	Nation-wide Time Dummy Variable Model	Nation-wide Characteristic Price Index Model
	No	City-specific Time Dummy Variable Model	City-specific Characteristic Price Index Model

Table 37: Assumptions of Econometric Models

From a theoretical point of view, the city-specific characteristic price index model is the most advantageous. However, *Tabachnick /Fidell (2006)* argue that a minimum of $N \geq 50 + 8m$ (where m is the number of independent variables) is necessary for a meaningful regression analysis to be performed.[709] The following table depicts the number of observations that are necessary for the different models:[710]

---

[708] See Table 37

[709] Cf. Tabachnick, B. G. /Fidell, L. S. (2006), p. 123

[710] See Table 38

Sample Size Requirements		Time-Dummy Variable Method	Characteristic Price Index Method
Nation-wide Models	Number of Independent Variables	47	38
	Number of Regression Equations	1	10 (one per time period)
	Required Sample Size per Equation	426	354
	Required Total Sample Size	**426**	**3540**
City-Specific Models	Number of Independent Variables	40	31
	Number of Regression Equations	5 (one per city)	50 (one per city and period)
	Required Sample Size per Equation	370	298
	Required Total Sample Size	**1850**	**14900**

Table 38: Sample Size Requirements

Unfortunately, the computation of city-specific characteristic price index models is not possible, as the data sample does not meet the sample size requirement for each year and city.[711] That leaves three alternative models. Here, the question as to which model's assumptions are more realistic has to be answered.

The following reasons clearly indicate that the first assumption is more restrictive and unrealistic. It has been shown that the real estate cycle theory holds true for the German rental office market. Real estate cycle phases influence the level of office rent, because office users, respective tenants, and landlords behave differently during the stages of the real estate cycle.[712] The literature review on office rent determinants, which is intimately connected with the real estate cycle theory, provides further evidence that the influence of some determinants (e.g., lease length and incentives) changes during the various stages of the real estate cycle.[713] In addition, the empirical findings based on the survey of German real estate professionals indicated only marginal differences between the different regional office markets.[714] Finally, the majority of independent variables are lease characteristics. It is questionable why tenants active in different business areas should assess the value of these lease characteristics differently. For instance, large corporations have their guidelines and requirements when renting office space, and they will negotiate each lease independently according to these requirements if the rental unit is located in Germany. Therefore, the nationwide characteristic price index model is favoured over the city-specific time dummy variable model. However, because of operative reasons, which are explained at a later stage,[715] the nationwide time dummy variable model is also computed.

---

711 See Table 20.

712 See Section 3.5

713 See Section 4.1

714 See Section 4.3.2.2

715 See Section 5.4.1.3 and 5.4.2

In summary, the following two basic econometric models are developed, which have either a linear, semilog, or double-log functional form:

$$RENT_a = \beta_0 + \beta_1 age1 + \beta_2 age2 + \beta_3 X06A + \beta_4 X08B + \beta_4 X22A + \beta_6 X24A + \beta_7 X31 + \sum_{h=1}^{H} \alpha_h Z_h + \sum_{i=1997}^{2006} \lambda_i B\_YEAR + \sum_{j=1}^{8} \gamma_j C\_X01_j + u_a$$

Equation 5-15: Nation-wide – Time Dummy Variable Model

$$RENT_{Year} = \beta_0 + \beta_1 age1 + \beta_2 age2 + \beta_3 X06A + \beta_4 X08B + \beta_4 X22A + \beta_6 X24A + \beta_7 X31 + \sum_{h=1}^{H} \alpha_h Z_h + \sum_{j=1}^{8} \gamma_j C\_X01_j + u_a$$

Equation 5-16: Nation-wide – Characteristic Price Index Model

where $\beta = [\beta_{0,} ..., \beta_7]$, $\alpha = [\alpha_{1,} ..., \alpha_M]$, $\lambda = [\lambda_{1997,} \lambda_{1998} ..., \lambda_{2006}]$, $\gamma = [\gamma_{1,} ..., \gamma_8]$ and $\delta = [\delta_{1,} ..., \delta_6]$ are vectors of parameters to be estimated. Z represents all dummy variables [*DX17, D_X18, D_X30, D_X32, D_X35*] and categorical variables [*C_X14, C_X19, C_X21, C_X23, C_X2527, C_X29A*]. B_YEAR_i is a vector of year dummies. C_X01_j= [*category 1 to category 8*] is a vector of city dummies. The term *u* stands for the residuals. The difference between Equation 5-15 and 5-16 is that the term $\sum_{i=1997}^{2006} \lambda_i B\_YEAR_i$ is dropped. Instead, a separate regression equation is computed for each year.

5.4.1.3 *Operative Proceedings*

Because five multiple imputed datasets are used, it is necessary to point out that, theoretically, 165 separate regression equations in total have to be calculated, their regression coefficients and standard errors have to be combined, and their statistical significance has to be tested.[716]

- 15 nationwide models with TDV method (5 imputed datasets x 3 functional forms)
- 150 nationwide characteristic price index models (5 imputed datasets x 10 time periods x 3 functional forms)

Furthermore, each regression equation has to be tested to see if it meets the regression assumptions, which necessitates another series of different tests. Because the amount of work is out of proportion to the scientific findings, a different operative approach is

[716] See Section 5.3.2.5

adopted. In the first step, the best functional form of the nationwide model with the TDV method is elicited, based on a random sample of the observed case datasets. Next, the best functional form of the nationwide model with the TDV method for the imputed datasets is found, and the result is compared with that of step one. It is expected that the same functional form will be found for both the complete case and the imputed datasets, which fits best the statistical assumptions. Otherwise, serious doubts will be cast upon the effectiveness of the multiple imputed datasets. The derived functional form is thereafter employed on all other models.

5.4.1.4 Statistical Tests

Hedonic models are based on multiple regression analysis and, as with any statistical procedure, this analysis relies on specific assumptions. In the following section, these assumptions and their diagnostic and graphical tests are briefly reviewed. What happens if these assumptions are not met is also discussed.

5.4.1.4.1 Normality

The first assumption for multiple regression analysis is that the residuals are normally distributed. Thus, unless the tests indicate that this condition holds, other significance tests like R^2 and t-statistics are likely to overstate the actual quality of fit.[717]

A common diagnostic test for analyzing whether the assumption of normally distributed residuals holds is the Jarque-Bera Test. This diagnostic test is based on the fact that the characteristics of the normal distribution can be described by the mean and the variance. Therefore, if the residuals are not normally distributed, their skewness and kurtosis will significantly depart from the normal distribution:

$$JB = \frac{(N-k)}{6}\left[S^2 + \frac{(K-3)^2}{4}\right]$$

Equation 5-17: Jarque-Bera Test

where K is kurtosis, S is skewness, N is the number of observations, and k is the number of variables.[718] For large samples, the Jarque-Bera Test does not provide accurate

[717] Cf. Tabachnick, B. G. /Fidell, L. S. (2006), p. 78-83, Evans, M. K. (2003), p. 146-147
[718] Cf. Evans, M. K. (2003), p. 147

results, and very slight divergence from normality will be declared significant.[719] Therefore, the residuals are checked graphically with q-q plots.

However, one should bear in mind that the importance of this assumption decreases with an increase in the number of observations. *Backhaus, et al. (2003)* state that if the number of observations is large enough (N>40), the significance tests are independent from the distribution of the residuals.[720]

5.4.1.4.2 Linearity

The second assumption for multiple regression analysis is that a linear relationship exists between the dependent and the independent variables. If this assumption is not met, then the regression coefficients are inefficient and biased. Several possibilities might lead to a nonlinear relationship, from different growth rates between the dependent variable and independent variables, to structural breaks, to interaction effects between the independent variables. However, a common solution is to transform the variables.[721]

A diagnostic test for linearity is the Ramsey regression equation specification error test (RESET).[722] It tests whether nonlinear transformations of the independent variables have been omitted. Consider the model $y_t = \beta_{1t} + \beta_2 X_{1t} + ...\beta_k X_{kt} + u_t$. The Ramsey test now takes the different powers of the values fitted by the above equation $\hat{y}_t^2, \hat{y}_t^3, ..., \hat{y}_t^k$ and includes them as independent variables in the regression equation. Through the F-Tests, the null hypothesis of whether all coefficients of the nonlinear terms are 0 is tested. If the null hypothesis is rejected, then the model suffers from nonlinearity. Some researchers argue that the Ramsey RESET also detects if important variables have been omitted.[723]

Another diagnostic test for linearity is the so-called Rainbow Test. It is based on the assumption that, even if the true relationship is nonlinear, a good linear fit can be achieved on a subsample in the centre of the data. The null hypothesis (linearity) is rejected if the overall fit is significantly inferior to the fit of the subsample.[724]

---

[719] Cf. Tabachnick, B. G. /Fidell, L. S. (2006), p. 80
[720] Cf. Backhaus, K., et al. (2003), p. 92
[721] Cf. Makridakis, S. /Wheelwright, S. C. (1989), p. 191-192, Backhaus, K., et al. (2003), p. 79-82
[722] Cf. Ramsey, J. B. (1969), p. 350-371
[723] Cf. Wuertz, D. (2006), p. 22, Evans, M. K. (2003), p. 150-152
[724] Cf. Wuertz, D. (2006), p. 22

Similar to those of the Jarque-Bera test, the results of Ramsey RESET diagnostic test have to be interpreted carefully with large datasets. Therefore, the assumption of linearity is primarily checked graphically. Component residual plots will detect whether the continuous independent variables have a linear relationship with the dependent variable.

5.4.1.4.3 Homoscedasticity

The third assumption in multiple regression analysis is that of constant variance of the regression errors. The technical term is homoscedasticity if the assumption is met, and heteroscedasticity if it is not. The main problem of heteroscedasticity is that the estimates of the standard errors are inconsistent.[725]

Besides a visual inspection of the residuals versus the fitted values of the regression model, the studentized *Breusch-Pagan / Cook Weisberg* test is undertaken. Thereby, the null hypothesis is that the error remains constant. The alternative hypothesis is that the error variance changes with the level of the fitted values. If the alternative hypothesis is statistically significant, then heteroscedasticity is present in the model.[726]

Another popular diagnostic test for heteroscedasticity is the *Goldfeld-Quant* test, which is also performed. This test compares the variances of two sub-models divided by a specified break point and rejects if the variances differ.[727]

5.4.1.4.4 Problem of Multicollinearity

Multicollinearity occurs if a linear relationship exists among the independent variables in a regression model. The problem of multicollinearity is that of redundant information and over-fitting. Therefore, the interpretation of the regression coefficients is limited.[728]

A common diagnostic test for multicollinearity is the variance inflation factor (VIF), which is defined as $VIF = \frac{1}{tolerance}$ where the tolerance is $tolerance = 1 - R_j^2$.

Thereby, R_j^2 is the squared multiple correlation coefficient of an independent variable X_j with the other independent variables. VIF reflects the fact that, as multicollinearity

---

[725] Cf. Tabachnick, B. G. /Fidell, L. S. (2006), p. 85-86, Evans, M. K. (2003), p. 148-149, Makridakis, S. /Wheelwright, S. C. (1989), p. 259, Backhaus, K., et al. (2003), p. 84-87

[726] Cf. Fox, J. (2006b), p. 81-82

[727] Cf. Wuertz, D. (2006), p. 21, Backhaus, K., et al. (2003), p. 84-87

[728] Cf. Tabachnick, B. G. /Fidell, L. S. (2006), p. 88-89, Backhaus, K., et al. (2003), p. 88-89, Hanke, J. E. /Reitsch, A. G. (2000), p. 259-262

increases, the precision of the regression coefficients decreases. Generally, VIF of greater than 5 indicates the problem of multicollinearity.[729] Because the independent variables contain different dimensions, the generalized variance inflation factor *GVIF^{1/(2times df)* is computed and reported, thereby adjusting for the different dimension of the confidence ellipsoid.[730]

5.4.1.5 Precision and Accuracy Measures

Cross-validation is often applied so that different regression models and their accuracy can be compared. To that end, the dataset is divided into two subsets. The analysis is initially performed on a single subset while the other subset is retained for the subsequent purpose of confirming and validating the results of the initial analysis. For this thesis, each multiple imputed dataset is therefore partitioned into two subsets (hereafter called in-sample and out-sample). As in other hedonic studies in real estate, the in-sample contains 90 percent of all observations and is used for the initial analysis, and the out-sample subset contains 10 percent of all observations and is used to analyze forecasting accuracy.[731]

Three measures - the mean square error (MSE), the root mean square error (RMSE), and the mean percentage error (MPE) - are computed based on the in-sample and out-sample subsets to compare the forecasting accuracy of the regression models. The mean square error penalizes forecasts if there are one or two large errors in the series. It is defined as

$$MSE = \frac{\sum_{t=1}^{n} u_t^2}{n}$$

Equation 5-18: Mean Square Error (MSE)

where u is the residual (error) and n represents the number of observations.[732]

The RMSE also measures the forecasting accuracy, but it is expressed in the same units as the original series. It measures the dispersion from the original series.[733]

---

[729] Cf. Backhaus, K., et al. (2003), p. 90

[730] Cf. Fox, J. (2006a), p. 99

[731] Cf. Bao, H. X. A. /Wan, A. T. K. (2004), p. , Anglin, P. M. /Gencay, R. (1996), p. 633-648, Fletcher, M., et al. (2004), p. 189-200

[732] Cf. Pecar, B. (1997), p. 152

[733] See Equation 5-19 and Ibid., p.

$$RMSE = \sqrt{\frac{\sum_{t=1}^{n} u_t^2}{n}}$$

Equation 5-19: Root Mean Square Error (RMSE)

Whereas the MSE and RMSE are only useful for comparing alternative models, the MPE gives evidence of how well the regression models estimate the dependent variable. It is computed as follows:

$$MPE = \frac{\sum_{t=1}^{n} \frac{u_t}{y_t} 100}{n}$$

Equation 5-20: Mean Percentage Error (MPE)

Thereby, *u* is the error, *n* the number of observations, and *y* the actual value of the dependent variable.[734]

Meeting the regression assumptions is especially important if the primary purpose of the regression analysis is to interpret the regression coefficients. In this thesis, however, the aim is to estimate a model that best explains the dependent variable. Therefore, the precision measures are more important.[735] In addition, a comparison of the precision and accuracy measures between the in-sample and out-sample gives an indication of the models' stability.[736]

5.4.2 Identification of the Best Functional Form

The identification of the best functional form consists of two steps.[737] The first step derives the best functional form based upon a random subsample of the observed dataset,[738] and the second step checks whether the functional form derived from step one also holds true for the imputed datasets.[739]

---

[734] Cf. Ibid., p. 153

[735] „Preferences has often been given to forming a model with high R-bar squared, low autocorrelation of the residuals and high 't' statistics [...], but whilst these may be desirable properties in any technical robust model, they may not yield the best predictive model." Chaplin, R. (1998), p. 23

[736] Cf. Söderberg, B. (2002), p. 173

[737] See Section 5.4.1.3

[738] See Figure 34

[739] See Figure 35

The observed dataset is divided randomly into two samples. The first dataset contains 80 percent of the cases; the second dataset, 20 percent.[740] Based on the second dataset, the nationwide TDV method[741] is computed with a linear, semilog, or double-log functional form.

From the residual diagnostic plots, it becomes obvious that, independent from the functional form, all models' residuals are not normally distributed and show mild heteroscedasticity.[742] Therefore, a fourth model is computed (henceforth denoted as the 'mix' model). In the mix model, the continuous variables are transformed so that they best meet the normal distribution.[743] However, the residual diagnostic plots still identify non-normal distributed residuals.[744] After component residual plots are used to check for linearity between the continuous variables and the dependent variable, the existence of a nonlinear relationship can be rejected.[745]

The observations lead to the finding that the models' residuals are not normally distributed are assigned as outliers within the dataset. As a matter of fact, the range of the dependent variable RENT is from 1.00 to 56.00 EUR/sqm/month. As a consequence, the models are recomputed based on a subsample that includes only lease contracts within 3.00 to 35.00 EUR/sqm/month.[746] The residuals of all the models, except for the model with a linear functional form, are normally distributed, and further evidence is given by the diagnostic tests.[747] The following figure summarizes the aforementioned operative proceedings of the first step for the identification of the best functional form.

---

740 The 80:20 split has been chosen in order to interpret the graphical diagnostic plots. Otherwise any graphical diagnostic plot with the full dataset (i.e. 22,005 observations) is difficult to read due to the high density and distribution. It resembles more a 'cloud'.

741 See Equation 5-15

742 See Appendix 6.1

743 The functional form of the mix model is similar to the double-log functional form. The only difference is that the variables X22A and X24A are not logarithmetic transformed.

744 See Appendix A.7.1.1

745 See Appendix A.7.2.1

746 The subsample's range has been based upon the calculation of the double interquartile range (2*IQR) of the dependent variable RENT and rounded off.

747 See Appendix A.6.4, A.6.5 and A.6.6

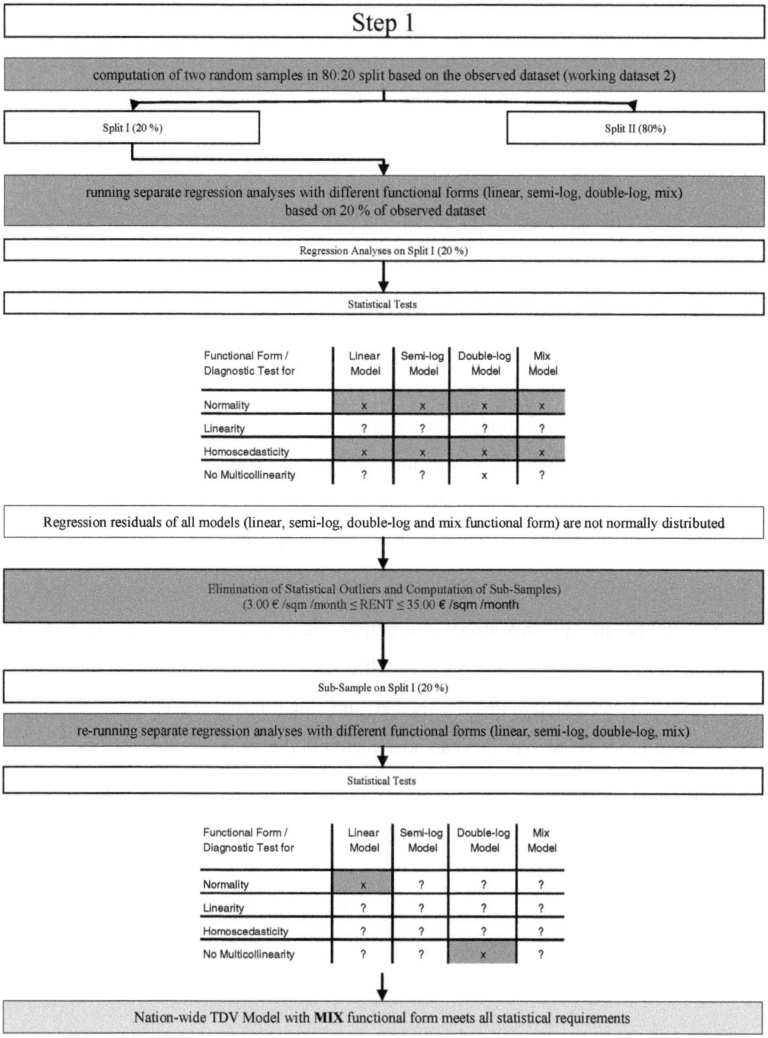

Functional Form / Diagnostic Test for	Linear Model	Semi-log Model	Double-log Model	Mix Model
Normality	x	x	x	x
Linearity	?	?	?	?
Homoscedasticity	x	x	x	x
No Multicollinearity	?	?	x	?

Functional Form / Diagnostic Test for	Linear Model	Semi-log Model	Double-log Model	Mix Model
Normality	x	?	?	?
Linearity	?	?	?	?
Homoscedasticity	?	?	?	?
No Multicollinearity	?	?	x	?

Diagnostic Test for	Test	Explanation
Normality	Residual Diagnostic Plot / Jarque Bera Test	√ diagnostic test passed
Linearity	Component Residual Plot / Rain Test / RESET Test	x diagnostic test failed
Homoscedasticity	Breusch-Pagan Test / Goldfelt-Quant Test	
Multicollinearity	VIF Test	

Figure 34: Identification of Best Functional Form - Step 1

In a second step, the different functional forms are tested with the five imputed datasets. As with the previous findings of the models based on the observed dataset's subsample, the residuals are not normally distributed.[748] If the models are recomputed based on imputed datasets' subsamples containing leases between 3.00 EUR/sqm and 35.00 EUR/sqm, the residuals of all the models, with the exception of the linear model, are normally distributed.[749] Therefore, because the linear functional form does not meet the regression assumptions, it is rejected.

Further diagnostic testing reveals that the semilog and the double-log models have a problem of multicollinearity affecting the interpretability of the regression models.[750] To finally determine which functional form should be used, the accuracy and precision are computed. Whereas only small differences for the average mean square error (MSE) and average root mean square error (RMSE) exist between the models, the mean percentage error (MPE) clearly rejects the linear model and indicates only small differences between the semilog, double-log, and mix models. However, it should be pointed out that only small differences in precision and accuracy exist between the in-samples and out-samples, which underpins the regression models' stability.[751]

Because the results of semilog and double-log models indicate a problem of multicollinearity and because the mix model is slightly more precise and more accurate, the mix model is chosen as the functional form for all further regression models. In other words, the results of the first step to identify the best functional form are confirmed. The operative proceeding of the second step can be depicted in the following figure.

---

748 See Appendix A.7.1.1.1

749 See Appendix A.7.2.1.1

750 See Appendix A.7.1.1.4 and A.7.2.1.4

751 See Appendix A.6.7

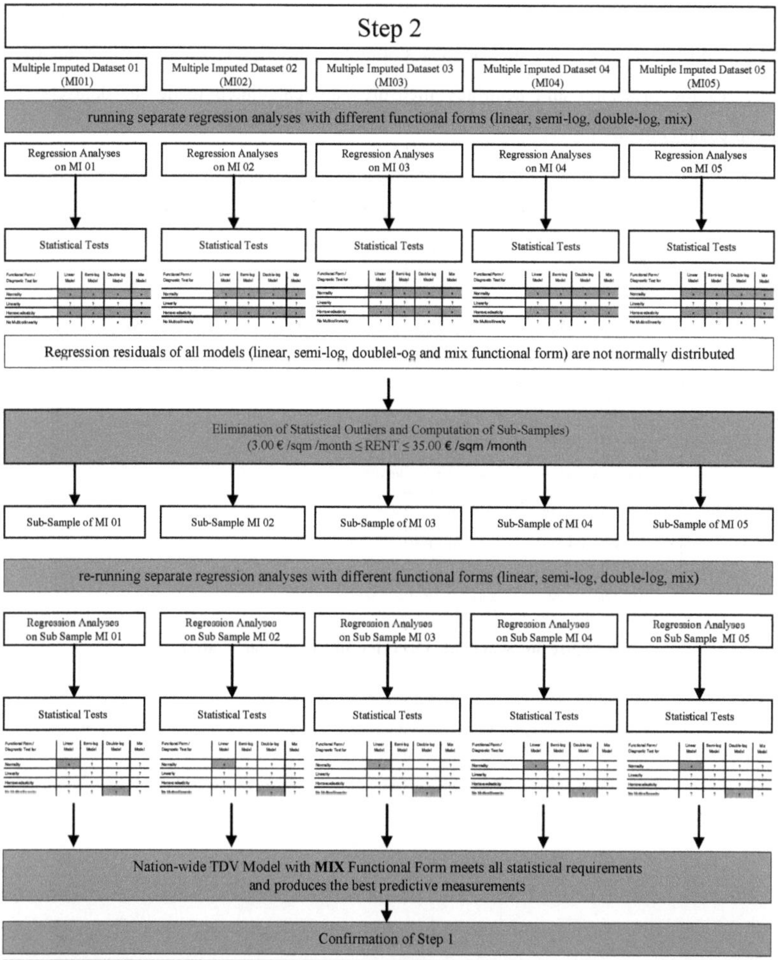

Diagnostic Test for	Test	Explanation
Normality	Residual Diagnostic Plot / Jarque Bera Test	√ diagnostic test passed
Linearity	Component Residual Plot / Rain Test / RESET Test	x diagnostic test failed
Homoscedasticity	Breusch-Pagan Test / Goldfelt-Quant Test	
Multicollinearity	VIF Test	

Figure 35: Identification of Best Functional Form - Step 2

All results based on the full imputed datasets and the subsamples of the imputed datasets are shown.[752] The following diagram gives an overview of the number of datasets

[752] Henceforth, all models which are computed based on the imputed datasets containing leases only between 3.00 EUR/m² and 35.00 EUR/m² are denoted with supplement *(sub sample)*.

and their denotations used for the various models.[753] The regression equations (110 in total) and diagnostic tests are always computed based on the in-sample datasets, whereas the precision and accuracy measures are calculated using all datasets (in-samples and out-samples).

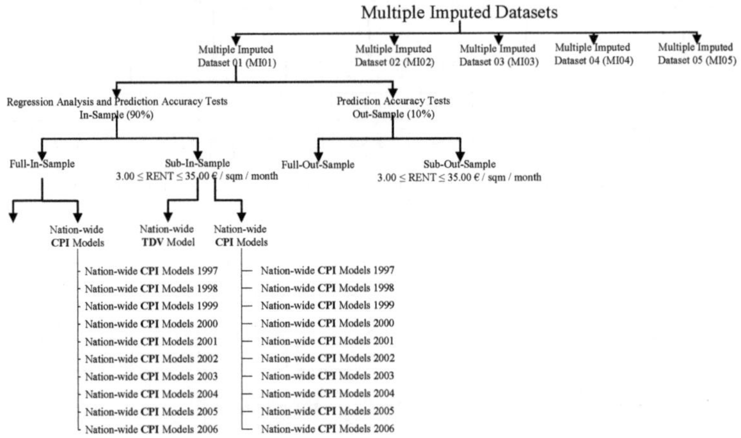

Figure 36: Schematic Overview of Regression Analysis

[753] See Figure 36

5.4.3 Empirical Findings

After deriving a suitable form for the various hedonic functions has been derived,[754] in the following sections, the various econometric models are computed, the regression assumptions checked, and the prediction accuracy calculated before an interpretation of the combined regression coefficients follows. Finally, the results of the different models are compared, and the implications for the computation of the hedonic office rent indices are presented.

5.4.3.1 Nationwide Time-Dummy Variable Model

5.4.3.1.1 Calculation and Checking for Assumptions

The conformance of the regression assumptions is primarily important if the regression coefficients are interpreted. Specifically, the regression assumption of the normal distribution of the residuals has to be met. In Table 39, a summary of the results of the diagnostic tests for the model based on the full and restricted imputed datasets is presented. In both cases, the Jarque-Bera tests indicate that the residuals are not normally distributed, and the Ramsey RESET tests indicate that the assumption of linearity is not met. However, as mentioned earlier, these diagnostic tests are sensitive to large sample sizes. An inspection of the univariate statistics of the residuals reveals that the residuals' skewness and kurtosis of the model based on the restricted imputed datasets (subsamples) are below 1,[755] and, as a consequence, a normal distribution of the residuals can be inferred.[756] Therefore, only the combined regression coefficients of the model based on the restricted imputed datasets (subsamples) can be interpreted. In other respects, the diagnostic tests reject the presence of multicollinearity and indicate only mild heteroscedasticity.

	Normality		Homoscedasticity		Linearity		No Multi-collinearity	Interpretation of Estimates & Standard Errors
	Jarque-Bera	Skewness / Kurtosis	Breusch-Pagan / Cook-Weisberg	Goldfeld-Quant	Ramsey Reset	Rainbow	Variance Inflation Factor	
nw.tdv.mix	No	No	Mild Heteroscedasticity	Yes	No	Yes	Yes	**not recommended**
iqr.nw.tdv.mix	No	Yes	Mild Heteroscedasticity	Yes	No	Yes	Yes	restricted

*iqr = model is computed based upon the restricted dataset (3.00€/m² <= RENT <= 35.00 €/m²)

Table 39: Summary of Diagnostic Tests of Nation-wide Time Dummy Variable Models

---

[754] See Section 5.4.2.

[755] See Appendix A.7.2.1.1

[756] Cf. Tabachnick, B. G. /Fidell, L. S. (2006), p. 81

5.4.3.1.2 *Prediction Accuracy of Models*

In the following tables, the precision and accuracy measures of the model based on the full and the subsamples are shown.[757] First, it must be highlighted that only a marginal difference between the precision measures of the in-samples and out-samples exists, which gives further evidence of the model's stability. Second, the root mean square error (RMSE) indicates a dispersion of 5.1 EUR/sqm around the mean of the actual values for the full in-samples and 4.1 EUR/sqm for the sub in-samples. Third, the mean percentage error (MPE) shows that the predicted values for the model based on the full in-samples are constantly above 10 percent and the predicted values for the model based on the restricted imputed datasets are above 6 percent. Finally, the nationwide time dummy variable model explains about 31 percent of the variances in office rents.

	Precision and Accuracy Measures (Full Sample)											
	in.mi01	in.mi02	in.mi03	in.mi04	in.mi05	Average	out.mi01	out.mi02	out.mi03	out.mi04	out.mi05	Average
Mean Square Error (MSE)	26.202	26.248	26.530	26.280	26.137	26.279	29.645	27.369	25.667	28.151	28.176	27.802
Root Mean Square Error (RMSE)	5.119	5.123	5.151	5.126	5.112	5.126	5.445	5.232	5.066	5.306	5.308	5.271
Mean Percentage Error (MPE)	-10.259	-10.083	-10.341	-9.636	-10.351	-10.134	-10.587	-9.891	-8.114	-13.210	-7.698	-9.900

Table 40: Precision and Accuracy Measures of Nation-wide Time-Dummy Model (Full Sample)

	Precision and Accuracy Measures (Sub-Sample)*											
	in.mi01	in.mi02	in.mi03	in.mi04	in.mi05	Average	out.mi01	out.mi02	out.mi03	out.mi04	out.mi05	Average
Mean Square Error (MSE)	17.709	17.605	17.566	17.555	17.553	17.598	16.864	17.083	17.796	17.932	17.729	17.481
Root Mean Square Error (RMSE)	4.208	4.196	4.191	4.190	4.190	4.195	4.107	4.133	4.219	4.235	4.211	4.181
Mean Percentage Error (MPE)	-6.125	-5.775	-6.074	-5.996	-5.921	-5.978	-5.583	-7.303	-4.826	-4.880	-5.747	-5.668

*iqr = model is computed based upon the restricted dataset (3.00€/m² <= RENT <= 35.00 €/m²)

Table 41: Precision and Accuracy Measures of Nation-wide Time-Dummy Model (Subsample)

	adjusted R²											
	in.mi01	in.mi02	in.mi03	in.mi04	in.mi05	Average	out.mi01	out.mi02	out.mi03	out.mi04	out.mi05	Average
nw.tdv.mix	0.309	0.318	0.317	0.318	0.315	0.315	0.310	0.276	0.275	0.284	0.301	0.289
iqr.nw.tdv.mix (subsample)	0.325	0.326	0.328	0.329	0.328	0.327	0.307	0.318	0.286	0.301	0.312	0.305

*iqr = model is computed based upon the restricted dataset (3.00€/m² <= RENT <= 35.00 €/m²)

Table 42: Adjusted R^2 of Nation-wide Time-Dummy Model

5.4.3.1.3 *Interpretation of Regression Coefficients*

The combined regression coefficients of the model based on the subsample show some interesting and unusual results.[758] However, it has to be pointed out that the nationwide time dummy variable model imposes some severe assumptions. First, it assumes that the

[757] See Table 40 and Table 41

[758] See Table 43

coefficients remain constant over the entire time span of 1997 to 2006 and that the coefficients also remain constant between the cities.

Time Variables	
Years	
Year 1998	-0.0099
Year 1999	0.0002
Year 2000	0.0049
Year 2001	**0.0188**
Year 2002	**0.0272**
Year 2003	0.0029
Year 2004	**-0.0137**
Year 2005	**-0.0175**
Year 2006	0.0001
Location Variables	
Cities	
Düsseldorf	**0.0400**
Frankfurt	**0.1239**
Hamburg	-0.0003
Cologne	**-0.0307**
Leipzig	**-0.2102**
Munich	**0.0871**
Others	**-0.1043**
Stuttgart	-0.0086
Building Variables	
Building Age	**-0.0610**
Building Area	**0.0144**
Building Height	-0.0038
Tenant Variables	
Value Added Tax	**0.0109**

Lease Variables	
Rental Area	**0.0460**
Lease Length	
between 13 and 36 months	**0.0229**
between 37 and 60 months	**0.0315**
between 61 and 120 months	**0.0357**
longer than 120 months	**0.0267**
indefinite lease length	**0.0141**
Extension Option	
extended once	**-0.0217**
extended several times	**-0.0190**
Extension Option Period	**0.0003**
Contract Extension Option	
automatically once	0.0412
automatically several times	**-0.0097**
Contract Extension Option Period	**-0.0006**
Break Options	
Tenant only	0.0127
Landlord only	**0.0485**
Both	**0.0195**
Contract Type	
indexation clause to the CPI or tu	**0.0471**
step-up leases	0.0156
step-up leases indexed to the CP	**0.0360**
free adaptation	0.0144
leases with no adaptation	0.0042
Rent Index Adaption Frequency	
every month	-0.0057
every two month	**-0.0979**
within 12 months	-0.0003
after 12 months	0.0052
Collective Contract	-0.0126
Subletting Allowed	0.0066
Owner Occupied	**0.0179**
Rentfree Months	-0.0049

All bold regression coefficients are statistical significant at a 10 percent level

Table 43: Combined Regression Coefficients of Nation-wide Time Dummy Model (Subsample)[759]

The time dummies behave as expected. The base period is the year 1997, and they indicate a constant rent increase for leases in Germany from 1999 till 2002. Thereafter, the level of rent decreases. For the years 2004 and 2005, the level of rent is even below the

---

759 All bold regression coefficients are statistically significant at a 10 percent level.

base year. Although not all regression coefficients are statistically significant, this finding is in line with the practitioners' view of the market.[760]

The regression coefficients of the city dummies also behave as expected.[761] The base city (the city of comparison) is Berlin. They demonstrate that the rent level in Düsseldorf, Frankfurt, and Munich has been, on average, higher than in Berlin, while the rent level in all other cities has been below that of Berlin.

Regarding the building variables, all regression coefficients are statistically significant, except for building height. The coefficient for age is negative, as expected, indicating that the level of rent decreases with the age of the building. The coefficient for building area is positive, as expected.

The regression estimate for leases in which the tenant carries a business subject to VAT is significant. However, it shows a positive sign. This positive relationship is counterintuitive and opposite to the correlation with the dependent variable. Obviously, this variable leads to a net suppression.[762]

Thereafter, Table 43 reports the regression estimates measuring the different lease factors. The coefficient for rental area is significant and unexpectedly positive, in contrast to the questionnaire's empirical findings. It seems that the rationale of economies of scale does not hold true for the German rental market.[763] Instead, the market for large rental units becomes very thin and is less competitive. Therefore, tenants who are searching for large rental units have to pay a premium.

The regression coefficients measuring the duration of the lease are statistically significant and reveal that leases that are longer than 13 months show a premium on rent. At first glance, this finding seems unusual, as it has been expected that shorter lease lengths lead to higher rent levels. The small number of leases shorter than 13 months (< 3.5%), however, indicates that these leases represent an exception. For instance, these leases could be only intermediate leases before a refurbishment takes place. In addition, the regression coefficients reveal that the highest rent premium is obtained for lease

---

[760] Cf. Gesellschaft für Immobilienwirtschaftliche Forschung (2007), p. 3-4

[761] Cf. Ibid.p. 3

[762] Net suppression is called the phenomenon in which variable suppresses the variance that is irrelevant to prediction of the dependent variable and enhances the effect of the other variables in the set of independent variables in a multiple regression analysis. Tabachnick, B. G. /Fidell, L. S. (2006), p. 154-155

[763] See Section 4.1.4.2

lengths between 5 and 10 years, followed by lease lengths between 3 and 5 years and leases lengths over 10 years. As mentioned earlier, the impact of lease length changes with the stages of the real estate cycle.[764] These changes, however, cannot be captured by the time dummy variable method.

The regression estimates for the extension options are negative and significant. A possible explanation is that the majority of the leases do not include such an option.[765] Therefore, this option might be included only when the tenant has greater negotiation power. In other words, this variable measures another effect. In contrast, the coefficient for the extension option period is significant and positive, as expected, indicating that, the longer the lease can be extended by the tenant, the higher the initial rent.

No predefined relationship has been formulated for the contract extension option. The regression analysis indicates that if the lease is extended automatically several times, it leads to a rent discount. Similarily, no hypothesis has been formulated for the coefficient for the contract extension option period, but, obviously, the longer the contract extension option period, the lower the initial rent.

The regression estimates measuring the different break options have some interesting results. Whenever a break option has been agreed upon, it leads to a rent premium, which is not surprising, because break options are usually perceived as an advantage for the tenants.[766] However, this finding also includes leases in which only the landlord has the right to terminate the lease. This finding is unusual, as such a break option provides an explicit advantage for the landlord, and therefore it is unlikely that the tenant is willing to pay a premium. This variable likely measures those situations in which landlords had a greater negotiation power, as the majority of leases have break options for tenants and landlords.[767]

For the categorical variable measuring the different contract types, a hypothesis has been formulated for only one category. In the event that the lease contains no adaptation clause, a rent premium has to be paid because the landlord bears all the inflation risk. Although the concerned regression coefficient is positive, it is not statistically signifi-

[764] See Section 4.1.4.1
[765] See Appendix A.3.1
[766] Cf. Bond, S. A., et al. (2005), p. 13
[767] See Appendix A.3.2

cant. Instead the regression coefficents for lease with an indexation clause to the CPI or if it is a step-up lease indexed to the CPI are statistically significant and indicate a positive relationship.

Closely related to the aforementioned contract type are the regression coefficients measuring the rent index adaptation frequency. Only one category proves to be statistically significant, namely, leases that are adapted every two months. These receive a higher discount than leases without any adaptation clause. This finding is in line with the theoretical expectations.[768]

Finally, from the set of dummy variables ('collective contract', 'subletting allowed', 'owner occupied' and 'rentfree months'), only the regression estimate for owner-occupied leases is statistically significant. The positive sign underpins the hypothesis that leases in which the landlord and the tenant are affiliated pay higher rents than for leases in which the lease parties do not have such an affiliation.

5.4.3.2 Nationwide Characteristic Price Index Models

5.4.3.2.1 Calculation and Checking for Assumptions

To compute the nationwide characteristic price index models, one must perform a separate regression analysis for each year. Therefore, 10 regression equations are computed for the time span of 1997 to 2006. Computing separate equations permits the impact of the independent variables to change during the different time periods. In the following table, the summary of the diagnostic test is depicted.[769] For the majority of years, only the residuals of the models based on the subsamples are normally distributed. In addition, some models show signs of severe or mild heteroscedasticity and fail the Ramsey RESET test.[770] Therefore, only the combined regression coefficients of the model based on the restricted imputed datasets (subsample) are interpreted.

---

[768] See Section 5.4.1.1

[769] See Table 44

[770] See Appendix A.8 for the results of all diagnostic tests

	Normality		Homoscedasticity		Linearity		No Multi-collinearity	Interpretation of Estimates & Standard Errors
	Jarque-Bera	Skewness / Kurtosis	Breusch-Pagan / Cook-Weisberg	Goldfeld-Quant	Ramsey Reset	Rainbow	Variance Inflation Factor	
nw.cp.1997	No	Yes	Yes	Yes	Yes	Yes	Yes	unrestricted
iqr.nw.cp 1997 (sub sample)	No	Yes	Yes	Yes	Yes	Yes	Yes	unrestricted
nw.cp.1998	No	No	Yes	Yes	Yes	Yes	Yes	not recommended
iqr.nw.cp 1998 (sub sample)	No	Yes	Yes	Yes	Yes	Yes	Yes	unrestricted
nw.cp.1999	No	No	Mild Hetero-scedasticity	Yes	Yes	Yes	Yes	not recommended
iqr.nw.cp1999 (sub sample)	No	Yes	Mild Hetero-scedasticity	Mild Hetero-scedasticity	Yes	Yes	Yes	restricted
nw.cp.2000	No	No	Yes	Yes	No	Yes	Yes	not recommended
iqr.nw.cp 2000 (sub sample)	No	Yes	Hetero-scedasticity	Yes	No	Yes	Yes	restricted
nw.cp.2001	No	Yes	Yes	Yes	No	Yes	Yes	restricted
iqr.nw.cp.2001 (sub sample)	No	Yes	Mild Hetero-scedasticity	Mild Hetero-scedasticity	No	Yes	Yes	restricted
nw.cp.2002	No	Yes	Yes	Mild Hetero-scedasticity	Yes	Yes	Yes	unrestricted
iqr.nw.cp.2002 (sub sample)	No	Yes	Mild Hetero-scedasticity	Yes	Yes	Yes	Yes	restricted
nw.cp.2003	No	Yes	Yes	Yes	Yes	Yes	Yes	unrestricted
iqr.nw.cp.2003 (sub sample)	No	Yes	Yes	Yes	Yes	Yes	Yes	unrestricted
nw.cp.2004	No	No	Yes	Yes	No	Yes	Mild Multi-collinearity	not recommended
iqr.nw.cp.2004 (sub sample)	No	Yes	Yes	Yes	No	Yes	Mild Multi-collinearity	restricted
nw.cp.2005	No	No	Hetero-scedasticity	Yes	No	Yes	Yes	not recommended
iqr.nw.cp.2005 (sub sample)	No	Yes	Yes	Yes	No	Yes	Yes	restricted
nw.cp.2006	No	No	Yes	Yes	Yes	Yes	Yes	not recommended
iqr.nw.cp.2006 (sub sample)	No	Yes	Mild Hetero-scedasticity	Yes	Yes	Yes	Yes	restricted

*iqr = model is computed based upon the restricted dataset (3.00€/m² <= RENT <= 35.00 €/m²)

Table 44: Summary of Diagnostic Tests of Nation-wide Characteristic Price Index Models

5.4.3.2.2 Prediction Accuracy of Models

The precision and accuracy measures for the nationwide characteristic price index models are shown in the following tables.[771] First, the comparison between the precision measures calculated based on the in-samples and out-samples indicates that the models are relatively stable. Second, the root mean square errors (RMSE) indicate a range of dispersion between 4.3 EUR/sqm and 5.8 EUR/sqm around the mean of the actual values for models based on the full in-samples and between 3.6 EUR/sqm and 4.5

[771] See Table 45 to Table 47

EUR/sqm for the models based on the sub in-samples. Third, the mean percentage errors (MPE) show that the predicted values for the models based on the full in-samples are consistently between 6.6 and 14.1 percent, and the predicted values for the models based on the restricted imputed datasets (sub in-samples) are between 4.8 and 6 percent. Finally, the adjusted R^2 improves in each year, except of 2004.[772] At a first glance the explanatory seems rather low. However, as described earlier the efficiency of office property markets is restricted and it has been expected that the regression analysis would carry some noise.[773] In addition, the explanatory power is in line with other reported variances from other research studies.[774]

	Mean Square Error (MSE)						Mean Square Error (MSE)					
	in.mi01	in.mi02	in.mi03	in.mi04	in.mi05	average	out.mi01	out.mi02	out.mi03	out.mi04	out.mi05	average
nw.cp.1997	21.809	21.345	21.961	21.029	21.715	**21.572**	22.085	29.136	23.289	29.925	23.379	**25.563**
iqr.nw.cp 1997 (subsample)	16.506	16.493	16.521	15.358	15.435	**16.063**	13.219	15.367	14.700	22.810	24.022	**18.024**
nw.cp.1998	27.614	24.965	26.038	24.776	26.363	**25.951**	12.099	35.523	20.710	37.751	23.065	**25.829**
iqr.nw.cp 1998 (subsample)	14.826	14.424	14.677	14.798	14.471	**14.639**	11.863	16.584	11.061	13.818	14.904	**13.646**
nw.cp.1999	18.494	18.627	18.287	18.761	18.280	**18.490**	23.096	22.341	22.665	18.136	22.411	**21.730**
iqr.nw.cp1999 (subsample)	13.783	14.405	13.992	14.106	13.783	**14.014**	15.848	11.294	13.261	11.628	14.635	**13.333**
nw.cp.2000	23.120	23.938	23.631	22.906	22.194	**23.158**	31.949	19.922	24.992	31.332	34.281	**28.495**
iqr.nw.cp 2000 (subsample)	12.709	12.699	12.597	12.803	12.504	**12.662**	15.119	14.266	17.048	14.257	16.012	**15.341**
nw.cp.2001	32.159	32.868	33.542	33.654	32.966	**33.038**	43.476	38.773	27.005	27.426	33.819	**34.100**
iqr.nw.cp.2001 (subsample)	15.460	15.036	15.648	15.451	15.502	**15.419**	14.143	18.722	11.657	15.161	13.521	**14.640**
nw.cp.2002	31.751	31.702	33.378	30.865	33.364	**32.212**	47.775	39.187	24.198	48.549	25.190	**36.980**
iqr.nw.cp.2002 (subsample)	20.691	20.493	20.940	19.977	21.058	**20.632**	17.482	20.134	17.318	26.514	15.793	**19.448**
nw.cp.2003	26.824	27.730	28.662	28.410	28.109	**27.947**	36.135	23.906	26.518	22.368	21.786	**26.143**
iqr.nw.cp.2003 (subsample)	18.499	18.319	18.407	18.455	18.165	**18.369**	17.298	15.828	16.822	15.442	17.322	**16.542**
nw.cp.2004	21.742	21.453	21.131	21.606	21.073	**21.401**	20.952	21.985	24.926	20.550	24.288	**22.540**
iqr.nw.cp.2004 (subsample)	17.855	17.702	17.216	17.371	17.438	**17.516**	16.502	16.327	20.664	18.888	17.686	**18.013**
nw.cp.2005	20.969	21.246	20.618	19.798	20.505	**20.627**	16.141	16.008	20.477	23.413	23.188	**19.845**
iqr.nw.cp.2005 (subsample)	15.666	15.744	15.505	15.342	15.763	**15.604**	14.500	13.939	17.696	14.937	16.904	**15.595**
nw.cp.2006	20.576	19.986	19.832	21.830	19.874	**20.420**	22.280	12.969	21.552	14.597	30.267	**20.333**
iqr.nw.cp.2006 (subsample)	17.528	17.015	17.235	17.982	18.124	**17.577**	20.810	12.211	16.661	14.003	14.063	**15.550**

Table 45: Mean Square Error (MSE) of Nation-wide Characteristic Price Index Models

[772] See Table 48

[773] See Section 3.4.3

[774] Cf. Slade, B. A. (2000), p. 368-370, Bond, S. A., et al. (2005), p. 26

	Root Mean Square Error (RMSE)						Root Mean Square Error (RMSE)					
	in.mi01	in.mi02	in.mi03	in.mi04	in.mi05	average	out.mi01	out.mi02	out.mi03	out.mi04	out.mi05	average
nw.cp.1997	4.670	4.620	4.686	4.586	4.660	**4.644**	4.700	5.398	4.826	5.470	4.835	**5.046**
iqr.nw.cp 1997 (subsample)	4.063	4.061	4.065	3.919	3.929	**4.007**	3.636	3.920	3.834	4.776	4.901	**4.213**
nw.cp.1998	5.255	4.996	5.103	4.978	5.134	**5.093**	3.478	5.960	4.551	6.144	4.803	**4.987**
iqr.nw.cp 1998 (subsample)	3.850	3.798	3.831	3.847	3.804	**3.826**	3.444	4.072	3.326	3.717	3.861	**3.684**
nw.cp.1999	4.300	4.316	4.276	4.331	4.275	**4.300**	4.806	4.727	4.761	4.259	4.734	**4.657**
iqr.nw.cp1999 (subsample)	3.713	3.795	3.741	3.756	3.713	**3.743**	3.981	3.361	3.642	3.410	3.826	**3.644**
nw.cp.2000	4.808	4.893	4.861	4.786	4.711	**4.812**	5.652	4.463	4.999	5.598	5.855	**5.313**
iqr.nw.cp 2000 (subsample)	3.565	3.564	3.549	3.578	3.536	**3.558**	3.888	3.777	4.129	3.776	4.001	**3.914**
nw.cp.2001	5.671	5.733	5.792	5.801	5.742	**5.748**	6.594	6.227	5.197	5.237	5.815	**5.814**
iqr.nw.cp.2001 (subsample)	3.932	3.878	3.956	3.931	3.937	**3.927**	3.761	4.327	3.414	3.894	3.677	**3.814**
nw.cp.2002	5.635	5.630	5.777	5.556	5.776	**5.675**	6.912	6.260	4.919	6.968	5.019	**6.016**
iqr.nw.cp.2002 (subsample)	4.549	4.527	4.576	4.470	4.580	**4.542**	4.181	4.487	4.161	5.140	3.074	**4.301**
nw.cp.2003	5.179	5.266	5.354	5.330	5.302	**5.286**	6.011	4.889	5.150	4.729	4.668	**5.089**
iqr.nw.cp.2003 (subsample)	4.301	4.280	4.290	4.296	4.262	**4.286**	4.159	3.978	4.101	3.930	4.162	**4.066**
nw.cp.2004	4.663	4.632	4.597	4.648	4.591	**4.626**	4.577	4.689	4.993	4.533	4.928	**4.744**
iqr.nw.cp.2004 (subsample)	4.225	4.207	4.149	4.168	4.176	**4.185**	4.062	4.041	4.546	4.346	4.205	**4.240**
nw.cp.2005	4.579	4.609	4.541	4.449	4.528	**4.541**	4.018	4.001	4.525	4.839	4.815	**4.440**
iqr.nw.cp.2005 (subsample)	3.958	3.968	3.938	3.917	3.970	**3.950**	3.808	3.733	4.207	3.865	4.111	**3.945**
nw.cp.2006	4.536	4.471	4.453	4.672	4.458	**4.518**	4.720	3.601	4.642	3.821	5.502	**4.457**
iqr.nw.cp.2006 (subsample)	4.187	4.125	4.151	4.241	4.257	**4.192**	4.562	3.494	4.082	3.742	3.750	**3.926**

Table 46: Root Mean Square Error (RMSE) of Nation-wide Characteristic Price Index Models

	Mean Percentage Error (MPE)						Mean Percentage Error (MPE)					
	in.mi01	in.mi02	in.mi03	in.mi04	in.mi05	average	out.mi01	out.mi02	out.mi03	out.mi04	out.mi05	average
nw.cp.1997	-6.234	-6.657	-6.575	-6.751	-6.739	**-6.591**	-11.382	-4.172	-4.246	-4.237	-7.700	**-6.347**
iqr.nw.cp 1997 (subsample)	-4.505	-5.224	-5.495	-5.227	-5.030	**-5.096**	-11.913	-3.290	-1.467	-4.407	-7.382	**-5.692**
nw.cp.1998	-11.185	-10.891	-10.005	-10.417	-11.514	**-10.802**	-8.194	-13.906	-18.016	-16.437	-6.128	**-12.536**
iqr.nw.cp 1998 (subsample)	-5.339	-4.802	-4.885	-5.311	-4.839	**-5.035**	-2.458	-12.083	-7.053	-6.099	-7.110	**-6.961**
nw.cp.1999	-7.332	-7.073	-6.815	-6.573	-6.225	**-6.804**	-0.457	-3.152	-6.365	-5.537	-7.465	**-4.595**
iqr.nw.cp1999 (subsample)	-5.050	-5.071	-5.290	-4.819	-4.054	**-4.857**	-1.491	-3.348	-1.299	-3.307	-8.687	**-3.626**
nw.cp.2000	-7.922	-7.424	-7.719	-7.316	-8.277	**-7.732**	-2.005	-4.213	-0.174	-6.546	-0.515	**-2.691**
iqr.nw.cp 2000 (subsample)	-5.023	-4.692	-4.679	-4.577	-4.957	**-4.786**	-1.165	-2.098	-0.806	-3.532	-1.843	**-1.889**
nw.cp.2001	-7.572	-7.302	-7.545	-6.989	-7.873	**-7.456**	-4.673	-7.794	-5.987	-8.662	-0.814	**-5.586**
iqr.nw.cp.2001 (subsample)	-5.046	-4.636	-4.889	-4.658	-5.175	**-4.881**	-2.696	-6.457	-4.731	-5.610	-0.716	**-4.042**
nw.cp.2002	-6.538	-7.300	-6.933	-7.753	-6.563	**-7.018**	-12.760	-7.572	-10.210	-2.298	-12.516	**-9.071**
iqr.nw.cp.2002 (subsample)	-5.520	-6.025	-5.995	-6.235	-5.653	**-5.885**	-10.401	-6.285	-5.966	-3.307	-9.073	**-7.006**
nw.cp.2003	-8.491	-8.267	-8.381	-7.891	-8.342	**-8.274**	-6.014	-8.330	-5.816	-8.166	-9.016	**-7.468**
iqr.nw.cp.2003 (subsample)	-6.321	-5.920	-6.360	-5.878	-6.262	**-6.148**	-4.668	-7.225	-4.363	-6.538	-6.756	**-5.910**
nw.cp.2004	-10.919	-9.899	-10.475	-10.534	-9.733	**-10.312**	-7.980	-13.712	-8.295	-7.478	-12.930	**-10.079**
iqr.nw.cp.2004 (subsample)	-6.742	-6.226	-6.665	-6.699	-6.188	**-6.504**	-7.626	-9.340	-4.997	-4.600	-7.212	**-6.755**
nw.cp.2005	-12.982	-14.509	-15.754	-11.828	-15.591	**-14.133**	-32.668	-11.580	-8.702	-36.802	-6.864	**-19.323**
iqr.nw.cp.2005 (subsample)	-5.663	-4.879	-5.654	-5.457	-5.348	**-5.400**	-5.853	-6.009	-5.646	-4.090	-4.540	**-5.228**
nw.cp.2006	-11.683	-10.715	-11.310	-10.557	-11.515	**-11.156**	-9.108	-7.059	-5.921	-2.099	-5.248	**-5.887**
iqr.nw.cp.2006 (subsample)	-5.458	-4.883	-5.532	-4.853	-5.852	**-5.316**	-4.354	-7.923	-4.912	-1.673	-3.708	**-4.514**

Table 47: Mean Percentage Error (MPE) of Nation-wide Characteristic Price Index Models

	Adjusted R²						Adjusted R²					
	in.mi01	in.mi02	in.mi03	in.mi04	in.mi05	average	out.mi01	out.mi02	out.mi03	out.mi04	out.mi05	average
nw.cp.1997	0.231	0.227	0.234	0.237	0.243	**0.234**	0.272	0.195	0.159	0.170	0.140	**0.187**
iqr.nw.cp 1997 (subsample)	0.267	0.274	0.286	0.282	0.298	**0.281**	0.386	0.233	0.123	0.253	0.115	**0.222**
nw.cp.1998	0.252	0.269	0.271	0.279	0.248	**0.264**	0.401	0.202	0.312	0.106	0.371	**0.278**
iqr.nw.cp 1998 (subsample)	0.312	0.319	0.334	0.314	0.311	**0.318**	0.375	0.221	0.178	0.268	0.371	**0.283**
nw.cp.1999	0.262	0.256	0.266	0.267	0.270	**0.264**	0.147	0.198	0.203	0.154	0.163	**0.173**
iqr.nw.cp1999 (subsample)	0.309	0.288	0.304	0.310	0.309	**0.304**	0.218	0.383	0.305	0.239	0.267	**0.283**
nw.cp.2000	0.293	0.327	0.317	0.321	0.322	**0.316**	0.368	0.209	0.263	0.259	0.307	**0.281**
iqr.nw.cp 2000 (subsample)	0.299	0.309	0.299	0.290	0.298	**0.299**	0.213	0.148	0.179	0.271	0.257	**0.214**
nw.cp.2001	0.374	0.376	0.382	0.379	0.370	**0.376**	0.338	0.298	0.326	0.310	0.418	**0.338**
iqr.nw.cp.2001 (subsample)	0.311	0.308	0.310	0.315	0.312	**0.311**	0.307	0.308	0.361	0.212	0.319	**0.301**
nw.cp.2002	0.353	0.356	0.351	0.344	0.348	**0.350**	0.284	0.313	0.325	0.344	0.355	**0.324**
iqr.nw.cp.2002 (subsample)	0.371	0.371	0.370	0.373	0.395	**0.376**	0.389	0.379	0.321	0.299	0.409	**0.359**
nw.cp.2003	0.373	0.385	0.378	0.381	0.377	**0.379**	0.338	0.322	0.370	0.375	0.367	**0.354**
iqr.nw.cp.2003 (subsample)	0.383	0.391	0.376	0.385	0.393	**0.386**	0.305	0.363	0.430	0.330	0.337	**0.353**
nw.cp.2004	0.273	0.285	0.288	0.283	0.288	**0.283**	0.310	0.264	0.239	0.305	0.288	**0.281**
iqr.nw.cp.2004 (subsample)	0.308	0.315	0.324	0.323	0.320	**0.318**	0.345	0.347	0.269	0.316	0.350	**0.325**
nw.cp.2005	0.371	0.366	0.369	0.405	0.361	**0.374**	0.298	0.431	0.328	0.261	0.363	**0.336**
iqr.nw.cp.2005 (subsample)	0.420	0.411	0.412	0.437	0.406	**0.417**	0.345	0.441	0.358	0.380	0.412	**0.387**
nw.cp.2006	0.365	0.394	0.372	0.378	0.370	**0.376**	0.337	0.325	0.383	0.334	0.324	**0.341**
iqr.nw.cp.2006 (subsample)	0.366	0.398	0.377	0.383	0.365	**0.378**	0.363	0.364	0.378	0.347	0.380	**0.367**

Table 48: Adjusted R² of Nation-wide Characteristic Price Index Models

5.4.3.2.3 Interpretation of Regression Coefficients

In the following table, the combined regression coefficients for the nationwide characteristic price index models are presented.[775] At first glance, it is obvious that the assumption that the impact of the independent variables remains constant does not hold true.

[775] See Table 49

	1997	1998	1999	2000	2001	2002	2003	2004	2005	2006
Location Variables										
Cities										
Düsseldorf	**-0.0437**	0.0237	**0.0812**	-0.0094	0.0051	**-0.0386**	**0.0449**	**0.0606**	**0.1090**	**0.0842**
Frankfurt	0.0257	**0.1600**	**0.1547**	**0.0752**	**0.0785**	**0.0842**	**0.1169**	**0.1227**	**0.2035**	**0.1464**
Hamburg	**-0.0539**	0.0037	0.0256	**-0.0592**	-0.0018	**-0.0431**	**-0.0337**	0.0178	**0.0423**	**0.0575**
Cologne	**-0.1101**	-0.0323	0.0072	**-0.0673**	**-0.0628**	-0.0292	**-0.0491**	-0.0027	0.0069	-0.0106
Leipzig	-0.1450	**-0.1089**	**-0.0788**	**-0.1676**	**-0.1862**	**-0.1917**	**-0.2470**	**-0.2011**	**-0.2301**	**-0.2282**
Munich	0.0109	**0.0875**	**0.0988**	**0.0423**	**0.0929**	**0.0593**	**0.0661**	**0.0862**	**0.1258**	**0.1122**
Others	**-0.1602**	**-0.0653**	**-0.0517**	**-0.1364**	**-0.1263**	**-0.1374**	**-0.1047**	**-0.1198**	**-0.0592**	**-0.0746**
Stuttgart	**-0.0950**	-0.0186	0.0110	-0.0273	-0.0478	**-0.0641**	-0.0328	0.0293	**0.0802**	0.0614
Building Variables										
Building Age	**-0.0504**	**-0.0628**	**-0.0481**	-0.0308	**-0.0475**	**-0.0603**	**-0.0753**	**-0.0786**	**-0.0696**	**-0.0548**
Building Area	0.0072	-0.0005	**-0.0310**	-0.0110	0.0101	0.0006	**0.0196**	**0.0388**	**0.0353**	0.0147
Building Height	0.0058	-0.0279	-0.0118	0.0034	-0.0192	0.0299	-0.0097	**-0.0387**	0.0150	0.0223
Tenant Variables										
Value Added Tax	0.0082	0.0072	0.0100	0.0136	0.0073	0.0035	0.0159	0.0137	**0.0194**	**0.0358**
Lease Variables										
Rental Area	**0.0456**	**0.0281**	**0.0496**	0.0693	**0.0488**	**0.0630**	**0.0572**	**0.0355**	**0.0158**	**0.0362**
Lease Length										
between 13 and 36 months	0.5015	**-0.0785**	**0.0763**	0.0475	0.0366	**-0.0520**	0.0047	0.0130	**0.0694**	0.0273
between 37 and 60 months	0.4959	**-0.0995**	**0.0817**	**0.0538**	0.0357	-0.0196	0.0258	0.0132	**0.0817**	**0.0590**
between 61 and 120 months	0.5020	**-0.0878**	**0.0776**	**0.0607**	0.0312	-0.0043	0.0237	**0.0306**	**0.0989**	**0.0718**
longer than 120 months	0.5278	**-0.1171**	**0.0819**	**0.0681**	0.0214	0.0082	-0.0160	-0.0331	**0.1461**	**0.0842**
indefinite lease length	0.4673	**-0.1026**	**0.0643**	**0.0702**	0.0108	**-0.0466**	-0.0195	0.0025	**0.0657**	0.0153
Extension Option										
extended once	0.0603	-0.0035	0.0416	0.0143	-0.0246	-0.0295	**-0.0651**	-0.0114	**-0.0504**	-0.0330
extended several times	0.0323	0.0156	0.0188	-0.0132	-0.0354	**-0.0546**	-0.0340	-0.0069	**-0.0366**	-0.0434
Extension Option Period	**-0.0012**	0.0004	-0.0007	-0.0001	0.0004	0.0005	**0.0008**	0.0000	0.0005	0.0007
Contract Extension Option										
automatically once	0.1143	0.1477	0.2112	0.0433	0.0203	**0.1388**	0.0799	**0.0651**	0.0235	**-0.0589**
automatically several times	-0.0268	0.0052	-0.0047	0.0059	0.0126	**0.0421**	-0.0248	**-0.0308**	-0.0142	-0.0356
Contract Extension Option Period	0.0004	**-0.0023**	-0.0031	0.0007	-0.0007	**-0.0020**	-0.0007	-0.0003	0.0002	-0.0005
Break Options										
Tenant only	0.0062	**-0.1140**	0.0510	-0.0425	-0.0402	0.0315	**0.1346**	-0.0870		
Landlord only	0.0334	0.0252	0.0347	**0.0357**	0.0383	**0.0614**	**0.0739**	**0.0811**	0.0005	0.0036
Both	**0.0337**	0.0103	**0.0398**	**0.0160**	**0.0464**	**0.0201**	**0.0289**	**0.0356**	-0.0159	**-0.0383**
Contract Type										
indexation clause to the CPI or turnover	0.1176	0.0607	0.0272	**0.0781**	**0.2138**	**0.1145**	0.0617	0.0344		
step-up leases	0.1815	0.0593	-0.0355	**0.0425**	**0.2582**	**0.1110**	0.0188	-0.0113	**-0.0599**	-0.0243
step-up leases indexed to the CPI	0.1184	**0.1274**	-0.0024	**0.0708**	**0.2093**	**0.1189**	**0.0978**	-0.0012	**-0.0324**	-0.0245
free adaptation	0.1210	-0.0068	-0.0175	-0.0033	0.1898	**0.0923**	0.0294	0.0219	**-0.0328**	0.0110
leases with no adaptation	0.1025	0.0140	-0.0640	-0.0083	**0.1989**	0.0737	0.0147	0.0135	**-0.0450**	0.0510
Rent Index Adaption Frequency										
every month	0.0285	**-0.0805**	-0.0379	**-0.0793**	0.0252	-0.0044	0.0087	0.0120	-0.0098	0.0408
every two month					**-0.1412**	**-0.1024**	**-0.1001**	**-0.0796**	**-0.0875**	-0.0483
within 12 months	0.0248	0.0168	-0.0347	**-0.0525**	0.0273	0.0081	0.0074	0.0097	0.0062	0.0137
after 12 months	-0.0009	**-0.0693**	**-0.0475**	-0.0244	**0.0441**	**0.0498**	0.0181	**0.0446**	0.0006	0.0035
Collective Contract	-0.0038	-0.0098	-0.0054	-0.0055	**-0.0153**	-0.0010	-0.0082	-0.0113	**-0.0223**	**-0.0451**
Subletting Allowed	0.0096	-0.0075	-0.0063	0.0167	-0.0056	0.0020	-0.0143	0.0085	0.0016	**0.0483**
Owner Occupied	0.0630	-0.0095	-0.0276	0.0238	**-0.0488**	**0.0794**	0.0255	0.0173	0.0162	**0.0601**
Rentfree Months	-0.0173	**0.0449**	**0.0346**	-0.0064	-0.0113	-0.0177	0.0129	**-0.0295**	-0.0103	-0.0238

*iqr = model is computed based upon the restricted dataset (3.00€/m² <= RENT <= 35.00 €/m²)

All bold regression coefficients are statistical significant at a 10 percent level

Table 49: Combined Regression Coefficients of Nation-wide Characteristic Price Index Models (Sub Sample)[776]

[776] All bold regression coefficients are statistical significant at a 10 percent level.

The dummy variables representing the cities show a relatively consistent picture. Most of their regression estimates are statistically significant and indicate that the level of rent in Frankfurt and Munich has been higher than in Berlin, the base of comparison, throughout the entire time span of 1997 to 2006. They also indicate that the level of rent in Düsseldorf, Hamburg, and Stuttgart caught up to and even surpassed the level in Berlin. This picture is also confirmed by the latest market report of the German Society of Property Researchers.[777]

Regarding the building variables, only the regression estimates for building age appear to be statistically significant throughout almost the entire time span. They underpin the hypothesis and show a negative relationship with the dependent variable. The other two building variables, namely, 'building height' and 'building area' are mainly not statistically significant. However, for the few time periods in which the regression estimates for building area are statistically significant, they change their mathematical sign. While in 1999 they show a negative relationship, in the latter years (2003 -2005) they indicate a positive relationship.

The regression estimates measuring whether tenants carry out a business subject to VAT are insignificant, except for 2005 and 2006. Here, the estimates indicate that tenants subject to VAT pay a rent premium which does not conform with the formulated hypothesis. The insignificance of the regression estimates might partly result from the fact that the impact of this variable is only important for the landlord only if the building is newer than 10 years. However, the average building age of the data sample is approximately 14 years.[778]

Thereafter, Table 49 reports the regression estimates of lease variables. The coefficient for rental area are positive and statistically significant. This finding provides some evidence against the hypothesis that, with large rental areas, higher economies of scales are obtained and, consequently, the level of rent is negatively correlated with the rental area. Instead, the finding indicates that the market for large rental spaces is thinner and therefore less competitive.

The interpretation regarding the lease length is quite difficult and is limited to the statistically significant regression estimates. First, the regression coefficients for the year

---

[777] Cf. Gesellschaft für Immobilienwirtschaftliche Forschung (2007), p. 3

[778] See Table 26

1998 have all negative relationships, as opposed to the majority of regression coefficients of the other time periods. Second, from 2004 to 2006, leases with a length of 5 to 10 years have paid higher rents than shorter leases. This is counterintuitive to the opinions of German market participants. In recessionary times, it is expected that the lease length will be negatively correlated with the level of rent.[779] However, this finding might also be an indication that market participants expected the overall economy to grow and, consequently, the level of rent to increase. Therefore, landlords asked a premium for long-term leases. The combined regression coefficients show that lease length is an important but ambiguous factor influencing the level of rent and that more in-depth research is necessary, a finding similar to that of the literature review.[780]

Although the regression coefficients for the variables 'extension option' and 'contract extension option' are significant only for a few years, they show some unusual results. The observation that leases with an extension option for the tenants receive a rent discount in the majority of years is counterintuitive, as is the observation that leases that have an automatic contract extension clause obtain a rent premium.

The regression estimates for break options in which both parties have the right to terminate the lease is positive and significant in the majority of years. This has been expected, as the tenant normally exercises a break option. To cover this additional risk, the landlord asks for a rent premium. However, the regression coefficients for a break option in which only the landlord has the right to terminate the lease are also positive, which is counterintuitive. One possible explanation is that this variable coincides with the effect of an unobserved variable (e.g., negotiation power or tenant quality).

The regression estimates for the categorical variable 'contract type' are statistically significant and show that it is important to control for contract types in the development of hedonic office rent indices.

Closely related to the variable 'contract type' is the variable 'rent index adaptation frequency'. The impact of rent index adaptation frequency fluctuates throughout the years. However, from 2001 up to 2006, its impact is relatively constant and statistically singnificant. If the rent index adaptation occurs every two months, a rent discount is ex-

---

[779] See Section 4.3.2.1.4

[780] See Section 4.1.4.1

pected, which is not the case for leases without any rent index adaptation. This finding is in line with the formulated hypthosesis.

Unfortunately, only a few regression estimates for the last set of dummy variables are statistically significant (i.e. 'collective contract', 'subletting allowed', 'owner occupied' and 'rentfree months'). For some years (2001, 2005, and 2006) the regression estimates for collective contracts indicate that leases negotiated under a collective contract pay less rent than other contracts, which is in line with the hypothesis. The regression estimates of the subletting option change their sign throughout the entire time span and are not significant, except in 2006. Here, the regression estimate is statistically significant and underpins the hypothesis of a positive relationship with the dependent variable. The signs of the regression coefficients for owner-occupied leases and rent-free months also change throughout the time span and are statistically insignificant in the majority of years. A possible explanation is that the effects of these variables coincide with the effect of another unobserved variable.

5.4.3.3 Comparison and Implications for Computation of Office Rent Indices

Two different econometric models have been computed, their regression assumptions tested, and their regression estimates interpreted. The majority of statistically significant regression estimates are in line with the formulated hypotheses. Some regression estimates do not have the expected mathematical sign and therefore cast some doubt on the models' use for index construction.[781] However, two main sources are put forward for this observation. First, the bivariate correlations already indicate that the variables do not behave as expected. Second, many important variables (e.g., tenant quality measures, negotiation power, and location variables) are left out of the regression equation because of unavailability. The latter source is referred to as the omitted variable problem and often has been encountered in hedonic real estate analysis.[782] Specifically, when leases are analyzed, "[...] there are often agreements made between tenants and landlords, that have a value but that value may be near impossible to obtain data on or measure."[783]

---

[781] Cf. Söderberg, B. (2002), p. 173

[782] Cf. Gatzlaff, D. /Geltner, D. (1998), p. 5, Zabel, J. E. (1999), p. 227, Pace, K. R., et al. (2002), p. 34, Curry, B., et al. (2001), p. 659-671

[783] Desyllas, J. (2000), p. 37

Moreover, in the special case of the nationwide characteristic price index models, some regression estimates changed their mathematical signs between the different time periods. Here, another explanation besides the omitted variable problem can be put forward. In each time period, different tenants enter the rental market and base their spending decisions on a different set of characteristics or assign different weights to them. In other words, the relationship between the lease characteristics and their implicit prices may change, causing the demand and supply curves in the implicit characteristics markets to shift. As a result, the regression estimates are not fixed parameters but weighted averages, implying that the regression estimates may not be stable over time and that the implied estimates of price and quality shift because of changes in the mix of tenants.[784]

Likewise, the fact that the regression coefficients of some variables are not statistically significant does not imply that market participants ignore these variables. Rather, it states that the sample analyzed did not provide clear evidence of how these variables were being considered. As *Janssen (2003)* points out, "[...] significance implies a certain consensus in the market regarding the influence on value. It is logical that there is consensus with respect to a few central aspects, and not surprising that opinions may differ for a number of not central ones."[785]

Besides, the traditional view that the regression parameters have to be stable and in line with economic theory to develop hedonic price indices has been challenged. *Pakes (2002)* argues that, if the purpose of hedonic analysis is merely to correct observed prices for changes in quality, then parameter stability and counterintuitive signs are irrelevant. He further states that the derivatives of a hedonic price function are formed from a complex equilibrium process and "[...] should not be interpreted as willingness to pay derivatives or cost derivates."[786] A similar position had been proposed earlier by *Griliches (1971)*.[787]

It goes without saying that, for the further development of the hedonic office rent indices, the nationwide characteristic price index models are used. As mentioned previously, the nationwide time dummy variable model has been computed only for operative reasons and is based on restrictive assumptions. Besides, the precision and accuracy

---

[784] Cf. Kokoski, M., et al. (2000), p. 8-9, Hulten, C. R. (2003), p. 10, Pakes, A. (2002), p. 7-9
[785] Janssen, C. (2003), p. 330
[786] Pakes, A. (2002), p. 14
[787] Cf. Griliches, Z. (1971), p. 8 quoted by Diewert, E. (2003), p. 31

measures, as well as the explained variances of nationwide characteristic price index models, improve each year.

5.5 Chapter Summary

This chapter tackles the objective to quantify the significant determinants of office rents in Germany (Objective II) and is the nucleus of this thesis.[788] It comprises the major empirical analysis, which is subdivided into two steps. Step one includes the presentation of the dataset and the data-mining process; step two includes the regression analysis and interpretation of the regression coefficients.

The key findings of step one are summarized as follows:

- The data source for the empirical analysis is the IPD Rental Database, provided by the IPD Germany. The initial data set contains 22,005 office leases with more than 60 independent variables across Germany and covers the time span from 1997 to 2006. These leases are retrieved from over 4,700 office buildings. The market coverage and representativeness of the data (measured by the sum of total rental space per year and city) is relatively high in comparison with the figures published by the German Society of Property Researchers.
- In a primary data-mining process, all auxiliary and independent variables that have more than 90 percent missing values have been disregarded (working dataset 1). In addition, some variables of interest were made anonymous for reasons of data protection by IPD. Thereafter, all selected variables underwent plausibility checks. Where it seemed necessary to decrease the percentage of missing values, the scale of the variables has been reduced or recombined into a new variable (working dataset 2).
- Nevertheless, some variables still had a high percentage of missing values. Therefore, different strategies to handle missing data and their assumptions have been presented and discussed. In principle, the strategies can be subdivided into two categories: single imputation and multiple imputation methods. A further analysis revealed that only the multiple imputation method is an appropriate strategy for handling the missing values in the dataset at hand.

[788] See Section 1.2

- The multiple imputation method involves creating multiple "complete" datasets by filling in values for the missing data. Each imputed (or filled-in) dataset is analyzed as if it were a complete dataset. The inferences from the imputed datasets are then combined into one result by averaging over the imputed datasets. The main advantage of the multiple imputation method is that it accounts for the uncertainty by replacing missing values and does not underestimate the standard errors. Hence, it does not overestimate the level of precision.
- The univariate and bivariate statistics of the multiple imputed datasets have been compared with the observed case dataset and the mean substitution dataset to check the quality of the multiple imputations. The univariate and the bivariate statistics revealed that the multiple imputed datasets outperformed the mean substitution method.

Step 2 of the empirical analysis represents the estimation stage of the hedonic analysis. The key findings are summarized as follows:

- The estimation stage had to cover the following issues: how the dimension of time is modeled, how the regional markets are modeled in the regression analysis, and which functional form to use.
- A mix model proved to be the most appropriate functional form, for it best met the statistical requirements and achieved the highest precision measures. In the mix model, all but two metric variables are logarithmically transformed. Furthermore, because of statistical outliers, another set of models has been computed that only includes leases between 3.00 and 35.00 EUR/sqm/month.
- Two econometric models are suggested and empirically tested for modeling the dimension time and the regional markets: the *nationwide time dummy variable model* and the *nationwide characteristic price index model.*
- The *nationwide time dummy variable model* consists of only one regression equation, in which the regional market and the time periods are captured by dummy variables, whereas the *nationwide characteristic price index model* formulates each time period separately, and only the regional markets enter as dummy variables in the regression equation. In city-specific models, a separate

regression equation is formulated for each city. However, these models are rejected because of data unavailability.

- For each model, namely, the nationwide time dummy variable model and the nationwide characteristic price index model, a regression analysis, which includes the calculation and checking of assumptions, the measurement of the precision accuracy, and an interpretation of the regression coefficients, has been performed.
- In most models, the regression coefficients show the expected sign. However, some unexpected results have been obtained for a few variables. These are probably due to a net suppression effect.
- From the regression analysis it became clear that the nationwide characteristic price index model based on the subsample (leases between 3.00 and 35.00 EUR/sqm/month) outperforms the other models. On the one hand, it best meets the statistical requirements of regression analysis, and, on the other hand, it imposes the least restrictive theoretical assumptions. Therefore, it is suggested that the nationwide characteristic price index model be used for the development of hedonic office rent indices in the next chapter (Composition Stage).

6 Development, Application and Evaluation of Hedonic Office Rent Indices

The previous chapters have been necessary to lay the groundwork for the development of the hedonic office rent indices for German metropolitan areas (Estimation Stage). This chapter computes the hedonic office rent indices (Composition Stage) and identifies the intertemporal and interregional rent changes. Finally, the hedonic office rent indices and the German Society of Property Researchers office rent indices are evaluated and compared.

6.1 Development of Hedonic Office Rent Indices

6.1.1 Choice of Index Formula and Weighting Procedure

Three different index construction methodologies, namely, the time dummy variable, the adjacent period dummy variable method, and the characteristic price index method, have been presented.[789] Although the estimated models in this thesis allow indices to be constructed based on both the characteristic price index methodology and the time dummy variable methodology, the following hedonic office rent indices focus on the characteristic price index methodology. As previously stated, the theory clearly advocates the characteristic price index method because the hedonic functional form of the time dummy variable method commands the index number formulae. In other words, a choice of the index-weighting scheme is not possible.[790]

The main issue is the choice of the characteristics' quantities, or the weighting procedure. In this thesis, the mean value of each characteristic per year is computed,[791] which permits the construction of indices based on the Laspeyres and Paasche index formulae. The Laspeyres index formula uses the mean value of each characteristic from the base period (year 1997), while the Paasche index formula allows the mean value of each characteristic to be computed per year.[792]

---

[789] See Section 2.2

[790] See Section 2.2.4

[791] See Table 50

[792] See Section 2.2.3

	1997	1998	1999	2000	2001	2002	2003	2004	2005	2006
Rent Index Adaption Frequency										
no adaptation	0.53	0.50	0.52	0.45	0.45	0.47	0.64	0.68	0.67	0.58
every month	0.03	0.04	0.05	0.07	0.06	0.07	0.07	0.04	0.08	0.09
every two month	0.00	0.00	0.00	0.00	0.01	0.01	0.02	0.13	0.11	0.13
within 12 months	0.37	0.41	0.37	0.42	0.43	0.40	0.23	0.12	0.10	0.12
after 12 months	0.07	0.05	0.06	0.06	0.05	0.06	0.04	0.03	0.05	0.08
Lease Length										
up to 12 months	0.00	0.03	0.02	0.01	0.02	0.02	0.03	0.05	0.06	0.07
between 13 and 36 months	0.09	0.09	0.10	0.09	0.09	0.10	0.14	0.15	0.14	0.16
between 37 and 60 months	0.24	0.28	0.25	0.32	0.33	0.31	0.28	0.22	0.20	0.25
between 61 and 120 months	0.44	0.33	0.34	0.29	0.30	0.30	0.20	0.17	0.15	0.17
longer than 120 months	0.12	0.08	0.06	0.07	0.07	0.06	0.05	0.03	0.03	0.05
indefinite lease	0.12	0.18	0.24	0.22	0.19	0.22	0.30	0.38	0.42	0.29
Extension										
no extension	0.93	0.93	0.89	0.88	0.84	0.80	0.82	0.77	0.73	0.59
extended once	0.05	0.03	0.09	0.07	0.11	0.15	0.11	0.09	0.12	0.19
extended several times	0.02	0.04	0.01	0.05	0.05	0.05	0.07	0.14	0.16	0.23
Contract Extension Option										
no contract	0.95	0.95	0.94	0.93	0.90	0.87	0.87	0.84	0.82	0.67
automatically	0.00	0.00	0.00	0.00	0.00	0.00	0.01	0.01	0.01	0.09
automatically several times	0.04	0.05	0.06	0.07	0.10	0.13	0.12	0.15	0.17	0.24
Break Options										
None	0.40	0.51	0.54	0.55	0.51	0.41	0.29	0.14	0.08	0.16
Tenant only	0.00	0.01	0.00	0.00	0.00	0.01	0.01	0.00	0.00	0.00
Landlord only	0.11	0.11	0.13	0.13	0.13	0.16	0.12	0.08	0.12	0.13
Both	0.49	0.38	0.33	0.31	0.35	0.42	0.59	0.78	0.80	0.72
Contract Type										
no specifications	0.01	0.01	0.01	0.03	0.00	0.00	0.01	0.00	0.00	0.00
indexation clause to the CPI	0.51	0.53	0.49	0.55	0.56	0.56	0.37	0.33	0.35	0.42
step-up leases	0.02	0.03	0.05	0.06	0.07	0.06	0.07	0.08	0.07	0.08
step-up leases indexed to the	0.07	0.02	0.04	0.02	0.03	0.03	0.03	0.03	0.05	0.01
free adaptation	0.09	0.10	0.14	0.11	0.13	0.18	0.34	0.46	0.50	0.39
leases with no adaptation	0.30	0.32	0.28	0.23	0.21	0.16	0.18	0.10	0.03	0.10
Dummy										
Collective	0.48	0.62	0.51	0.62	0.53	0.59	0.52	0.25	0.49	0.45
Subletting	0.59	0.69	0.59	0.66	0.53	0.54	0.42	0.13	0.10	0.07
Value Added	0.68	0.62	0.71	0.73	0.58	0.71	0.63	0.80	0.66	0.72
Owner Occupied	0.01	0.03	0.02	0.02	0.03	0.03	0.03	0.06	0.11	0.06
Rentfree Months	0.09	0.12	0.13	0.14	0.13	0.16	0.13	0.10	0.14	0.11
Continuous Variables										
Building Age	10.51	13.39	13.82	13.69	14.28	12.78	12.51	17.47	16.92	18.34
Building Area	14210.00	12690.00	11160.00	11280.00	13540.00	14120.00	12640.00	10990.00	9220.00	8502.00
Building Height	5.67	5.73	5.88	5.00	5.28	5.84	5.10	4.58	5.85	5.55
Extension Option Period	3.54	3.98	4.90	5.79	8.53	10.57	9.03	11.91	13.57	19.86
Contract Extension Option	0.64	1.13	0.76	1.04	1.27	2.17	2.39	6.62	5.54	10.92
Rental Area	828.80	813.70	665.40	644.30	656.60	768.00	1015.00	1186.00	871.90	770.70

Table 50: Mean Value of each Characteristic per Year

The mean values of each characteristic present only a fictitious lease contract. For instance, it is not possible for a dummy variable to take the value of 0.5. Another approach would be to define a standard German lease contract and to calculate an index based on its quantities. However, the definition of standard German lease contract is a difficult endeavour, as has been observed in other countries.[793]

6.1.2 Calculation of Hedonic Office Rent Indices

The indices are calculated based on the regression equations of the nationwide characteristic price index model (subsample) because this model imposes the least restrictive theoretical assumptions and best meets the regression analysis requirements.[794]

The following indices based on the nationwide characteristic price index model are computed for each city and denoted as:

- *Laspeyres Hedonic Office Rent Index (L-HORIX)*

  The 'Laspeyres Hedonic Office Rent Index' (L-HORIX) uses the mean value of each characteristic from the year 1997.[795] It answers the question of how much it would cost an office user in the current period to rent the same average office rental unit that he could have rented in the year 1997.

- *Paasche Hedonic Office Rent Index (P-HORIX)*

  The 'Paasche Hedonic Office Rent Index' (P-HORIX) uses the subsequent period as a reference point. Therefore, it uses the mean value of each characteristic per year.[796] It answers the question of how much it would have cost an office user in the base period to rent the same average office rental unit that he can rent in the current period.

- *IPD Rental Database Average Office Rent Index (RD-ORIX)*

  This office rent index is the arithmetic average of the leases provided by the IPD Rental Database and is included for comparative purposes only.

The L-HORIX and the P-HORIX could also be computed based on the characteristics' quantities of each year and city. This endeavour is not undertaken because it implies that, for each city, a different type of lease is assumed. Hence, an interregional comparison of office rents would be impossible.

---

[793] Cf. French, N. /Wiseman, G. (2003), p. 24, International Monetary Fund (2004), p. 161
[794] See Section 5.4.3.3
[795] See Table 50
[796] See Table 50

6.1.3 Selection of the Comparative Office Rent Indices - German Society of Property Researchers Office Rent Indices (GIF-ORIX)

In the introductory chapter, various office rent indices for the major German office markets were presented.[797] These office rent indices published by major real estate consultancies showed significant variances, making the choice for the comparative index difficult. Although these real estate consultancies want to increase the transparency of the real estate market, it has to be kept in mind that they are also profit oriented and often use office rent indices as a marketing tool. In other words, office rent indices published by real estate consultancies cannot be acquitted completely of subjectivity.[798]

The office rent indices published by the German Society of Property Researchers, however, are an exception and can be viewed as the most representative view of the German real estate market. First, the German Society of Property Researchers is a nonprofit organization. Second, their office rent indices represent the result of an annual meeting of major real estate consultancies organized by an independent presenter. Before the meeting takes place, all participants have to fill out a record sheet.[799] Here, they report the average and prime office rents according to the definitions of the German Society of Property Researchers. Using these record sheets, the participants compare and discuss their negotiated office leases of the past year, trying to find a consensus on the weighted average and prime office rent for the major office property markets. The discussion mainly covers the major office leases agreemnents (i.e. letta ble area greater than 500 sqm). As a matter of fact, the published figures do not necessarily represent a mathematical average.[800] Although the office rent indices published by the German Society of Property Researchers obviously miss a scientific and statistical construction methodology, they have a major advantage in that they represent a common market view on office rents. Therefore, the office rent indices of the German Society of Property Researchers, denoted as GIF-ORIX, is used by way of comparison. However, it does not imply that the aforementioned critism does not hold,[801] it rather implies that for the purpose of comparison it is the best available option.

---

[797] See Sections 1.1 and 4.2

[798] Cf. Dröge, F. (2005), p. 89-90

[799] See Appendix A.9

[800] See Appendix A.10 Interview with Günter Muncke

[801] See Section 1.1

6.2 Application

In this section the last objective of this thesis is tackled.[802] It uses the different office rent indices to measure the interregional and intertemporal changes in office rents. It also offers a brief insight into the various opportunities of hedonic office rent indices for real estate research and management.

Moreover, the major goal of any real estate price index from a statistical point of view is to provide "[...] the ratio of the market price of purchasing a reference real estate bundle in a base period, given the prices prevailing at that time, and at a latter 'current' period, given whatever changes in price had occurred in the interval."[803] This goal is achieved only by the Laspeyres and the Paasche hedonic office rent indices. Therefore, the application will mainly focus on these indices.

In an analysis of the interregional office rent change, the same type of lease and the same quantities of each lease characteristic have to be employed. Hence, the interregional rent change for each hedonic office rent index is presented separately.

The intertemporal rent change is analysed on a city level. Thereby, it allows for the observation of whether different types of lease contracts show a similar or different pattern over time. In addition, the volatility measured by the standard deviation of the annual percentage rental growth rate is calculated, and a correlation analysis is also undertaken. An overview of the calculated indices is given in the following table:[804]

	Hedonic Office Rent Indices (HORIX)		Rental Database (RD-ORIX)	German Society of Property Researchers Indices (GIF-ORIX)
Index Construction Methodology	Hedonic Method (Constant Quality Approach)		Unweighted Average	Expert Judgement
Index Formula	Laypeyres (L-HORIX)	Paasche (P-HORIX)	-	-
Data Base	IPD Rental Database		IPD Rental Database	Real Estate Research and Consulting Companies
Underlying Lease and Property Characteristics Contract	Average Characteristics of 1997	Average Characteristics of current period	Average Characteristics between 1997 to 2006	Average Characteristics of current period
Base Year	1997	1997	-	-
Berlin **(BER)**	*BER-L-HORIX*	*BER-P-HORIX*	*BER-RD-ORIX*	*BER-GIF-ORIX*
Düsseldorf **(DUS)**	*DUS-L-HORIX*	*DUS-P-HORIX*	*DUS-RD-ORIX*	*DUS-GIF-ORIX*
Frankfurt **(FRA)**	*FRA-L-HORIX*	*FRA-P-HORIX*	*FRA-RD-ORIX*	*FRA-GIF-ORIX*
Hamburg **(HAM)**	*HAM-L-HORIX*	*HAM-P-HORIX*	*HAM-RD-ORIX*	*HAM-GIF-ORIX*
Munich **(MUC)**	*MUC-L-HORIX*	*MUC-P-HORIX*	*MUC-RD-ORIX*	*MUC-GIF-ORIX*

Table 51: Overview of Office Rent Indices

---

[802] See Section

[803] Cf. Lum, S. K. (2004), p. 33

[804] In the following in order to increase the readability only the abbreviations of the various indices are used. See Table 51

6.2.1 Interregional Rent Change

6.2.1.1 Laspeyres Hedonic Office Rent Index (L-HORIX)

The L-HORIX shows that, apart from those in Berlin, office rents of a lease with the average characteristics from 1997 increased. Specifically, the office rents in Frankfurt and Düsseldorf developed quite well. For 1999, office rents in Frankfurt and Düsseldorf were always above the level of 1997.[805] The office rents in Hamburg and Munich moved sideways and in a more cyclical manner. Here, the recessionary stage of the German rental market, to which market participants often refer, can be observed. Office rents reached their peak in 2001, and it has been surpassed only in 2006. Furthermore, they moved closely together, which is evidenced by the results of the correlation analysis.[806] The index for Berlin confirms the opinion of many market participants that Berlin's office market plays a different role in the German office market. Here, office rents never reached the same level as in 1997. In addition, the univariate statistics provide further evidence that the Berlin office market is most volatile and, as a consequence, the most risky one.[807]

---

[805] See Figure 37 and Appendix A.11.1.1

[806] See Appendix A.11.1.2

[807] See Table 52

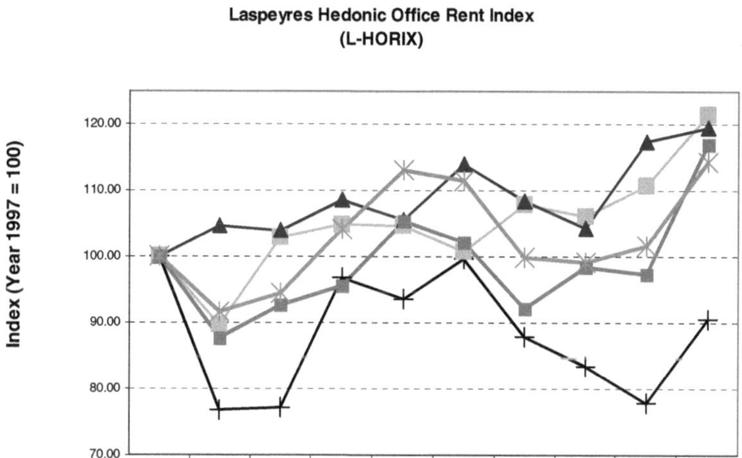

	1997	1998	1999	2000	2001	2002	2003	2004	2005	2006
Berlin	100.00	76.80	77.17	96.81	93.50	99.64	87.90	83.38	77.92	90.53
Düsseldorf	100.00	89.68	102.87	104.77	104.61	100.80	107.77	106.01	110.76	121.52
Frankfurt	100.00	104.61	103.86	108.48	105.58	113.99	108.42	104.24	117.34	119.53
Hamburg	100.00	87.68	92.66	95.62	105.40	102.13	92.07	98.33	97.23	116.99
Munich	100.00	91.61	94.49	104.08	112.95	111.40	99.82	99.17	101.53	114.30

Figure 37: Interregional Rent Change – Laspeyres Hedonic Office Rent Index (L-HORIX)

Univariate Statistics	Laspeyres Hedonic Office Rent Index (L-HORIX)				
	Berlin	Düsseldorf	Frankfurt	Hamburg	Munich
Mean of Annual Growth Rate	-0.16%	2.43%	2.15%	2.20%	1.77%
Standard Deviation	14.62%	7.51%	5.82%	10.14%	7.92%

Table 52: Univariate Statistics - Laspeyres Hedonic Office Rent Index (L-HORIX)

6.2.1.2 Paasche Hedonic Office Rent Index (P-HORIX)

The P-HORIX reveals some interesting results. The office rents in Frankfurt experienced an impressive increase up until 2002. A lease with the average characteristics' quantities of the year 2002 would have been approximately 18 percent more expensive than in the base period, 1997. After their peak in 2002, office rents in Frankfurt fell below the level of 1998. Office rents in Munich performed impressively and even outperformed the P-HORIX for Frankfurt in 2001. Similarly, the level of office rents fell constantly beginning in 2002, and only in 2006 was the base period's level reached again. In other words, a tenant would have paid for a lease with the average characteristics' quantities of 2006 the same price per square metre as in 1997. The level of office rents in Düsseldorf moved sideways, whereas the office rent index for Hamburg follows the office index of Munich.[808] The correlation analysis provides further evidence of this observation.[809] The office rents in Berlin fell drastically in 1998, reached their peak in 2002, and then fell again, at an increasing rate. The volatility measures give further support that the office market in Berlin is high risk, while the office market of Frankfurt has a low-risk profile.[810]

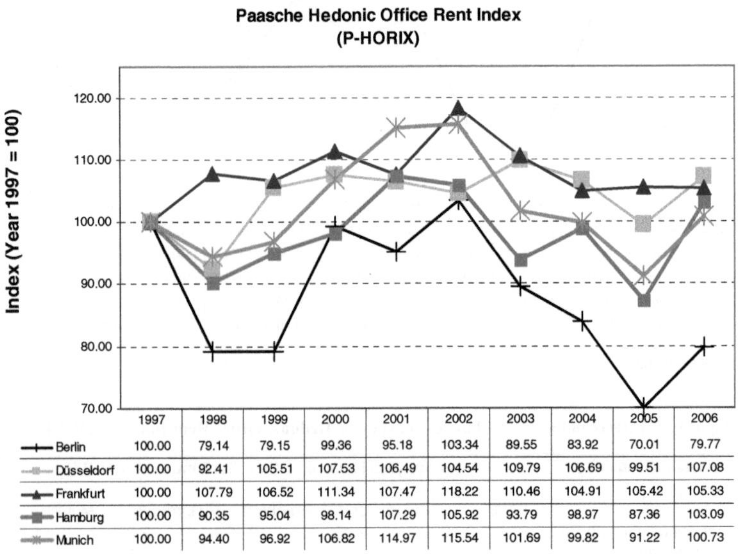

	1997	1998	1999	2000	2001	2002	2003	2004	2005	2006
Berlin	100.00	79.14	79.15	99.36	95.18	103.34	89.55	83.92	70.01	79.77
Düsseldorf	100.00	92.41	105.51	107.53	106.49	104.54	109.79	106.69	99.51	107.08
Frankfurt	100.00	107.79	106.52	111.34	107.47	118.22	110.46	104.91	105.42	105.33
Hamburg	100.00	90.35	95.04	98.14	107.29	105.92	93.79	98.97	87.36	103.09
Munich	100.00	94.40	96.92	106.82	114.97	115.54	101.69	99.82	91.22	100.73

Figure 38: Interregional Rent Change – Paasche Hedonic Office Rent Index (P-HORIX)

Univariate Statistics	Paasche Hedonic Office Rent Index (P-HORIX)				
	Berlin	Düsseldorf	Frankfurt	Hamburg	Munich
Mean of Annual Growth Rate	-1,47%	0,98%	0,72%	0,80%	0,38%
Standard Deviation	15,19%	7,02%	5,69%	10,23%	8,14%

Table 53: Univariate Statistics - Hedonic Office Rent Index (P-HORIX)

[808] See Figure 38 and Appendix A.11.2.1

[809] See Appendix A.11.2.2

[810] See Table 53

6.2.2 Intertemporal Rent Change / Comparison of Indices

In this section, the different indices are compared on a city level. As stated previously, each index can be thought of as a different type of lease contract. Therefore, this section identifies whether different types of lease contracts show a similar pattern over time. However, because the German Society of Property Researchers has published its figures only since the beginning of 2001, the analysis is limited, and further information is necessary for the interpretation of the graphs and the univariate and correlation analyses. In the following sections, some graphs show the intertemporal rent change based on the monthly rent per square metre. Here, the focus should be not on the absolute numbers, as they are not comparable, but rather on the upward or downward trends of the indices. In addition, because of the short time series, the univariate and correlation analyses should be treated with caution.

Finally, it is important to note that the comparison does not intend to make a judgment of accuracy of the various indices. Rather, it intends to demonstrate how different index methodologies and different lease contracts might lead to different results.

6.2.2.1 Berlin

In the following figures, the hedonic office rent indices for Berlin (*BER-L-HORIX* and *BER-P-HORIX*) are presented. Moreover, office rents published by the German Society of Property Researchers (*BER-GIF-ORIX*) and the rental database average (*BER-RD-ORIX*) are depicted.[811] With the exception of the office rents in 2001 published by the German Society of Property Researchers, all indices move closely together and head for the same direction. The results of the correlation analysis further underpin this observation.[812] Beginning in 1998, office rents increased in Berlin and reached their peak in 2002. Afterward, they declined constantly, and the rental market only slowly recovered in 2006.

---

[811] See Figure 39 and Appendix A.12.1.1

[812] See Appendix A.12.1.2

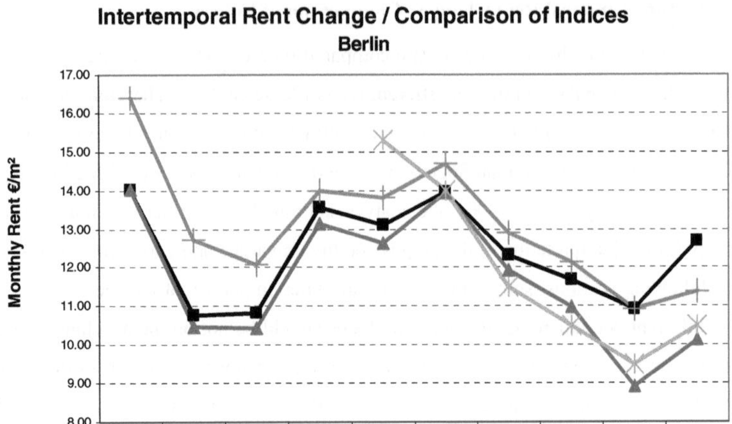

	1997	1998	1999	2000	2001	2002	2003	2004	2005	2006
L-HORIX	14.02	10.77	10.82	13.57	13.11	13.97	12.32	11.69	10.92	12.69
P-HORIX	14.02	10.47	10.43	13.13	12.62	13.92	11.93	10.97	8.92	10.14
RD-ORIX	16.40	12.73	12.08	13.98	13.81	14.68	12.90	12.14	10.93	11.39
GIF-ORX					15.30	14.00	11.50	10.50	9.50	10.50

Figure 39: Comparison of Indices - Monthly Rent EUR/sqm- Berlin

The univariate statistics reveal that the *BER-GIF-ORIX* shows the most negative picture of Berlin. For 2001 and 2006, the mean annual growth was -6.81 percent, with a volatility of 10.44 percent. *BER-L-HORIX* presents the most optimistic picture. It measures a decrease of only 0.69 percent and a volatility of 10.21percent.[813]

	Mean Annual Rental Growth Rate (1997 to 2006)	Standard Deviation (1997 to 2006)	Mean Annual Rental Growth Rate (2001 to 2006)	Standard Deviation (2001 to 2006)
L-HORIX	-0.16%	14.62%	-0.69%	10.21%
P-HORIX	-1.47%	15.19%	-2.98%	12.04%
RD-ORIX	-3.38%	11.22%	-3.12%	7.47%
GIF-ORIX			-6.81%	10.44%

Table 54: Univariate Statistics of Indices – Berlin

Figure 40 also presents the importance of controlling for lease characteristics and its implications for benchmarking in portfolio management. For instance, in 2006, the *BER-L-HORIX* takes a value of 90.53 and the *BER-P-HORIX* a value of 79.77. That implies that a 1997 lease with the average quantities declined by approximately 10 percent in comparison with the base period, and a 2006 lease with the average quantities declined by approximately 20 percent in comparison with the base period.

[813] See Table 54

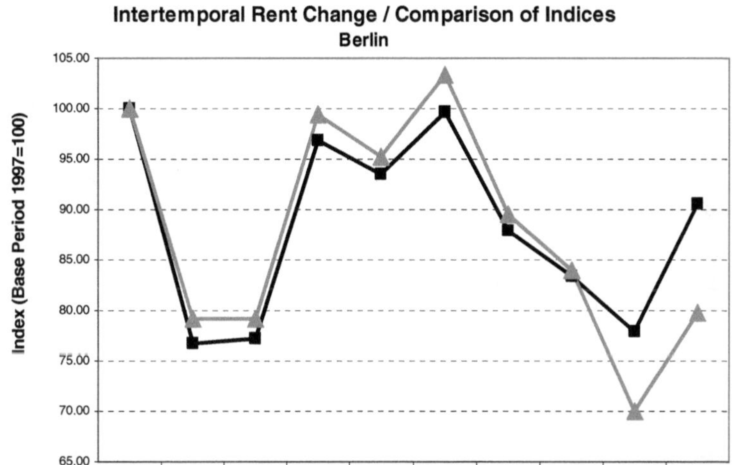

	1997	1998	1999	2000	2001	2002	2003	2004	2005	2006
L-HORIX	100.00	76.80	77.17	96.81	93.50	99.64	87.90	83.38	77.92	90.53
P-HORIX	100.00	79.14	79.15	99.36	95.18	103.34	89.55	83.92	70.01	79.77

Figure 40: Comparison of Indices – Index – Berlin

6.2.2.2 Düsseldorf

Depending on the choice of the underlying lease contract, one gets a different picture of the office rental market in Düsseldorf. The *DUS-L-HORIX* and *DUS-RD-ORIX* move closely together, and both reach a record high in 2006. The *DUS-GIF-ORIX* decreases almost constantly after 2001 and only stabilizes in 2005. The *DUS-P-HORIX* shows a development similar to the *DUS-L-HORIX* up to 2004. Here, the indices diverge and follow different directions. While the *DUS-P-HORIX* continues to fall, the *DUS-L-HORIX* continues its positive development.[814] The correlation analysis provides further indication of the varying development of office rents.[815]

[814] See Figure 41 and Appendix A.12.2.1

[815] See Appendix A.12.2.2

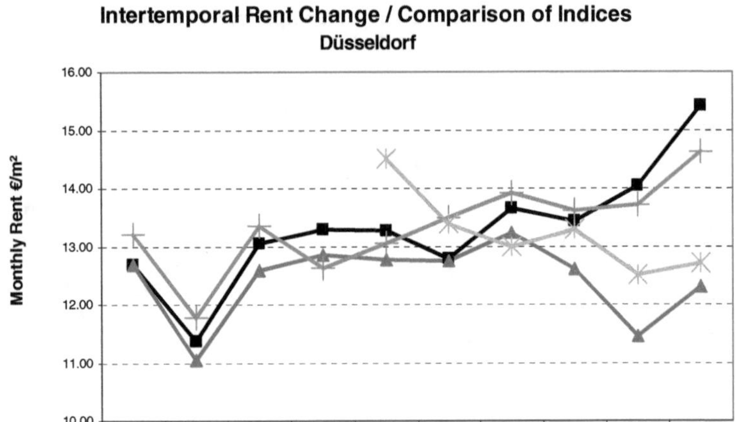

	1997	1998	1999	2000	2001	2002	2003	2004	2005	2006
L-HORIX	12.68	11.37	13.04	13.28	13.26	12.78	13.66	13.44	14.04	15.41
P-HORIX	12.68	11.06	12.58	12.85	12.77	12.74	13.23	12.61	11.46	12.31
RD-ORIX	13.21	11.78	13.36	12.62	13.05	13.49	13.92	13.62	13.71	14.62
GIF-ORX					14.50	13.40	13.00	13.30	12.50	12.70

Figure 41: Comparison of Indices - Monthly Rent EUR/sqm - Düsseldorf

The univariate analysis reports a similar volatility for all four indices between 2001 and 2006. However, regarding the average rental growth rates, the indices are discordant. While the *DUS-L-HORIX* and *DUS-RD-ORIX* show a positive rental growth rate (approximately 2.5 percent), the *DUS-P-HORIX* reports stagnation and the *DUS-GIF-ORIX* a decrease of 2.5 percent.[816]

	Mean Annual Rental Growth Rate (1997 to 2006)	Standard Deviation (1997 to 2006)	Mean Annual Rental Growth Rate (2001 to 2006)	Standard Deviation (2001 to 2006)
L-HORIX	2.43%	7.51%	2.61%	5.24%
P-HORIX	0.98%	7.02%	0.05%	5.30%
RD-ORIX	1.36%	6.99%	2.52%	2.98%
GIF-ORIX			-2.54%	4.43%

Table 55: Univariate Statistics of Indices – Düsseldorf

In Figure 42, *DUS-L-HORIX* and *DUS-P-HORIX* index numbers are compared. The *DUS-L-HORIX* takes the value of 110.76 in the year 2005, and the *DUS-P-HORIX* takes a value of 99.51. In other words, a 2005 lease with the average characteristics has approximately the same value as in 1997. A lease with the average characteristics from 1997, however, is worth 10 percent more in 2005. In addition, the figure strongly indi-

816 See Table 55

cates that in 2004 market participants started to value office lease characteristics differently. These observations reinforce the necessity for portfolio managers to control for lease characteristics before they analyse their portfolio.

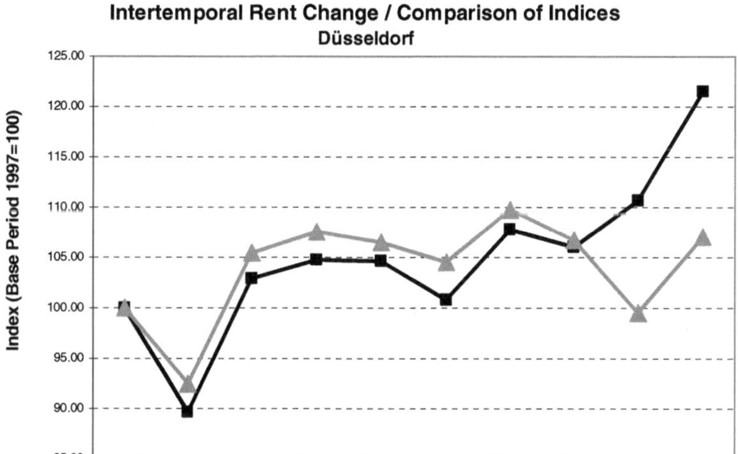

	1997	1998	1999	2000	2001	2002	2003	2004	2005	2006
L-HORIX	100.00	89.68	102.87	104.77	104.61	100.80	107.77	106.01	110.76	121.52
P-HORIX	100.00	92.41	105.51	107.53	106.49	104.54	109.79	106.69	99.51	107.08

Figure 42: Comparison of Indices – Index – Düsseldorf

6.2.2.3 Frankfurt

The *FRA-GIF-ORIX* reports a decrease in office rents.[817] In 2001, the *FRA-GIF-ORIX* measures 20.50 EUR/sqm per month, which decreases to 15.00 EUR/sqm in 2005. Specifically, the negative annual growth rates for 2002 and 2004 are more than 10 percent. From the *FRA-L-HORIX* and *FRA-P-HORIX,* the office rental market in Frankfurt cannot be considered bearish, as it can from the *FRA-GIF-ORIX.* Here, the annual growth rates are much lower. The *FRA-L-HORIX* even shows an office rent increase in 2004. The correlation analysis supports this opposite development of office rents.[818]

[817] See Figure 43 and Appendix A.12.3.1

[818] See Appendix A.12.3.2

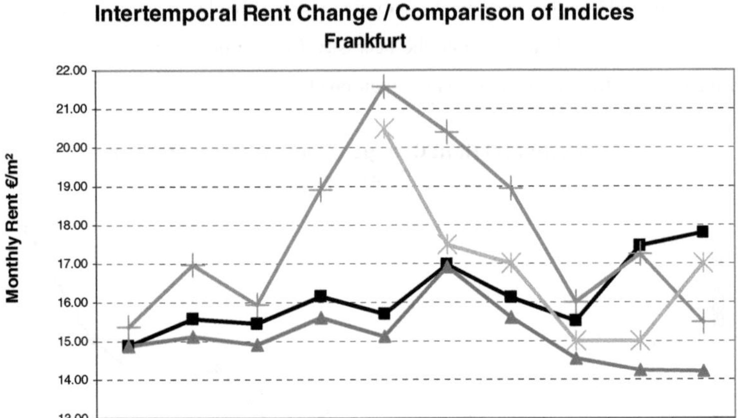

	1997	1998	1999	2000	2001	2002	2003	2004	2005	2006
L-HORIX	14.88	15.56	15.45	16.14	15.71	16.96	16.13	15.51	17.46	17.78
P-HORIX	14.88	15.13	14.90	15.61	15.12	16.90	15.62	14.55	14.25	14.21
RD-ORIX	15.37	16.96	15.94	18.91	21.57	20.39	18.95	16.00	17.24	15.48
GIF-ORX					20.50	17.50	17.00	15.00	15.00	17.00

Figure 43: Comparison of Indices - Monthly Rent EUR/sqm - Frankfurt

The univariate statistics of the various office rent indices indicate that the *FRA-RD-ORIX* is the most volatile (11.30%), followed by the *FRA-GIF-ORIX* (11.04%). All other office rent indices indicate volatilities below 7.08 percent for the time span 2001 to 2006.[819] In addition, the mean annual growth rates are, with the exception of the *FRA-L-HORIX*, negative. In other words, the general recession of office rents has not affected leases with the average characteristics from 1997.

	Mean Annual Rental Growth Rate (1997 to 2006)	Standard Deviation (1997 to 2006)	Mean Annual Rental Growth Rate (2001 to 2006)	Standard Deviation (2001 to 2006)
L-HORIX	2.15%	5.82%	1.83%	7.08%
P-HORIX	0.72%	5.69%	-0.78%	5.95%
RD-ORIX	0.72%	12.09%	-2.75%	11.30%
GIF-ORIX			-3.18%	11.04%

Table 56: Univariate Statistics of Indices – Frankfurt

The development of the various office rent indices is also depicted in Figure 44. The level of office rents for a lease with the average characteristics of 1997 increased by approximately 19.5 percent from the year 1997 to 2006 *(FRA-L-HORIX)*, whereas the level of office rents for a lease with the average characteristics of 2006 grew by only 5.3

---

[819] See Table 56

percent *(FRA-P-HORIX)*. Furthermore, the graph shows that both indices move closely together until 2004; then they diverge from the pattern. Obviously, the market participants attributed leases with the average characteristics from 1997 a much higher value than current leases with average characteristics.

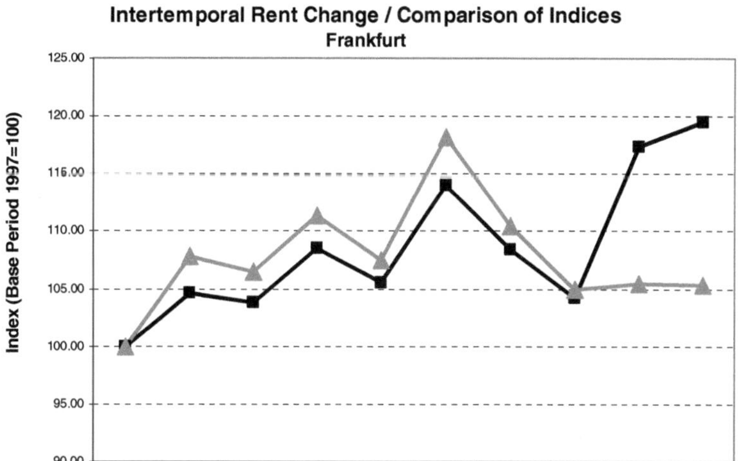

	1997	1998	1999	2000	2001	2002	2003	2004	2005	2006
L-HORIX	100.00	104.61	103.86	108.48	105.58	113.99	108.42	104.24	117.34	119.53
P-HORIX	100.00	107.79	106.52	111.34	107.47	118.22	110.46	104.91	105.42	105.33

Figure 44: Comparison of Indices – Index – Frankfurt

6.2.2.4 Hamburg

The *HAM-GIF-ORIX* reports a relatively stable development of office rents in Hamburg. Between 2001 and 2006, the level of office rents lies between 12.00 EUR/sqm per month (in 2004) and 13.80 EUR/sqm per month (in 2001). The other indices report a similar stability of office rents. With the exception of 2006, the rental spreads for the other indices are approximately 2.50 EUR/sqm.[820] A matter of particular interest is the development of the annual rental growth rates for the years 2004 and 2005.[821] Although the *HAM-GIF-ORIX* reports a rent decrease, all other indices show a rent increase in 2004. In 2005, the opposite happens. Here, the *HAM-GIF-ORIX* reports a rent increase; all other indices indicate a rent decrease. Otherwise, all indices move in the same direc-

[820] See Figure 45

[821] See Appendix A.12.4.1

tion but not with the same amplitude. The correlation analysis partly supports this observation.[822]

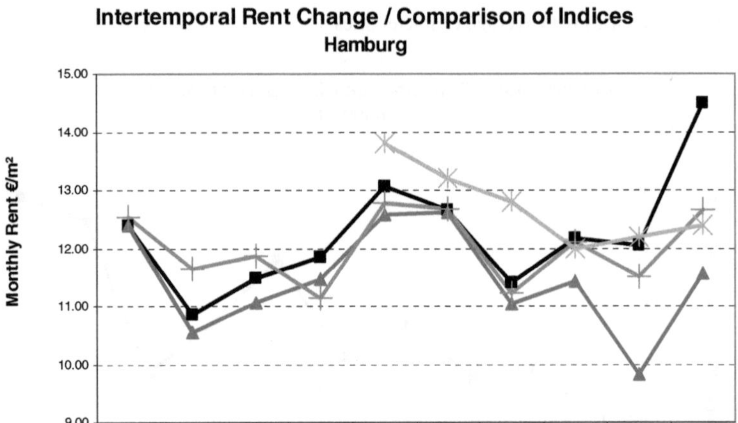

	1997	1998	1999	2000	2001	2002	2003	2004	2005	2006
L-HORIX	12.38	10.86	11.48	11.84	13.05	12.65	11.40	12.18	12.04	14.49
P-HORIX	12.38	10.56	11.07	11.46	12.57	12.61	11.04	11.43	9.83	11.58
RD-ORIX	12.54	11.65	11.87	11.15	12.77	12.67	11.23	12.11	11.51	12.66
GIF-ORX					13.80	13.20	12.80	12.00	12.20	12.40

Figure 45: Comparison of Indices - Monthly Rent EUR/sqm - Hamburg

However, the univariate analysis challenges the contention of the stability of Hamburg's office market. The *HAM-GIF-ORIX* reports a volatility of 3.58 percent, whereas all other office rent indices measure volatilities of more than 9.5 percent. Further discrepancies exist with respect to the mean rental growth rate between 2001 and 2006. Here, the *HAM-GIF-ORIX* states a negative growth rate of 2.06, whereas all other indices report positive growth rates.[823]

	Mean Annual Rental Growth Rate (1997 to 2006)	Standard Deviation (1997 to 2006)	Mean Annual Rental Growth Rate (2001 to 2006)	Standard Deviation (2001 to 2006)
L-HORIX	2.20%	10.14%	3.88%	10.78%
P-HORIX	0.80%	10.23%	1.40%	11.83%
RD-ORIX	0.44%	8.79%	2.55%	9.89%
GIF-ORIX			-2.06%	3.58%

Table 57: Univariate Statistics of Indices – Hamburg

[822] See Appendix A.12.4.2

[823] See Table 57

A look at the development of the office rent indices normalized for the year 1997 demonstrates that, up to 2004, all indices move closely together. However, from 2005 they diverge unexpectedly. For instance, for 2005 the *HAM-L-HORIX* takes the value 97.23, indicating a deflation of office rents for leases with the average characteristics from 1997. In contrast, the *HAM-P-HORIX* takes the value of 87.36. In other words, the rental value of a lease with the average characteristics of the year 2005 decreased by more than 12%, in comparison with the rental value of a lease with the average characteristics of the year 1997, which decreased by approximately 2.8 percent. A similar observation also has been made for Frankfurt's office market. [824]

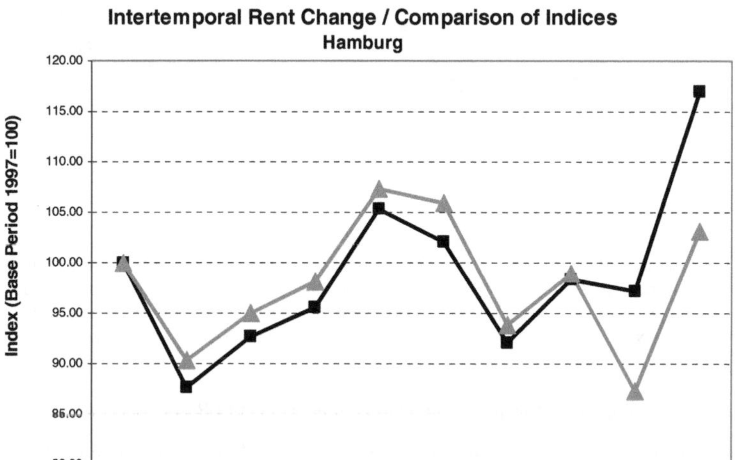

	1997	1998	1999	2000	2001	2002	2003	2004	2005	2006
L-HORIX	100.00	87.68	92.66	95.62	105.40	102.13	92.07	98.33	97.23	116.99
P-HORIX	100.00	90.35	95.04	98.14	107.29	105.92	93.79	98.97	87.36	103.09

Figure 46: Comparison of Indices – Index – Hamburg

6.2.2.5 *Munich*

The German Society of Property Researchers *(MUC-GIF-ORIX)* reports the highest office rent of 17.3 EUR/sqm per month in 2002 and the lowest of 13.2 EUR/sqm per month in 2004. In the ensuing years, the level of office rents increased again.[825] Although not in absolute number, all other indices follow the same pattern. The correlation

[824] See Figure 46

[825] See Figure 47 and Appendix A.12.5.1

analysis provides further evidence for this contention.[826] However, one striking exception exists. In 2005, the *MUC-P-HORIX* decouples itself from the other indices. Although all other indices report a rental increase, the *MUC-P-HORIX* reports a rental decrease.

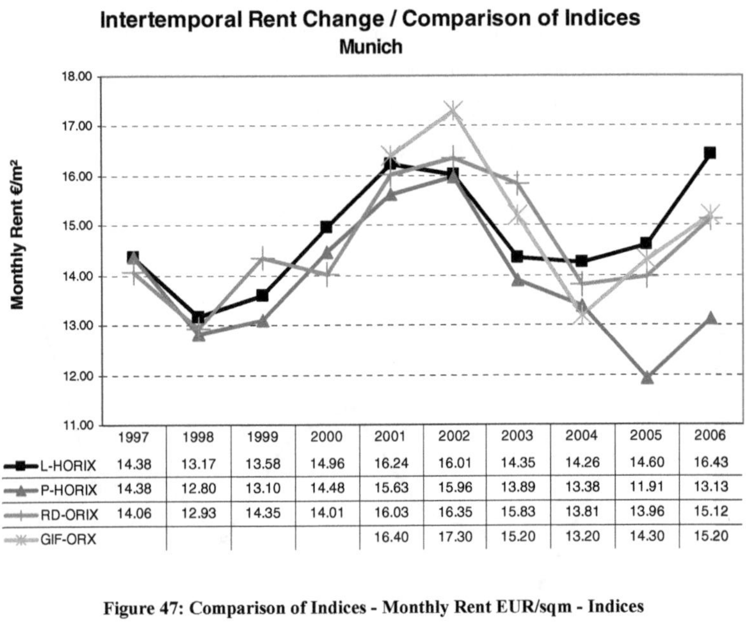

	1997	1998	1999	2000	2001	2002	2003	2004	2005	2006
L-HORIX	14.38	13.17	13.58	14.96	16.24	16.01	14.35	14.26	14.60	16.43
P-HORIX	14.38	12.80	13.10	14.48	15.63	15.96	13.89	13.38	11.91	13.13
RD-ORIX	14.06	12.93	14.35	14.01	16.03	16.35	15.83	13.81	13.96	15.12
GIF-ORX					16.40	17.30	15.20	13.20	14.30	15.20

Figure 47: Comparison of Indices - Monthly Rent EUR/sqm - Indices

The univariate analysis of the indices is inconclusive. Although the volatility of all indices is between 7.92 and 10.66 percent, significantly different annual rental growth rates are reported. Whereas the *MUC-L-HORIX* and *MUC-RD-ORIX* measure a positive growth rate of between 1.64 and 1.84 percent, the *MUC-P-HORIX* and *MUC-GIF-ORIX* report a negative growth rate for the period between 2001 and 2006.[827]

	Mean Annual Rental Growth Rate (1997 to 2006)	Standard Deviation (1997 to 2006)	Mean Annual Rental Growth Rate (2001 to 2006)	Standard Deviation (2001 to 2006)
L-HORIX	1.77%	7.92%	1.84%	7.92%
P-HORIX	0.38%	8.14%	-0.65%	8.14%
RD-ORIX	1.16%	8.88%	1.64%	8.88%
GIF-ORIX			-1.04%	10.66%

Table 58: Univariate Statistics of Indices – Munich

[826] See Appendix A.12.5.2

[827] See Table 58

In 2004, the development of the various office rent indices changes, as it did in Hamburg's and Frankfurt's office markets. Although the *MUC-P-HORIX* continues to decline, all other indices indicate a rental increase. Furthermore, the *MUC-L-HORIX* takes a value of 101.53 in the year 2005, meaning that office rents for leases with the average characteristics from 1997 experienced only a mild increase of less than 2 percent in comparison with the base period. In contrast, the *MUC-P-HORIX* takes a value of 91.22.[828] In other words, office rents for leases with the average characteristics from 2005 decreased by approximately 9 percent. Again this simple example shows the importance of constant quality rent indices.

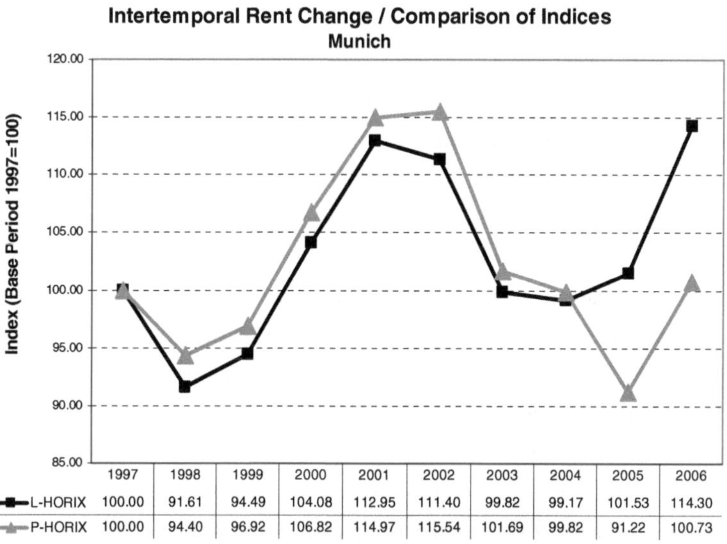

	1997	1998	1999	2000	2001	2002	2003	2004	2005	2006
L-HORIX	100.00	91.61	94.49	104.08	112.95	111.40	99.82	99.17	101.53	114.30
P-HORIX	100.00	94.40	96.92	106.82	114.97	115.54	101.69	99.82	91.22	100.73

Figure 48: Comparison of Indices – Index – Munich

[828] See Figure 48

6.2.3 Fields of Application for Real Estate Practitioners

At the beginning of this thesis, the descriptive and operational fields of application for real estate rent indices have been presented.[829] Moreover, the application of the L-HORIX and P-HORIX and their comparison with the GIF-ORIX reveal that, in the majority of cases, the L-HORIX and P-HORIX show a different development of the office rental market than the GIF-ORIX. They measure a different average rental growth in the rental markets and risk in terms of volatility.[830] These observations lead to the question of which implications can be deduced for real estate practitioners and which practical use for real estate practitioners is obtained by the application of L-HORIX and P-HORIX.

6.2.3.1 Descriptive Field of Application

Regarding the descriptive field of application, real estate indices might serve as market indicator, economic indicator and forecasting tool. As the quality of the underlying lease contracts is incorporated, the HORIX are perfectly suited as market indicator. In comparison to the current published office rents, which indicate only a trend in the real estate market, these indices actually track rental prices. For instance, it is possible to track office rental prices for leases with different qualities. In section 6.2.2, different rent indices were compared. Each index measures the development of office rents of a different lease agreement. Although these indices represent hypothetical lease contracts, they clearly show that the office rental markets in Germany did not behave similarly for all leases. This observation cannot be made by the office rent indices published at present.[831] The major advantage, however, is that the interregional comparison of leases with the same quality can be performed. In other words, real estate practitioners gain consistency and flexibility in their analysis of the office rental market.

The HORIX are also useful as economic indicator. For instance, with the application of Laspeyres index formula it is possible to analyse whether office rents of a standard lease contract increased or decreased in the past. In other words, the developed hedonic office rent indices can be interpreted as sign of inflation or deflation for office leases. Again,

[829] See Section 1.4
[830] See Section 6.2.1 and 6.2.2
[831] See Section 1.1

this task cannot be performed with the published office rents, as the quality of the underlying lease contracts is unknown.

As forecasting tool, the use of the HORIX is limited. Here, it would rely on the restrictive assumption that the influence of the office rent determinants that have been observed in the past, also apply for the future. From the hedonic analysis, however, it has become obvious that the impact of office rent determinants is not constant and changes over time.[832]

6.2.3.2 Operational Field of Application

In the operational field of application, real estate indices are useful as benchmarking instrument and have a large target audience in real estate.

The HORIX help real estate developers to obtain a more precise estimation of office rents for their development calculation, as they can calculate an index that reflects the past development of the office rental market for a similiar office building they intend to construct. However, it must be pointed out that due to the small number of building characteristics incorporated in the HORIX, the usefullness for real estate developers is limited.

For real estate investors the HORIX are of great value. For instance, an investors could benchmark the lease agreements of the office property that they intend to buy with the market for lease agreements with same quality. Thereby, it is possible to analyze whether their office property is under- or overrented. In addition, real estate investors can calculate different scenarios analyzing whether different lease agreements would have resulted in a higher cash flow of the office property at hand. This scenario analysis also permits to be analysed the quality and the performance of the current asset management.

The aforementioned advantages of the HORIX also apply for tenants as well as for real estate valuers and portfolio managers.

For portfolio managers the HORIX allow further quantitative analysis and contributes to the further development of the construction of efficient lease portfolio and risk man-

---

[832] See Section 5.4.3.3

agement in real estate leasing practice - an overlooked area of real estate research.[833] The observation that different lease agreements performed differently in terms of rental growth and risk unfolds the possibilities in terms of modern portfolio theory (MPT). In MPT, investors are assumed to construct their portfolios by bringing together assets that will provide an acceptable level of return whilst diversifying some of the risks. Carrying forward this approach on income-producing assets such as office properties, lease agreements can be interpreted as assets because they comprise risk and return of the property (in the form of rent).[834] Therefore, the HORIX permit portfolio managers to construct an efficient frontier[835] in terms of an efficient lease portfolio and to benchmark the lease portfolio.

In addition, portfolio managers need to forecast the expected returns, volatility and correlations for all assets prior to the investment period. Expectations are based on a number of different information sources, such as historical data, current market price, market sentiment and personal intuition.[836] As the HORIX showed different developments of office rent in German metropolitan areas in terms of growth rates and volatility, portfolio managers might obtain an different view of the office property and thereby form different expectations that, in return, will affect their investment decisions.

---

[833] Cf. Wang, J. (2005), p. 13

[834] Cf. Pretorius, F., et al. (2003), p. 3

[835] Each possible asset combination can be plotted in risk-term space, and the collection of all such possible portfolios defines a region in space. The line along the upper edge of this region is known as efficient frontier of efficient set. Cf. Brueggeman, W. B. /Fisher, J. D. (2007), p. 662, Ross, S. A., et al. (2002), p. 255

[836] Cf. French, N. (2001), p. 401-403

6.3 Evaluation and Comparison with German Society of Property Researchers Office Rent Indices

It is not possible to evaluate and compare the office rent indices to determine which index represents the true market development because a representative benchmark does not exist. Instead, the evaluation and comparison are undertaken by defining a set of requirements that an index must meet to be accepted by market participants. After these evaluation criteria have been explained, they are used to compare and evaluate the hedonic office rent indices *(L-HORIX and P-HORIX)* on the one hand and the German Society of Property Researchers office rent index *(GIF-ORIX)* on the other.

6.3.1 Evaluation Criteria

Thomas (1997) identifies six criteria that an index must meet to achieve market acceptance:[837]

- Quality and Quantity of Input Data

The reliability of an index is, to a large degree, dependent on the quality and quantity of the input data.[838] *Hargity /Yu (1993)* and *Bourassa, et al. (2006)* reason that the quality and quantity of the input data are appropriate for use in an index construction if the data are relevant and provide adequate coverage, if the sample size of data is statistically adequate, and if the data are objective and free from bias.[839]

- Index Construction Methodology

The index construction methodology should account for the fact that office properties and office leases are heterogeneous. This requirement can be met in two possible ways: either the index is based on a homogeneous sample of office leases, meaning all office leases have the same quality, or the index accommodates the heterogeneity of office leases with a statistical procedure.[840]

---

[837] Cf. Thomas, M. (1997), p. 44-46
[838] Cf. Ibid.p. 44
[839] Cf. Bourassa, S. C., et al. (2006), p. 86-87, Hargity, S. E. /Yu, S.-M. (1993), p. 227-228
[840] Cf. Maurer, R. /Sebastian, S. (2000), p. 1, Thomas, M. (1997), p. 44, Beyerle, T. (2006a), p. 4

- Service Concept

A reliable service concept is necessary for data collection and index calculation.[841] This requirement is closely related to the following evaluation criteria. It claims that the procedure for data collection and for index calculation is easily understandable, transparent, reliable, and comprehensible.

- Simplicity

The requirement of simplicity is twofold. On the one hand, the mathematical construction of the index has to be easy to understand. On the other hand, the ascertainment of the input has to be simple.[842]

- Transparency

Transparency implies that the input data and the index formula are publicly available. However, as has been highlighted throughout this thesis, German data protection laws, as well as the secretive handling of information among German market participants, prevent the fulfillment of this requirement.[843]

- Comprehensibility

Comprehensibility implies theoretical and practical comprehensibility. Theoretical comprehensibility implies that the index construction is understandable for a third party under the prerequisite that the requirements 'simplicity' and 'transparency' are met. Practical comprehensibility implies that a third party can actually rebuild the index. However, as mentioned, German data protection laws and the secretive handling of information among German market participants prevent the fulfillment of practical comprehensibility.[844]

It must be kept in mind that it is possible for these requirements to be mutually exclusive sometimes. For instance, a complex statistical and mathematical index construction methodology is often chosen to account for the heterogeneity of office leases. Although the requirement of an appropriate index construction methodology is met, the choice is at odds with the requirements of 'simplicity' and 'transparency.' In addition, the relative

---

[841] Cf. Thomas, M. (1997), p. 44

[842] Cf. Bourassa, S. C., et al. (2006), p. 87, Thomas, M. (1997), p. 44-45, Geßner, S. (1997), p. 4

[843] See Sections 3.4 and 4.2.2

[844] Cf. Thomas, M. (1997), p. 45-46

importance of the individual criteria depends to a large extent on the purpose for which the index is constructed.[845]

6.3.2 Evaluation and Comparison

In this section, the evaluation criteria set the basis for the comparison between the developed hedonic office rent indices *(HORIX)* and the German Society of Property Researchers index *(GIF-ORIX)*. A distinction between the various hedonic office rent indices is not undertaken because they are based on the same regression parameters and differ only in their index formula (weighting procedure of characteristics).[846]

6.3.2.1 Quality and Quantity of Input Data

Both types of indices, namely, the HORIX, which are based on leases of the IPD Rental Database, and the GIF-ORIX, which is based on leases of real estate consultants and agents, use data with adequate market coverage, and the sample sizes are statistically adequate. However, some differences concerning the requirements that the data be objective and free from bias exist. As described, the IPD Rental Database primarily retrieves its leases directly from institutional owners' databases, which the owners use for accounting and for drawing financial reports.[847] Therefore, it can be concluded that the data are fairly objective and free from bias. In contrast, the figures published by the GIF-ORIX represent the result of a consensus meeting; therefore, the objectivity of the data cannot be ascertained.

6.3.2.2 Index Construction Methodology

In comparison to the GIF-ORIX, the HORIX clearly meet the requirements of an appropriate index construction methodology. The HORIX account for the heterogeneity of office leases. Some criticism may arise because the hedonic office rent indices do not control for all factors that determine the heterogeneity of office leases. Specifically, some spatial and tenant quality characteristics are not included. However, the comparative index, namely, GIF-ORIX, does not explicitly account for any characteristics. In fact, the GIF-ORIX represents only the nominal office rent, without any adjustments for

---

845 Cf. Fenwick, D. (2005), p. 368-370

846 See Section 6.1.1

847 See Section 5.1

incentives.[848] In other words, users of the HORIX have control over some lease characteristics and therefore can use them for benchmarking purposes in portfolio management and valuation. Users of the GIF-ORIX have no control and consequently can use this index only to determine a trend in the rental market.

6.3.2.3 Service Concept

The service concept of the IPD Rental Database for data collection is reliable. First, it retrieves primary leases from the investor owners' databases and, second, the data undergo some quality checks before being stored in the rental database. Because the procedure is standardized and described in detail, a high degree of reliability and transparency is assumed. In comparison with the leases of the German Society of Property Researchers, no certain conclusions can be made. However, all consensus meetings are based on the prefilled record sheet, and, because all participants agree unanimously on the result, the outcome is highly representative. In addition, an independent party presents the consensus meeting.[849] Nevertheless, it cannot be denied that, during the meeting, some participants have more influence on the outcome than others.

The service concept of index construction is, in the case of the HORIX, transparent, as it has been described in detail; however, it is not easy to understand. In fact, previous statistical knowledge is necessary to understand the multiple imputation method and the regression analysis. The service concept of the GIF-ORIX is easy to understand, as it is the result of a consensus meeting of the major real estate agents in the respective market. It is not transparent because no details about the consensus meetings are publicly available.[850]

6.3.2.4 Simplicity

The index calculation of the GIF-ORIX is simpler than the HORIX, as the GIF-ORIX only represents the absolute index number indicating the average rent per month per square meter that an office user has to pay in a city. The index calculation of the HORIX is more complex in three ways. First, data are checked and transformed, and missing data are filled in by the multiple imputation method. Second, a regression analysis is performed. Third, depending on which index formula is chosen, the quanti-

---

[848] See Appendix A.9 and A.10 Interview with Günter Muncke

[849] See Appendix A.10 Interview with Günter Muncke

[850] See Appendix A.10 Interview with Günter Muncke

ties of the independent variables have to be determined, and only then is the index number computed.

However, two issues should be taken in consideration. On the one hand, the calculation of a relative index number (e.g., Laspeyres or Paasche) is more complicated per se than that of an absolute index number. On the other hand, the absolute index number is appropriate only in the case of homogeneous goods.[851] In addition, it is much too simplistic to track prices of office leases.

6.3.2.5 Transparency

The HORIX are more transparent than the GIF-ORIX. Although the original input data and detailed information of each separate lease are not available for either type of index, in this thesis the input data are described in detail, and an index user gains a deep insight into many lease characteristics on an aggregated level. Moreover, the parameter estimates and inserted quantities are listed in detail. Therefore, it is possible for a third party to recalculate the indices or to compute an individual index using different quantities.

6.3.2.6 Comprehensibility

The GIF-ORIX is easy to comprehend because it demands no previous knowledge of statistics and economics. Although some statistical knowledge is advantageous for comprehending the hedonic office rent indices, previous statistical knowledge is necessary only to the extent that a third party wants to understand the index. For the basic index construction methodology, only common sense is necessary, but for an in-depth understanding of the regression analysis and multiple imputation procedure, sound statistical and economic knowledge is a prerequisite.

It is clear that the GIF-ORIX does not meet the requirement for practical comprehensibility at all. The HORIX meet them to a certain degree, as the regression parameter, the used quantities, and the index formula are presented.

---

[851] Cf. Brachinger, H. W. (2003), p. 1

6.4 Implications for Real Estate Practitioners

At first glance, the various applications of the HORIX in terms of interregional and intertemporal rent changes may cause more confusion than clarity. The observation that the P-HORIX and L-HORIX of each city do not always move in the same direction with the same amplitude does not indicate that the indices are incorrectly specified or developed. On the contrary, this observation reinforces the necessity to control for the quality of leases, as each index can be interpreted as a different type of lease.

Consequently, all real estate practitioners who attempt to benchmark a specific office lease have to examine the type of office lease and the quality of the office lease they have at hand. In addition, real estate researchers who want to describe the development of the regional office rental market have to specify which type of office lease they are referring to.

The fact that the L-HORIX and P-HORIX have moved apart since 2004 raises the question of which index formulae, Laspeyres or Paasche, should be used as a market indicator. From a practical and a user point of view, the Laspeyres should be favoured because of its simpler calculation. Moreover, because the characteristics (weights) of the office rent determinants are fixed, their interpretation is easier for market participants with no additional knowledge of index numbers. As the Paasche index involves the reweighing of the office rent determinants for each year, its interpretation becomes more difficult. Therefore, users should instead analyze whether the average of the lease characteristics of the base period (here, 1997) still represents the average of the current period. If not, then the complete index should be calculated with a new weighted scheme.

From the evaluation and comparison with the GIF-ORIX, it should not be concluded that indices have to be disregarded or replaced by the HORIX. Nevertheless, it becomes evident that the developed HORIX are useful in many aspects for real estate practitioners. For instance, using regression coefficients, portfolio managers and valuers can compute their own index for benchmarking purposes. The HORIX also provide for the analysis of how different lease and property characteristics are valued across the various time periods.

6.5 Chapter Summary

This chapter tackles the last objectives of this thesis by developing and applying different hedonic office rent indices for German metropolitan areas (Objective III & IV).[852] The key findings are as follows:

- Based upon the findings of chapter five, the regression parameters of the nationwide character price index model are used to develop hedonic office rent indices (HORIX). This choice allowed for the construction of various hedonic indices with different index formulae, based on different lease characteristics' quantities.

- Two types of hedonic office rent indices (HORIX) for each major office market have been developed. The first type uses the Laspeyres index formula (L-HORIX); the second type uses the Paasche index formula (P-HORIX). Therefore, ten hedonic office rent indices (HORIX) are computed.[853] In addition, the average office rent based on the IPD Rental Database (RD-ORIX) and the average office rent published by the German Society of Property Researchers (GIF-ORIX) are presented for comparative purposes.

- The office rent indices of the German Society of Property Researchers (GIF-ORIX) have been chosen for comparison because they are objective and represent the market view on office rents.

- These hedonic office rent indices (HORIX) are applied to discover the intertemporal and interregional rent changes. The interregional comparison indicated that Berlin's rental market decoupled itself from the rental market of Düsseldorf, Frankfurt, Hamburg, and Munich. For the analysis of the intertemporal rent change, both indices (L-HORIX and P–HORIX) were employed to show how the rent levels of different office lease agreements developed. For all rental markets, but with different velocity, the analysis revealed that in 2004 market participants differed between office lease agreements and started to place different values on them.

[852] See Section

[853] See Table 51

- The application made clear that, depending on the choice of office lease agreement, different pictures of the various rental markets could be drawn. Therefore, all market participants should be aware of this fact when analyzing German office property markets.
- Moreover, a short insight of the practical use of the hedonic office rent indices (HORIX) for real estate practitioners has been provided. The hedonic office rent indices (HORIX) can be applied in the descriptive field of application as market indicator or economic indicator as well as in the operative field of application for benchmarking purposes.
- Finally, the hedonic office rent indices (HORIX) and the German Society of Property Researchers office rent index (GIF-ORIX) were compared. Therefore, six requirements that are essential for an index to obtain market acceptance served as evaluation criteria: quality and quantity of input data, index construction methodology, service concept, simplicity, transparency, and comprehensibility.
- Although the hedonic office rent indices (HORIX) still have some limitations, the evaluation and comparison underlined that the hedonic office rent indices (HORIX) have some practical advantages over the German Society of Property Researchers office rent index (GIF-ORIX), which shows the trend of office rents rather than the exact movement. In addition, the hedonic office rent indices serves as market and economic indicator as well as benchmarking instrument for real estate investors, valuers, portfolio managers and tenants.
- Finally, the implications the hedonic office rent indices (HORIX) have been discussed. The HORIX based on the Laspeyres index formulae are recommended for practitioners because of their simplicity regarding calculation and interpretation.

7 Conclusion

7.1 Summary of the Findings

The aim of this thesis was to develop office rent indices for the major office property markets that take into account the heterogeneity of office leases and thus are considered constant quality indices or hedonic indices (HORIX).

The primary motive for undertaking this thesis was the fact that although German and foreign investors have been interested in the German property market and, specifically, the office property market in the recent past, the market still lacks proper office rent indices based on a robust and scientific methodology. Despite the role that office properties play in the economy and the overall property market, portfolio managers, institutional investors, property valuation companies, and office users (tenants) have to be satisfied with the office rent indices published by real estate consultancies. Their rent indices, however, merely represent a time series of average or prime office rents for the major German cities, thereby ignoring the fact that office properties, as well as office leases, are heterogeneous goods. Office leases are heterogeneous. Therefore, the underlying office property is heterogeneous, because each office lease contains various clauses and options. Office rent indices based on simple average computations ignore the heterogeneity of office leases and thereby challenge the scientific community. More important, they are imprecise and biased, and might lead to false investment decisions.

Against this background, the second chapter introduced the theory of the hedonic price indices as a solution to this dilemma. Hedonic prices indices are built on the hedonic hypothesis, which assumes that, for any good, there is a functional relationship between its price and its characteristics. When applied to office rents, this hypothesis implies that office rents can be explained as a function of the characteristics of the underlying properties and the individual lease characteristics. If these building characteristics are known and quantifiable, the hedonic function can be solved by a statistical technique such as regression analysis.

Chapter two outlined in more detail the two stages in the construction of hedonic price indices: the estimation stage and the composition stage. The estimation stage deals with the identification of the characteristics that can ensue either from the demand side (office users' perspective) or from the supply side (landlords' perspective). Because the existing stock of office rental units dominates the office market and the short-term supply of office space is fixed, a demand-side approach was adopted. Moreover, this chapter looked into which functional form hedonic price indices can be based on.

The composition stage deals with the various index construction methodologies and considers their assumptions, drawbacks, and advantages. At this point, it was made clear that, although some construction methodologies are more advantageous from a theoretical point of view, the choice of index construction methodology is often beyond the researcher's influence and is merely a question of data availability.

In chapter three, the fundamentals of the office property market were outlined. First, it was explained why an office lease should be considered a heterogeneous good. On the one hand, the heterogeneity of office leases stems from the lease agreement itself, which contains various clauses in different combinations. On the other hand, the characteristics of the underlying property of any office lease agreement render each office lease a heterogeneous good. Second, the office property market was delineated from other commercial property markets. Third, office market dynamics demonstrated that, in office property market economics, office rents play the role that price normally does, namely, that of acting as a key signal to agents active in the market. Therefore, office rents are at the centre of the analysis. Fourth, an analysis of the efficiency of office property markets revealed that the markets are inefficient, and, consequently, the level of accuracy of a hedonic office rent index cannot be compared with the indices of other assets markets (e.g., stocks and bonds). Finally, the theory on real estate office cycles indicated that the set of characteristics forming the hedonic function varies during the real estate cycle phases; thereby affecting the index construction methodology.

The first three chapters laid out the theoretical framework; chapter four attempted to identify the office rent determinants, in other words, the necessary set of characteristics forming the hedonic function (estimation stage). First, the international literature on office rent determinants was reviewed. The literature review considered not only quantitative research studies about hedonic office rent indices but also studies analyzing office rent in general. The office rent determinants comprise location, building, equipment and layout, and lease characteristics. The literature review further revealed that although that some research studies attempted to analyze the same office rent determinant, they produced different, sometimes even contradictory, results. This finding could be attributed partly to the fact that these research studies were conducted in different markets and across different time periods. However, this finding also clearly indicates the necessity of analyzing the German office property markets separately. This necessity was fulfilled in the following section of this chapter. Here, a descriptive analysis of the major office property markets, namely, Berlin, Düsseldorf, Frankfurt, Hamburg, and Munich, and of their economic demand forces was presented. The results indicated that these office property markets differ not only in size but also in the existence of submarkets and demand forces. Furthermore, a report on the availability of data about the German office market and an insight into the legal foundation of German office leases were given. Although office market data significantly improved and real estate research received much attention in the recent past, data availability is still lagging far behind more mature markets, such as the UK or the US. The analysis demonstrated that the legal environment of German office leases differs in many aspects from the environment in other countries.

Because no picture could be painted to show conclusively that office rent determinants are important for Germany, a survey of real estate professionals was conducted in May 2006 to shed light on which office rent determinants are important in Germany. Out of 1,732 professionals, 102 returned the survey (response rate = 5.9%). Although the low response rate permitted only a limited statistical analysis, it clearly indicated that location and lease characteristics were considered the most important office rent determinants and that participants in the different office property markets value the same office rent determinants.

Chapter five, the nucleus of the thesis, presented the major empirical analysis and the estimation stage of the construction of the hedonic rent indices.

First, the data source was described. The initial dataset contained 22,005 office leases of more than 4,700 office buildings with more than 60 auxiliary and independent variables across Germany covering the time span from 1997 to 2006. The Rental Database of the Investment Property Databank Germany (IPD) provided the data. The IPD Rental Database directly retrieves the office lease data from the database systems (e.g., SAP and

Oracle) of mainly institutional investors. Therefore, the high quality of the data was assumed. Moreover, a comparison of the sum of total rental space per year and city with the published figures of the German Society of Property Researchers (gif) indicated that market coverage and representativeness of the data were more than satisfactory.

Second, the initial dataset underwent an extensive data-mining process. All variables having more than 90 percent missing values were disregarded (working dataset 1). In addition, when it was necessary to decrease the percentage of missing values, the scale of variables was reduced or recombined into a new variable (working dataset 2). However, because of data protection and contractual agreements with its clients (and data providers), the IPD Rental Database managers needed to make some variables of interest anonymous, specifically, spatial relationships (final working dataset). In fact, the office leases were aggregated to the city level, rendering all spatial econometric analysis impossible.

Third, as some variables still showed a high percentage of missing values, a brief review of how to handle missing data was given. In principle, two broad strategies exist, namely, single and multiple imputation methods. In this thesis, the multiple imputation method was adopted. Basically, the multiple imputation method involves three steps. The first step (imputation) generates several completed datasets (so-called multiple imputed datasets). The missing values are replaced with an algorithm. In the second step (complete data analysis), standard regression analysis is applied to the multiple imputed datasets. The third step (combination) combines the regression results of the second step. The main advantage of multiple imputation is that it accounts for the uncertainty in replacing missing values, does not underestimate the standard errors, and, as a consequence, does not overestimate the level of precision. However, it also adds complexity to the statistical analysis. As this thesis is one of the first research studies to employ this method in the field of real estate, the quality of the multiple imputation was checked. Univariate and bivariate statistics revealed that the multiple imputed dataset outperformed the conventional single imputation methods for missing values.

Thereafter, the dataset entered the estimation stage of the construction of the hedonic office rent indices. Here, the question of how to model the dimension of time and the regional markets was answered. Two models were built. In the first model (nationwide time dummy variable model), the dimension of time and the regional markets entered as dummy variables, imposing the restrictive assumptions that the influence of office rent determinants does not change over time and regions. In the second model (nationwide characteristic price index model), only the regional markets were reflected with dummy variables. A further relaxation of the assumptions was not possible, as expected, because of data unavailability.

As statistical outliers were detected, another set of models was computed with a reduced sample that included only office leases between 3.00 and 35.00 EUR/sqm/month. An interpretation of the models' regression coefficients followed, revealing which office rent determinants have a large influence on office rents. In most cases, the office rent determinants showed the expected sign. Nevertheless, a few independent variables did not have the expected relationship. This observation could be partly assigned to the fact that some important office rent determinants did not enter the regression analysis, leading to a net suppression effect. Finally, a series of graphical and statistical tests was undertaken on all models to check the assumptions and the accuracy of the results. The second model (nationwide characteristic price index model) produced the best results and was suggested for further use.

In chapter six, the hedonic office rent indices (HORIX) for the major German office property markets were computed. In other words, this chapter represented the composition stage of the construction of hedonic indices. Based on the nationwide characteristic price index model, two different types of hedonic office rent indices were calculated for Berlin, Düsseldorf, Frankfurt, Hamburg, and Munich. The first model used the Laspeyres index formulae and the second model the Paasche index formulae because they each answer a different question. The Laspeyres hedonic office rent indices (L-HORIX) show how the office rent of an average office rental unit with average lease characteristics from 1997 developed, and the Paasche hedonic office rent indices (P-HORIX) show how the office rents of an average office rental unit with average lease characteristics from the current year developed in comparison with 1997. In simpler terms, both indices measure the development of office rents for different kinds of lease agreements with different underlying office rental units.

Both types of hedonic indices (L-HORIX and P-HORIX) were applied, and both demonstrated the interregional and the intertemporal rent changes. Looking at the interregional rent change, both indices showed that the Berlin office rental market was under more pressure than the other markets. They also revealed that Düsseldorf best performed in terms of mean annual growth rates (from 1997 to 2006), followed by Hamburg, Frankfurt, and Munich. However, when the standard deviation was added into the picture as a measurement of volatility and risk, the indices showed that Frankfurt's office rental market was least volatile, followed by Munich, Düsseldorf, Hamburg, and Berlin (from 1997 to 2006).

The intertemporal rent change analyzed separately each office property market. Here, the office rent indices (GIF-ORIX) published by the German Society of Property Researchers were included in the analysis. Given that the indices measure a different type of office lease agreement, different pictures, ranging from positive to negative development, of the office rental markets could be drawn. This observation reinforced the contention that office leases have different qualities and, in the analysis of office rental markets, it is of the utmost importance to scrutinize which type of office lease agreement one has in mind.

Finally, the hedonic office rent indices (HORIX) and indices published by the German Society of Property Researchers (GIF-ORIX) were evaluated and compared. The six criteria normally required for market acceptance were used for the evaluation: quality and quantity of input data, index construction methodology, service concept, simplicity, transparency, and comprehensibility. Measured by these criteria, the HORIX outperformed the GIF-ORIX, although further improvements are needed. Nevertheless, it has been made clear that the office rent indices published by the German Society of Property Researchers have the an advantage in that they are based on the opinions of major real estate consultancies and therefore have a wider market acceptance.

7.2 Limitations of the Study

It is important and valuable to make clear the limitations of this research study. It must be pointed out that these limitations do not undermine the validity of the main findings, but they do suggest in which direction further research for the development of office rent indices might go.

- Missing Rental Area Definition

The unit of measurement of the dependent variable was EUR per square metre per month (EUR/sqm/month). Unfortunately, it could not be specified which rental area definition the leases were based on. As a consequence, the meaningfulness of the developed hedonic office rent indices (HORIX) is reduced. However, many office lease agreements fail to specify the rental area definition, which is often a source for legal disputes.

- Omitted Variables

Another limitation of this study is that many important variables that have been identified as having an influence on the level of office rent could not be included in the hedonic regression analysis. The omission of these variables, which is due to data unavailability, hampers the usefulness of the developed hedonic office rent indices. For example, the explanatory power of the regression models in terms of explained variances is below 50 percent. In other words, more than 50 percent of the variances in office rents remain unexplained. In addition, the omitted variables are probably responsible for the fact that some independent variables showed an unexpected relationship with office rents.

- Delimitation of Regional Office Markets and Spatial Relationships

Closely related to the problem of omitted variables is the limitation that the developed hedonic office rent indices do not include any spatial relationships. For instance, no variables that measure the quality of infrastructure have been included. Furthermore, the differences between the regional office markets are controlled only by dummy variables. Because of data unavailability, separate regression analyses for regional office markets or even office submarkets could not be run.

- Functional Form

The functional form of the regression models assumes linearity between the dependent variable and the independent variables. The assumption of linearity has been checked with diagnostic plots and tests, and it has been ensured (because of data transformation) that the linearity assumption is met. Nonetheless, the question of whether other regression models (e.g., spline smoothing) not based on the linearity assumption would have obtained a higher explanatory power remains. Therefore, further progress in the statistical area of multiple imputation and nonparametric regression techniques is necessary.

- Complexity of Data Mining

A significant drawback for the market acceptance of the developed hedonic office rent indices is the complexity of the data-mining process. Although the variable transformations are common in any statistical analysis, the application of the multiple imputation method to fill in the missing values is complex. Moreover, as long as missing values remain in the dataset, it is necessary to recompute the multiple imputed datasets if the hedonic office rent indices are computed for subsequent years.

7.3 Suggestions for further Research

This thesis is the first research study to develop hedonic office rent indices for German metropolitan areas. Throughout the thesis, limitations and problems have been openly addressed, if not always resolved. Some of them provide a good starting point for further real estate research studies. In addition, the real estate data situation will continue to improve in the upcoming years. The IPD Rental Database is a major step forward and provides a strong database structure. In this light, new attempts to develop office rent indices for German metropolitan areas should focus on the following issues:

Future research studies should attempt to relax the severe assumption of the nationwide models constructed in this thesis that the influence on office rent determinants is constant between regional markets. Instead separate office rent indices for each regional market should be built. Moreover, it would be worthwhile to analyze which office rent determinants are valued differently between the regional markets by market participants. Against this background, submarkets and delimitations of German office property markets should be scrutinized.

Closely related to the above-mentioned issue is the challenge to use spatial econometrics in the future construction of office rent indices, as they provide a powerful tool for quantifying the influence of unobserved office rent determinants. Another interesting statistical technique is the use of nonparameter regression methodology, which relaxes the assumption of linearity.

Appendix

A.1 Overview of Research Studies Office Rent Determinants

General Information							Location Factors and Spatial Relationships					Building Factors				Equipment and Lacoet Factors of Office Spase	Lease Factors					Market Situation and Bargaining Power
							Importance of Face-to-Face Contacts			*Importance of Face-to-Face Contacts*	*Representativeness of Location*											
Author	Published	Study Years	Study Area	Type of Study	Sample Size (Number of Observations)	Dependent Variable	Transporation Modes	Quality of Surroundings	Labour Market Proximity			Quality	Prestige and Representativeness	Environmental Aspects	Internal Services / Amenities		Lease Length	Size of Rental Area	Rent Review Provisions	Options and Incentives	Type and Quality of the Tenan	
Archer / Smith	2003	2000	Houston (US)	Quantitative Analysis	647	Rent				X		X	X									
Arge	2005	-	Norwegen	Qualititaive Analysis (Survey)	11 office developers	-																
Bender et al.	1999	-	Geneva (Switzerland)	Qualitative Analysis (Survey / AHP)	1800 office users	-	X				X											
Benjamin et al.	1992	(collected over 4 years)	Greensboro (US)	Quantitative Analysis	320	Rents											X	X			X	
Bollinger et al.	1998	1990-1996	Atlanta (US)	Quantitative Analysis	658-907 per year	Rent	X	X		X		X	X		X							
Bond et al.	2005	1994-2004	London (UK)	Quantitative Analysis	935	Rent						X					X	X		X		
Bottom et al.	1997	1996	London (UK)	Qualitative Analysis (Survey)	76 respondents	-	X					X										
Clapp	1980	-	Los Angeles (US)	Quantitative Analysis	105	Rent	X		X	X	X		X		X							
Colwell / Munneke	2006	1995-1997	Illinois (US)	Quantitative Analysis	477	Price																X
Colwell et al.	1998	1986 to 1993	Chicago (US)	Quantitative Analysis	427	Parcel Prices	X	X		X		X	X									
Crosby et al.	2006	2003-2004	England and Wales (UK)	Quantitative and qualititative Analysis (Survey)	428 respondents	-											X					
D'Arcy et al.	1997	1983-1994	22 European Cities	Quantitative Analysis	264	Rent																X
Desyllas	2000	1991-1997	Berlin (Germany)	Quantitative Analysis	437	Rent						X					X	X				
Downs / Slade	1999	1987-1996	Phoenix (US)	Quantitative Analysis	935	Price				X		X	X									
Dunse / Jones	1998	1994-1995	Glasgow (UK)	Quantitative Analysis	477	Rents						X			X			X				
Dunse et al.	2002	1992-1998	Glasgow and Edinburgh (UK)	Quantitative Analysis	539	Rent	X			X		X				X						
Englund et al.	2003	1998-2002	Stockholm, Gothenburg, Milo (Sweden)	Quantitative Analysis	4387	Rent						X					X		X		X	
Gat	1998	1997	Tel Aviv (Israel)	Quantitative Analysis	50 (office buildings)	Asking Rent (averaged over office buildings)	X			X		X	X									
Glasgock et al.	1990	1984-1988	Baton Rouge (US)	Quantitative Analysis	675	Rent						X	X		X							
Glasgock et al.	1993	1984-1990	Baton Rouge (US)	Quantitative Analysis	127	Rent															X	
Gunnelin / Söderberg	2003	1977-1991	Stockholm (Sweden)	Quantitative Analysis	1349	Rent						X					X	X			X	

Table 59: Overview of Research Studies (Part I)

General Information							Location Factors and Spatial Relationships					Building Factors				Equipment and Lacout Factors of Office Space	Lease Factors					Market Situation and Bargaining Power
							Importance of Face-to-Face Contacts			*Importance of Face-to-Face Contacts*	*Representativeness of Location*											
Author	Published	Study Years	Study Area	Type of Study	Sample Size (Number of Observations)	Dependent Variable	Transporation Modes	Quality of Surroundings	Labour Market Proximity			Quality	Prestige and Representativeness	Environmental Aspects	Internal Services / Amenities		Lease Length	Size of Rental Area	Rent Review Provisions	Options and Incentives	Type and Quality of the Tenan	
Heyser	2006	2001	Munich (Germany)	Quantitative Analysis	89	Rent	X	X		X		X			X							
Hodgson	2006	1997-2004	Phoenix (US)	Quantitative Analysis	1846	Price				X		X	X									
Ihlandfeldt	1990	1980-1983	Atlanta (US)	Quantitative Analysis	-	-		X		X												
Laverne / Winson-Geidemann	2003	1995-2001	Cleveland (US)	Quantitative Analysis	270	Rent						X										
Leishman et al.	2003	2002	Edinburgh (UK)	Qualitative Analysis (Survey)	61 responses	Office Occupiers and Lease Agents			X							X						
Mills	1992	1990	Chicago (US)	Quantitative Analysis	543	Rents									X							
Mooradian / Yang	2000	~1990	US	Quantitative Analysis	311	Rents														X		
Munnecke / Slade	2001	1988-1986	Phoenix (US)	Quantitative Analysis	890	Price				X		X	X									
Nitsch	2006	-	Munich (Germany)	Quantitative Analysis	46	Rent	X	X		X		X			X							
O'Mara	1999	1990-1996	US	Qualitative Analysis (Case Study / Survey)	40 cases	Informatin-age Companies			X													
Orr et al.	2003	1994-1998	Scotland (UK)	Quantitative Analysis	333 (retail, office industrial transactions)	Rent																X
Oven / Pekdemir	2004	2003	Istanbul (Turkey)	Quantitative Analysis (Factor Analysis)	52	Rent	X	X		X												
Ryan	2005	1986-1995	San Diego (US)	Quantitative Analysis	520	Rent	X	X		X												
Shiers	1999	1996-1997	UK	Qualitative Analysis (Case Study)	23	-								X								
Sivitanidou	1996	1987-1992	Los Angeles (US)	Quantitative Analysis	539	Property Value	X	X			X	X			X							
Slade	2000	1991-1996	Phoenix (US)	Quantitative Analysis	Unknown (483 properties)	Rent						X			X							
St. Lawrence	2004	-	UK	Qualitative Analysis (Case Studies)	7 cases	-								X								
Stanton / Wallace	2002	1987-1996	US metropolitan reas	Quantitative Analysis	130	Rents											X			X	X	
Vandell et al.	1989	1979-1986	Boston (UK)	Quantitative Analysis	56	Rent						X										
Webb / Fisher	1996	1985-1991	Chicago (US)	Quantitative Analysis	225	Rent						X							X		X	X
Wheaton / Torto	1995	1979-1991	50 metropolitan reas (US)	Quantitative Analysis	~60,000	Rent						X	X					X				

Table 60: Overview of Research Studies (Part II)

A.2 Survey among German Real Estate Professionals

A.2.1 Pre-Test Interview Partners

Interview Partner:	Ulrich Denk
Name of Company	BulwienGesa AG – Berlin
Position	Project Manager
Field of Business Activity	Research
Date / Type	21.03.2006 / Telephone

Interview Partner:	Stefan Börger
Name of Company	Grossmann + Berger GmbH – Hamburg
Position	Senior Investment Consultant
Field of Business Activity	Investment
Date / Tyoe	21.03.2006 / Telephone

Interview Partner:	Heiko Fischer
Name of Company	CB Richard Ellis – Hamburg
Position	Managing Director
Field of Business Activity	Agency
Date / Phone	22.03.2006 / Telephone

Interview Partner:	Drazenko Grahovac MRICS
Name of Company	CB Richard Ellis – Valuation Services – Berlin
Position	Head of Valuation - Berlin
Field of Business Activity	Valuation
Date / Phone	24.02.2006 / Personal

Interview Partner:	Frank Kamping MRICS
Name of Company	BRANDI IGH Ingenieure GmbH – Cologne
Position	Managing Director
Field of Business Activity	Technical Consulting Services
Date / Type	28.02.2006 / Telephone

Interview Partner:	Peter Marquardt
Name of Company	ReSolution - Cologne
Position	Project Manager
Field of Business Activity	Asset Management
Date / Type	23.02.2006 / Telephone

Interview Partner:	Andreas Paduch
Name of Company	CB Richard Ellis – Global Corporate Services – London
Position	Associate Director
Field of Business Activity	Corporate Real Estate
Date / Type	15.02.2006 / Telephone

Interview Partner:	Professor Dr. Andrea Pelzeter
Name of Company	Berufsakademie in der Fachhochschule für Wirtschaft Berlin
Position	Senior Professor
Field of Business Activity	Research & Education
Date / Type	22.02.2006 / Personal

Interview Partner:	Dr. Barbara Pierschke
Name of Company	ebs Immobilienakademie – Berlin / Essen
Position	Managing Director
Field of Business Activity	Research & Education
Date / Type	10.03.2006 / Personal

Interview Partner:	Joachim Schmidt
Name of Company	Schmalz Rechtsanwälte – Frankfurt
Position	Lawyer
Field of Business Activity	Real Estate & Construction
Date / Type	16.03.2006 / Telephone

A.2.2 Questionnaire's Survey

Untersuchung der werttreibenden Einflussfaktoren auf Büromieten
Eine empirische Untersuchung

Ziel der Studie

In der wissenschaftlichen Literatur wird eine Reihe von Einflussfaktoren auf Büromieten genannt. Diese lassen sich in den Kategorien Standort-, Gebäude-, Ausstattungs- und Mietvertragsfaktoren aber auch makroökonomischen Faktoren zuordnen. ***In dieser Studie soll verifiziert werden, ob die genannten Faktoren in der Praxis auf Büromieten einen Einfluss ausüben und welche Einflussstärke diese Faktoren gegebenenfalls haben.*** Für die deutschen Büroimmobilienmärkte ist dieser Untersuchungsgegenstand bisher weitgehend unerforscht. Diese Studie ist insofern für alle Marktteilnehmer von Bedeutung, da die Ergebnisse den Prozeß der Mietpreisbildung und somit die Bewertung von Immobilien transparenter darstellen.

Bei der Untersuchung handelt es sich um einen essentiellen Bestandteil des Promotionsvorhabens von Herrn Simon Kempf, Doktorand von Prof. Dr. Schulte HonRICS CRE und wissenschaftlicher Mitarbeiter am Stiftungslehrstuhl für Immobilienökonomie der European Business School (**ebs**).

Aufbau und Durchführung der Befragung

Der Fragebogen ist in drei Teile gegliedert. Das Ausfüllen wird lediglich **15-20 Minuten** Ihrer Zeit in Anspruch nehmen.

Vertraulichkeit

Es wird versichert, dass alle Bedingungen zum Datenschutz strengstens eingehalten werden und alle Angaben ausschließlich statistisch neutral in aggregierter Form ausgewertet werden.

Ergebnisdarstellung

Die Untersuchungsergebnisse sollen im Rahmen der im Juni 2006 stattfindenden Konferenz der European Real Estate Society in Weimar vorgestellt werden. Gerne stelle ich Ihnen die Ergebnisse auch vorab zur Verfügung.

Sollen Ihnen die Ergebnisse zugeschickt werden? Ja ☐ Nein ☐

Preisauslobung

Unter den ***ersten 50 vollständig ausgefüllten Fragebögen*** wird ein ***Assortiment von Champagner*** (1er CRU LOCRET-LACHAUD aus der Wiege der Champagne) verlost.

Möchten Sie an der Verlosung teilnehmen: Ja ☐ Nein ☐

Wenn Sie an den Ergebnissen interessiert sind oder an der Verlosung teilnehmen möchten, tragen Sie bitte Ihre Email-Adresse ein: ______________________@______________

Definitionen

In dieser Befragung wird der Einfluss auf die **Netto-Kaltmiete** untersucht. Die Netto-Kaltmiete entspricht der Grundmiete mit separater Umlegung von Heizung und Warmwasser sowie weiterer Umlage sonstiger Nebenkosten.

Bitte schicken Sie den ausgefüllten Fragebogen bis 15. Mai 2006 per FAX an:

030 – 439096 - 50

Vielen Dank für Ihre Unterstützung!

TEIL 1: ANGABEN ZUM BÜROMARKT

Bitte spezifizieren Sie Ihren Kenntnisstand über die folgenden Büroimmobilienmärkte?

	sehr hoch	hoch	mittel	unterdurchschnittlich	gering	„Nicht mein Markt"
Berlin	☐	☐	☐	☐	☐	☐
Düsseldorf	☐	☐	☐	☐	☐	☐
Frankfurt am Main	☐	☐	☐	☐	☐	☐
Hamburg	☐	☐	☐	☐	☐	☐
München	☐	☐	☐	☐	☐	☐
Stuttgart	☐	☐	☐	☐	☐	☐

Für die nächsten Fragen (Teil 2.1 bis 2.5) ist es wichtig, dass nur **ein Büroimmobilienmarkt** *im Fokus Ihrer Antworten liegt. Bitte wählen Sie daher denjenigen Büromarkt, über welchen Sie die größten Fachkenntnisse besitzen!*

Berlin	Düsseldorf	Frankfurt am Main	Hamburg	München	Stuttgart
☐	☐	☐	☐	☐	☐

In welcher Rolle treten Sie hauptsächlich im Markt auf? (Einfachnennung)

als Vermieter	als Mieter	als Makler	als Dienstleister
☐	☐	☐	☐

TEIL 2.1: SPEZIFIZIERUNG DER STANDORTFAKTOREN

Bestimmen Sie bitte nach Ihrer Meinung die **Einflussstärke (Mietaufschlag oder –abschlag)** *der nachfolgenden* **Standortfaktoren** *auf die* **Netto-Kaltmiete.**

	Positiv (Mietaufschlag)				Kein Einfluss	Negativ (Mietabschlag)			
	sehr stark	stark	mittel	schwach		schwach	mittel	stark	sehr stark
Verkehrsinfrastruktur	++++	+++	++	+	0	-	--	---	----
Nähe zu ÖPNV	☐	☐	☐	☐	☐	☐	☐	☐	☐
Nähe zu internationalem Flughafen	☐	☐	☐	☐	☐	☐	☐	☐	☐
Nähe zu Fernverkehrsbahnhof	☐	☐	☐	☐	☐	☐	☐	☐	☐
Nähe zum Autobahnanschluss	☐	☐	☐	☐	☐	☐	☐	☐	☐
Verfügbarkeit von Parkplätzen	☐	☐	☐	☐	☐	☐	☐	☐	☐
Verfügbarkeit von kostenfreien Parkplätzen	☐	☐	☐	☐	☐	☐	☐	☐	☐
Lagekriterien	++++	+++	++	+	0	-	--	---	----
Nähe zu Restaurants	☐	☐	☐	☐	☐	☐	☐	☐	☐
Nähe zu Einkaufsläden für den täglichen Bedarf	☐	☐	☐	☐	☐	☐	☐	☐	☐
Nähe zu Hotels	☐	☐	☐	☐	☐	☐	☐	☐	☐
Nähe zu branchenähnlichen Unternehmen	☐	☐	☐	☐	☐	☐	☐	☐	☐
Nähe zu vor- od. nachgelagerten Produktionsstufen	☐	☐	☐	☐	☐	☐	☐	☐	☐
Atmosphäre	++++	+++	++	+	0	-	--	---	----
Gutes Image des Umfelds	☐	☐	☐	☐	☐	☐	☐	☐	☐
Schlechtes Image des Umfelds	☐	☐	☐	☐	☐	☐	☐	☐	☐
Hohe Aufenthalts- und Umweltqualität	☐	☐	☐	☐	☐	☐	☐	☐	☐
Niedrige Aufenthalts- und Umweltqualität	☐	☐	☐	☐	☐	☐	☐	☐	☐
Hohe Verkehrs- / Emissionsbelastung	☐	☐	☐	☐	☐	☐	☐	☐	☐
Niedrige Verkehrs- / Emissionsbelastung	☐	☐	☐	☐	☐	☐	☐	☐	☐
Gute Sichtbarkeit des Gebäudes	☐	☐	☐	☐	☐	☐	☐	☐	☐
Schlechte Sichtbarkeit des Gebäudes	☐	☐	☐	☐	☐	☐	☐	☐	☐

TEIL 2.2: SPEZIFIZIERUNG DER GEBÄUDEFAKTOREN

Bestimmen Sie bitte nach Ihrer Meinung die **Einflussstärke (Mietaufschlag oder –abschlag)** *der nachfolgenden* **Gebäudefaktoren** *auf die* **Netto-Kaltmiete.**

	Positiv (Mietaufschlag)				Kein Einfluss	Negativ (Mietabschlag)			
	sehr stark	stark	mittel	schwach		schwach	mittel	stark	sehr stark
Flexibilität **(Zuschnitt / Rastermaß)**	++++	+++	++	+	0	-	--	---	----
Hoch	☐	☐	☐	☐	☐	☐	☐	☐	☐
Mittel	☐	☐	☐	☐	☐	☐	☐	☐	☐
Niedrig	☐	☐	☐	☐	☐	☐	☐	☐	☐
Wahl der Definitionseinheit der Nutzfläche	++++	+++	++	+	0	-	--	---	----
nach gif-Richtlinie	☐	☐	☐	☐	☐	☐	☐	☐	☐
nach DIN 277	☐	☐	☐	☐	☐	☐	☐	☐	☐
Sonstige:	☐	☐	☐	☐	☐	☐	☐	☐	☐
Bau- / Sanierungs- / Modernisierungsdatum	++++	+++	++	+	0	-	--	---	----
Vor 1990	☐	☐	☐	☐	☐	☐	☐	☐	☐
1990 – 1995	☐	☐	☐	☐	☐	☐	☐	☐	☐
1996 – 2000	☐	☐	☐	☐	☐	☐	☐	☐	☐
2001 – 2005	☐	☐	☐	☐	☐	☐	☐	☐	☐
Ab 2006	☐	☐	☐	☐	☐	☐	☐	☐	☐
Architektur, Design, Gestaltung	++++	+++	++	+	0	-	--	---	----
Qualitätsvolle architektonische Außengestaltung	☐	☐	☐	☐	☐	☐	☐	☐	☐
Qualitätsniedrige architektonische Außengestaltung	☐	☐	☐	☐	☐	☐	☐	☐	☐
Repräsentativer Eingangsbereich	☐	☐	☐	☐	☐	☐	☐	☐	☐
Hohe Qualität der verwendeten Baustoffe	☐	☐	☐	☐	☐	☐	☐	☐	☐
Niedrige Qualität der verwendeten Baustoffe	☐	☐	☐	☐	☐	☐	☐	☐	☐
Hoher Prestigewert (Baustil, historischer Wert, Außenwirkung aufs Unternehmen)	☐	☐	☐	☐	☐	☐	☐	☐	☐
Niedriger Prestigewert (Baustil, historischer Wert, Außenwirkung aufs Unternehmen)	☐	☐	☐	☐	☐	☐	☐	☐	☐
Raumklima	++++	+++	++	+	0	-	--	---	----
Keine Klimatisierung (Fensterbelüftung)	☐	☐	☐	☐	☐	☐	☐	☐	☐
Teilklimatisierung (Spitzenklimatisierung)	☐	☐	☐	☐	☐	☐	☐	☐	☐
Vollklimatisierung	☐	☐	☐	☐	☐	☐	☐	☐	☐
Notstromversorgung der Büroeinheit	++++	+++	++	+	0	-	--	---	----
Vorhanden	☐	☐	☐	☐	☐	☐	☐	☐	☐
Nicht vorhanden	☐	☐	☐	☐	☐	☐	☐	☐	☐
Sicherheitssysteme	++++	+++	++	+	0	-	--	---	----
Vorhanden	☐	☐	☐	☐	☐	☐	☐	☐	☐
Nachrüstbar / Vorgerüstet	☐	☐	☐	☐	☐	☐	☐	☐	☐
Nicht vorhanden	☐	☐	☐	☐	☐	☐	☐	☐	☐
IT-Infrastruktur	++++	+++	++	+	0	-	--	---	----
Nicht vorhanden (Konventionelle Cad 5 oder Cad 7)	☐	☐	☐	☐	☐	☐	☐	☐	☐
Glasfaser	☐	☐	☐	☐	☐	☐	☐	☐	☐
Serverraum nicht vorhanden	☐	☐	☐	☐	☐	☐	☐	☐	☐
Serverraum im Keller	☐	☐	☐	☐	☐	☐	☐	☐	☐
Serverraum auf der Etage	☐	☐	☐	☐	☐	☐	☐	☐	☐
Ökologische Ausrichtung des Gebäudes	++++	+++	++	+	0	-	--	---	----
Sparsamer Energieverbrauch (Hoher Dämmschutz etc.)	☐	☐	☐	☐	☐	☐	☐	☐	☐
Fassaden- und Dachbegrünung	☐	☐	☐	☐	☐	☐	☐	☐	☐
Solarzellen	☐	☐	☐	☐	☐	☐	☐	☐	☐
Wärmepumpe/Blockheizkraft	☐	☐	☐	☐	☐	☐	☐	☐	☐
Nachrüstbarkeit der IT-Infrastruktur	++++	+++	++	+	0	-	--	---	----
Einfache Nachrüstbarkeit (Doppelböden, Schächte, Reserveflächen)	☐	☐	☐	☐	☐	☐	☐	☐	☐
Aufwändige Nachrüstbarkeit	☐	☐	☐	☐	☐	☐	☐	☐	☐
Sonstiges	++++	+++	++	+	0	-	--	---	----
Aufzug vorhanden	☐	☐	☐	☐	☐	☐	☐	☐	☐

TEIL 2.3: SPEZIFIZIERUNG DER AUSSTATTUNGSFAKTOREN DER GEMIETETEN BÜROEINHEIT

Bestimmen Sie bitte nach Ihrer Meinung die **Einflussstärke (Mietaufschlag oder –abschlag)** *der nachfolgenden* **Ausstattungsfaktoren** *auf die* **Netto-Kaltmiete**.

	Positiv (Mietaufschlag)				Kein Einfluss	Negativ (Mietabschlag)			
	sehr stark	stark	mittel	schwach		schwach	mittel	stark	sehr stark
Bürozuschnitt	++++	+++	++	+	0	-	--	---	----
Großraumbüro	☐	☐	☐	☐	☐	☐	☐	☐	☐
Gruppenbüro (max. 20 Personen)	☐	☐	☐	☐	☐	☐	☐	☐	☐
Zellenbüro	☐	☐	☐	☐	☐	☐	☐	☐	☐
Kombibüro	☐	☐	☐	☐	☐	☐	☐	☐	☐
Flexibler Zuschnitt	☐	☐	☐	☐	☐	☐	☐	☐	☐
Reversibler Zuschnitt	☐	☐	☐	☐	☐	☐	☐	☐	☐
Bodenbelag	++++	+++	++	+	0	-	--	---	----
Teppich	☐	☐	☐	☐	☐	☐	☐	☐	☐
Parkett	☐	☐	☐	☐	☐	☐	☐	☐	☐
Steinfußboden im Empfangsbereich (Marmor etc.)	☐	☐	☐	☐	☐	☐	☐	☐	☐
Regelung der Raumqualität (Lüftung, Kälte etc.)	++++	+++	++	+	0	-	--	---	----
Raumindividuelle Regelung	☐	☐	☐	☐	☐	☐	☐	☐	☐
Arbeitsplatzindividuelle Regelung	☐	☐	☐	☐	☐	☐	☐	☐	☐
Marktsituation	++++	+++	++	+	0	-	--	---	----
Büroeinheit wurde vor Fertigstellung vermietet	☐	☐	☐	☐	☐	☐	☐	☐	☐
Büroeinheit stand nach Fertigstellung bis zu 9 Monate leer	☐	☐	☐	☐	☐	☐	☐	☐	☐
Büroeinheit stand nach Fertigstellung länger als 9 Monate leer	☐	☐	☐	☐	☐	☐	☐	☐	☐
Vermietungsstand des Bürogebäudes	++++	+++	++	+	0	-	--	---	----
Erste vermietete Büroeinheit (erster Mieter / Ankermieter)	☐	☐	☐	☐	☐	☐	☐	☐	☐
Letzte vermietete Büroeinheit (letzter Mieter)	☐	☐	☐	☐	☐	☐	☐	☐	☐
Sonstige	++++	+++	++	+	0	-	--	---	----
Erweiterung der Mietfläche (Zuschaltbarkeit von Mieteinheiten)	☐	☐	☐	☐	☐	☐	☐	☐	☐
Erstbezug (neue Fläche)	☐	☐	☐	☐	☐	☐	☐	☐	☐

TEIL 2.4: SPEZIFIZIERUNG DER MIETVERTRAGSFAKTOREN

Bestimmen Sie bitte nach Ihrer Meinung die **Einflussstärke (Mietaufschlag oder –abschlag)** *der nachfolgenden* **Mietvertragsfaktoren** *auf die* **Netto-Kaltmiete**.

	Positiv (Mietaufschlag)				Kein Einfluss	Negativ (Mietabschlag)			
	sehr stark	stark	mittel	schwach		schwach	mittel	stark	sehr stark
Vertragsdauer	++++	+++	++	+	0	-	--	---	----
bis 3 Jahre	☐	☐	☐	☐	☐	☐	☐	☐	☐
bis 5 Jahre	☐	☐	☐	☐	☐	☐	☐	☐	☐
bis 10 Jahre	☐	☐	☐	☐	☐	☐	☐	☐	☐
über 10 Jahre	☐	☐	☐	☐	☐	☐	☐	☐	☐
Größe der gemieteten Fläche	++++	+++	++	+	0	-	--	---	----
bis 500 m² BGF	☐	☐	☐	☐	☐	☐	☐	☐	☐
500 - 1000 m² BGF	☐	☐	☐	☐	☐	☐	☐	☐	☐
1001 – 5000 m² BGF	☐	☐	☐	☐	☐	☐	☐	☐	☐
Über 5000 m² BGF	☐	☐	☐	☐	☐	☐	☐	☐	☐
Optionen	++++	+++	++	+	0	-	--	---	----
Mietverlängerung	☐	☐	☐	☐	☐	☐	☐	☐	☐
Breakoption mit Penalty	☐	☐	☐	☐	☐	☐	☐	☐	☐
Untervermietung an verbundene Unternehmen ohne Zustimmung des Vermieters möglich	☐	☐	☐	☐	☐	☐	☐	☐	☐
Kaufoption des Gebäudes	☐	☐	☐	☐	☐	☐	☐	☐	☐
Flächenanpassung	++++	+++	++	+	0	-	--	---	----
Expansion ohne Umzug mit Vormietrecht	☐	☐	☐	☐	☐	☐	☐	☐	☐
Expansion ohne Umzug mit Anbietungsverpflichtung des Vermieters	☐	☐	☐	☐	☐	☐	☐	☐	☐
Reduzierung / Teilflächenrückgabemöglichkeit	☐	☐	☐	☐	☐	☐	☐	☐	☐
Incentives	++++	+++	++	+	0	-	--	---	----
Freistellung der bestehenden Mietvertragsverpflichtungen des „alten" Mietgegenstandes durch den „neuen" Vermieter	☐	☐	☐	☐	☐	☐	☐	☐	☐
Übernahme der Umzugskosten durch den Vermieter	☐	☐	☐	☐	☐	☐	☐	☐	☐
Vereinbarung von mietfreien Zeiten	☐	☐	☐	☐	☐	☐	☐	☐	☐
Übernahme der Kosten des Mieterausbaus (Sonderausbauten)	☐	☐	☐	☐	☐	☐	☐	☐	☐
Sicherheiten	++++	+++	++	+	0	-	--	---	----
Barkaution / Bürgschaft	☐	☐	☐	☐	☐	☐	☐	☐	☐
Patronatserklärung	☐	☐	☐	☐	☐	☐	☐	☐	☐

Mietanpassungsklauseln	++++	+++	++	+	0	-	--	---	----
Staffelmiete	☐	☐	☐	☐	☐	☐	☐	☐	☐
Wertsicherungsklausel (Gleit-, Spannungs-, Leistungsvorbehalt/Verhandlungsklausel)	☐	☐	☐	☐	☐	☐	☐	☐	☐
Nebenkostenübernahme des Mieters	++++	+++	++	+	0	-	--	---	----
Betriebskosten werden vom Mieter übernommen	☐	☐	☐	☐	☐	☐	☐	☐	☐
Verwaltungskosten werden zusätzlich vom Mieter übernommen	☐	☐	☐	☐	☐	☐	☐	☐	☐
Objektüberwachungskosten werden vom Mieter übernommen	☐	☐	☐	☐	☐	☐	☐	☐	☐
Instandhaltung und -setzung innerhalb des Mietgegenstandes werden vom Mieter übernommen	☐	☐	☐	☐	☐	☐	☐	☐	☐
Instandhaltung und -setzung an Dach+Fach, technische Gebäudeeinrichtungen und Außenanlagen werden anteilig vom Mieter übernommen	☐	☐	☐	☐	☐	☐	☐	☐	☐
Instandhaltung und -setzung an Dach+Fach, technische Gebäudeeinrichtungen und Außenanlagen werden komplett vom Mieter übernommen	☐	☐	☐	☐	☐	☐	☐	☐	☐
Vereinbarung eines Vollwartungsauftrages	☐	☐	☐	☐	☐	☐	☐	☐	☐
Rechtsform des Mieters	++++	+++	++	+	0	-	--	---	----
Natürliche Person	☐	☐	☐	☐	☐	☐	☐	☐	☐
Juristische Person	☐	☐	☐	☐	☐	☐	☐	☐	☐
Vorsteuerabzugsfähigkeit (Vermieter hat zur Umsatzsteuer optiert)	++++	+++	++	+	0	-	--	---	----
Mieter ist vorsteuerabzugsberechtigt	☐	☐	☐	☐	☐	☐	☐	☐	☐
Mieter ist nicht vorsteuerabzugsberechtigt	☐	☐	☐	☐	☐	☐	☐	☐	☐
Umsatz des Mieters ist teilweise vorsteuerschädlich	☐	☐	☐	☐	☐	☐	☐	☐	☐
Unternehmenshauptsitz des Mieters	++++	+++	++	+	0	-	--	---	----
Deutschland	☐	☐	☐	☐	☐	☐	☐	☐	☐
Europa (EU 25)	☐	☐	☐	☐	☐	☐	☐	☐	☐
Außerhalb Europas	☐	☐	☐	☐	☐	☐	☐	☐	☐
Branche des Mieters	++++	+++	++	+	0	-	--	---	----
Banken & Investment-Firmen, Versicherungsunternehmen	☐	☐	☐	☐	☐	☐	☐	☐	☐
Rechtsberatung, Wirtschaftsprüfung, Buchhaltung	☐	☐	☐	☐	☐	☐	☐	☐	☐
Sonstige Dienstleistungen	☐	☐	☐	☐	☐	☐	☐	☐	☐
Medien / Unterhaltung / Werbung	☐	☐	☐	☐	☐	☐	☐	☐	☐
EDV (IT & Telekommunikation / Forschung & Software)	☐	☐	☐	☐	☐	☐	☐	☐	☐
Öffentliche Institutionen	☐	☐	☐	☐	☐	☐	☐	☐	☐
Verbände / Stiftungen /Vereine	☐	☐	☐	☐	☐	☐	☐	☐	☐
Sonstige (Verarbeitendes Gewerbe, Groß- und Einzelhandel, etc.)	☐	☐	☐	☐	☐	☐	☐	☐	☐
Bereitstellung von Mieterservices	++++	+++	++	+	0	-	--	---	----
Reinigung der Büroflächen	☐	☐	☐	☐	☐	☐	☐	☐	☐
Sicherheitsdienst	☐	☐	☐	☐	☐	☐	☐	☐	☐
Wäschedienst	☐	☐	☐	☐	☐	☐	☐	☐	☐
Catering	☐	☐	☐	☐	☐	☐	☐	☐	☐
Möblierungsmanagement	☐	☐	☐	☐	☐	☐	☐	☐	☐
Umzugsservice	☐	☐	☐	☐	☐	☐	☐	☐	☐
Kinderbetreuung	☐	☐	☐	☐	☐	☐	☐	☐	☐
Einkaufsdienste	☐	☐	☐	☐	☐	☐	☐	☐	☐
Concierge	☐	☐	☐	☐	☐	☐	☐	☐	☐
Sonstiges	++++	+++	++	+	0	-	--	---	----
Baukostenzuschuss des Mieters	☐	☐	☐	☐	☐	☐	☐	☐	☐
Befreiung des Mieters von Rückbauverpflichtungen	☐	☐	☐	☐	☐	☐	☐	☐	☐

TEIL 2.5: SPEZIFIZIERUNG DER MAKROÖKONOMISCHEN FAKTOREN

Bitte kreuzen Sie an, welche **Relevanz** *nach Ihrer Meinung folgende* **makroökonomische Faktoren** *in der Mietpreisfindung spielen.*

	hoch	mittel	niedrig	keine
Allgemein				
Gesamtwirtschaftliche Entwicklung (Wachstum, Konjunktur, Inflation)	☐	☐	☐	☐
Marktentwicklung der Stadt	☐	☐	☐	☐
Struktur und Entwicklung des Immobilienangebots				
Marktumfang / Bestand	☐	☐	☐	☐
Leerstand	☐	☐	☐	☐
Geplante Projekte, Bauvolumen	☐	☐	☐	☐
Verhandlungsmacht des Vermieters	☐	☐	☐	☐
Struktur und Entwicklung der Immobiliennachfrage				
Flächenbedarfsentwicklung (Neuansiedlung, Expansion von Mietern)	☐	☐	☐	☐
Anzahl / Struktur aktueller Mieter	☐	☐	☐	☐
Anzahl / Struktur potentieller Mieter	☐	☐	☐	☐
Nachfragemacht der Mieter	☐	☐	☐	☐

TEIL 2.6: ZUSAMMENFASSUNG

Zusammenfassend soll der Einfluss der Kategorien untersucht werden. Bitte kreuzen Sie an, inwiefern die Kategorien nach Ihrer Meinung einen Einfluss auf Büroimmobilienmietpreise haben.

	sehr hoch	hoch	mittel	niedrig	sehr niedrig	Kein Einfluss
Standortfaktoren (ÖPNV Anschluss, Nahversorgungsmöglichkeiten, Image, etc.)	☐	☐	☐	☐	☐	☐
Gebäudefaktoren (Baudatum, Architektur, Klimaanlage, Aufzug etc.)	☐	☐	☐	☐	☐	☐
Ausstattungsfaktoren der Mieteinheit (Bürozuschnitt, Bodenbelag, Stockwerk, etc.)	☐	☐	☐	☐	☐	☐
Mietvertragskonditionen (Vertragsdauer, Mietanpassungsklauseln, Incentives, Services etc.)	☐	☐	☐	☐	☐	☐
Makroökonomische Faktoren (Regionale Entwicklung, Branchenstruktur, gesamtwirtschaftliche Entwicklung)	☐	☐	☐	☐	☐	☐
Sonstige Faktoren:	☐	☐	☐	☐	☐	☐

***Bitte ordnen Sie die fünf Kategorien nach Ihrer Einflussstärke** (1 = am stärksten; 5 = am schwächsten).*

	Rang
Standortfaktoren ÖPNV Anschluss, Nahversorgungsmöglichkeiten, Image, etc.	
Gebäudefaktoren Baudatum, Architektur, Klimaanlage, Aufzug etc.	
Ausstattungsfaktoren der Mieteinheit Bürozuschnitt, Bodenbelag, Stockwerk, etc.	
Mietvertragskonditionen Vertragsdauer, Mietanpassungsklauseln, Incentives, Services etc.	
Makroökonomische Faktoren Regionale Entwicklung, Branchenstruktur, gesamtwirtschaftliche Entwicklung	

TEIL 3: ANGABEN ZUR PERSON

Welcher Branche ist Ihr Arbeitgeber zuzuordnen?

	Haupttätigkeit *(Einfachnennung)*	Nebentätigkeit *(Mehrfachnennungen möglich)*
Projektentwickler / Bauträger	☐	☐
Investor / Bestandhalter	☐	☐
Non Property Company	☐	☐
Corporate Real Estate Management	☐	☐
Private Real Estate Management	☐	☐
Bauunternehmen	☐	☐
Bank / Versicherung	☐	☐
Öffentliche Hand	☐	☐
Dienstleister (bitte spezifizieren; siehe nächste Frage)	☐	☐
Sonstige:	☐	☐

Wenn Ihr Arbeitgeber ein Dienstleister ist, spezifizieren Sie bitte, welche Dienstleistungen Ihr Unternehmen anbietet.

(Mehrfachnennung möglich)

Architekt / Fachplaner	☐	Makler	☐	Projektsteuerer	☐
Sachverständiger	☐	Berater	☐	Facilities Manager / Immobilienverwalter	☐

Wie viele Jahre Berufserfahrung haben Sie im Immobilienbereich?

unter 3 Jahren	3 -5 Jahre	5 – 10 Jahre	über 10 Jahre
☐	☐	☐	☐

In welchem Bereich liegt der Schwerpunkt Ihrer Tätigkeit im Unternehmen? (Mehrfachnennungen möglich)

Projektentwicklung	☐	Immobilienanalyse	☐
Facilities Management / Immobilienverwaltung	☐	Immobilieninvestition	☐
Immobilienfinanzierung	☐	Immobilienmarketing (inkl. Vertrieb)	☐
Immobilienbewertung	☐	Corporate Real Estate Management	☐
Portfoliomanagement	☐	Private Real Estate Management	☐
Public Real Estate Management	☐	Sonstige:	☐
Bau-Projektmanagement	☐		

Vielen Dank!

Per Fax an 030 439096 50 Seite 1 von 5

A.2.3 Office Rent in German Cities

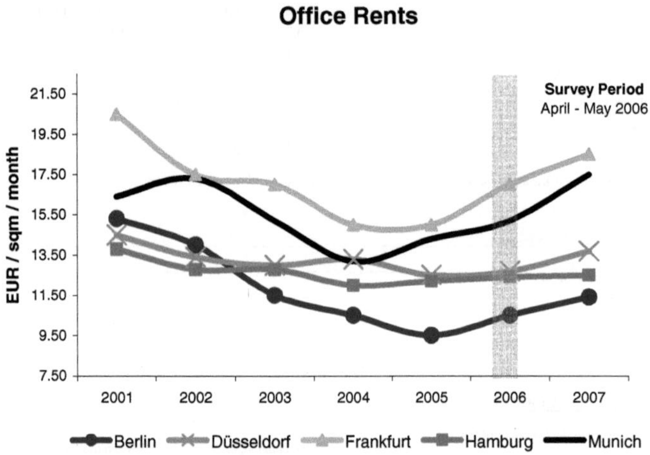

Source: Gesellschaft für Immobilienwirtschaftliche Forschung (gif)

Figure 49: Office Rents in German Cities

A.2.4 Statistical Results

A.2.4.1 Descriptive Statistics

	Count	Mean	Median	Range	Std Deviation	Percentile 05	Percentile 25	Percentile 75
2.1 Proximity to Public Transportation	96	2,691	3,000	3,000	0,880	1,000	2,000	3,000
2.1 Proximity to Airport	96	1,833	2,000	8,000	1,149	0,000	1,000	3,000
2.1 Proximity to Railway Station	96	1,854	2,000	8,000	1,105	0,000	1,000	2,000
2.1 Proximity to Highway Access	96	2,010	2,000	5,000	1,021	0,850	1,000	3,000
2.1 Availability of Parking Space	96	2,938	3,000	6,000	0,927	1,850	3,000	3,000
2.1 Availability of Free Parking Space	96	2,125	2,000	4,000	1,117	0,000	1,000	3,000
2.1 Proximity to Restaurants	96	1,604	2,000	5,000	1,100	0,000	1,000	2,000
2.1 Proximity to Shops	96	1,552	2,000	4,000	0,961	0,000	1,000	2,000
2.1 Proximity to Hotels	96	0,979	1,000	5,000	1,046	-0,150	0,000	2,000
2.1 Proximity to Companies of the same Sector	96	1,260	1,000	6,000	1,163	-0,150	0,000	2,000
2.1 Proximity to Companies	96	0,979	1,000	6,000	1,117	0,000	0,000	2,000
2.1 Atmoshere-Good Image of Surroundings	96	2,916	3,000	3,000	0,834	1,000	3,000	3,000
2.1 Atmoshere-Bad Image of Surroundings	96	-2,802	-3,000	7,000	1,148	-4,000	-4,000	-2,000
2.1 Atmosphere-High Comfort of Surroundings	96	2,095	2,000	7,000	1,063	1,000	1,000	3,000
2.1 Atmosphere-Low Comfort of Surroundings	96	-2,063	-2,000	7,000	1,303	-4,000	-3,000	-2,000
2.1 Atmosphere-High Emission of Traffic Polution and Noise	96	-1,646	-2,000	7,000	1,596	-4,000	-3,000	-1,000
2.1 Atmosphere-Low Emission of Traffic Polution and Noise	96	1,000	1,000	6,000	1,082	-0,200	0,000	2,000
2.1 Atmosphere-Good Visibility of Office Building	96	1,896	2,000	7,000	1,174	0,000	1,000	3,000
2.1 Atmosphere-Bad Visibility of Office Building	96	-1,448	-1,000	6,000	1,113	-3,000	-2,000	-1,000

Table 61: Descriptive Statistics of Location Factors

	Count	Mean	Median	Range	Std Deviation	Percentile 05	Percentile 25	Percentile 75
2.2 Flexibility-High	96	2,448	2,000	3,000	0,905	1,000	2,000	3,000
2.2 Flexibility-Medium	96	0,484	0,000	4,000	1,040	-1,000	0,000	1,000
2.2 Flexibility-Low	96	-1,600	-2,000	7,000	1,462	-4,000	-3,000	-1,000
2.2 Unit of Area Measurement- GIF	96	0,585	0,000	6,000	1,186	-1,000	0,000	1,000
2.2 Unit of Area Measurement-DIN 227	96	0,372	0,000	6,000	1,107	-1,250	0,000	1,000
2.2 Unit of Area Measurement-Others	96	-0,225	0,000	5,000	0,865	-2,000	0,000	0,000
2.2 Year of Construction - before 1990	96	-1,585	-2,000	8,000	1,589	-4,000	-3,000	-1,000
2.2 Year of Construction - between 1991 and 1995	96	-0,354	0,000	7,000	1,330	-2,000	-1,000	0,000
2.2 Year of Construction - between 1996 and 2000	96	0,438	0,000	5,000	1,094	-1,000	0,000	1,000
2.2 Year of Construction - between 2001 and 2005	96	1,719	2,000	6,000	1,023	0,000	1,000	2,000
2.2 Year of Construction - after 2006	96	2,510	3,000	5,000	1,095	0,000	2,000	3,000
2.2 Architecture - High Quality of Exterior Design	96	2,188	2,000	7,000	1,108	1,000	2,000	3,000
2.2 Architecture - Low Quality of Exterior Design	96	-1,621	-2,000	6,000	1,044	-3,000	-2,000	-1,000
2.2 Architecture - Representative Entrance Area	96	2,031	2,000	4,000	0,934	0,000	1,000	3,000
2.2 Architecture - High Quality of Construction Materials	96	1,604	2,000	6,000	0,946	0,000	1,000	2,000
2.2 Architecture - Low Quality of Construction Materials	96	-1,660	-2,000	6,000	1,093	-3,000	-2,000	-1,000
2.2 Architecture - High Prestige	96	2,490	3,000	7,000	1,124	1,000	2,000	3,000
2.2 Architecture - Low Prestige	96	-1,832	-2,000	7,000	1,226	-4,000	-3,000	-1,000
2.2 Climate Control - No Air-Conditioning	96	-0,656	-1,000	8,000	1,398	-3,000	-2,000	0,000
2.2 Climate Control - Partial Air-Conditioning	96	1,281	1,000	7,000	1,254	-1,000	1,000	2,000
2.2 Climate Control - Full Air-Conditioning	96	1,063	1,000	7,000	1,666	-3,000	0,250	2,000
2.2 Emergeny Power - provided	96	0,737	1,000	4,000	0,828	0,000	0,000	1,000
2.2 Emergeny Power - not provided	96	-0,452	0,000	5,000	0,860	-2,200	-1,000	0,000
2.2 Security Systems - provided	96	1,396	1,000	4,000	0,888	0,000	1,000	2,000
2.2 Security Systems - upgradable	96	0,604	0,000	6,000	1,041	-1,000	0,000	1,000
2.2 Security Systems - not provided	96	-0,802	-1,000	6,000	0,969	-2,000	-1,000	0,000
2.2 IT Infrastructure - not provide	96	-0,979	-1,000	8,000	1,940	-4,000	-2,000	0,000
2.2 IT Infrastructure - fibre optics	96	1,151	1,000	7,000	1,215	-1,300	0,000	2,000
2.2 IT Infrastructure - Server Room provided	96	-1,474	-2,000	7,000	1,359	-3,200	-2,000	-1,000
2.2 IT Infrastructure - Server Room in the Basement	96	-0,564	0,000	6,000	1,063	-2,000	-1,000	0,000
2.2 IT Infrastructure - Server Room on the same Level	96	0,747	1,000	5,000	1,041	-1,000	0,000	2,000
2.2 Ecology - Economic Power Consumption	96	1,579	2,000	7,000	1,154	0,000	1,000	2,000
2.2 Ecology - Planting Vegetation on the Facade	96	0,463	0,000	6,000	0,897	0,000	0,000	1,000
2.2 Ecology - Solar Cells	96	0,543	0,000	4,000	0,771	0,000	0,000	1,000
2.2 Ecology - Heat Pump	96	0,543	0,000	3,000	0,799	0,000	0,000	1,000
2.2 Upgradeability of IT - simple	96	1,547	1,000	7,000	1,319	0,000	1,000	2,000
2.2 Upgradeability of IT - complex	96	-1,926	-2,000	6,000	1,257	-4,000	-3,000	-1,000
2.2 Availability of Elevator	96	1,832	2,000	4,000	1,326	0,000	1,000	3,000

Table 62: Descriptive Statistics of Building Factors

	Count	Mean	Median	Range	Std Deviation	Percentile 05	Percentile 25	Percentile 75
2.4 Lease Length - up to 3 years	96	1,200	1,000	8,000	1,342	-0,200	0,000	2,000
2.4 Lease Length - up to 5 years	96	0,389	0,000	5,000	1,055	-1,000	0,000	1,000
2.4 Lease Length - up to 10 years	96	-0,884	-1,000	6,000	1,228	-2,200	-2,000	0,000
2.4 Lease Length - over 10 years	96	-1,874	-2,000	8,000	1,496	-4,000	-3,000	-1,000
2.4 Rental Space - up to 500 m²	96	0,916	1,000	6,000	1,117	-1,000	0,000	2,000
2.4 Rental Space - between 500 and 1000 m²	96	0,116	0,000	6,000	1,030	-2,000	0,000	1,000
2.4 Rental Space - between 1001 and 5000 m²	96	-0,958	-1,000	5,000	1,157	-3,000	-2,000	0,000
2.4 Rental Space - over 5000 m²	96	-1,726	-2,000	7,000	1,498	-4,000	-3,000	-1,000
2.4 Options - Lease Extension	96	0,337	0,000	5,000	0,985	-1,000	0,000	1,000
2.4 Options - Breakoption with Penality	96	0,582	1,000	5,000	1,106	-2,000	0,000	1,000
2.4 Options - Subletting	96	0,389	0,000	6,000	0,879	0,000	0,000	1,000
2.4 Options - Purchase Option	96	0,368	0,000	6,000	0,864	-1,000	0,000	1,000
2.4 Adjustment of Rental Space - Expansion with First Right to Rent	96	1,064	1,000	4,000	0,982	0,000	0,000	2,000
2.4 Adjustment of Rental Space - Expansion with Obligation of Landlord to offer	96	0,828	1,000	4,000	0,880	0,000	0,000	1,000
2.4 Adjustment of Space - Reduction	96	1,362	1,000	6,000	1,199	-0,500	1,000	2,000
2.4 Incentives - "New" landlord takes over "old" lease contracts	96	1,587	2,000	6,000	1,215	-0,350	1,000	2,000
2.4 Incentives - Landlord takes over relocation expenses	96	1,400	1,000	5,000	1,015	0,000	1,000	2,000
2.4 Incentives - Rent Free Periods	96	1,505	2,000	6,000	1,090	0,000	1,000	2,000
2.4 Incentives - Landlord takes over tenant's fit out	96	1,747	2,000	6,000	1,091	0,000	1,000	2,000
2.4 Collateral - Suretyship	96	-0,106	0,000	4,000	0,558	-1,000	0,000	0,000
2.4 Collateral - Letter of Comfort	96	-0,106	0,000	7,000	0,886	-1,250	0,000	0,000
2.4 Lease contract with stepped rent	96	-0,452	0,000	7,000	1,379	-3,000	-1,000	0,000
2.4 Lease contract with escalation clause	96	-0,074	0,000	5,000	0,937	-2,000	-1,000	0,000
2.4 Additional Charges - Operating Expenses	96	-0,221	0,000	7,000	0,840	-2,000	0,000	0,000
2.4 Additional Charges - Administration Costs	96	-0,771	-1,000	7,000	0,957	-2,000	-1,000	0,000
2.4 Additional Charges - Security Costs	96	-0,737	-1,000	7,000	1,013	-2,000	-1,000	0,000
2.4 Additional Charges - Maintenance and Repair within rental unit	96	-0,737	-1,000	6,000	1,023	-3,000	-1,000	0,000
2.4 Additional Charges - Maintenance and Repair (Dach+Fach) pro rata	96	-1,427	-1,000	8,000	1,296	-4,000	-2,000	-1,000
2.4 Additional Charges - Maintenance and Repair (Dach+Fach) total	96	-2,552	-3,000	8,000	1,352	-4,000	-3,750	-2,000
2.4 Additional Charges - Agreement on Full Maintenance Contract	96	-1,539	-2,000	7,000	1,523	-4,000	-3,000	0,000
2.4 Legal Form - Sole Proprietor	96	0,138	0,000	6,000	0,784	-1,000	0,000	0,000
2.4 Legal Form - Corporate Body	96	0,064	0,000	3,000	0,459	-1,000	0,000	0,000
2.4 Value added tax on input - tenant is allowed to charge VAT on input	96	0,258	0,000	6,000	0,943	-1,000	0,000	0,000
2.4 Value added tax on input - tenant is not allowed to charge VAT on input	96	0,368	0,000	8,000	1,845	-4,000	0,000	2,000
2.4 Value added tax on input - tenant is partially allowed to charge VAT on input	96	0,309	0,000	7,000	1,552	-3,000	0,000	1,000
2.4 Location of Tenant's Headquarters - Germany	96	0,128	0,000	4,000	0,609	-0,250	0,000	0,000
2.4 Location of Tenant's Headquarters - EU 25	96	0,245	0,000	3,000	0,581	-0,250	0,000	1,000
2.4 Location of Tenant's Headquarters - outside of Europe	96	0,223	0,000	7,000	1,069	-1,250	0,000	1,000
2.4 Business Sector of Tenant - Banks, Investmentfirms, Insurances	96	0,594	0,000	6,000	1,286	-1,150	0,000	2,000
2.4 Business Sector of Tenant - Barister, Auditing, Accounting	96	0,750	1,000	7,000	1,322	-1,000	0,000	2,000
2.4 Business Sector of Tenant - Other Services	96	0,340	0,000	5,000	0,741	-0,250	0,000	1,000
2.4 Business Sector of Tenant - Media, Entertainment, Advertisement	96	0,474	0,000	4,000	0,885	-1,000	0,000	1,000
2.4 Business Sector of Tenant - IT / Computing	96	0,421	0,000	5,000	0,906	-1,000	0,000	1,000
2.4 Business Sector of Tenant - Public Institutions	96	-0,375	-1,000	7,000	1,503	-3,000	-1,000	0,750
2.4 Business Sector of Tenant - Foundation for Public Utility, Syndicates	96	-0,188	0,000	6,000	1,259	-2,150	-1,000	1,000
2.4 Business Sector of Tenant - Others	96	0,073	0,000	6,000	0,785	-1,000	0,000	0,000
2.4 Tenant Services - Cleaning of Rental Space	96	0,734	1,000	3,000	0,750	0,000	0,000	1,000
2.4 Tenant Services - Security Services	96	0,883	1,000	2,000	0,686	0,000	0,000	1,000
2.4 Tenant Services - Laundry Services	96	0,340	0,000	4,000	0,578	0,000	0,000	1,000
2.4 Tenant Services - Canteen	96	0,638	1,000	2,000	0,584	0,000	0,000	1,000
2.4 Tenant Services - Furnishment Services	96	0,553	0,000	2,000	0,633	0,000	0,000	1,000
2.4 Tenant Services - Moving Services	96	0,628	1,000	3,000	0,656	0,000	0,000	1,000
2.4 Tenant Services - Day Care	96	0,755	1,000	3,000	0,825	0,000	0,000	1,000
2.4 Tenant Services - Shopping Services	96	0,447	0,000	5,000	0,713	0,000	0,000	1,000
2.4 Tenant Services - Concierge	96	0,713	1,000	4,000	0,771	0,000	0,000	1,000
2.4 Others - Building Cost Subsidy	96	-0,446	-1,000	7,000	1,848	-3,000	-2,000	2,000
2.4 Exemption of tenant's obligation to restore to original condition	96	1,228	1,000	7,000	1,070	-0,350	1,000	2,000

Table 63: Descriptive Statistics of Lease Factors

	Count	Mean	Median	Range	Std Deviation	Percentile 05	Percentile 25	Percentile 75
2.5 Macroeconomic Development of Germany	96	2,400	3,000	3,000	0,690	1,000	2,000	3,000
2.5 Macroeconomic Development of City	96	2,621	3,000	2,000	0,530	2,000	2,000	3,000
2.5 Structure of Real Estate Supply - Market Size	96	2,411	2,000	3,000	0,644	1,000	2,000	3,000
2.5 Structure of Real Estate Supply - Vacancy	96	2,737	3,000	2,000	0,488	2,000	3,000	3,000
2.5 Structure of Real Estate Supply - Planned Projects	96	2,021	2,000	2,000	0,655	1,000	2,000	2,000
2.5 Structure of Real Estate Supply - Bargaining Power of Landlord	96	2,053	2,000	3,000	0,830	1,000	1,000	3,000
2.5 Structure of Real Estate Demand - Development of Land Requirement	96	2,202	2,000	3,000	0,727	1,000	2,000	3,000
2.5 Structure of Real Estate Demand - Number of Tenants	96	1,851	2,000	3,000	0,733	1,000	1,000	2,000
2.5 Structure of Real Estate Demand - Number of potential Tenants	96	1,883	2,000	3,000	0,716	1,000	1,000	2,000
2.5 Structure of Real Estate Demand - Bargaining Power of Tenant	96	2,474	3,000	3,000	0,727	1,000	2,000	3,000

Table 64: Descriptive Statistics of Macroeconomic Factors

	Count	Mean	Median	Range	Std Deviation	Percentile 05	Percentile 25	Percentile 75
2.6 Location Factors	96	4,084	4,000	3,000	0,794	2,800	4,000	5,000
2.6 Building Factors	96	3,684	4,000	3,000	0,657	2,800	3,000	4,000
2.6 Equipment and Layout Factors	96	3,674	4,000	3,000	0,691	3,000	3,000	4,000
2.6 Lease Factors	96	3,705	4,000	3,000	0,966	2,000	3,000	4,000
2.6 Macroeconomic Factors	96	3,358	3,000	4,000	1,051	1,800	3,000	4,000
2.6 Ranking - Location Factors	96	2,215	2,000	4,000	1,309	1,000	1,000	3,000
2.6 Ranking - Building Factors	96	3,204	3,000	4,000	0,962	2,000	3,000	4,000
2.6 Ranking - Equipment and Layout Factors	96	3,011	3,000	4,000	1,166	1,000	2,000	4,000
2.6 Ranking - Lease Factors	96	2,902	3,000	4,000	1,476	1,000	1,000	4,000
2.6 Ranking - Macroeconomic Factors	96	3,587	5,000	4,000	1,691	1,000	2,000	5,000

Table 65: Descriptive Statistics of Summary Factors

A.2.4.2 Univariate Analysis - Differences between Office Markets

The following tables show the statistical results of the univariate analysis. The univariate analysis comprises three steps. First, it was checked whether the attributes met the Levene's test for homogeneity of variances. Second, if the assumption of homogeneity of variances has not been violated, the hyptothesis are tested using the Fisher exact test. Third, due to the small sample size, significance tests for Brown-Forsythe and Welch are applied. Only those results are reported which meet all statistical tests.

A.2.4.2.1 Location Factors

Test of Homogeneity of Variances

	Levene Statistic	df1	df2	Sig.
2.1 Proximity to Public Transportation	0,212	3	78	0,888
2.1 Proximity to Airport	2,916	3	80	0,039
2.1 Proximity to Railway Station	1,207	3	80	0,313
2.1 Proximity to Highway Access	2,574	3	80	0,060
2.1 Availability of Parking Space	1,626	3	80	0,190
2.1 Availability of Free Parking Space	0,453	3	80	0,716
2.1 Proximity to Restaurants	1,489	3	80	0,224
2.1 Proximity to Shops	2,941	3	80	0,038
2.1 Proximity to Hotels	0,325	3	80	0,808
2.1 Proximity to Companies of the same Sector	0,422	3	80	0,738
2.1 Proximity to Companies	0,874	3	78	0,458
2.1 Atmoshere-Good Image of Surroundings	1,052	3	79	0,374
2.1 Atmoshere-Bad Image of Surroundings	3,446	3	80	0,020
2.1 Atmosphere-High Comfort of Surroundings	3,114	3	79	0,031
2.1 Atmosphere-Low Comfort of Surroundings	1,597	3	79	0,197
2.1 Atmosphere-High Emission of Traffic Polution and Noise	2,107	3	80	0,106
2.1 Atmosphere-Low Emission of Traffic Polution and Noise	1,753	3	79	0,163
2.1 Atmosphere-Good Visibility of Office Building	1,296	3	80	0,282
2.1 Atmosphere-Bad Visibility of Office Building	2,974	3	80	0,037

Table 66: Levene's Test for Homogeneity y of Variances - Location Factors by Office Markets

ANOVA

		Sum of Squares	df	Mean Square	F	Sig.
2.1 Proximity to Public Transportation	Between Groups	6,858	3	2,286	3,028	0,034
	Within Groups	58,898	78	0,755		
	Total	65,756	81			
2.1 Proximity to Railway Station	Between Groups	13,833	3	4,611	3,990	0,011
	Within Groups	92,452	80	1,156		
	Total	106,286	83			
2.1 Proximity to Restaurants	Between Groups	15,202	3	5,067	4,530	0,006
	Within Groups	89,500	80	1,119		
	Total	104,702	83			
2.1 Atmosphere-High Emission of Traffic Polution and Noise	Between Groups	20,398	3	6,799	2,768	0,047
	Within Groups	196,495	80	2,456		
	Total	216,893	83			

Table 67: ANOVA Results for Location Factors

		Statistic(a)	df1	df2	Sig.
2.1 Proximity to Public Transportation	Welch	2,557	3	30,001	0,074
	Brown-Forsythe	2,743	3	52,764	0,052
2.1 Proximity to Railway Station	Welch	4,501	3	32,475	0,009
	Brown-Forsythe	3,257	3	33,030	0,034
2.1 Availability of Parking Space	Welch	0,693	3	30,801	0,564
	Brown-Forsythe	0,728	3	52,599	0,540
2.1 Proximity to Restaurants	Welch	4,376	3	34,012	0,010
	Brown-Forsythe	4,448	3	55,637	0,007
2.1 Atmosphere-High Emission of Traffic Polution and Noise	Welch	2,436	3	32,926	0,082
	Brown-Forsythe	2,512	3	49,077	0,069

Table 68: Robust Tests for Location Factors

2.1 Proximity to Public Transportation

Tukey HSD[a,b]

1.2 Specification of Office Market	N	Subset for alpha = .05 1	2
Düsseldorf	12	2,08	
Berlin	35	2,63	2,63
Frankfurt	21		2,90
Hamburg	14		3,00
Sig.		,260	,592

Means for groups in homogeneous subsets are displayed.

a. Uses Harmonic Mean Sample Size = 17,320.

b. The group sizes are unequal. The harmonic mean of the group sizes is used. Type I error levels are not guaranteed.

Table 69: Post-hoc Turkey Test (Proximity to Public Transportation)

2.1 Proximity to Railway Station

Tukey HSD[a,b]

1.2 Specification of Office Market	N	Subset for alpha = .05 1	2
Düsseldorf	14	1,36	
Berlin	35	1,71	1,71
Hamburg	14	1,71	1,71
Frankfurt	21		2,52
Sig.		,748	,112

Means for groups in homogeneous subsets are displayed.

a. Uses Harmonic Mean Sample Size = 18,261.

b. The group sizes are unequal. The harmonic mean of the group sizes is used. Type I error levels are not guaranteed.

Table 70: Post-hoc Turkey Test (Proximity to Railway Station)

2.1 Proximity to Restaurants

Tukey HSD[a,b]

1.2 Specification of Office Market	N	Subset for alpha = .05 1	2
Düsseldorf	14	1,07	
Frankfurt	21	1,14	
Berlin	35	1,71	1,71
Hamburg	14		2,29
Sig.		,264	,366

Means for groups in homogeneous subsets are displayed.

a. Uses Harmonic Mean Sample Size = 18,261.

b. The group sizes are unequal. The harmonic mean of the group sizes is used. Type I error levels are not guaranteed.

Table 71: Post-hoc Turkey Test (Proximity to Restaurants)

2.1 Atmosphere-High Emission of Traffic Polution and Noise

Tukey HSD[a,b]

1.2 Specification of Office Market	N	Subset for alpha = .05	
		1	2
Hamburg	14	-2,14	
Berlin	35	-1,69	-1,69
Frankfurt	21	-1,24	-1,24
Düsseldorf	14		-,57
Sig.		,308	,147

Means for groups in homogeneous subsets are displayed.

a. Uses Harmonic Mean Sample Size = 18,261.

b. The group sizes are unequal. The harmonic mean of the group sizes is used. Type I error levels are not guaranteed.

Table 72: Post-hoc Turkey Test (Atmosphere-High Emission of Traffic Pollution and Noise)

A.2.4.2.2 Lease Factors

Test of Homogeneity of Variances

	Levene Statistic	df1	df2	Sig.
2.4 Lease Length - up to 3 years	1,697	3	79	0,174
2.4 Lease Length - up to 5 years	3,821	3	79	0,013
2.4 Lease Length - up to 10 years	1,324	3	79	0,272
2.4 Lease Length - over 10 years	0,142	3	79	0,934
2.4 Rental Space - up to 500 m²	0,633	3	79	0,596
2.4 Rental Space - between 500 and 1000 m²	0,711	3	79	0,548
2.4 Rental Space - between 1001 and 5000 m²	0,719	3	79	0,544
2.4 Rental Space - over 5000 m²	0,909	3	79	0,441
2.4 Options - Lease Extension	2,046	3	79	0,114
2.4 Options - Breakoption with Penality	0,438	3	76	0,726
2.4 Options - Subletting	4,612	3	79	0,005
2.4 Options - Purchase Option	0,681	3	79	0,566
2.4 Adjustment of Rental Space - Expansion with First Right to Rent	0,677	3	79	0,569
2.4 Adjustment of Rental Space - Expansion with Obligation of Landlord to offer	3,109	3	78	0,031
2.4 Adjustment of Space - Reduction	2,312	3	78	0,083
2.4 Incentives - "New" landlord takes over "old" lease contracts	0,491	3	77	0,690
2.4 Incentives - Landlord takes over relocation expenses	1,919	3	79	0,133
2.4 Incentives - Rent Free Periods	1,676	3	79	0,179
2.4 Incentives - Landlord takes over tenant's fit out	0,572	3	79	0,635
2.4 Collateral - Suretyship	3,084	3	78	0,032
2.4 Collateral - Letter of Comfort	1,662	3	78	0,182
2.4 Lease contract with stepped rent	0,399	3	78	0,754
2.4 Lease contract with escalation clause	0,880	3	79	0,455
2.4 Additional Charges - Operating Expenses	0,510	3	80	0,677
2.4 Additional Charges - Administration Costs	1,163	3	80	0,329
2.4 Additional Charges - Security Costs	1,470	3	79	0,229
2.4 Additional Charges - Maintenance and Repair within rental unit	0,142	3	79	0,934
2.4 Additional Charges - Maintenance and Repair (Dach+Fach) pro rata	0,564	3	80	0,641
2.4 Additional Charges - Maintenance and Repair (Dach+Fach) total	0,623	3	80	0,602
2.4 Additional Charges - Agreement on Full Maintenance Contract	0,611	3	76	0,610
2.4 Legal Form - Sole Proprietor	2,885	3	78	0,041
2.4 Legal Form - Corporate Body	3,041	3	78	0,034
2.4 Value added tax on input - tenant is allowed to charge VAT on input	4,268	3	77	0,008
2.4 Value added tax on input - tenant is not allowed to charge VAT on input	1,527	3	79	0,214
2.4 Value added tax on input - tenant is partially allowed to charge VAT on input	0,745	3	79	0,528
2.4 Location of Tenant's Headquarters - Germany	3,861	3	78	0,012
2.4 Location of Tenant's Headquarters - EU 25	3,232	3	78	0,027
2.4 Location of Tenant's Headquarters - outside of Europe	0,551	3	78	0,649
2.4 Business Sector of Tenant - Banks, Investmentfirms, Insurances	0,929	3	80	0,430
2.4 Business Sector of Tenant - Barister, Auditing, Accounting	0,177	3	80	0,911
2.4 Business Sector of Tenant - Other Services	2,746	3	78	0,049
2.4 Business Sector of Tenant - Media, Entertainment, Advertisement	1,373	3	79	0,257
2.4 Business Sector of Tenant - IT / Computing	1,055	3	79	0,373
2.4 Business Sector of Tenant - Public Institutions	2,262	3	80	0,088
2.4 Business Sector of Tenant - Foundation for Public Utility, Syndicates	2,282	3	80	0,085
2.4 Business Sector of Tenant - Others	4,924	3	80	0,003
2.4 Tenant Services - Cleaning of Rental Space	1,028	3	78	0,385
2.4 Tenant Services - Security Services	0,728	3	78	0,538
2.4 Tenant Services - Laundry Services	4,024	3	78	0,010
2.4 Tenant Services - Canteen	1,619	3	78	0,192
2.4 Tenant Services - Furnishment Services	1,800	3	78	0,154
2.4 Tenant Services - Moving Services	2,118	3	78	0,105
2.4 Tenant Services - Day Care	1,724	3	78	0,169
2.4 Tenant Services - Shopping Services	6,103	3	78	0,001
2.4 Tenant Services - Concierge	1,465	3	78	0,230
2.4 Others - Building Cost Subsidy	5,055	3	77	0,003
2.4 Exemption of tenant's obligation to restore to original condition	1,281	3	77	0,287

Table 73: Levene's Test for Homogeneity of Variances - Lease Factors by Office Markets

ANOVA

		Sum of Squares	df	Mean Square	F	Sig.
2.4 Lease Length - up to 10 years	Between Groups	13,508	3	4,503	3,207	0,028
	Within Groups	110,902	79	1,404		
	Total	124,410	82			
2.4 Rental Space - up to 500 m²	Between Groups	13,181	3	4,394	4,177	0,008
	Within Groups	83,108	79	1,052		
	Total	96,289	82			
2.4 Rental Space - between 500 and 1000 m²	Between Groups	10,073	3	3,358	3,513	0,019
	Within Groups	75,495	79	0,956		
	Total	85,568	82			
2.4 Rental Space - between 1001 and 5000 m²	Between Groups	9,712	3	3,237	2,579	0,059
	Within Groups	99,179	79	1,255		
	Total	108,892	82			
2.4 Options - Breakoption with Penality	Between Groups	12,540	3	4,180	4,001	0,011
	Within Groups	79,410	76	1,045		
	Total	91,950	79			

Table 74: ANOVA Results for Lease Factors

Robust Tests of Equality of Means(b,c,d)

		Statistic(a)	df1	df2	Sig.
2.4 Lease Length - up to 10 years	Welch	3,861	3	37,114	0,017
	Brown-Forsythe	3,594	3	66,612	0,018
2.4 Rental Space - up to 500 m²	Welch	3,756	3	36,035	0,019
	Brown-Forsythe	4,435	3	62,891	0,007
2.4 Rental Space - between 500 and 1000 m²	Welch	5,646	3	38,891	0,003
	Brown-Forsythe	4,717	3	76,986	0,004
2.4 Rental Space - between 1001 and 5000 m²	Welch	2,104	3	36,176	0,117
	Brown-Forsythe	2,784	3	67,612	0,047
2.4 Options - Breakoption with Penality	Welch	3,656	3	30,948	0,023
	Brown-Forsythe	3,791	3	51,141	0,016

Table 75: Robust Tests for Lease Factors

2.4 Lease Length - up to 10 years

Tukey HSD[a,b]

1.2 Specification of Office Market	N	Subset for alpha = .05	
		1	2
Düsseldorf	14	-1,64	
Hamburg	14	-1,00	-1,00
Berlin	34	-,91	-,91
Frankfurt	21		-,38
Sig.		,253	,398

Means for groups in homogeneous subsets are displayed.

a. Uses Harmonic Mean Sample Size = 18,191.

b. The group sizes are unequal. The harmonic mean of the group sizes is used. Type I error levels are not guaranteed.

Table 76: Post-hoc Turkey Test (Lease Length – up to 10 years)

2.4 Rental Space - up to 500 m²

Tukey HSD[a,b]

1.2 Specification of Office Market	N	Subset for alpha = .05	
		1	2
Hamburg	14	,36	
Düsseldorf	14	,64	,64
Berlin	34	,68	,68
Frankfurt	21		1,48
Sig.		,784	,076

Means for groups in homogeneous subsets are displayed.

a. Uses Harmonic Mean Sample Size = 18,191.

b. The group sizes are unequal. The harmonic mean of the group sizes is used. Type I error levels are not guaranteed.

Table 77: Post-hoc Turkey Test (Rental Space – up to 500 m²)

2.4 Rental Space - between 500 and 1000 m²

Tukey HSD[a,b]

1.2 Specification of Office Market	N	Subset for alpha = .05	
		1	2
Hamburg	14	-,36	
Düsseldorf	14	-,21	-,21
Berlin	34	,03	,03
Frankfurt	21		,62
Sig.		,634	,057

Means for groups in homogeneous subsets are displayed.

a. Uses Harmonic Mean Sample Size = 18,191.

b. The group sizes are unequal. The harmonic mean of the group sizes is used. Type I error levels are not guaranteed.

Table 78: Post-hoc Turkey Test (Rental Space – between 500 and 1000 m²)

2.4 Rental Space - between 1001 and 5000 m²

Tukey HSD[a,b]

1.2 Specification of Office Market	N	Subset for alpha = .05
		1
Hamburg	14	-1,21
Berlin	34	-1,18
Düsseldorf	14	-1,07
Frankfurt	21	-,38
Sig.		,121

Means for groups in homogeneous subsets are displayed.

a. Uses Harmonic Mean Sample Size = 18,191.

b. The group sizes are unequal. The harmonic mean of the group sizes is used. Type I error levels are not guaranteed.

Table 79: Post-hoc Turkey Test (Rental Space – between 1001 and 5000 m²)

2.4 Options - Breakoption with Penalty

Tukey HSD[a,b]

1.2 Specification of Office Market	N	Subset for alpha = .05	
		1	2
Hamburg	12	-,08	
Düsseldorf	14	-,07	
Berlin	34	,65	,65
Frankfurt	20		,90
Sig.		,166	,888

Means for groups in homogeneous subsets are displayed.

a. Uses Harmonic Mean Sample Size = 17,081.

b. The group sizes are unequal. The harmonic mean of the group sizes is used. Type I error levels are not guaranteed.

Table 80: Post-hoc Turkey Test (Options – Break option with Penalty)

A.2.4.3 Univariate Analysis - Differences between Market Participants' Perceptions

A.2.4.3.1 Building Factors

Test of Homogeneity of Variances

	Levene Statistic	df1	df2	Sig.
2.2 Flexibility-High	2,077	3	78	0,110
2.2 Flexibility-Medium	1,074	3	77	0,365
2.2 Flexibility-Low	0,397	3	77	0,755
2.2 Unit of Area Measurement- GIF	0,471	3	76	0,703
2.2 Unit of Area Measurement-DIN 227	0,374	3	76	0,772
2.2 Unit of Area Measurement-Others	1,969	3	60	0,128
2.2 Year of Construction - before 1990	3,741	3	76	0,015
2.2 Year of Construction - between 1991 and 1995	0,748	3	78	0,527
2.2 Year of Construction - between 1996 and 2000	0,015	0	70	0,000
2.2 Year of Construction - between 2001 and 2005	1,236	3	78	0,302
2.2 Year of Construction - after 2006	0,258	3	78	0,856
2.2 Architecture - High Quality of Exterior Design	0,406	3	78	0,749
2.2 Architecture - Low Quality of Exterior Design	3,310	3	77	0,024
2.2 Architecture - Representative Entrance Area	0,897	3	78	0,447
2.2 Architecture - High Quality of Construction Materials	0,138	3	78	0,937
2.2 Architecture - Low Quality of Construction Materials	1,214	3	76	0,311
2.2 Architecture - High Prestige	0,232	3	78	0,873
2.2 Architecture - Low Prestige	0,366	3	77	0,778
2.2 Climate Control - No Air-Conditioning	0,131	3	78	0,941
2.2 Climate Control - Partial Air-Conditioning	1,728	3	78	0,168
2.2 Climate Control - Full Air-Conditioning	9,127	3	78	0,000
2.2 Emergeny Power - provided	0,667	3	77	0,575
2.2 Emergeny Power - not provided	6,548	3	77	0,001
2.2 Security Systems - provided	3,450	3	78	0,021
2.2 Security Systems - upgradable	1,090	3	78	0,358
2.2 Security Systems - not provided	1,545	3	78	0,210
2.2 IT Infrastructure - not provide	0,470	3	77	0,704
2.2 IT Infrastructure - fibre optics	3,007	3	76	0,035
2.2 IT Infrastructure - Server Room provided	1,820	3	77	0,150
2.2 IT Infrastructure - Server Room in the Basement	5,201	3	77	0,003
2.2 IT Infrastructure - Server Room on the same Level	0,567	3	77	0,638
2.2 Ecology - Economic Power Consumption	1,725	3	77	0,169
2.2 Ecology - Planting Vegetation on the Facade	6,356	3	77	0,001
2.2 Ecology - Solar Cells	1,130	3	77	0,342
2.2 Ecology - Heat Pump	2,546	3	77	0,062
2.2 Upgradeability of IT - simple	0,224	3	77	0,880
2.2 Upgradeability of IT - complex	1,417	3	77	0,244
2.2 Availability of Elevator	2,051	3	77	0,114

Table 81: Levene's Test of Homogeneity of Variances - Building Factors by Market Participants' Perceptions

ANOVA

		Sum of Squares	df	Mean Square	F	Sig.
2.2 Climate Control - No Air-Conditioning	Between Groups	27,430	3	9,143	5,409	0,002
	Within Groups	131,851	78	1,690		
	Total	159,280	81			

Table 82: ANOVA Results for Building Factors

Robust Tests of Equality of Means(b)

		Statistic(a)	df1	df2	Sig.
2.2 Climate Control - No Air-Conditioning	Welch	4,947	3	17,586	0,011
	Brown-Forsythe	5,053	3	28,717	0,006

Table 83: Robust Tests for Building Factors

2.2 Climate Control - No Air-Conditioning

Tukey HSD[a,b]

1.3 Activity in the Real Estate Market	N	Subset for alpha = .05 1	2
Broker	8	-1,50	
Service Provider	29	-1,14	-1,14
Tenant	7	-,71	-,71
Landlord	38		-,03
Sig.		,448	,159

Means for groups in homogeneous subsets are displayed.

a. Uses Harmonic Mean Sample Size = 12,171.

b. The group sizes are unequal. The harmonic mean of the group sizes is used. Type I error levels are not guaranteed.

Table 84: Post-hoc Turkey Test (Climate Control – No Air Conditioning)

A.2.4.3.2 Equipment and Layout Factor of an Office Unit

Test of Homogeneity of Variances

	Levene Statistic	df1	df2	Sig.
2.3 Office Layout - Open Plan Office	0,498	3	75	0,685
2.3 Office Layout - Group Office	1,887	3	75	0,139
2.3 Office Layout - Cellular Design	4,858	3	73	0,004
2.3 Office Layout - "Kombibüro"	1,164	3	75	0,329
2.3 Office Layout - flexible	0,881	3	76	0,455
2.3 Office Layout - reversible	0,346	3	70	0,792
2.3 Flooring - carpet	0,765	3	77	0,517
2.3 Flooring - parquet	0,188	3	77	0,905
2.3 Flooring - marble	0,548	3	76	0,651
2.3 Regulation of Air Condition - Per Room	3,406	3	77	0,022
2.3 Regulation of Air Condition - Per Workspace	0,128	3	77	0,943
2.3 Market Situation - Rental before Completion	0,909	3	75	0,441
2.3 Market Situation - Rental within 9 months of Completion	0,212	3	75	0,888
2.3 Market Situation - Rental after 9 months of Completion	0,718	3	75	0,544
2.3 Occupancy Level - First Tenant	1,582	3	73	0,201
2.3 Occupancy Level - Last Tenant	2,436	3	73	0,072
2.3. Others - Expansion of Rental Space	1,581	3	76	0,201
2.3 Others - First time use	2,841	3	76	0,043

Table 85: Levene's Test for Homogeneity of Variances - Equipment/Layout Factors by Market Participants' Perceptions

ANOVA

2.3 Flooring - parquet	Between Groups	11,432	3	3,811	4,880	0,004
	Within Groups	60,124	77	0,781		
	Total	71,556	80			

Table 86: ANOVA Results for Equipment/Layout Factors of Office Unit

Robust Tests of Equality of Means

		Statistic(a)	df1	df2	Sig.
2.3 Flooring - parquet	Welch	4,301	3	17,535	0,019
	Brown-Forsythe	4,519	3	29,846	0,010

Table 87: Robust Tests for Equipment/Layout Factors

2.3 Flooring - parquet

Tukey HSD[a,b]

1.3 Activity in the Real Estate Market	N	Subset for alpha = .05	
		1	2
Broker	8	,00	
Service Provider	29		1,03
Tenant	7		1,29
Landlord	37		1,30
Sig.		1,000	,884

Means for groups in homogeneous subsets are displayed.

a. Uses Harmonic Mean Sample Size = 12,145.

b. The group sizes are unequal. The harmonic mean of the group sizes is used. Type I error levels are not guaranteed.

Table 88: Post-hoc Turkey Test (Flooring - Parquet)

A.2.4.3.3 Lease Factors

Test of Homogeneity of Variances

	Levene Statistic	df1	df2	Sig.
2.4 Lease Length - up to 3 years	1,206	3	77	0,313
2.4 Lease Length - up to 5 years	0,049	3	77	0,985
2.4 Lease Length - up to 10 years	2,020	3	77	0,118
2.4 Lease Length - over 10 years	1,352	3	77	0,264
2.4 Rental Space - up to 500 m²	1,427	3	77	0,241
2.4 Rental Space - between 500 and 1000 m²	2,160	3	77	0,100
2.4 Rental Space - between 1001 and 5000 m²	1,936	3	77	0,131
2.4 Rental Space - over 5000 m²	0,652	3	77	0,584
2.4 Options - Lease Extension	1,071	3	77	0,367
2.4 Options - Breakoption with Penality	2,003	3	74	0,121
2.4 Options - Subletting	0,298	3	77	0,827
2.4 Options - Purchase Option	0,688	3	77	0,562
2.4 Adjustment of Rental Space - Expansion with First Right to Rent	5,556	3	77	0,002
2.4 Adjustment of Rental Space - Expansion with Obligation of Landlord to offer	0,694	3	76	0,558
2.4 Adjustment of Space - Reduction	0,644	3	76	0,589
2.4 Incentives - "New" landlord takes over "old" lease contracts	0,805	3	75	0,495
2.4 Incentives - Landlord takes over relocation expenses	1,515	3	77	0,217
2.4 Incentives - Rent Free Periods	1,786	3	77	0,157
2.4 Incentives - Landlord takes over tenant's fit out	2,063	3	77	0,112
2.4 Collateral - Suretyship	1,232	3	76	0,304
2.4 Collateral - Letter of Comfort	12,016	3	76	0,000
2.4 Lease contract with stepped rent	0,235	3	76	0,872
2.4 Lease contract with escalation clause	0,480	3	77	0,697
2.4 Additional Charges - Operating Expenses	4,668	3	78	0,005
2.4 Additional Charges - Administration Costs	0,779	3	78	0,509
2.4 Additional Charges - Security Costs	0,104	3	77	0,957
2.4 Additional Charges - Maintenance and Repair within rental unit	0,298	3	77	0,826
2.4 Additional Charges - Maintenance and Repair (Dach+Fach) pro rata	0,530	3	78	0,663
2.4 Additional Charges - Maintenance and Repair (Dach+Fach) total	0,984	3	78	0,405
2.4 Additional Charges - Agreement on Full Maintenance Contract	0,994	3	74	0,401
2.4 Legal Form - Sole Proprietor	4,222	3	76	0,008
2.4 Legal Form - Corporate Body	2,425	3	76	0,072
2.4 Value added tax on input - tenant is allowed to charge VAT on input	0,627	3	75	0,600
2.4 Value added tax on input - tenant is not allowed to charge VAT on input	1,527	3	77	0,214
2.4 Value added tax on input - tenant is partially allowed to charge VAT on input	1,315	3	77	0,275
2.4 Location of Tenant's Headquarters - Germany	2,998	3	76	0,036
2.4 Location of Tenant's Headquarters - EU 25	1,117	3	76	0,348
2.4 Location of Tenant's Headquarters - outside of Europe	2,074	3	76	0,111
2.4 Business Sector of Tenant - Banks, Investmentfirms, Insurances	1,908	3	78	0,135
2.4 Business Sector of Tenant - Barister, Auditing, Accounting	0,997	3	78	0,399
2.4 Business Sector of Tenant - Other Services	2,874	3	76	0,042
2.4 Business Sector of Tenant - Media, Entertainment, Advertisement	1,106	3	77	0,352
2.4 Business Sector of Tenant - IT / Computing	0,914	3	77	0,438
2.4 Business Sector of Tenant - Public Institutions	1,040	3	78	0,380
2.4 Business Sector of Tenant - Foundation for Public Utility, Syndicates	0,951	3	78	0,420
2.4 Business Sector of Tenant - Others	1,070	3	78	0,367
2.4 Tenant Services - Cleaning of Rental Space	0,965	3	76	0,414
2.4 Tenant Services - Security Services	3,277	3	76	0,026
2.4 Tenant Services - Laundry Services	3,529	3	76	0,019
2.4 Tenant Services - Canteen	0,766	3	76	0,517
2.4 Tenant Services - Furnishment Services	1,208	3	76	0,313
2.4 Tenant Services - Moving Services	0,877	3	76	0,457
2.4 Tenant Services - Day Care	0,160	3	76	0,923
2.4 Tenant Services - Shopping Services	2,448	3	76	0,070
2.4 Tenant Services - Concierge	0,815	3	76	0,490
2.4 Others - Building Cost Subsidy	0,573	3	75	0,635
2.4 Exemption of tenant's obligation to restore to original condition	0,193	3	75	0,901

Table 89: Levene's Test for Homogeneity of Variances - Lease Factors by Market Participants' Perceptions

ANOVA

		Sum of Squares	df	Mean Square	F	Sig.
2.4 Rental Space - between 1001 and 5000 m²	Between Groups	11,159	3	3,720	2,931	0,039
	Within Groups	97,730	77	1,269		
	Total	108,889	80			
2.4 Collateral - Letter of Comfort	Between Groups	5,319	3	1,773	2,344	0,080
	Within Groups	57,481	76	0,756		
	Total	62,800	79			
2.4 Lease contract with stepped rent	Between Groups	16,585	3	5,528	3,823	0,013
	Within Groups	109,902	76	1,446		
	Total	126,488	79			
2.4 Additional Charges - Administration Costs	Between Groups	10,967	3	3,656	4,551	0,005
	Within Groups	62,655	78	0,803		
	Total	73,622	81			
2.4 Additional Charges - Security Costs	Between Groups	7,434	3	2,478	2,558	0,061
	Within Groups	74,591	77	0,969		
	Total	82,025	80			

Table 90: ANOVA Results for Lease Factors

Robust Tests of Equality of Means(b)

		Statistic(a)	df1	df2	Sig.
2.4 Rental Space - between 1001 and 5000 m²	Welch	4,774	3	18,838	0,012
	Brown-Forsythe	3,184	3	26,817	0,040
2.4 Collateral - Letter of Comfort	Welch	0,653	3	19,282	0,591
	Brown-Forsythe	1,151	3	8,175	0,385
2.4 Lease contract with stepped rent	Welch	3,787	3	17,639	0,029
	Brown-Forsythe	3,552	3	29,075	0,026
2.4 Additional Charges - Administration Costs	Welch	3,553	3	16,963	0,037
	Brown-Forsythe	3,626	3	23,288	0,028
2.4 Additional Charges - Security Costs	Welch	2,001	3	18,099	0,150
	Brown-Forsythe	2,522	3	28,252	0,078

Table 91: Robust Tests for Lease Factors

2.4 Rental Space - between 1001 and 5000 m²

Tukey HSD[a,b]

1.3 Activity in the Real Estate Market	N	Subset for alpha = .05	
		1	2
Broker	8	-2,00	
Tenant	7	-1,00	-1,00
Service Provider	29	-1,00	-1,00
Landlord	37		-,70
Sig.		,136	,915

Means for groups in homogeneous subsets are displayed.

a. Uses Harmonic Mean Sample Size = 12,145.

b. The group sizes are unequal. The harmonic mean of the group sizes is used. Type I error levels are not guaranteed.

Table 92: Post-hoc Turkey Test (Rental Space – between 1001 and 5000 m²)

2.4 Collateral - Letter of Comfort

Tukey HSD[a,b]

1.3 Activity in the Real Estate Market	N	Subset for alpha = .05	
		1	2
Tenant	7	-1,00	
Service Provider	28	-,21	-,21
Broker	8	-,13	-,13
Landlord	37		-,05
Sig.		,072	,969

Means for groups in homogeneous subsets are displayed.

a. Uses Harmonic Mean Sample Size = 12,099.

b. The group sizes are unequal. The harmonic mean of the group sizes is used. Type I error levels are not guaranteed.

Table 93: Post-hoc Turkey Test (Collateral – Letter of Comfort)

2.4 Additional Charges - Administration Costs

Tukey HSD[a,b]

1.3 Activity in the Real Estate Market	N	Subset for alpha = .05	
		1	2
Tenant	7	-1,57	
Broker	8	-1,00	-1,00
Service Provider	29	-,93	-,93
Landlord	38		-,39
Sig.		,299	,349

Means for groups in homogeneous subsets are displayed.

a. Uses Harmonic Mean Sample Size = 12,171.

b. The group sizes are unequal. The harmonic mean of the group sizes is used. Type I error levels are not guaranteed.

Table 94: Post-hoc Turkey Test (Additional Charges – Administration Costs)

2.4 Additional Charges - Security Costs

Tukey HSD[a,b]

1.3 Activity in the Real Estate Market	N	Subset for alpha = .05	
		1	2
Tenant	7	-1,57	
Broker	8	-,88	-,88
Service Provider	29	-,79	-,79
Landlord	37		-,49
Sig.		,217	,765

Means for groups in homogeneous subsets are displayed.

a. Uses Harmonic Mean Sample Size = 12,145.

b. The group sizes are unequal. The harmonic mean of the group sizes is used. Type I error levels are not guaranteed.

Table 95: Post-hoc Turkey Test (Additional Charges – Security Costs)

2.4 Lease contract with stepped rent

Tukey HSD[a,b]

1.3 Activity in the Real Estate Market	N	Subset for alpha = .05	
		1	2
Tenant	7	-2,00	
Service Provider	27	-,74	-,74
Broker	8		-,38
Landlord	38		-,37
Sig.		,057	,872

Means for groups in homogeneous subsets are displayed.

a. Uses Harmonic Mean Sample Size = 12,077.

b. The group sizes are unequal. The harmonic mean of the group sizes is used. Type I error levels are not guaranteed.

Table 96: Post-hoc Turkey Test (Lease contract with stepped rent)

A.3 Descriptive Statistics of IPD Rental Database

A.3.1 Descriptive Statistics of Variables C_X07 and C_X15

Building Area Definition					
	Description	Frequency	Percent	Valid Percent	Cumulative Percent
Category 0	Unknown / Inconsistent	18,290	83.1	83.1	83.1
Category 1	gif	41	0.2	0.2	83.3
Category 2	GEA	2,561	11.6	11.6	94.9
Category 3	GIA	557	2.5	2.5	97.5
Category 4	DIN 283	9	0.0	0.0	97.5
Category 5	Other	547	2.5	2.5	100.0
	Total	22,005	100.0	100.0	

Table 97: Descriptive Statistics of Building Area Definition (C_X07)

Rental Unit Area Definition					
	Description	Frequency	Percent	Valid Percent	Cumulative Percent
Category 0	Unknown / Inconsistent	17,374	79.0	79.0	79.0
Category 1	gif	85	0.4	0.4	79.3
Category 2	GEA	3,116	14.2	14.2	93.5
Category 3	GIA	882	4.0	4.0	97.5
Category 4	DIN 283	17	0.1	0.1	97.6
Category 5	Other	531	2.4	2.4	100.0
	Total	22,005	100.0	100.0	

Table 98: Descriptive Statistics of Rental Area Definition (C_X15)

A.3.2 Descriptive Statistics per City (Dummy and Categorical Variables)

		Cities: Berlin	Düsseldorf	Frankfurt am Main	Hamburg	Cologne	Leipzig	Munich	Others	Stuttgart	Total
Rent Index Adaption Frequency (C_X14)	no adaptation specified	1,925	792	2,198	1,075	460	322	929	4,658	200	12,559
	every month	24	226	154	151	64	14	136	510	42	1,321
	every two month	44	13	34	44	4	14	45	922	27	1,147
	between 3 and 12 months	406	674	804	792	236	30	484	2,347	132	5,905
	after 12 months	47	102	104	235	80	5	91	382	27	1,073
	Total	2,446	1,807	3,294	2,297	844	385	1,685	8,819	428	22,005
Lease Length (C_X19)	up to 12 months	55	50	69	103	43	33	59	335	9	756
	between 13 and 36 months	234	224	266	291	98	130	149	1,217	46	2,655
	between 37 and 60 months	566	468	779	776	245	101	501	2,229	123	5,788
	between 61 and 120 months	311	501	925	620	153	27	481	2,229	127	5,374
	longer than 120 months	71	82	297	103	33	5	110	441	13	1,155
	indefinite lease length	1,209	482	958	404	272	89	385	2,368	110	6,277
	Total	2,446	1,807	3,294	2,297	844	385	1,685	8,819	428	22,005
Extension Option (C_X21)	no extension	2,123	1,409	2,728	1,783	700	362	1,331	6,972	351	17,759
	extended once	208	255	349	307	97	12	246	765	26	2,265
	extended several times	115	143	217	207	47	11	108	1,082	51	1,981
	Total	2,446	1,807	3,294	2,297	844	385	1,685	8,819	428	22,005
Contract Extension Option (C_X23)	no contract extension	2,250	1,530	2,961	1,919	674	338	1,493	7,149	336	18,650
	automatically once	18	12	50	27	5	1	25	87	0	225
	automatically several times	178	265	283	351	165	46	167	1,583	92	3,130
	Total	2,446	1,807	3,294	2,297	844	385	1,685	8,819	428	22,005
Break Options (C_X2527)*	None	587	575	991	1,013	364	106	661	2,558	208	7,062
	Tenant only	4	23	10	11	1	0	8	26	0	84
	Landlord only	162	399	329	308	64	35	177	1,049	55	2,579
	Both	1,693	810	1,963	967	415	244	839	5,194	165	12,290
	Total	2,446	1,807	3,294	2,297	844	385	1,685	8,819	428	22,005
Contract Type (C_X29A)	no specifications	7	4	13	21	5	0	3	77	3	133
	indexation clause to the CPI or turnover	581	1,005	1,112	1,207	398	75	808	4,306	231	9,723
	step-up leases	252	100	171	135	98	7	80	578	11	1,432
	step-up leases indexed to the CPI	40	58	94	166	19	0	82	249	3	711
	free adaptation	1,227	364	1,427	265	183	233	332	2,251	67	6,349
	leases with no adaptation	339	276	477	503	141	70	380	1,358	113	3,657
	Total	2,446	1,807	3,294	2,297	844	385	1,685	8,819	428	22,005
Collective Contract (D_X17)	Missing Values	1,994	1,172	2,723	1,480	471	283	1,014	4,528	256	13,921
	0	265	290	175	297	189	46	256	3,015	95	4,628
	1	187	345	396	520	184	56	415	1,276	77	3,456
	Total	2,446	1,807	3,294	2,297	844	385	1,685	8,819	428	22,005
Subletting Allowed (D_X18)	Missing Values	2,145	1,434	2,911	1,878	669	303	1,416	5,456	310	16,522
	0	221	166	168	221	140	49	160	2,762	81	3,968
	1	80	207	215	198	35	33	109	601	37	1,515
	Total	2,446	1,807	3,294	2,297	844	385	1,685	8,819	428	22,005
Value Added Tax (D_x30)	Missing Values	958	1,124	2,160	1,577	495	108	1,127	4,616	270	12,435
	0	474	170	698	135	80	171	159	818	47	2,752
	1	1,014	513	436	585	269	106	399	3,385	111	6,818
	Total	2,446	1,807	3,294	2,297	844	385	1,685	8,819	428	22,005
Owner Occupied (D_X32)	0	2,086	1,692	3,255	2,244	776	375	1,546	8,602	394	20,970
	1	360	115	39	53	68	10	139	217	34	1,035
	Total	2,446	1,807	3,294	2,297	844	385	1,685	8,819	428	22,005
Rentfree Months (D_X35)	0	2,221	1,501	2,933	1,992	723	353	1,421	7,775	354	19,273
	1	225	306	361	305	121	32	264	1,044	74	2,732
	Total	2,446	1,807	3,294	2,297	844	385	1,685	8,819	428	22,005

*Based on D_X25 and D_X27

Table 99: Descriptive Statistics per City (Part I)

A.3.3 Descriptive Statistics per City (Continuous Variables)

		Building Age	Building Area	Building Height	Extension Option Period	Contractual Extension Period	Rental Area
Berlin	Minimum	0.00	116.00	0.00	0	0	6
	Mean	8.12	16,026.50	6.24	48	17	890
	Maximum	55.00	71,969.00	14.00	180	120	34,088
Düsseldorf	Minimum	0.00	200.00	0.00	0	0	2
	Mean	16.17	14,547.72	6.73	59	12	814
	Maximum	55.00	89,760.00	11.00	180	60	28,995
Frankfurt am Main	Minimum	0.00	146.00	0.00	0	0	1
	Mean	12.77	18,399.36	8.47	54	28	1,218
	Maximum	53.00	87,719.00	25.00	120	120	88,167
Hamburg	Minimum	0.00	150.00	0.00	0	0	3
	Mean	14.97	12,663.80	6.62	48	17	642
	Maximum	56.00	49,150.00	27.00	120	60	57,604
Köln	Minimum	0.00	194.00	0.00	0	0	7
	Mean	21.39	6,470.70	4.88	42	16	681
	Maximum	54.00	58,320.00	20.00	139	72	19,079
Leipzig	Minimum	0.00	865.00	0.00	0	0	7
	Mean	6.35	13,837.53	5.33	38	11	505
	Maximum	40.00	56,393.00	10.00	60	60	12,276
Munich	Minimum	0.00	126.00	0.00	0	0	3
	Mean	13.90	15,774.33	6.27	47	23	732
	Maximum	56.00	54,399.00	17.00	120	60	40,017
Stuttgart	Minimum	0.00	105.00	0.00	0	0	5
	Mean	13.31	9,095.47	4.70	47	26	1,050
	Maximum	52.00	54,945.00	7.00	60	60	20,920
Others	Minimum	0.00	100.00	0.00	0	0	1
	Mean	15.46	9,083.30	4.10	49	29	871
	Maximum	56.00	292,266.00	18.00	173	146	80,989
Total	*Minimum*	*0.00*	*100.00*	*0.00*	*0*	*0*	*1*
	Mean	*14.62*	*11,886.20*	*5.18*	*50*	*24*	*876*
	Maximum	*56.00*	*292,266.00*	*27.00*	*180*	*146*	*88,167*

Table 100: Descriptive Statistics per City (Part II)

A.4 Missing Value Analysis

A.4.1 EM correlations (Little MCAR test)

EM Correlations[a]

	RENT	AGE1	M_X04A	M_X06A	M_X08B	M_X22A	M_X24A	M_X31	D_X17	D_X18	D_X25	D_X27	D_X30	D_X32	D_X35
RENT	1														
AGE1	-.160	1													
M_X04A	.164	-.964	1												
M_X06A	.190	-.201	.210	1											
M_X08B	.066	.021	-.021	.115	1										
M_X22A	.017	.032	.000	-.049	.065	1									
M_X24A	-.092	.096	-.061	-.053	.032	.478	1								
M_X31	.064	-.035	.042	.141	-.001	.022	.078	1							
D_X17	.061	-.096	.089	.004	.241	.095	-.042	-.053	1						
D_X18	.074	-.088	.070	.042	.133	.098	-.064	-.033	.549	1					
D_X25	-.042	.041	-.001	-.071	-.050	-.078	.127	.086	-.151	-.179	1				
D_X27	.011	-.025	.067	-.083	-.020	.228	.150	.083	-.019	.018	.770	1			
D_X30	-.034	-.005	.017	.000	-.051	.075	.092	.019	-.091	-.033	.002	.048	1		
D_X32	-.017	.047	-.043	-.032	.029	-.063	-.034	.041	.061	.003	.031	-.007	-.071	1	
D_X35	.018	-.037	.035	-.039	.041	.264	.053	-.014	.061	.089	-.117	.102	-.010	-.045	1

a. Little's MCAR test: Chi-Square = 3709.058, DF = 388, Sig. = .000

Table 101: EM correlations

A.4.2 Separate Variance t Test

Separate Variance t Tests[a]

		RENT	AGE1	M_X04A	M_X06A	M_X08B	M_X22A	M_X24A	M_X31	D_X12	D_X17	D_X18	D_X25	D_X27	D_X30	D_X32	D_X35
AGE1	t	-5.0	.	-116.4	-6.8	8.4	5.9	4.5	-5.2	36.2	15.8	8.8	-38.7	-33.1	21.7	-14.6	2.2
	df	6338.4	.	2205.5	2115.8	1110.4	6781.9	7049.2	5495.9	7813.1	1632.0	928.4	7826.9	8623.5	4984.6	5088.4	6828.8
	P(2-tail)	.000	.	.000	.000	.000	.000	.000	.000	.000	.000	.000	.000	.000	.000	.000	.031
	# Present	17556	17673	17673	14627	6310	17673	17673	17673	17673	6976	4843	17673	17673	6559	17673	17673
	# Missing	4297	0	326	1805	716	4332	4332	4332	4332	1108	640	4332	4332	3011	4332	4332
	Mean(Present)	11.8998	14.6228	1987.2392	11608.8647	5.2642	10.0947	3.7390	823.75	.4760	.46	.29	.51	.63	.78	.03	.1265
	Mean(Missing)	12.4462	.	2002.0153	14133.6277	4.4120	7.8980	2.8313	1087.13	.2128	.24	.15	.79	.85	.56	.10	.1147
M_X04A	t	-.9	.	.	.2	8.3	5.2	3.0	-4.8	36.4	16.3	9.5	-42.1	-38.2	21.8	-15.1	.9
	df	6196.4	.	.	1991.6	1077.7	6005.5	6078.1	4972.5	7018.0	1591.0	898.0	7224.3	8251.0	4908.5	4599.1	5992.9
	P(2-tail)	.346	.	.	.809	.000	.000	.003	.000	.000	.000	.000	.000	.000	.000	.000	.381
	# Present	17882	17673	17999	14835	6334	17999	17999	17999	17999	7002	4867	17999	17999	6589	17999	17999
	# Missing	3971	0	0	1597	692	4006	4006	4006	4006	1082	616	4006	4006	2981	4006	4006
	Mean(Present)	11.9895	14.6228	1987.5068	11893.8440	5.2599	10.0286	3.6746	828.79	.4731	.46	.29	.51	.63	.78	.03	.1251
	Mean(Missing)	12.0873	.	.	11815.2079	4.4220	8.0162	3.0467	1085.90	.2047	.23	.14	.81	.87	.56	.11	.1201
M_X06A	t	-16.8	15.6	-17.9	.	-18.3	24.5	28.0	-3.0	90.3	-106.2	.	-103.6	-73.0	30.9	-15.6	31.1
	df	9772.3	4801.6	4979.2	.	255.0	14529.5	19956.0	8849.1	18429.2	7842.0	.	20064.2	20000.6	3587.4	6914.5	18488.4
	P(2-tail)	.000	.000	.000	.	.000	.000	.000	.003	.000	.000	.	.000	.000	.000	.000	.000
	# Present	16280	14627	14835	16432	6831	16432	16432	16432	16432	7843	5483	16432	16432	7123	16432	16432
	# Missing	5573	3046	3164	0	195	5573	5573	5573	5573	241	0	5573	5573	2447	5573	5573
	Mean(Present)	11.6009	15.2834	1986.7416	11886.2014	5.1167	11.4222	4.5336	845.31	.5435	.41	.28	.43	.58	.60	.03	.1539
	Mean(Missing)	13.1944	11.4501	1991.0945	.	7.3026	4.4728	.6907	964.90	.0727	1.00	.	.94	.94	.46	.10	.0364
M_X08B	t	-26.0	25.1	-16.2	-28.9	.	49.8	44.4	8.4	20.3	27.7	-3.1	9.2	40.2	28.2	3.4	29.3
	df	16761.8	11593.8	11798.8	16386.4	.	9417.9	7152.8	10847.3	13380.5	1810.8	140.7	13992.0	17780.5	3809.7	12534.8	9590.0
	P(2-tail)	.000	.000	.000	.000	.	.000	.000	.000	.000	.000	.003	.000	.000	.000	.001	.000
	# Present	6942	6310	6334	6831	7026	7026	7026	7026	7026	7026	5347	7026	7026	7026	7026	7026
	# Missing	14911	11363	11665	9601	0	14979	14979	14979	14979	1058	136	14979	14979	2544	14979	14979
	Mean(Present)	10.5571	18.0970	1985.2577	8692.6255	5.1773	21.7982	10.7143	1103.09	.5233	.47	.27	.61	.84	.79	.05	.2336
	Mean(Missing)	12.6824	12.6935	1988.7281	14158.3936	.	3.9698	.2047	768.89	.3777	.14	.40	.54	.60	.48	.04	.0728
D_X17	t	-21.4	24.9	-15.6	-30.1	.	65.0	44.6	7.4	24.4	.	.	2.2	45.4	28.6	3.0	43.8
	df	19182.4	13123.0	13383.4	15470.8	.	9013.2	8212.4	14135.2	16378.2	.	.	16944.0	20795.3	3351.8	15704.2	9965.0
	P(2-tail)	.000	.000	.000	.000	.	.000	.000	.000	.000	.	.	.026	.000	.000	.003	.000
	# Present	7932	6976	7002	7843	7026	8084	8084	8084	8084	8084	5483	8084	8084	7254	8084	8084
	# Missing	13921	10697	10997	8589	0	13921	13921	13921	13921	0	0	13921	13921	2316	13921	13921
	Mean(Present)	10.8877	17.7823	1985.5140	8870.0538	5.1773	23.7578	9.4854	1047.57	.5306	.43	.28	.57	.84	.79	.05	.2684
	Mean(Missing)	12.6452	12.5623	1988.7757	14640.3807	.	1.4768	.1196	775.73	.3625	.	.	.56	.58	.47	.04	.0404
D_X18	t	-21.1	17.6	-11.2	-17.2	-20.5	36.7	34.3	12.1	14.6	-33.8	.	2.1	47.1	34.5	-11.0	24.7
	df	10659.2	7947.2	8024.2	12893.3	3557.2	7327.7	5800.3	7084.7	9208.6	5059.5	.	9416.7	14161.3	7064.4	13812.3	7125.9
	P(2-tail)	.000	.000	.000	.000	.000	.000	.000	.000	.000	.000	.	.032	.000	.000	.000	.000
	# Present	5399	4843	4867	5483	5347	5483	5483	5483	5483	5483	5483	5483	5483	5483	5483	5483
	# Missing	16454	12830	13132	10949	1679	16522	16522	16522	16522	2601	0	16522	16522	4087	16522	16522
	Mean(Present)	10.5893	17.6250	1985.6030	9623.2805	4.7623	20.6589	10.8822	1304.98	.5092	.31	.28	.57	.88	.85	.02	.2384
	Mean(Missing)	12.4725	13.4895	1988.2124	13019.4187	6.4991	6.0128	1.1305	733.10	.3960	.68	.	.56	.61	.53	.05	.0862
D_X30	t	-20.6	23.2	-14.1	-30.3	.	43.5	44.2	11.2	-5.3	81.2	.	35.4	59.9	.	22.9	28.4
	df	21817.7	12286.9	12508.6	16399.0	.	14993.0	9773.4	17416.9	20694.8	7253.0	.	21265.8	21690.0	.	12529.1	15126.2
	P(2-tail)	.000	.000	.000	.000	.	.000	.000	.000	.000	.000	.	.000	.000	.	.000	.000
	# Present	9477	6559	6589	7123	7026	9570	9570	9570	9570	7254	5483	9570	9570	9570	9570	9570
	# Missing	12376	11114	11410	9309	0	12435	12435	12435	12435	830	0	12435	12435	0	12435	12435
	Mean(Present)	11.0565	17.7317	1985.6106	8645.3061	5.1773	17.2394	8.0875	1095.71	.4043	.48	.28	.69	.87	.71	.09	.1990
	Mean(Missing)	12.7353	12.7880	1988.6018	14366.0487	.	3.8308	.0762	706.20	.4396	.00	.	.46	.53	.	.02	.0666

For each quantitative variable, pairs of groups are formed by indicator variables (present, missing).

a. Indicator variables with less than 5% missing are not displayed.

Table 102: Separate Variance t Test

A.4.3 Frequency Distribution before Transformation

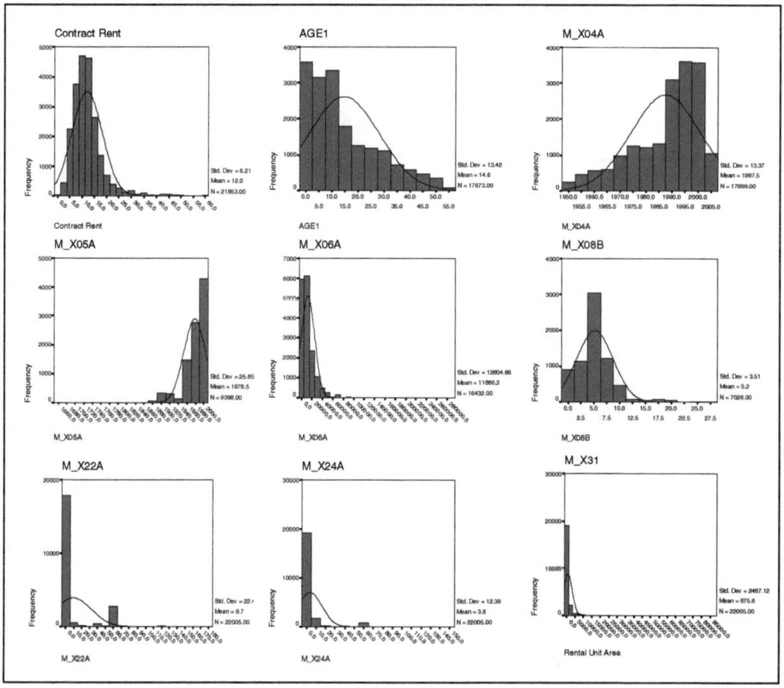

Figure 50: Frequency Distribution (before Transformation)

A.4.4 Frequency Distribution after Transformation

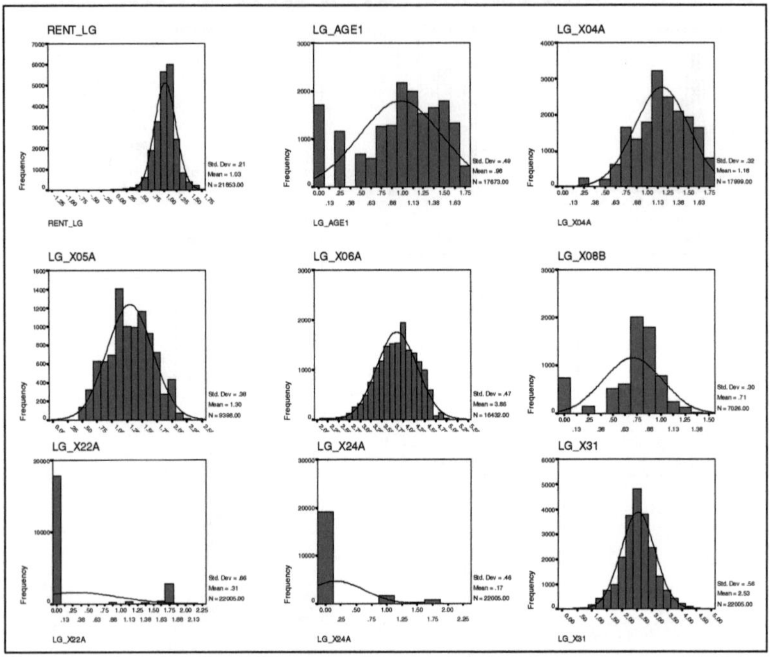

Figure 51: Frequency Distribution (after Transformation)

A.5 Choice of Predictors for Multiple Imputation

A.5.1 Choice of Predictors for RENT_LG

Variable	RENT_LG
Observed Values	21,853
Missing Values	152

Variable Name	Pearson Correlation Coefficient / Chi-Quadrat	df	p-Value	Correlation with response variable	p-Value	% Usuables		% Relevants		Removed in step
lg_age1	-0.28		0.000	-0.02	0.002	117	76.97%	17556	80.34%	
lg_x04a	-0.26		0.000	-0.04	0.000	117	76.97%	17882	81.83%	
lg_x05a	-0.23		0.000	-0.05	0.000	126	82.89%	9272	42.43%	4
lg_x06a	0.26		0.000	-0.01	0.169	152	100.00%	16280	74.50%	
lg_x08b	0.18		0.000	0.03	0.022	84	55.26%	6942	31.77%	4
lg_x22a	0.00		0.540	0.02	0.001	152	100.00%	21,853	100.00%	1
lg_x24a	-0.10		0.000	-0.02	0.010	152	100.00%	21,853	100.00%	
lg_x31	0.19		0.000	0.00	0.738	152	100.00%	21,853	100.00%	
c_x01	916.09	8	0.000	31.09	0.000	152	100.00%	21,853	100.00%	
c_x07	374.38	5	0.000	12.80	0.025	152	100.00%	21,853	100.00%	
c_x14	290.80	4	0.000	12.70	0.013	152	100.00%	21,853	100.00%	
c_x15	380.45	5	0.000	12.09	0.034	152	100.00%	21,853	100.00%	
c_x19	116.98	5	0.000	245.85	0.000	152	100.00%	21,853	100.00%	
c_x21	83.04	2	0.000	9.77	0.008	152	100.00%	21,853	100.00%	
c_x23	92.55	2	0.000	6.88	0.032	152	100.00%	21,853	100.00%	
c_x29a	30.90	5	0.000	71.32	0.000	152	100.00%	21,853	100.00%	
d_x12	0.04		0.000	0.00	0.937	152	100.00%	21,853	100.00%	
d_x17	0.24		0.000	0.03	0.005	152	100.00%	7,932	36.30%	4
d_x18	0.35		0.000	0.13	0.000	84	55.26%	5,399	24.71%	4
d_x25	-0.05		0.000	-0.05	0.000	152	100.00%	21,853	100.00%	
d_x27	0.02		0.011	0.06	0.000	152	100.00%	21,853	100.00%	
d_x30	-0.06		0.000	0.05	0.000	93	61.18%	9,477	43.37%	4
d_x32	0.01		0.389	0.03	0.000	152	100.00%	21,853	100.00%	1
d_x35	0.03		0.000	-0.02	0.000	152	100.00%	21,853	100.00%	
b_year	68.70	9	0.000	204.42	0.000	152	100.00%	21,853	100.00%	

Table 103: Choice of Predictors for Rent (RENT_LG)

A.5.2 Choice of Predictors for LG_AGE1

Variable	LG_AGE1
Observed Values	17,673
Missing Values	4,332

Variable Name	Pearson Correlation Coefficient / Chi-Quadrat	df	p-Value	Correlation with response variable	p-Value	% Usuables		% Relevants		Removed in step
rent_lg	-0.28		0.000	0.03	0.000	4,297	99.19%	17,556	99.34%	
lg_x04a	0.93		0.000	-0.21	0.000	326	7.53%	17,673	100.00%	4
lg_x05a	0.75		0.000	0.38	0.000	703	16.23%	8,695	49.20%	4
lg_x06a	-0.33		0.000	0.01	0.387	1,805	41.67%	14,627	82.76%	
lg_x08b	-0.02		0.108	-0.04	0.001	716	16.53%	6,310	35.70%	4
lg_x22a	0.01		0.054	-0.05	0.000	4,332	100.00%	17,673	100.00%	1
lg_x24a	0.10		0.000	-0.06	0.000	4,332	100.00%	17,673	100.00%	
lg_x31	-0.15		0.000	0.08	0.000	4,332	100.00%	17,673	100.00%	
c_x01	86.70	8	0.000	2725.34	0.000	4,332.00	100.00%	17,673	100.00%	
c_x07	304.11	5	0.000	170.43	0.000	4,332.00	100.00%	17,673	100.00%	
c_x14	149.68	4	0.000	1125.53	0.000	4,332.00	100.00%	17,673	100.00%	
c_x15	330.71	5	0.000	233.45	0.000	4,332.00	100.00%	17,673	100.00%	
c_x19	169.09	5	0.000	1946.51	0.000	4,332.00	100.00%	17,673	100.00%	
c_x21	28.57	2	0.000	86.85	0.000	4,332.00	100.00%	17,673	100.00%	
c_x23	82.34	2	0.000	149.30	0.000	4,332.00	100.00%	17,673	100.00%	
c_x29a	28.63	5	0.000	2767.22	0.000	4,332.00	100.00%	17,673	100.00%	
d_x12	0.00		0.937	-0.21	0.000	4,332.00	100.00%	17,673	100.00%	1
d_x17	-0.31		0.000	-0.15	0.000	1,108.00	25.58%	6,976	39.47%	4
d_x18	-0.33		0.000	-0.10	0.000	640.00	14.77%	4,843	27.40%	4
d_x25	0.06		0.000	0.23	0.000	4,332.00	100.00%	17,673	100.00%	
d_x27	-0.05		0.000	0.18	0.000	4,332.00	100.00%	17,673	100.00%	
d_x30	-0.08		0.000	-0.23	0.000	3,011.00	69.51%	6,559	37.11%	4
d_x32	0.06		0.000	0.13	0.000	4,332.00	100.00%	17,673	100.00%	
d_x35	-0.08		0.000	-0.01	0.036	4,332.00	100.00%	17,673	100.00%	
b_year	72.95		0.000	1609.55	0.000	4,332.00	100.00%	17,673	100.00%	

Table 104: Choice of Predictors for Building Age (LG_AGE1)

A.5.3 Choice of Predictors for LG_X04A

Variable	LG_X04A
Observed Values	17,999
Missing Values	4,006

Variable Name	Pearson Correlation Coefficient / Chi-Quadrat	df	p-Value	Correlation with response variable	p-Value		% Usuables		% Relevants	Removed in step
rent_lg	-0.26		0.000	0.01	0.078	3,971	99.13%	17,882	99.35%	
lg_age1	0.93		0.000	.(a)	.	0	0.00%	17,673	98.19%	
lg_x05a	0.77		0.000	0.45	0.000	590	14.73%	8,808	48.94%	4
lg_x06a	-0.32		0.000	-0.04	0.000	1,597	39.87%	14,835	82.42%	
lg_x08b	0.00		0.862	-0.04	0.003	692	17.27%	6,334	35.19%	4
lg_x22a	-0.03		0.000	-0.05	0.000	4006	100.00%	17999	100.00%	
lg_x24a	0.07		0.000	-0.05	0.000	4006	100.00%	17999	100.00%	
lg_x31	-0.14		0.000	0.08	0.000	4006	100.00%	17999	100.00%	
c_x01	94.54	8	0.000	2873.05	0.000	4006	100.00%	17999	100.00%	
c_x07	233.45	5	0.000	149.29	0.000	4006	100.00%	17999	100.00%	
c_x14	107.63	4	0.000	1132.86	0.000	4006	100.00%	17999	100.00%	
c_x15	198.32	5	0.000	198.86	0.000	4006	100.00%	17999	100.00%	
c_x19	111.87	5	0.000	2226.08	0.000	4006	100.00%	17999	100.00%	
c_x21	17.17	2	0.000	76.97	0.000	4006	100.00%	17999	100.00%	
c_x23	45.38	2	0.000	120.73	0.000	4006	100.00%	17999	100.00%	
c_x29a	23.42	5	0.000	2999.50	0.000	4006	100.00%	17999	100.00%	
d_x12	0.03		0.000	-0.21	0.000	4006	100.00%	17999	100.00%	
d_x17	-0.28		0.000	-0.16	0.000	1,082	27.01%	7,570	42.06%	4
d_x18	-0.21		0.000	-0.10	0.000	616	15.38%	5,348	29.71%	4
d_x25	0.01		0.045	0.24	0.000	4006	100.00%	17999	100.00%	
d_x27	-0.10		0.000	0.20	0.000	4006	100.00%	17999	100.00%	
d_x30	-0.09		0.000	-0.23	0.000	2,981	74.41%	6,589	36.61%	4
d_x32	0.05		0.000	0.14	0.000	4006	100.00%	17999	100.00%	
d_x35	-0.07		0.000	-0.01	0.386	4006	100.00%	17999	100.00%	
b_year	73.48		0.000	2059.55	0.000	4006	100.00%	17999	100.00%	

Table 105: Choice of Predictors for Economic Year of Construction (LG_X04A)

A.5.4 Choice of Predictors for LG_X05A

Variable	LG_X05A
Observed Values	9,398
Missing Values	12,607

Variable Name	Pearson Correlation Coefficient / Chi-Quadrat	df	p-Value	Correlation with response variable	p-Value		% Usuables		% Relevants	Removed in step
rent_lg	-0.23		0.000	0.09	0.000	12,581	99.79%	9,272	98.66%	
lg_age1	0.75		0.000	-0.11	0.000	8,978	71.21%	8,695	92.52%	
lg_x04a	0.77		0.000	-0.01	0.080	9,191	72.90%	8,808	93.72%	
lg_x06a	-0.23		0.000	0.26	0.000	8,558	67.88%	7,874	83.78%	
lg_x08b	0.07		0.000	-0.13	0.000	164	1.30%	6,862	73.02%	4
lg_x22a	-0.05		0.000	-0.47	0.000	12,607	100.00%	9,398	100.00%	
lg_x24a	0.05		0.000	-0.40	0.000	12,607	100.00%	9,398	100.00%	
lg_x31	-0.15		0.000	-0.10	0.000	12,607	100.00%	9,398	100.00%	
c_x01	23.63	8	0.000	880.22	0.000	12,607	100.00%	9,398	100.00%	
c_x07	174.29	5	0.000	5278.09	0.000	12,607	100.00%	9,398	100.00%	
c_x14	62.39	4	0.000	3577.69	0.000	12,607	100.00%	9,398	100.00%	
c_x15	111.18	5	0.000	6725.83	0.000	12,607	100.00%	9,398	100.00%	
c_x19	29.25	5	0.000	246.27	0.000	12,607	100.00%	9,398	100.00%	
c_x21	8.49	2	0.000	5177.27	0.000	12,607	100.00%	9,398	100.00%	
c_x23	8.44	2	0.000	3794.02	0.000	12,607	100.00%	9,398	100.00%	
c_x29a	15.01	5	0.000	2666.37	0.000	12,607	100.00%	9,398	100.00%	
d_x12	-0.03		0.001	-0.10	0.000	12,607	100.00%	9,398	100.00%	
d_x17	-0.17		0.000	-0.13	0.000	514	4.08%	7,570	80.55%	
d_x18	-0.27		0.000	-0.10	0.000	135	1.07%	5,348	56.91%	4
d_x25	0.06		0.000	-0.14	0.000	12,607	100.00%	9,398	100.00%	4
d_x27	-0.16		0.000	-0.34	0.000	12,607	100.00%	9,398	100.00%	
d_x30	-0.09		0.000	-0.29	0.000	2,447	19.41%	7,120	75.76%	4
d_x32	-0.01		0.596	0.01	0.039	12,607	100.00%	9,398	100.00%	1
d_x35	-0.05		0.000	-0.26	0.000	12,607	100.00%	9,398	100.00%	
b_year	15.36		0.000	2172.90	0.000	12,607	100.00%	9,398	100.00%	

Table 106: Choice of Predictors for Historic Year of Construction (LG_X05A)

A.5.5 Choice of Predictors for LG_X06A

Variable	LG_X06A
Observed Values	16,432
Missing Values	5,573

Variable Name	Pearson Correlation Coefficient / Chi-Quadrat	df	p-Value	Correlation with response variable	p-Value	% Usuables		% Relevants		Removed in step
rent_lg	0.26		0.000	0.13	0.000	5,573	100.00%	16,280	99.07%	
lg_age1	-0.33		0.000	-0.12	0.000	3,046	54.66%	14,627	89.02%	
lg_x04a	-0.32		0.000	-0.14	0.000	3,164	56.77%	14,835	90.28%	
lg_x05a	-0.23		0.000	-0.09	0.000	1,524	27.35%	7,874	47.92%	4
lg_x08b	0.38		0.000	0.11	0.000	195	3.50%	7,874	47.92%	4
lg_x22a	-0.07		0.000	-0.15	0.000	5,573	100.00%	16,432	100.00%	
lg_x24a	-0.11		0.000	-0.18	0.000	5,573	100.00%	16,432	100.00%	
lg_x31	0.16		0.000	0.08	0.000	5,573	100.00%	16,432	100.00%	
c_x01	179.00	8	0.000	3233.53	0.000	5,573	100.00%	16,432	100.00%	
c_x07	243.83	5	0.000	1426.99	0.000	5,573	100.00%	16,432	100.00%	
c_x14	112.14	4	0.000	0071.55	0.000	5,573	100.00%	16,432	100.00%	
c_x15	347.39	5	0.000	1765.23	0.000	5,573	100.00%	16,432	100.00%	
c_x19	110.01	5	0.000	1641.55	0.000	5,573	100.00%	16,432	100.00%	
c_x21	62.98	2	0.000	599.89	0.000	5,573	100.00%	16,432	100.00%	
c_x23	115.35	2	0.000	815.43	0.000	5,573	100.00%	16,432	100.00%	
c_x29a	232.69	5	0.000	7115.54	0.000	5,573	100.00%	16,432	100.00%	
d_x12	0.01		0.308	-0.41	0.000	5,573	100.00%	16,432	100.00%	1
d_x17	0.08		0.000	0.20	0.000	241	4.32%	7,843	47.73%	4
d_x18	0.25		0.000	.(a)	.	0	0.00%	5,483	33.37%	4
d_x25	-0.16		0.000	0.45	0.000	5,573	100.00%	16,432	100.00%	
d_x27	-0.11		0.000	0.33	0.000	5,573	100.00%	16,432	100.00%	
d_x30	0.07		0.000	-0.33	0.000	2,447	43.91%	7,123	43.35%	4
d_x32	-0.05		0.000	0.13	0.000	5,573	100.00%	16,432	100.00%	
d_x35	-0.02		0.036	-0.15	0.000	5,573	100.00%	16,432	100.00%	
b_year	61.12		0.000	1531.96	0.000	5,573	100.00%	16,432	100.00%	

Table 107: Choice of Predictors for Building Area (LG_X06A)

A.5.6 Choice of Predictor for LG_X08B

Variable	LG_X08B
Observed Values	7,026
Missing Values	14,979

Variable Name	Pearson Correlation Coefficient / Chi-Quadrat	df	p-Value	Correlation with response variable	p-Value	% Usuables		% Relevants		Removed in step
rent_lg	0.18		0.000	0.18	0.000	14,911	99.55%	6,942	98.80%	
lg_age1	-0.02		0.108	-0.18	0.000	11,363	75.86%	6,310	89.81%	1
lg_x04a	0.00		0.862	-0.09	0.000	11,665	77.88%	6,334	90.15%	1
lg_x05a	0.07		0.000	-0.15	0.000	2,536	16.93%	6,862	97.67%	4
lg_x06a	0.38		0.000	0.29	0.000	9,601	64.10%	6,831	97.22%	
lg_x22a	0.18		0.000	-0.44	0.000	14,979	100.00%	7,026	100.00%	
lg_x24a	0.12		0.000	-0.51	0.000	14,979	100.00%	7,026	100.00%	
lg_x31	-0.08		0.000	-0.09	0.000	14,979	100.00%	7,026	100.00%	
c_x01	120.68	8	0.000	1401.02	0.000	14,979	100.00%	7,026	100.00%	
c_x07	354.16	5	0.000	9252.76	0.000	14,979	100.00%	7,026	100.00%	
c_x14	108.72	4	0.000	5462.54	0.000	14,979	100.00%	7,026	100.00%	
c_x15	224.39	5	0.000	11863.88	0.000	14,979	100.00%	7,026	100.00%	
c_x19	40.80	5	0.000	459.80	0.000	14,979	100.00%	7,026	100.00%	
c_x21	110.64	2	0.000	4840.32	0.000	14,979	100.00%	7,026	100.00%	
c_x23	71.49	2	0.000	6025.85	0.000	14,979	100.00%	7,026	100.00%	
c_x29a	102.48	5	0.000	2129.83	0.000	14,979	100.00%	7,026	100.00%	
d_x12	0.14		0.000	-0.14	0.000	14,979	100.00%	7,026	100.00%	
d_x17	0.37		0.000	-0.23	0.000	1,058	7.06%	7,026	100.00%	4
d_x18	0.25		0.000	0.05	0.001	136	0.91%	5,347	76.10%	4
d_x25	-0.20		0.000	-0.06	0.000	14,979	100.00%	7,026	100.00%	
d_x27	-0.07		0.000	-0.24	0.000	14,979	100.00%	7,026	100.00%	
d_x30	-0.09		0.000	-0.30	0.000	2,544	16.98%	7,026	100.00%	4
d_x32	0.08		0.000	-0.02	0.000	14,979	100.00%	7,026	100.00%	
d_x35	0.10		0.000	-0.23	0.000	14,979	100.00%	7,026	100.00%	
b_year	19.30		0.000	2925.34	0.000	14,979	100.00%	7,026	100.00%	

Table 108: Choice of Predictors for Number of Storeys (LG_X08B)

A.5.7 Choice of Predictor for D_X17

Variable	D_X17
Observed Values	8,084
Missing Values	13,921

Variable Name	Pearson Correlation Coefficient / Chi-Quadrat	df	p-Value	Correlation with response variable	p-Value	% Usuables		% Relevants		Removed in step
rent_lg	0.24		0.000	0.15	0.000	13,921	100.00%	7,932	98.12%	
lg_age1	-0.31		0.000	-0.17	0.000	10,697	76.84%	6,976	86.29%	
lg_x04a	-0.28		0.000	-0.08	0.000	10,997	79.00%	7,002	86.62%	
lg_x05a	-0.17		0.000	-0.12	0.000	1,828	13.13%	7,570	93.64%	4
lg_x06a	0.08		0.000	0.29	0.000	8,589	61.70%	7,843	97.02%	
lg_x08b	0.37		0.000 .(a)	.		0	0.00%	7,026	86.91%	4
lg_x22a	0.22		0.000	-0.53	0.000	13,921	100.00%	8,084	100.00%	
lg_x24a	0.16		0.000	-0.47	0.000	13,921	100.00%	8,084	100.00%	
lg_x31	-0.17		0.000	-0.09	0.000	13,921	100.00%	8,084	100.00%	
c_x01	104.13	8	0.000	1473.49	0.000	13,921	100.00%	8,084	100.00%	
c_x07	2436.18	5	0.000	7459.51	0.000	13,921	100.00%	8,084	100.00%	
c_x14	745.02	4	0.000	5512.72	0.000	13,921	100.00%	8,084	100.00%	
c_x15	2573.37	5	0.000	9554.26	0.000	13,921	100.00%	8,084	100.00%	
c_x19	182.26	5	0.000	384.19	0.000	13,921	100.00%	8,084	100.00%	
c_x21	426.09	2	0.000	6564.12	0.000	13,921	100.00%	8,084	100.00%	
c_x23	328.86	2	0.000	5276.88	0.000	13,921	100.00%	8,084	100.00%	
c_x29a	150.82	5	0.000	1995.70	0.000	13,921	100.00%	8,084	100.00%	
d_x12	0.18		0.000	-0.16	0.000	13,921	100.00%	8,084	100.00%	
									0.00%	
d_x18	0.87		0.000 .(a)	.		0	0.00%	5,483	67.83%	4
d_x25	-0.41		0.000	-0.01	0.026	13,921	100.00%	8,084	100.00%	
d_x27	-0.05		0.000	-0.27	0.000	13,921	100.00%	8,084	100.00%	
d_x30	-0.17		0.000	-0.31	0.000	2,316	16.64%	7,254	89.73%	4
d_x32	0.16		0.000	-0.02	0.003	13,921	100.00%	8,084	100.00%	
d_x35	0.13		0.000	-0.33	0.000	13,921	100.00%	8,084	100.00%	
b_year	73.82		0.000	3047.70	0.000	13,921	100.00%	8,084	100.00%	

Table 109: Choice of Predictors for Collective Contract (D_X17)

A.5.8 Choice of Predictor for D_X18

Variable	D_X18
Observed Values	5,483
Missing Values	16,522

Variable Name	Pearson Correlation Coefficient / Chi-Quadrat	df	p-Value	Correlation with response variable	p-Value	% Usuables		% Relevants		Removed in step
rent_lg	0.350		0.000	0.159	0.000	16,454	99.59%	5,399	98.47%	
lg_age1	-0.329		0.000	-0.114	0.000	12,830	77.65%	4,843	88.33%	
lg_x04a	-0.211		0.000	-0.051	0.000	13,132	79.48%	4,867	88.77%	
lg_x05a	-0.270		0.000	-0.054	0.000	4,050	24.51%	5,348	97.54%	4
lg_x06a	0.253		0.000	0.189	0.000	10,949	66.27%	5,483	100.00%	
lg_x08b	0.246		0.000	0.259	0.000	1,679	10.16%	5,347	97.52%	4
lg_x22a	0.332		0.000	-0.343	0.000	16,522	100.00%	5,483	100.00%	
lg_x24a	0.125		0.000	-0.378	0.000	16,522	100.00%	5,483	100.00%	
lg_x31	-0.073		0.000	-0.159	0.000	16,522	100.00%	5,483	100.00%	
c_x01	80.370	8	0.000	1499.079	0.000	16,522	100.00%	5,483	100.00%	
c_x07	2780.704	5	0.000	13109.596	0.000	16,522	100.00%	5,483	100.00%	
c_x14	1118.763	4	0.000	4624.520	0.000	16,522	100.00%	5,483	100.00%	
c_x15	2641.215	5	0.000	13030.293	0.000	16,522	100.00%	5,483	100.00%	
c_x19	151.927	5	0.000	254.804	0.000	16,522	100.00%	5,483	100.00%	
c_x21	578.702	2	0.000	3400.125	0.000	16,522	100.00%	5,483	100.00%	
c_x23	227.221	2	0.000	3033.225	0.000	16,522	100.00%	5,483	100.00%	
c_x29a	166.722	5	0.000	1827.141	0.000	16,522	100.00%	5,483	100.00%	
d_x12	0.273		0.000	-0.099	0.000	16,522	100.00%	5,483	100.00%	
d_x17	0.868		0.000	0.353	0.000	2,601	15.74%	5,483	100.00%	4
d_x25	-0.712		0.000	-0.014	0.033	16,522	100.00%	5,483	100.00%	
d_x27	0.142		0.000	-0.252	0.000	16,522	100.00%	5,483	100.00%	
d_x30	-0.070		0.000	-0.347	0.000	4,087	24.74%	5,483	100.00%	4
d_x32	0.013		0.331	0.061	0.000	16,522	100.00%	5,483	100.00%	1
d_x35	0.296		0.000	-0.200	0.000	16,522	100.00%	5,483	100.00%	
b_year	164.350		0.000	2233.009	0.000	16,522	100.00%	5,483	100.00%	

Table 110: Choice of Predictors for Subletting Allowed (D_X18)

A.5.9 Choice of Predictor for D_X30

Variable	D_X30									
Observed Values	9,570									
Missing Values	12,435									
Variable Name	Pearson Correlation Coefficient / Chi-Quadrat	df	p-Value	Correlation with response variable	p-Value	% Usuables		% Relevants		Removed in step
rent_lg	-0.06		0.000	0.14	0.000	12,376	99.53%	9,477	99.03%	
lg_age1	-0.08		0.000	-0.16	0.000	11,114	89.38%	11,114	116.13%	
lg_x04a	-0.09		0.000	-0.08	0.000	11,410	91.76%	6,589	68.85%	
lg_x05a	-0.09		0.000	-0.15	0.000	2,278	18.32%	7,120	74.40%	4
lg_x06a	0.07		0.000	0.30	0.000	9,309	74.86%	7,123	74.43%	
lg_x08b	-0.09		0.000 .(a)	.		0	0.00%	7,026	73.42%	
lg_x22a	0.14		0.000	-0.35	0.000	12,435	100.00%	9,570	100.00%	
lg_x24a	0.12		0.000	-0.42	0.000	12,435	100.00%	9,570	100.00%	
lg_x31	0.04		0.000	-0.14	0.000	12,435	100.00%	9,570	100.00%	
c_x01	135.20	8	0.000	843.30	0.000	12,435	100.00%	9,570	100.00%	
c_x07	195.51	5	0.000	5807.65	0.000	12,435	100.00%	9,570	100.00%	
c_x11	71.08	4	0.000	4520.15	0.000	12,435	100.00%	9,570	100.00%	
c_x15	190.10	5	0.000	7390.44	0.000	12,435	100.00%	9,570	100.00%	
c_x19	56.51	5	0.000	885.39	0.000	12,435	100.00%	9,570	100.00%	
c_x21	83.06	2	0.000	3135.79	0.000	12,435	100.00%	9,570	100.00%	
c_x23	50.98	2	0.000	4194.08	0.000	12,435	100.00%	9,570	100.00%	
c_x29a	60.34	5	0.000	5099.21	0.000	12,435	100.00%	9,570	100.00%	
d_x12	0.10		0.000	0.04	0.000	12,435	100.00%	9,570	100.00%	
d_x17	-0.17		0.000	-0.29	0.000	830	6.67%	7,254	75.80%	4
d_x18	-0.07		0.000 .(a)	.		0	0.00%	5,483	57.29%	4
d_x25	-0.01		0.211	-0.23	0.000	12,435	100.00%	9,570	100.00%	1
d_x27	0.12		0.000	-0.36	0.000	12,435	100.00%	9,570	100.00%	
d_x32	-0.13		0.000	-0.17	0.000	12,435	100.00%	9,570	100.00%	
d_x35	-0.03		0.004	-0.20	0.000	12,435	100.00%	9,570	100.00%	
b_year	25.89		0.000	6054.48	0.000	12,435	100.00%	9,570	100.00%	

Table 111: Choice of Predictors for Value Added Tax (D_X30)

A.6 Identification of Best Functional Form (Nation-wide Models based on observed datasets)

A.6.1 Residual Diagnostic Plots for Linear, Semi-log and Double log Models

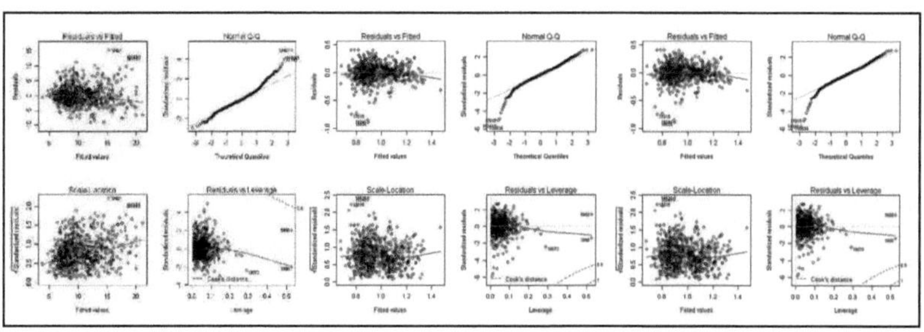

Figure 52: Residual Diagnostic Plots of Nation-wide TDV Models (linear, semi—log, double-log) based on observed dataset

A.6.2 Residual Diagnostic Plots Mix-Models

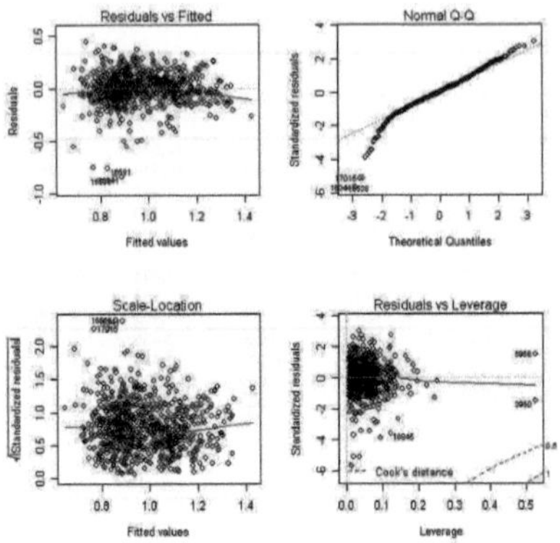

Figure 53: Residual Diagnostic Plots of Nation-wide TDV Models (Mix) based on observed dataset

A.6.3 Component Residual Plots for Nation-wide TDV Mix Models

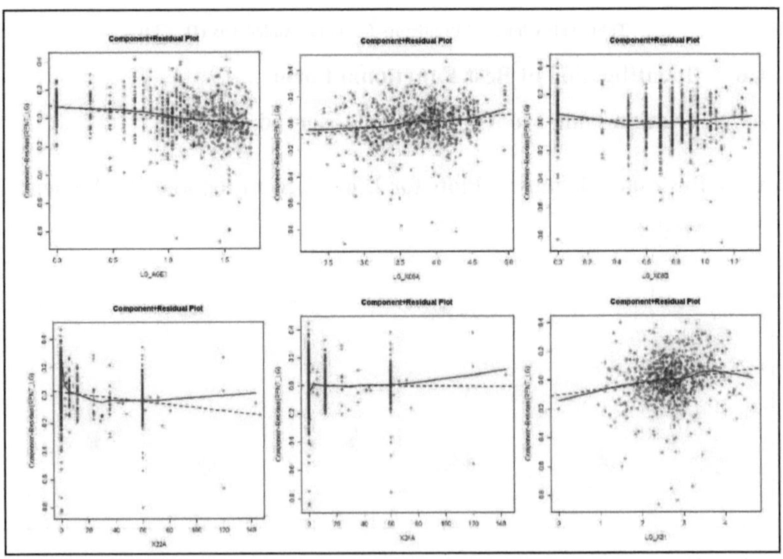

Figure 54: Component Residual Plots for Nation-wide TDV Model (Mix) based on observed dataset

A.6.4 Residual Diagnostic Plots for Linear, Semi-log, Double log, Mix Models (RENT with 3.00 to 35.00 EUR/sqm/month)

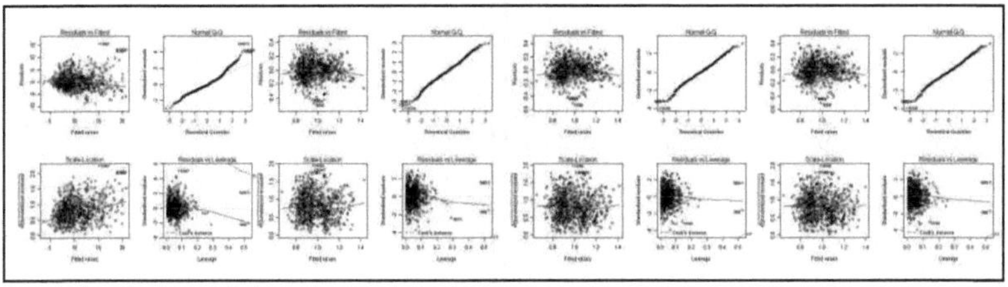

Figure 55: Residual Diagnostic Plots Nation-wide TDV Models (linear, semi-log, double log, mix) based on observed dataset

A.6.5 Diagnostic Tests for Multicollinearity

VIF-TEST		NW.TDV.CCA.LINEAR	
		GVIF^(1/2Df)	
Variables	df	Full-Sample	Sub-Sample
C_YEAR	9	1.11	1.11
C_X01	8	1.09	1.09
C_X14	4	1.99	1.99
C_X19	5	1.16	1.16
C_X21	2	1.85	1.85
C_X23	2	1.54	1.54
C_X2527	2	2.30	2.31
C_X29A	3	1.98	1.98
D_X18	1	2.42	2.44
D_X30	1	1.17	1.16
D_X32	1	1.07	1.07
D_X35	1	1.20	1.20
AGE1	1	4.09	4.08
I(AGE1^2)	1	3.76	3.75
X06A	1	1.36	1.36
X08B	1	1.28	1.28
X22A	1	3.23	3.20
X24A	1	2.75	2.74
X31	1	1.17	1.17

VIF-TEST		NW.TDV.CCA.SEMI	
		GVIF^(1/2Df)	
Variables	df	Full-Sample	Sub-Sample
C_YEAR	9	1.11	1.11
C_X01	8	1.09	1.09
C_X14	4	1.99	1.99
C_X19	5	1.16	1.16
C_X21	2	1.85	1.85
C_X23	2	1.54	1.54
C_X2527	2	2.30	2.31
C_X29A	3	1.98	1.98
D_X18	1	2.42	2.44
D_X30	1	1.17	1.16
D_X32	1	1.07	1.07
D_X35	1	1.20	1.20
AGE1	1	4.09	4.08
I(AGE1^2)	1	3.76	3.75
X06A	1	1.36	1.36
X08B	1	1.28	1.28
X22A	1	3.23	3.20
X24A	1	2.75	2.74
X31	1	1.17	1.17

Table 112: Diagnostic Tests for Multicollinearity (Linear and Semi-log Model)

VIF-TEST		NW.TDV.CCA.DOUBLE GVIF^(1/2Df)	
Variables	df	Full-Sample	Sub-Sample
C_YEAR	9	1.11	1.12
C_X01	8	1.08	1.08
C_X14	4	1.99	1.99
C_X19	5	1.16	1.16
C_X21	2	2.54	2.53
C_X23	2	2.28	2.28
C_X2527	2	2.37	2.39
C_X29A	3	1.98	1.97
D_X18	1	2.46	2.49
D_X30	1	1.17	1.17
D_X32	1	1.07	1.07
D_X35	1	1.21	1.21
LG_AGE1	1	1.51	1.52
LG_X06A	1	1.30	1.30
LG_X08B	1	1.28	1.28
LG_X22A	1	5.47	5.45
LG_X24A	1	5.31	5.31
LG_X31	1	1.15	1.14

VIF-TEST		NW.TDV.CCA.MIX GVIF^(1/2Df)	
Variables	df	Full-Sample	Sub-Sample
C_YEAR	9	1.11	1.12
C_X01	8	1.08	1.08
C_X14	4	1.99	1.99
C_X19	5	1.16	1.16
C_X21	2	1.85	1.84
C_X23	2	1.54	1.55
C_X2527	2	2.35	2.37
C_X29A	3	1.98	1.97
D_X18	1	2.45	2.49
D_X30	1	1.17	1.17
D_X32	1	1.07	1.07
D_X35	1	1.21	1.21
LG_AGE1	1	1.51	1.51
LG_X06A	1	1.30	1.30
LG_X08B	1	1.28	1.28
X22A	1	3.22	3.19
X24A	1	2.74	2.73
LG_X31	1	1.15	1.14

Table 113: Tests for Multicollinearity (Double-log and Mix Model)

A.6.6 Summary of Diagnostic Tests

Full-Sample	Heteroscedasticity				Linearity				Normality		Residuals	
	Goldfeld-Quant	p-value	Breusch-Pagan /	p-value	Rain-Test	p-value	RESET-Test	p-value	JarqueBera Test	p-value	Skewness	Kurtosis
Linear Model	2.3991	0.0000	40.4293	0.0000	1.0189	0.4257	0.8596	0.4237	172.6541	0.0000	0.7118	1.6480
Semi-log	1.3884	0.0007	10.9099	0.0010	0.6116	1.0000	11.3517	0.0000	828.8806	0.0000	-0.9376	4.3923
Double-log	1.4512	0.0001	9.5154	0.0020	0.6370	1.0000	12.9149	0.0000	905.9129	0.0000	-0.9571	4.6116
Mix	1.4600	0.0001	9.6148	0.0019	0.6417	1.0000	13.3586	0.0000	859.5470	0.0000	-0.9373	4.4876

Sub-Sample	Heteroscedasticity				Linearity				Normality		Residuals	
	Goldfeld-Quant	p-value	Breusch-Pagan /	p-value	Rain-Test	p-value	RESET-Test	p-value	JarqueBera Test	p-value	Skewness	Kurtosis
Linear Model	0.86	0.93	46.47	0.00	1.04	0.34	1.66	0.19	196.94	0.00	0.79	1.73
Semi-log	1.13	0.12	6.07	0.01	0.70	1.00	8.95	0.00	10.24	0.01	-0.09	0.50
Double-log	1.17	0.06	3.98	0.05	0.76	1.00	10.57	0.00	15.23	0.00	-0.08	0.63
Mix	1.17	0.07	3.88	0.05	0.76	1.00	10.77	0.00	14.32	0.00	-0.08	0.61

Table 114: Diagnostic Tests for Nation-wide TDV Models (observed dataset)

A.6.7 Precision Measures

A.6.7.1 Mean Square Error (MSE)

	MSE						MSE					
	in.mi01	in.mi02	in.mi03	in.mi04	in.mi05	Average	out.mi01	out.mi02	out.mi03	out.mi04	out.mi05	Average
nw.tdv.linear	25.679	25.643	26.005	25.729	25.644	25.740	28.596	26.765	24.870	27.552	27.204	26.997
nw.tdv.semi	26.597	26.607	26.895	26.632	26.529	26.652	29.794	27.503	26.041	28.525	28.437	28.060
nw.tdv.double	26.219	26.261	26.546	26.301	26.153	26.296	29.669	27.388	25.675	28.157	28.194	27.817
nw.tdv.mix	26.202	26.248	26.530	26.280	26.137	26.279	29.645	27.369	25.667	28.151	28.176	27.802

Table 115: Mean Square Error (MSE) Nation-wide TDV Models (imputed datasets)

A.6.7.2 Root Mean Square Error (RMSE)

	RMSE						RMSE					
	in.mi01	in.mi02	in.mi03	in.mi04	in.mi05	Average	out.mi01	out.mi02	out.mi03	out.mi04	out.mi05	Average
nw.tdv.linear	5.067	5.064	5.099	5.072	5.064	5.073	5.348	5.173	4.987	5.249	5.216	5.195
nw.tdv.semi	5.157	5.158	5.186	5.161	5.151	5.163	5.458	5.244	5.103	5.341	5.333	5.296
nw.tdv.double	5.120	5.125	5.152	5.128	5.114	5.128	5.447	5.233	5.067	5.306	5.310	5.273
nw.tdv.mix	5.119	5.123	5.151	5.126	5.112	5.126	5.445	5.232	5.066	5.306	5.308	5.271

Table 116: Root Mean Square Error (RMSE) Nation-wide TDV Models (imputed datasets)

A.6.7.3 Mean Percentage Error (MPE)

	MPE						MPE					
	in.mi01	in.mi02	in.mi03	in.mi04	in.mi05	Average	out.mi01	out.mi02	out.mi03	out.mi04	out.mi05	Average
nw.tdv.linear	-18.682	-18.441	-18.837	-18.149	-18.793	-18.580	-19.427	-18.437	-16.620	-20.986	-15.937	-18.281
nw.tdv.semi	-10.376	-10.213	-10.463	-9.834	-10.470	-10.271	-10.862	-10.096	-8.296	-12.983	-7.868	-10.021
nw.tdv.double	-10.273	-10.101	-10.354	-9.843	-10.304	-10.147	-10.600	9.875	-8.140	-13.300	-7.714	-9.928
nw.tdv.mix	-10.259	-10.083	-10.341	-9.636	-10.351	-10.134	-10.587	-9.891	-8.114	-13.210	-7.698	-9.900

Table 117: Mean Percentage Error (MPE) Nation-wide TDV Models (imputed datasets)

A.7 Nation-wide TDV Models (based on imputed datasets)

A.7.1 Full-Sample

A.7.1.1 Diagnostic Tests of Nationwide TDV Models

A.7.1.1.1 Residual Normality

Full-Sample		Jarque-Bera Test				
		in.mi01	in.mi02	in.mi03	in.mi04	in.mi05
nw.tdv.linear	χ^2	82852.886	78100.967	81334.741	75110.962	79090.127
nw.tdv.semi	χ^2	25452.903	31884.654	32098.314	21786.822	32005.431
nw.tdv.double	χ^2	29266.990	36120.889	36500.201	24284.687	36845.602
nw.tdv.mix	χ^2	29180.660	35939.272	36319.801	24210.865	36694.825
nw.tdv.linear	p-value	0.000	0.000	0.000	0.000	0.000
nw.tdv.semi	p-value	0.000	0.000	0.000	0.000	0.000
nw.tdv.double	p-value	0.000	0.000	0.000	0.000	0.000
nw.tdv.mix	p-value	0.000	0.000	0.000	0.000	0.000

Table 118: Jarque Bera Residual Normality Test for Nationwide TDV Model (Imputed Dataset / Full Sample / All Models)

Full-Sample	Residual Skewness				
	in.mi01	in.mi02	in.mi03	in.mi04	in.mi05
nw.tdv.linear	1.965	1.926	1.967	1.925	1.944
nw.tdv.semi	-0.826	-0.886	-0.866	-0.789	-0.872
nw.tdv.double	-0.809	-0.870	-0.846	-0.767	-0.858
nw.tdv.mix	-0.809	-0.870	-0.846	-0.768	-0.859
	Residual Kurtosis				
	in.mi01	in.mi02	in.mi03	in.mi04	in.mi05
nw.tdv.linear	9.216	8.933	9.114	8.728	8.984
nw.tdv.semi	5.302	5.957	5.991	4.889	5.978
nw.tdv.double	5.731	6.382	6.431	5.203	6.457
nw.tdv.mix	5.721	6.365	6.414	5.194	6.443

Table 119: Descriptive Statistics for Nationwide TDV Model Residuals (Imputed Dataset / Full Sample / All Models)

A.7.1.1.2 Heteroscedasticity

		Breusch Pagan / Cook Weisberg Test				
		in.mi01	in.mi02	in.mi03	in.mi04	in.mi05
nw.tdv.linear	p-value	0.000	0.000	0.000	0.000	0.000
nw.tdv.semi	p-value	0.180	0.136	0.186	0.260	0.063
nw.tdv.double	p-value	0.035	0.026	0.030	0.049	0.011
nw.tdv.mix	p-value	0.033	0.024	0.028	0.046	0.010

Table 120: Breusch Pagan Heterogeneity Tests for Nationwide TDV Model Residuals (Imputed Dataset / Full Sample / All Models)

Full-Sample		Goldfeld-Quant Test				
		in.mi01	in.mi02	in.mi03	in.mi04	in.mi05
nw.tdv.linear	p-value	0.000	0.000	0.000	0.000	0.000
nw.tdv.semi	p-value	0.994	0.999	1.000	0.992	1.000
nw.tdv.double	p-value	1.000	1.000	1.000	1.000	1.000
nw.tdv.mix	p-value	1.000	1.000	1.000	1.000	1.000

Table 121: Goldfeld-Quant Heterogeneity Tests for Nationwide TDV Model Residuals (Imputed Dataset / Full Sample / All Models)

A.7.1.1.3 Linearity

		RAMSEY RESET TEST				
		in.mi01	in.mi02	in.mi03	in.mi04	in.mi05
nw.tdv.linear	p-value	0.000	0.000	0.000	0.000	0.000
nw.tdv.semi	p-value	0.000	0.000	0.000	0.000	0.000
nw.tdv.double	p-value	0.000	0.000	0.000	0.000	0.000
nw.tdv.mix	p-value	0.000	0.000	0.000	0.000	0.000

Table 122: RAMSEY Reset Linearity Tests for Nationwide TDV Model Residuals (Imputed Dataset / Full Sample / All Models)

Full-Sample		Rainbow Test				
		in.mi01	in.mi02	in.mi03	in.mi04	in.mi05
nw.tdv.linear	p-value	1.000	1.000	1.000	1.000	1.000
nw.tdv.semi	p-value	0.013	0.052	0.195	0.376	0.112
nw.tdv.double	p-value	0.001	0.010	0.043	0.145	0.028
nw.tdv.mix	p-value	0.001	0.010	0.044	0.141	0.027

Table 123: Rainbow Linearity Tests for Nationwide TDV Model Residuals (Imputed Dataset / Full Sample / All Models)

A.7.1.1.4 Multicollinearity

A.7.1.1.4.1 Linear Model

VIF-TEST		Nation-wide TDV Linear Model (Full Sample) GVIF^(1/2Df)				
Variables	df	in.mi01	in.mi02	in.mi03	in.mi04	in.mi05
C_YEAR	9	1.04	1.04	1.04	1.04	1.04
C_X01	8	1.04	1.04	1.04	1.04	1.04
C_X14	4	1.42	1.42	1.42	1.42	1.42
C_X19	5	1.07	1.07	1.07	1.07	1.07
C_X21	2	1.66	1.65	1.66	1.65	1.65
C_X23	2	1.38	1.39	1.39	1.39	1.39
C_X2527	3	1.29	1.28	1.30	1.29	1.29
C_X29A	5	1.29	1.29	1.29	1.29	1.29
D_X17	1	1.22	1.20	1.24	1.21	1.21
D_X18	1	1.42	1.42	1.46	1.45	1.43
D_X30	1	1.12	1.11	1.11	1.11	1.11
D_X32	1	1.08	1.08	1.08	1.08	1.08
D_X35	1	1.10	1.10	1.10	1.10	1.10
AGE1	1	3.31	3.33	3.32	3.33	3.33
I(AGE1^2)	1	3.21	3.22	3.21	3.22	3.22
X06A	1	1.13	1.13	1.14	1.13	1.14
X08B	1	1.09	1.10	1.09	1.09	1.08
X22A	1	2.46	2.44	2.46	2.43	2.42
X24A	1	1.97	1.98	1.97	1.96	1.97
X31	1	1.04	1.04	1.04	1.04	1.04

Table 124: Variance Inflation Test for Nationwide TDV Model (Imputed Dataset / Full Sample / Linear Model)

A.7.1.1.4.2 Semi-log Model

VIF-TEST		Nation-wide TDV Semi-log Model (Full Sample) GVIF^(1/2Df)				
Variables	df	in.mi01	in.mi02	in.mi03	in.mi04	in.mi05
C_YEAR	9	1.04	1.04	1.04	1.04	1.04
C_X01	8	1.04	1.04	1.04	1.04	1.04
C_X14	4	1.42	1.42	1.42	1.42	1.42
C_X19	5	1.07	1.07	1.07	1.07	1.07
C_X21	2	1.66	1.65	1.66	1.65	1.65
C_X23	2	1.38	1.39	1.39	1.39	1.39
C_X2527	3	1.29	1.28	1.30	1.29	1.29
C_X29A	5	1.29	1.29	1.29	1.29	1.29
D_X17	1	1.22	1.20	1.24	1.21	1.21
D_X18	1	1.42	1.42	1.46	1.45	1.43
D_X30	1	1.12	1.11	1.11	1.11	1.11
D_X32	1	1.08	1.08	1.08	1.08	1.08
D_X35	1	1.10	1.10	1.10	1.10	1.10
AGE1	1	3.31	3.33	3.32	3.33	3.33
I(AGE1^2)	1	3.21	3.22	3.21	3.22	3.22
X06A	1	1.13	1.13	1.14	1.13	1.14
X08B	1	1.09	1.10	1.09	1.09	1.08
X22A	1	2.46	2.44	2.46	2.43	2.42
X24A	1	1.97	1.98	1.97	1.96	1.97
X31	1	1.04	1.04	1.04	1.04	1.04

Table 125: Variance Inflation Test for Nationwide TDV Model (Imputed Dataset / Full Sample / Semi-log Model)

A.7.1.1.4.3 Double-log Model

VIF-TEST		Nation-wide TDV Double-log Model (Full Sample)				
				GVIF^(1/2Df)		
Variables	df	in.mi01	in.mi02	in.mi03	in.mi04	in.mi05
C_YEAR	9	1.04	1.04	1.04	1.04	1.04
C_X01	8	1.04	1.04	1.04	1.04	1.04
C_X14	4	1.42	1.42	1.42	1.42	1.42
C_X19	5	1.07	1.07	1.07	1.07	1.07
C_X21	2	2.42	2.40	2.42	2.41	2.39
C_X23	2	2.19	2.19	2.21	2.20	2.20
C_X2527	3	1.30	1.29	1.31	1.30	1.30
C_X29A	5	1.30	1.29	1.29	1.29	1.29
D_X17	1	1.22	1.21	1.25	1.21	1.22
D_X18	1	1.42	1.42	1.46	1.45	1.43
D_X30	1	1.12	1.11	1.11	1.11	1.11
D_X32	1	1.08	1.08	1.08	1.08	1.08
D_X35	1	1.10	1.10	1.10	1.10	1.10
LG_AGE1	1	1.16	1.16	1.15	1.16	1.16
LG_X06A	1	1.21	1.21	1.22	1.20	1.21
LG_X08B	1	1.15	1.16	1.16	1.16	1.16
LG_X22A	1	5.35	5.29	5.36	5.34	5.26
LG_X24A	1	4.86	4.87	4.93	4.92	4.89
LG_X31	1	1.09	1.09	1.10	1.09	1.10

Table 126: Variance Inflation Test for Nationwide TDV Model (Imputed Dataset / Full Sample / Double-log Model)

A.7.1.1.4.4 Mix Model

VIF-TEST		Nation-wide TDV Mix Model (Full Sample)				
				GVIF^(1/2Df)		
Variables	df	in.mi01	in.mi02	in.mi03	in.mi04	in.mi05
C_YEAR	9	1.04	1.04	1.04	1.04	1.04
C_X01	8	1.04	1.04	1.04	1.04	1.04
C_X14	4	1.42	1.42	1.42	1.42	1.42
C_X19	5	1.07	1.07	1.07	1.07	1.07
C_X21	2	1.66	1.66	1.66	1.65	1.65
C_X23	2	1.39	1.39	1.39	1.39	1.39
C_X2527	3	1.29	1.29	1.31	1.30	1.30
C_X29A	5	1.30	1.29	1.29	1.29	1.29
D_X17	1	1.22	1.21	1.25	1.21	1.22
D_X18	1	1.42	1.42	1.46	1.45	1.43
D_X30	1	1.12	1.11	1.11	1.11	1.11
D_X32	1	1.08	1.08	1.08	1.08	1.08
D_X35	1	1.10	1.10	1.10	1.10	1.10
LG_AGE1	1	1.16	1.16	1.15	1.16	1.16
LG_X06A	1	1.21	1.21	1.22	1.20	1.21
LG_X08B	1	1.15	1.16	1.16	1.16	1.16
X22A	1	2.46	2.44	2.46	2.43	2.42
X24A	1	1.97	1.98	1.97	1.96	1.97
LG_X31	1	1.09	1.09	1.10	1.09	1.10

Table 127: Variance Inflation Test for Nationwide TDV Model (Imputed Dataset / Full Sample / Mix Model)

A.7.1.2 Precision and Accuracy Measures of Nationwide TDV Models

A.7.1.2.1 Mean Square Error (MSE)

	MSE						MSE					
	in.mi01	in.mi02	in.mi03	in.mi04	in.mi05	Average	out.mi01	out.mi02	out.mi03	out.mi04	out.mi05	Average
nw.tdv.linear	25.679	25.643	26.005	25.729	25.644	25.740	28.596	26.765	24.870	27.552	27.204	26.997
nw.tdv.semi	26.597	26.607	26.895	26.632	26.529	26.652	29.794	27.503	26.041	28.525	28.437	28.060
nw.tdv.double	26.219	26.261	26.546	26.301	26.153	26.296	29.669	27.388	25.675	28.157	28.194	27.817
nw.tdv.mix	26.202	26.248	26.530	26.280	26.137	26.279	29.645	27.369	25.667	28.151	28.176	27.802

Table 128: Mean Square Error (MSE) for Nationwide TDV Model (Imputed Dataset / Full Sample / All Models)

A.7.1.2.2 Root Mean Square Error (RMSE)

	RMSE						RMSE					
	in.mi01	in.mi02	in.mi03	in.mi04	in.mi05	Average	out.mi01	out.mi02	out.mi03	out.mi04	out.mi05	Average
nw.tdv.linear	5.067	5.064	5.099	5.072	5.064	5.073	5.348	5.173	4.987	5.249	5.216	5.195
nw.tdv.semi	5.157	5.158	5.186	5.161	5.151	5.163	5.458	5.244	5.103	5.341	5.333	5.296
nw.tdv.double	5.120	5.125	5.152	5.128	5.114	5.128	5.447	5.233	5.067	5.306	5.310	5.273
nw.tdv.mix	5.119	5.123	5.151	5.126	5.112	5.126	5.445	5.232	5.066	5.306	5.308	5.271

Table 129: Root Mean Square Error (RMSE) for Nationwide TDV Model (Imputed Dataset / Full Sample / All Models)

A.7.1.2.3 Mean Percentage Error (MPE)

	MPE						MPE					
	in.mi01	in.mi02	in.mi03	in.mi04	in.mi05	Average	out.mi01	out.mi02	out.mi03	out.mi04	out.mi05	Average
nw.tdv.linear	-18.682	-18.441	-18.837	-18.149	-18.793	-18.580	-19.427	-18.437	-16.620	-20.986	-15.937	-18.281
nw.tdv.semi	-10.376	-10.213	-10.463	-9.834	-10.470	-10.271	-10.862	-10.096	-8.296	-12.983	-7.868	-10.021
nw.tdv.double	-10.273	-10.101	-10.354	-9.643	-10.364	-10.147	-10.609	-9.875	-8.140	-13.300	-7.714	-9.928
nw.tdv.mix	-10.259	-10.083	-10.341	-9.636	-10.351	-10.134	-10.587	-9.891	-8.114	-13.210	-7.698	-9.900

Table 130: Mean Percentage Error (MSE) for Nationwide TDV Model (Imputed Dataset / Full Sample / All Models)

A.7.2 Sub-Sample (3.00 EUR/sqm <= RENT <= 35.00 EUR /sqm)

A.7.2.1 Diagnostic Tests of Nationwide TDV Models

A.7.2.1.1 Residual Normality

Sub-Sample		Jarque-Bera Test				
		in.mi01	in.mi02	in.mi03	in.mi04	in.mi05
iqr.nw.tdv.linear	χ^2	12812.4897	12240.9474	12669.1474	12201.6008	12871.9058
iqr.nw.tdv.semi	χ^2	776.8185	738.6484	739.9745	725.8169	680.5051
iqr.nw.tdv.double	χ^2	857.7154	785.6978	785.8168	791.4832	746.5538
iqr.nw.tdv.mix	χ^2	853.3783	782.0893	783.6087	786.8635	741.4818
iqr.nw.tdv.linear	p-value	0.0000	0.0000	0.0000	0.0000	0.0000
iqr.nw.tdv.semi	p-value	0.0000	0.0000	0.0000	0.0000	0.0000
iqr.nw.tdv.double	p-value	0.0000	0.0000	0.0000	0.0000	0.0000
iqr.nw.tdv.mix	p-value	0.0000	0.0000	0.0000	0.0000	0.0000

Table 131: Jarque Bera Residual Normality Test for Nationwide TDV Model (Imputed Dataset / Sub Sample / All Models)

Sub-Sample	Residual Skewness				
	in.mi01	in.mi02	in.mi03	in.mi04	in.mi05
iqr.nw.tdv.linear	1.1525	1.1412	1.1542	1.1339	1.1632
iqr.nw.tdv.semi	-0.2129	-0.2102	-0.2063	-0.2191	-0.1870
iqr.nw.tdv.double	-0.1629	-0.1602	-0.1550	-0.1695	-0.1370
iqr.nw.tdv.mix	-0.1640	-0.1610	-0.1561	-0.1707	-0.1381
	Residual Kurtosis				
	in.mi01	in.mi02	in.mi03	in.mi04	in.mi05
iqr.nw.tdv.linear	3.2535	3.1595	3.2242	3.1629	3.2498
iqr.nw.tdv.semi	0.8844	0.8600	0.8647	0.8417	0.8391
iqr.nw.tdv.double	0.9786	0.9338	0.9374	0.9312	0.9224
iqr.nw.tdv.mix	0.9751	0.9308	0.9352	0.9273	0.9184

Table 132: Descriptive Statistics for Nationwide TDV Model Residuals (Imputed Dataset / Sub Sample / All Models)

A.7.2.1.2 Heteroscedasticity

		Breusch Pagan / Cook Weisberg Test				
		in.mi01	in.mi02	in.mi03	in.mi04	in.mi05
iqr.nw.tdv.linear	p-value	0.0000	0.0000	0.0000	0.0000	0.0000
iqr.nw.tdv.semi	p-value	0.6698	0.9388	0.7701	0.9004	0.4376
iqr.nw.tdv.double	p-value	0.0347	0.0258	0.0300	0.0490	0.0111
iqr.nw.tdv.mix	p-value	0.0327	0.0237	0.0276	0.0462	0.0102

Table 133: Breusch Pagan Heterogeneity Tests for Nationwide TDV Model Residuals (Imputed Dataset / Sub Sample / All Models)

Sub-Sample		Goldfeld-Quant Test				
		in.mi01	in.mi02	in.mi03	in.mi04	in.mi05
iqr.nw.tdv.linear	p-value	0.0000	0.0000	0.0000	0.0000	0.0000
iqr.nw.tdv.semi	p-value	0.0774	0.1618	0.2624	0.2860	0.4444
iqr.nw.tdv.double	p-value	0.6986	0.8566	0.9796	0.9848	0.9924
iqr.nw.tdv.mix	p-value	0.7040	0.8524	0.9847	0.9875	0.9850

Table 134: Goldfeld-Quant Heterogeneity Tests for Nationwide TDV Model Residuals (Imputed Dataset / Sub Sample / All Models)

A.7.2.1.3 Linearity

		RAMSEY RESET TEST				
		in.mi01	in.mi02	in.mi03	in.mi04	in.mi05
iqr.nw.tdv.linear	p-value	0.0000	0.0000	0.0000	0.0000	0.0000
iqr.nw.tdv.semi	p-value	0.0000	0.0000	0.0000	0.0000	0.0000
iqr.nw.tdv.double	p-value	0.0000	0.0000	0.0000	0.0000	0.0000
iqr.nw.tdv.mix	p-value	0.0000	0.0000	0.0000	0.0000	0.0000

Table 135: RAMSEY Reset Linearity Tests for Nationwide TDV Model Residuals (Imputed Dataset / Sub Sample / All Models)

Sub-Sample		Rainbow Test				
		in.mi01	in.mi02	in.mi03	in.mi04	in.mi05
iqr.nw.tdv.linear	p-value	1.0000	1.0000	1.0000	1.0000	1.0000
iqr.nw.tdv.semi	p-value	0.9980	0.9994	1.0000	0.9997	1.0000
iqr.nw.tdv.double	p-value	0.9822	0.9934	0.9987	0.9953	0.9999
iqr.nw.tdv.mix	p-value	0.9813	0.9934	0.9988	0.9953	0.9999

Table 136: Rainbow Linearity Tests for Nationwide TDV Model Residuals (Imputed Dataset / Sub Sample / All Models)

A.7.2.1.4 Multicollinearity

A.7.2.1.4.1 Linear Model

VIF-TEST		Nation-wide TDV Linear Model (Sub-Sample)				
		GVIF^(1/2Df)				
Variables	df	in.mi01	in.mi02	in.mi03	in.mi04	in.mi05
C_YEAR	9	1.04	1.04	1.04	1.04	1.04
C_X01	8	1.04	1.04	1.04	1.04	1.04
C_X14	4	1.42	1.42	1.42	1.42	1.42
C_X19	5	1.07	1.07	1.07	1.07	1.07
C_X21	2	1.66	1.65	1.66	1.65	1.64
C_X23	2	1.38	1.39	1.39	1.39	1.39
C_X2527	3	1.29	1.28	1.31	1.29	1.29
C_X29A	5	1.30	1.29	1.29	1.29	1.29
D_X17	1	1.22	1.20	1.24	1.21	1.21
D_X18	1	1.42	1.42	1.46	1.45	1.44
D_X30	1	1.12	1.11	1.11	1.11	1.11
D_X32	1	1.08	1.08	1.08	1.08	1.08
D_X35	1	1.10	1.10	1.10	1.10	1.10
AGE1	1	3.31	3.32	3.32	3.33	3.32
I(AGE1^2)	1	3.20	3.22	3.21	3.22	3.21
X06A	1	1.13	1.13	1.13	1.12	1.13
X08B	1	1.09	1.10	1.10	1.09	1.08
X22A	1	2.45	2.44	2.46	2.43	2.42
X24A	1	1.97	1.98	1.97	1.96	1.97
X31	1	1.04	1.04	1.04	1.04	1.04

Table 137: Variance Inflation Test for Nationwide TDV Model (Imputed Dataset / Sub Sample / Linear Model)

A.7.2.1.4.2 Semi-log Model

VIF-TEST		Nation-wide TDV Semi-log Model (Sub-Sample)				
		GVIF^(1/2Df)				
Variables	df	in.mi01	in.mi02	in.mi03	in.mi04	in.mi05
C_YEAR	9	1.04	1.04	1.04	1.04	1.04
C_X01	8	1.04	1.04	1.04	1.04	1.04
C_X14	4	1.42	1.42	1.42	1.42	1.42
C_X19	5	1.07	1.07	1.07	1.07	1.07
C_X21	2	1.66	1.65	1.66	1.65	1.64
C_X23	2	1.38	1.39	1.39	1.39	1.39
C_X2527	3	1.29	1.28	1.31	1.29	1.29
C_X29A	5	1.30	1.29	1.29	1.29	1.29
D_X17	1	1.22	1.20	1.24	1.21	1.21
D_X18	1	1.42	1.42	1.46	1.45	1.44
D_X30	1	1.12	1.11	1.11	1.11	1.11
D_X32	1	1.08	1.08	1.08	1.08	1.08
D_X35	1	1.10	1.10	1.10	1.10	1.10
AGE1	1	3.31	3.32	3.32	3.33	3.32
I(AGE1^2)	1	3.20	3.22	3.21	3.22	3.21
X06A	1	1.13	1.13	1.13	1.12	1.13
X08B	1	1.09	1.10	1.10	1.09	1.08
X22A	1	2.45	2.44	2.46	2.43	2.42
X24A	1	1.97	1.98	1.97	1.96	1.97
X31	1	1.04	1.04	1.04	1.04	1.04

Table 138: Variance Inflation Test for Nationwide TDV Model (Imputed Dataset / Sub Sample / Semi-log Model)

A.7.2.1.4.3 Double-log Model

VIF-TEST		Nation-wide TDV Double-log Model (Sub-Sample)				
		GVIF^(1/2Df)				
Variables	df	in.mi01	in.mi02	in.mi03	in.mi04	in.mi05
C_YEAR	9	1.04	1.04	1.04	1.04	1.04
C_X01	8	1.04	1.04	1.04	1.04	1.04
C_X14	4	1.42	1.42	1.42	1.42	1.42
C_X19	5	1.07	1.07	1.07	1.07	1.07
C_X21	2	2.42	2.40	2.42	2.41	2.39
C_X23	2	2.19	2.19	2.21	2.20	2.20
C_X2527	3	1.30	1.29	1.31	1.30	1.30
C_X29A	5	1.30	1.30	1.30	1.30	1.30
D_X17	1	1.22	1.21	1.25	1.22	1.22
D_X18	1	1.42	1.42	1.46	1.46	1.44
D_X30	1	1.12	1.11	1.11	1.11	1.11
D_X32	1	1.08	1.08	1.08	1.08	1.08
D_X35	1	1.10	1.10	1.10	1.10	1.10
LG_AGE1	1	1.15	1.16	1.15	1.15	1.15
LG_X06A	1	1.20	1.20	1.21	1.20	1.20
LG_X08B	1	1.15	1.16	1.16	1.16	1.15
LG_X22A	1	5.35	5.30	5.36	5.34	5.26
LG_X24A	1	4.86	4.87	4.92	4.91	4.89
LG_X31	1	1.09	1.09	1.10	1.09	1.10

Table 139: Variance Inflation Test for Nationwide TDV Model (Imputed Dataset / Sub Sample / Double-log Model)

A.7.2.1.4.4 Mix Model

VIF-TEST		Nation-wide TDV Mix Model (Sub Sample)				
		GVIF^(1/2Df)				
Variables	df	in.mi01	in.mi02	in.mi03	in.mi04	in.mi05
C_YEAR	9	1.04	1.04	1.04	1.04	1.04
C_X01	8	1.04	1.04	1.04	1.04	1.04
C_X14	4	1.42	1.42	1.42	1.42	1.42
C_X19	5	1.07	1.07	1.07	1.07	1.07
C_X21	2	1.66	1.65	1.66	1.65	1.65
C_X23	2	1.39	1.39	1.39	1.39	1.39
C_X2527	3	1.29	1.29	1.31	1.30	1.30
C_X29A	5	1.30	1.30	1.30	1.30	1.30
D_X17	1	1.22	1.21	1.25	1.21	1.22
D_X18	1	1.42	1.42	1.46	1.46	1.44
D_X30	1	1.12	1.11	1.11	1.11	1.11
D_X32	1	1.08	1.08	1.08	1.08	1.08
D_X35	1	1.10	1.10	1.10	1.10	1.10
LG_AGE1	1	1.15	1.16	1.15	1.15	1.15
LG_X06A	1	1.20	1.20	1.21	1.20	1.20
LG_X08B	1	1.15	1.16	1.16	1.16	1.15
X22A	1	2.46	2.44	2.46	2.43	2.42
X24A	1	1.97	1.98	1.97	1.96	1.97
LG_X31	1	1.09	1.09	1.10	1.09	1.10

Table 140: Variance Inflation Test for Nationwide TDV Model (Imputed Dataset / Sub Sample / Mix Model)

A.7.2.2 Precision and Accuracy Measures of Nationwide TDV Models

A.7.2.2.1 Mean Square Error (MSE)

	MSE						MSE					
	in.mi01	in.mi02	in.mi03	in.mi04	in.mi05	Average	out.mi01	out.mi02	out.mi03	out.mi04	out.mi05	Average
iqr.nw.tdv.linear	17.454	17.282	17.296	17.266	17.322	17.324	16.365	17.009	17.350	17.637	17.118	17.096
iqr.nw.tdv.semi	18.104	17.947	17.926	17.904	17.948	17.966	16.930	17.431	18.293	18.299	17.922	17.775
iqr.nw.tdv.double	17.728	17.622	17.585	17.579	17.572	17.617	16.891	17.101	17.803	17.937	17.750	17.496
iqr.nw.tdv.mix	17.709	17.605	17.566	17.555	17.553	17.598	16.864	17.083	17.796	17.932	17.729	17.481

Table 141: Mean Square Error (MSE) for Nationwide TDV Model (Imputed Dataset / Sub Sample / All Models)

A.7.2.2.2 Root Mean Square Error (RMSE)

	RMSE						RMSE					
	in.mi01	in.mi02	in.mi03	in.mi04	in.mi05	Average	out.mi01	out.mi02	out.mi03	out.mi04	out.mi05	Average
iqr.nw.tdv.linear	4.178	4.157	4.159	4.155	4.162	4.162	4.045	4.124	4.165	4.200	4.137	4.134
iqr.nw.tdv.semi	4.255	4.236	4.234	4.231	4.236	4.239	4.115	4.175	4.277	4.278	4.233	4.216
iqr.nw.tdv.double	4.210	4.198	4.193	4.193	4.192	4.197	4.110	4.135	4.219	4.235	4.213	4.183
iqr.nw.tdv.mix	4.208	4.196	4.191	4.190	4.190	4.195	4.107	4.133	4.219	4.235	4.211	4.181

Table 142: Root Mean Square Error (RMSE) for Nationwide TDV Model (Imputed Dataset / Sub Sample / All Models)

A.7.2.2.3 Mean Percentage Error (MPE)

	MPE						MPE					
	in.mi01	in.mi02	in.mi03	in.mi04	in.mi05	Average	out.mi01	out.mi02	out.mi03	out.mi04	out.mi05	Average
iqr.nw.tdv.linear	-11.394	-11.048	-11.333	-11.300	-11.244	-11.264	-11.021	-12.743	-10.180	-10.225	-10.923	-11.018
iqr.nw.tdv.semi	-6.279	-5.945	-6.216	-6.179	-6.094	-6.143	-5.850	-7.516	-4.976	-5.029	-5.825	-5.839
iqr.nw.tdv.double	-6.131	-5.780	-6.074	-5.999	-5.922	-5.981	-5.566	-7.286	-4.846	-4.895	-5.760	-5.671
iqr.nw.tdv.mix	-6.125	-5.775	-6.074	-5.996	-5.921	-5.978	-5.583	-7.303	-4.826	-4.880	-5.747	-5.668

Table 143: Mean Percentage Error (MSE) for Nationwide TDV Model (Imputed Dataset / Sub Sample / All Models)

A.8 Diagnostic Tests for Nation-wide Characteristic Price Index Models

A.8.1 Nation-wide Characteristic Price Index Model (Year 1997)

A.8.1.1 Residual Normality

Jarque-Bera Test					
	in.mi01	in.mi02	in.mi03	in.mi04	in.mi05
nw.cp.1997	341.4681	372.8135	356.7233	393.4566	408.4182
iqr.nw.cp 1997	90.9015	103.5214	103.7412	108.7838	100.0460

Table 144: Jarque-Bera Normality Tests Nation-wide Characteristic Price Index Model (Imputed Datasets / Full + Sub Sample / Year 1997)

Residual Skewness					
	in.mi01	in.mi02	in.mi03	in.mi04	in.mi05
nw.cp.1997	-0.4483	-0.4260	-0.4360	-0.5764	-0.4345
iqr.nw.cp 1997	-0.2102	-0.2696	-0.2631	-0.4011	-0.2653

Residual Kurtosis					
	in.mi01	in.mi02	in.mi03	in.mi04	in.mi05
nw.cp.1997	2.8336	3.0130	2.9360	3.0111	3.1181
iqr.nw.cp 1997	1.4836	1.5679	1.5741	1.5057	1.5222

Table 145: Descriptive Statistics for Residuals of Nation-wide Characteristic Price Index Model (Imputed Datasets / Full + Sub Sample / Year 1997)

A.8.1.2 Heteroscedasticity

Breusch-Pagan / Cook Weisberg Test					
	in.mi01	in.mi02	in.mi03	in.mi04	in.mi05
nw.cp.1997	0.3091	0.6013	0.2114	0.3826	0.4044
iqr.nw.cp 1997	0.1125	0.5331	0.1504	0.2354	0.2789

Table 146: Breusch-Pagan Heteroscedasticity Test for Nation-wide Characteristic Price Index Model (Imputed Datasets / Full + Sub Sample / Year 1997)

Goldfeld-Quant Test					
	in.mi01	in.mi02	in.mi03	in.mi04	in.mi05
nw.cp.1997	0.7154	0.3897	0.3751	0.1464	0.7068
iqr.nw.cp 1997	0.4487	0.1049	0.0299	0.0129	0.2157

Table 147: Goldfeld-Quant Heteroscedasticity Test for Nation-wide Characteristic Price Index Model (Imputed Datasets / Full + Sub Sample / Year 1997)

A.8.1.3 Linearity

RAMSEY RESET					
	in.mi01	in.mi02	in.mi03	in.mi04	in.mi05
nw.cp.1997	0.2582	0.2935	0.5982	0.2631	0.2750
iqr.nw.cp 1997	0.0340	0.0123	0.1634	0.1035	0.0450

Table 148: Ramsey Reset Linearity Test for Nation-wide Characteristic Price Index Model (Imputed Datasets / Full + Sub Sample / Year 1997)

Rainbow Test					
	in.mi01	in.mi02	in.mi03	in.mi04	in.mi05
nw.cp.1997	0.2886	0.3519	0.2254	0.3774	0.2019
iqr.nw.cp 1997	0.5472	0.4425	0.3772	0.7250	0.3599

Table 149: Rainbow Linearity Test for Nation-wide Characteristic Price Index Model (Imputed Datasets / Full + Sub Sample / Year 1997)

A.8.1.4 Multicollinearity

VIF-TEST		Nation-wide CP.1997 Mix Model (Full Sample)				
		GVIF^(1/2Df)				
Variables	df	in.mi01	in.mi02	in.mi03	in.mi04	in.mi05
C_X01	8	1.07	1.08	1.08	1.08	1.08
C_X14	3	1.43	1.45	1.45	1.44	1.44
C_X19	5	1.07	1.07	1.08	1.07	1.07
C_X21	2	1.60	1.55	1.58	1.63	1.58
C_X23	2	1.71	1.68	1.69	1.73	1.70
C_X2527	3	1.28	1.29	1.33	1.28	1.30
C_X29A	5	1.21	1.22	1.22	1.22	1.22
D_X17	1	1.17	1.17	1.20	1.14	1.16
D_X18	1	1.46	1.45	1.57	1.39	1.48
D_X30	1	1.11	1.12	1.09	1.10	1.09
D_X32	1	1.12	1.12	1.14	1.13	1.12
D_X35	1	1.32	1.31	1.33	1.36	1.32
LG_AGE1	1	1.18	1.18	1.17	1.18	1.18
LG_X06A	1	1.26	1.24	1.26	1.25	1.25
LG_X08B	1	1.12	1.08	1.13	1.11	1.10
X22A	1	1.98	1.88	1.88	1.95	1.92
X24A	1	2.37	2.34	2.35	2.41	2.39
LG_X31	1	1.11	1.10	1.12	1.10	1.11

Table 150: Variance Inflation Test for Nation-wide Characteristic Price Index Model (Imputed Datasets / Full Sample / Year 1997)

VIF-TEST		Nation-wide CP.1997 Mix Model (Sub Sample)				
		GVIF^(1/2Df)				
Variables	df	in.mi01	in.mi02	in.mi03	in.mi04	in.mi05
C_X01	8	1.07	1.08	1.08	1.08	1.08
C_X14	3	1.43	1.45	1.45	1.45	1.44
C_X19	5	1.07	1.07	1.08	1.07	1.07
C_X21	2	1.60	1.55	1.58	1.63	1.58
C_X23	2	1.71	1.68	1.69	1.73	1.70
C_X2527	3	1.28	1.29	1.33	1.29	1.30
C_X29A	5	1.21	1.22	1.22	1.22	1.22
D_X17	1	1.17	1.17	1.21	1.14	1.16
D_X18	1	1.46	1.45	1.56	1.38	1.49
D_X30	1	1.11	1.12	1.09	1.10	1.09
D_X32	1	1.12	1.12	1.14	1.13	1.12
D_X35	1	1.32	1.31	1.33	1.36	1.32
LG_AGE1	1	1.18	1.18	1.18	1.19	1.19
LG_X06A	1	1.26	1.25	1.26	1.25	1.25
LG_X08B	1	1.12	1.08	1.13	1.11	1.10
X22A	1	1.99	1.88	1.88	1.95	1.92
X24A	1	2.37	2.34	2.35	2.41	2.39
LG_X31	1	1.11	1.11	1.12	1.10	1.12

Table 151: Variance Inflation Test for Nation-wide Characteristic Price Index Model (Imputed Datasets / Sub Sample / Year 1997)

A.8.2 Nation-wide Characteristic Price Index Model (Year 1998)

A.8.2.1 Residual Normality

	Jarque-Bera Test				
	in.mi01	in.mi02	in.mi03	in.mi04	in.mi05
nw.cp.1998	2630.2460	2797.4224	2853.1477	2340.2896	2683.1762
iqr.nw.cp 1998	80.8290	70.2708	70.9394	102.5444	101.0230

Table 152: Jarque-Bera Normality Tests Nation-wide Characteristic Price Index Model (Imputed Datasets / Full + Sub Sample / Year 1998)

	Residual Skewness				
	in.mi01	in.mi02	in.mi03	in.mi04	in.mi05
nw.cp.1998	-1.1683	-1.2879	-1.1064	-1.1307	-1.1904
iqr.nw.cp 1998	-0.1696	-0.2934	-0.1491	-0.2459	-0.2047

	Residual Kurtosis				
	in.mi01	in.mi02	in.mi03	in.mi04	in.mi05
nw.cp.1998	7.0669	7.2063	7.3770	6.6563	7.1448
iqr.nw.cp 1998	1.2772	1.0781	1.1910	1.4058	1.4223

Table 153: Descriptive Statistics for Residuals of Nation-wide Characteristic Price Index Model (Imputed Datasets / Full + Sub Sample / Year 1998)

A.8.2.2 Heteroscedasticity

Breusch-Pagan / Cook Weisberg Test					
	in.mi01	in.mi02	in.mi03	in.mi04	in.mi05
nw.cp.1998	0.6240	0.9835	0.6842	0.7864	0.4531
iqr.nw.cp 1998	0.3006	0.0267	0.2169	0.1523	0.2698

Table 154: Breusch-Pagan Heteroscedasticity Test for Nation-wide Characteristic Price Index Model (Imputed Datasets / Full + Sub Sample / Year 1998)

Goldfeld-Quant Test					
	in.mi01	in.mi02	in.mi03	in.mi04	in.mi05
nw.cp.1998	1.0000	1.0000	1.0000	1.0000	1.0000
iqr.nw.cp 1998	0.2907	0.1649	0.3964	0.1694	0.1634

Table 155: Goldfeld-Quant Heteroscedasticity Test for Nation-wide Characteristic Price Index Model (Imputed Datasets / Full + Sub Sample / Year 1998)

A.8.2.3 Linearity

RAMSEY RESET					
	in.mi01	in.mi02	in.mi03	in.mi04	in.mi05
nw.cp.1998	0.0061	0.0344	0.0115	0.0002	0.0241
iqr.nw.cp 1998	0.0335	0.0458	0.1265	0.0588	0.1692

Table 156: Ramsey Reset Linearity Test for Nation-wide Characteristic Price Index Model (Imputed Datasets / Full + Sub Sample / Year 1998)

Rainbow Test					
	in.mi01	in.mi02	in.mi03	in.mi04	in.mi05
nw.cp.1998	1.0000	1.0000	1.0000	1.0000	1.0000
iqr.nw.cp 1998	1.0000	1.0000	0.9996	1.0000	0.9997

Table 157: Rainbow Linearity Test for Nation-wide Characteristic Price Index Model (Imputed Datasets / Full + Sub Sample / Year 1998)

A.8.2.4 Multicollinearity

VIF-TEST		Nation-wide CP.1998 Mix Model (Full Sample)				
		GVIF^(1/2Df)				
Variables	df	in.mi01	in.mi02	in.mi03	in.mi04	in.mi05
C_X01	8	1.07	1.07	1.07	1.08	1.07
C_X14	3	1.57	1.57	1.60	1.57	1.58
C_X19	5	1.10	1.10	1.11	1.10	1.10
C_X21	2	1.80	1.78	1.77	1.81	1.82
C_X23	2	1.36	1.37	1.37	1.37	1.36
C_X2527	3	1.31	1.31	1.32	1.29	1.29
C_X29A	5	1.29	1.29	1.30	1.29	1.29
D_X17	1	1.14	1.15	1.18	1.13	1.12
D_X18	1	1.55	1.57	1.58	1.49	1.46
D_X30	1	1.11	1.10	1.10	1.12	1.10
D_X32	1	1.08	1.10	1.10	1.10	1.10
D_X35	1	1.20	1.21	1.20	1.22	1.19
LG_AGE1	1	1.21	1.21	1.19	1.19	1.20
LG_X06A	1	1.24	1.24	1.24	1.25	1.23
LG_X08B	1	1.08	1.11	1.12	1.10	1.12
X22A	1	2.80	2.76	2.74	2.83	2.93
X24A	1	1.74	1.73	1.74	1.69	1.69
LG_X31	1	1.10	1.10	1.10	1.10	1.10

Table 158: Variance Inflation Test for Nation-wide Characteristic Price Index Model (Imputed Datasets / Full Sample / Year 1998)

VIF-TEST		Nation-wide CP.1998 Mix Model (Sub Sample)				
		GVIF^(1/2Df)				
Variables	df	in.mi01	in.mi02	in.mi03	in.mi04	in.mi05
C_X01	8	1.07	1.07	1.07	1.08	1.07
C_X14	3	1.58	1.58	1.61	1.58	1.60
C_X19	5	1.10	1.11	1.11	1.11	1.10
C_X21	2	1.81	1.78	1.78	1.81	1.83
C_X23	2	1.36	1.37	1.37	1.37	1.36
C_X2527	3	1.31	1.31	1.33	1.29	1.30
C_X29A	5	1.29	1.29	1.31	1.30	1.30
D_X17	1	1.13	1.15	1.17	1.13	1.13
D_X18	1	1.55	1.59	1.61	1.51	1.47
D_X30	1	1.12	1.10	1.10	1.11	1.10
D_X32	1	1.09	1.10	1.10	1.10	1.10
D_X35	1	1.20	1.21	1.21	1.22	1.19
LG_AGE1	1	1.21	1.21	1.19	1.19	1.20
LG_X06A	1	1.24	1.24	1.25	1.25	1.23
LG_X08B	1	1.08	1.11	1.12	1.10	1.13
X22A	1	2.80	2.76	2.74	2.84	2.93
X24A	1	1.74	1.73	1.74	1.69	1.69
LG_X31	1	1.10	1.10	1.10	1.10	1.10

Table 159: Variance Inflation Test for Nation-wide Characteristic Price Index Model (Imputed Datasets / Sub Sample / Year 1998)

A.8.3 Nation-wide Characteristic Price Index Model (Year 1999)

A.8.3.1 Residual Normality

Jarque-Bera Test					
	in.mi01	in.mi02	in.mi03	in.mi04	in.mi05
nw.cp.1999	1596.9599	1455.8951	1183.9396	1266.1002	1702.5615
iqr.nw.cp1999	189.6060	173.4274	175.9400	152.6126	173.5187

Table 160: Jarque-Bera Normality Tests Nation-wide Characteristic Price Index Model (Imputed Datasets / Full + Sub Sample / Year 1999)

Residual Skewness					
	in.mi01	in.mi02	in.mi03	in.mi04	in.mi05
nw.cp.1999	-0.6913	-0.6455	-0.5050	-0.6315	-0.6669
iqr.nw.cp1999	-0.1927	-0.1333	-0.1323	-0.2083	-0.1021

Residual Kurtosis					
	in.mi01	in.mi02	in.mi03	in.mi04	in.mi05
nw.cp.1999	4.6660	4.4770	4.0822	4.1517	4.8871
iqr.nw.cp1999	1.6413	1.5931	1.6058	1.4547	1.6120

Table 161: Descriptive Statistics for Residuals of Nation-wide Characteristic Price Index Model (Imputed Datasets / Full + Sub Sample / Year 1999)

A.8.3.2 Heteroscedasticity

Breusch-Pagan / Cook Weisberg Test					
	in.mi01	in.mi02	in.mi03	in.mi04	in.mi05
nw.cp.1999	0.0008	0.0013	0.0037	0.0050	0.0014
iqr.nw.cp1999	0.0070	0.0049	0.0064	0.0166	0.0088

Table 162: Breusch-Pagan Heteroscedasticity Test for Nation-wide Characteristic Price Index Model (Imputed Datasets / Full + Sub Sample / Year 1999)

Goldfeld-Quant Test					
	in.mi01	in.mi02	in.mi03	in.mi04	in.mi05
nw.cp.1999	0.2492	0.4055	0.3890	0.1544	0.2704
iqr.nw.cp1999	0.0171	0.0497	0.0561	0.0124	0.0275

Table 163: Goldfeld-Quant Heteroscedasticity Test for Nation-wide Characteristic Price Index Model (Imputed Datasets / Full + Sub Sample / Year 1999)

A.8.3.3 Linearity

RAMSEY RESET					
	in.mi01	in.mi02	in.mi03	in.mi04	in.mi05
nw.cp.1999	0.9372	0.9062	0.8392	0.9580	0.9610
iqr.nw.cp1999	0.4861	0.9762	0.5884	0.9352	0.5620

Table 164: Ramsey Reset Linearity Test for Nation-wide Characteristic Price Index Model (Imputed Datasets / Full + Sub Sample / Year 1999)

Rainbow Test					
	in.mi01	in.mi02	in.mi03	in.mi04	in.mi05
nw.cp.1999	0.7127	0.8752	0.9392	0.7662	0.9855
iqr.nw.cp1999	0.9994	0.9997	1.0000	0.9996	1.0000

Table 165: Rainbow Linearity Test for Nation-wide Characteristic Price Index Model (Imputed Datasets / Full + Sub Sample / Year 1999)

A.8.3.4 Multicollinearity

VIF-TEST		Nation-wide CP.1999 Mix Model (Full Sample)				
		GVIF^(1/2Df)				
Variables	df	in.mi01	in.mi02	in.mi03	in.mi04	in.mi05
C_X01	8	1.06	1.06	1.05	1.05	1.05
C_X14	3	1.56	1.57	1.56	1.57	1.59
C_X19	5	1.06	1.06	1.06	1.06	1.06
C_X21	2	1.51	1.51	1.50	1.50	1.51
C_X23	1	4.10	2.32	2.25	2.44	2.21
C_X2527	3	1.36	1.38	1.41	1.37	1.42
C_X29A	5	1.33	1.33	1.32	1.33	1.34
D_X17	1	1.19	1.17	1.20	1.17	1.17
D_X18	1	1.59	1.70	1.80	1.61	1.86
D_X30	1	1.12	1.11	1.10	1.10	1.10
D_X32	1	1.05	1.04	1.05	1.06	1.06
D_X35	1	1.23	1.23	1.23	1.24	1.23
LG_AGE1	1	1.19	1.17	1.17	1.18	1.17
LG_X06A	1	1.20	1.17	1.18	1.20	1.17
LG_X08B	1	1.09	1.09	1.11	1.10	1.09
X22A	1	2.13	2.14	2.13	2.10	2.12
X24A	1	4.10	5.02	4.78	5.57	4.56
LG_X31	1	1.06	1.06	1.06	1.07	1.07

Table 166: Variance Inflation Test for Nation-wide Characteristic Price Index Model (Imputed Datasets / Full Sample / Year 1999)

VIF-TEST		Nation-wide CP.1999 Mix Model (Sub Sample)				
		GVIF^(1/2Df)				
Variables	df	in.mi01	in.mi02	in.mi03	in.mi04	in.mi05
C_X01	8	1.06	1.06	1.05	1.05	1.05
C_X14	3	1.57	1.59	1.57	1.58	1.61
C_X19	5	1.06	1.06	1.06	1.06	1.06
C_X21	2	1.51	1.51	1.51	1.50	1.51
C_X23	2	4.10	2.32	2.25	2.44	2.21
C_X2527	3	1.36	1.37	1.41	1.37	1.42
C_X29A	5	1.33	1.33	1.33	1.33	1.35
D_X17	1	1.19	1.18	1.21	1.17	1.18
D_X18	1	1.58	1.70	1.80	1.62	1.87
D_X30	1	1.12	1.11	1.11	1.10	1.10
D_X32	1	1.05	1.04	1.05	1.06	1.05
D_X35	1	1.23	1.23	1.23	1.24	1.23
LG_AGE1	1	1.19	1.18	1.17	1.18	1.17
LG_X06A	1	1.20	1.17	1.18	1.20	1.17
LG_X08B	1	1.09	1.09	1.11	1.11	1.09
X22A	1	2.13	2.14	2.13	2.10	2.12
X24A	1	4.10	5.02	4.78	5.57	4.56
LG_X31	1	1.06	1.06	1.06	1.07	1.07

Table 167: Variance Inflation Test for Nation-wide Characteristic Price Index Model (Imputed Datasets / Sub Sample / Year 1999)

A.8.4 Nation-wide Characteristic Price Index Model (Year 2000)

A.8.4.1 Residual Normality

Jarque-Bera Test					
	in.mi01	in.mi02	in.mi03	in.mi04	in.mi05
nw.cp.2000	1784.0015	1672.7111	1672.8527	1788.6898	1914.5792
iqr.nw.cp 2000	129.4517	155.9637	142.4965	120.7684	146.7550

Table 168: Jarque-Bera Normality Tests Nation-wide Characteristic Price Index Model (Imputed Datasets / Full + Sub Sample / Year 2000)

Residual Skewness					
	in.mi01	in.mi02	in.mi03	in.mi04	in.mi05
nw.cp.2000	-0.7655	0.7689	-0.7901	-0.7616	-0.8679
iqr.nw.cp 2000	-0.3060	-0.3218	-0.3338	-0.2377	-0.2792

Residual Kurtosis					
	in.mi01	in.mi02	in.mi03	in.mi04	in.mi05
nw.cp.2000	4.5358	4.3611	4.3370	4.5169	4.6543
iqr.nw.cp 2000	1.1516	1.2771	1.1898	1.1595	1.2742

Table 169: Descriptive Statistics for Residuals of Nation-wide Characteristic Price Index Model (Imputed Datasets / Full + Sub Sample / Year 2000)

A.8.4.2 Heteroscedasticity

Breusch-Pagan / Cook Weisberg Test					
	in.mi01	in.mi02	in.mi03	in.mi04	in.mi05
nw.cp.2000	0.3601	0.4064	0.3706	0.5651	0.4612
iqr.nw.cp 2000	0.0023	0.0079	0.0011	0.0021	0.0000

Table 170: Breusch-Pagan Heteroscedasticity Test for Nation-wide Characteristic Price Index Model (Imputed Datasets / Full + Sub Sample / Year 2000)

Goldfeld-Quant Test					
	in.mi01	in.mi02	in.mi03	in.mi04	in.mi05
nw.cp.2000	1.0000	1.0000	1.0000	1.0000	1.0000
iqr.nw.cp 2000	0.9977	0.9897	0.9987	0.9874	0.9330

Table 171: Goldfeld-Quant Heteroscedasticity Test for Nation-wide Characteristic Price Index Model (Imputed Datasets / Full + Sub Sample / Year 2000)

A.8.4.3 Linearity

RAMSEY RESET					
	in.mi01	in.mi02	in.mi03	in.mi04	in.mi05
nw.cp.2000	0.0233	0.0011	0.0025	0.0000	0.0002
iqr.nw.cp 2000	0.0000	0.0000	0.0000	0.0000	0.0000

Table 172: Ramsey Reset Linearity Test for Nation-wide Characteristic Price Index Model (Imputed Datasets / Full + Sub Sample / Year 2000)

Rainbow Test					
	in.mi01	in.mi02	in.mi03	in.mi04	in.mi05
nw.cp.2000	0.6384	0.4345	0.6824	0.7693	0.8636
iqr.nw.cp 2000	0.2839	0.0714	0.5385	0.3167	0.2174

Table 173: Rainbow Linearity Test for Nation-wide Characteristic Price Index Model (Imputed Datasets / Full + Sub Sample / Year 2000)

A.8.4.4 Multicollinearity

VIF-TEST		Nation-wide CP.2000 Mix Model (Full Sample)				
		GVIF^(1/2Df)				
Variables	df	in.mi01	in.mi02	in.mi03	in.mi04	in.mi05
C_X01	8	1.06	1.06	1.05	1.06	1.06
C_X14	3	1.58	1.57	1.58	1.57	1.60
C_X19	5	1.06	1.06	1.05	1.06	1.05
C_X21	2	1.67	1.64	1.66	1.65	1.63
C_X23	2	1.54	1.51	1.53	1.55	1.70
C_X2527	3	1.29	1.31	1.35	1.30	1.31
C_X29A	5	1.33	1.32	1.33	1.32	1.34
D_X17	1	1.16	1.14	1.18	1.16	1.14
D_X18	1	1.43	1.52	1.67	1.50	1.48
D_X30	1	1.09	1.08	1.07	1.07	1.08
D_X32	1	1.07	1.06	1.08	1.07	1.07
D_X35	1	1.27	1.25	1.25	1.27	1.27
LG_AGE1	1	1.21	1.22	1.21	1.19	1.21
LG_X06A	1	1.22	1.23	1.22	1.22	1.23
LG_X08B	1	1.11	1.12	1.10	1.10	1.12
X22A	1	2.61	2.50	2.54	2.50	2.48
X24A	1	2.05	1.96	1.98	2.05	2.56
LG_X31	1	1.10	1.10	1.10	1.10	1.10

Table 174: Variance Inflation Test for Nation-wide Characteristic Price Index Model (Imputed Datasets / Full Sample / Year 2000)

VIF-TEST		Nation-wide CP.2000 Mix Model (Sub Sample)				
		GVIF^(1/2Df)				
Variables	df	in.mi01	in.mi02	in.mi03	in.mi04	in.mi05
C_X01	8	1.06	1.06	1.05	1.06	1.06
C_X14	3	1.60	1.59	1.60	1.59	1.61
C_X19	5	1.06	1.06	1.06	1.06	1.06
C_X21	2	1.67	1.64	1.66	1.65	1.64
C_X23	2	1.54	1.50	1.52	1.54	1.70
C_X2527	3	1.29	1.31	1.35	1.31	1.31
C_X29A	5	1.34	1.33	1.34	1.33	1.34
D_X17	1	1.16	1.14	1.19	1.16	1.15
D_X18	1	1.43	1.53	1.67	1.51	1.51
D_X30	1	1.09	1.08	1.07	1.07	1.08
D_X32	1	1.07	1.07	1.08	1.07	1.07
D_X35	1	1.27	1.24	1.25	1.27	1.27
LG_AGE1	1	1.21	1.22	1.21	1.19	1.21
LG_X06A	1	1.22	1.23	1.22	1.22	1.24
LG_X08B	1	1.11	1.11	1.10	1.11	1.12
X22A	1	2.60	2.49	2.54	2.49	2.47
X24A	1	2.04	1.96	1.97	2.05	2.56
LG_X31	1	1.11	1.10	1.10	1.10	1.10

Table 175: Variance Inflation Test for Nation-wide Characteristic Price Index Model Imputed Datasets / Sub Sample / Year 2000)

A.8.5 Nation-wide Characteristic Price Index Model (Year 2001)

A.8.5.1 Residual Normality

Jarque-Bera Test					
	in.mi01	in.mi02	in.mi03	in.mi04	in.mi05
nw.cp.2001	692.9271	825.1531	836.9157	733.8008	794.4734
iqr.nw.cp.2001	155.5170	175.3429	147.5865	145.3693	132.3321

Table 176: Jarque-Bera Normality Tests Nation-wide Characteristic Price Index Model (Imputed Datasets / Full + Sub Sample / Year 2001)

Residual Skewness					
	in.mi01	in.mi02	in.mi03	in.mi04	in.mi05
nw.cp.2001	-0.3559	-0.4286	-0.4159	-0.3558	-0.3803
iqr.nw.cp.2001	-0.1697	-0.1964	-0.1631	-0.1279	-0.1121

Residual Kurtosis					
	in.mi01	in.mi02	in.mi03	in.mi04	in.mi05
nw.cp.2001	2.6562	2.8789	2.9036	2.7218	2.8372
iqr.nw.cp.2001	1.2851	1.3586	1.2536	1.2524	1.2028

Table 177: Descriptive Statistics for Residuals of Nation-wide Characteristic Price Index Model (Imputed Datasets / Full + Sub Sample / Year 2001)

A.8.5.2 Heteroscedasticity

Breusch-Pagan / Cook Weisberg Test					
	in.mi01	in.mi02	in.mi03	in.mi04	in.mi05
nw.cp.2001	0.1925	0.0447	0.1026	0.0452	0.1321
iqr.nw.cp.2001	0.0256	0.0391	0.0251	0.0063	0.0053

Table 178: Breusch-Pagan Heteroscedasticity Test for Nation-wide Characteristic Price Index Model (Imputed Datasets / Full + Sub Sample / Year 2001)

Goldfeld-Quant Test					
	in.mi01	in.mi02	in.mi03	in.mi04	in.mi05
nw.cp.2001	0.9950	0.8597	0.9820	0.9488	0.9407
iqr.nw.cp.2001	0.0681	0.0268	0.0971	0.2542	0.0494

Table 179: Goldfeld-Quant Heteroscedasticity Test for Nation-wide Characteristic Price Index Model (Imputed Datasets / Full + Sub Sample / Year 2001)

A.8.5.3 Linearity

RAMSEY RESET					
	in.mi01	in.mi02	in.mi03	in.mi04	in.mi05
nw.cp.2001	0.0000	0.0000	0.0000	0.0000	0.0003
iqr.nw.cp.2001	0.0000	0.0000	0.0000	0.0000	0.0000

Table 180: Ramsey Reset Linearity Test for Nation-wide Characteristic Price Index Model (Imputed Datasets / Full + Sub Sample / Year 2001)

Rainbow Test					
	in.mi01	in.mi02	in.mi03	in.mi04	in.mi05
nw.cp.2001	0.8226	0.9277	0.8907	0.9809	0.9463
iqr.nw.cp.2001	0.2009	0.3322	0.1561	0.3981	0.2104

Table 181: Rainbow Linearity Test for Nation-wide Characteristic Price Index Model (Imputed Datasets / Full + Sub Sample / Year 2001)

A.8.5.4 Multicollinearity

VIF-TEST		Nation-wide CP.2001 Mix Model (Full Sample)				
		GVIF^(1/2Df)				
Variables	df	in.mi01	in.mi02	in.mi03	in.mi04	in.mi05
C_X01	8	1.06	1.06	1.06	1.06	1.06
C_X14	4	1.49	1.48	1.49	1.49	1.48
C_X19	5	1.07	1.07	1.08	1.07	1.07
C_X21	2	1.67	1.65	1.67	1.66	1.66
C_X23	2	1.49	1.47	1.48	1.48	1.51
C_X2527	3	1.39	1.36	1.41	1.39	1.38
C_X29A	5	1.34	1.33	1.34	1.34	1.33
D_X17	1	1.20	1.18	1.20	1.18	1.20
D_X18	1	1.58	1.51	1.73	1.65	1.51
D_X30	1	1.13	1.11	1.14	1.12	1.13
D_X32	1	1.12	1.12	1.13	1.12	1.13
D_X35	1	1.23	1.23	1.22	1.23	1.23
LG_AGE1	1	1.24	1.24	1.24	1.24	1.26
LG_X06A	1	1.26	1.26	1.25	1.24	1.27
LG_X08B	1	1.13	1.13	1.13	1.15	1.14
X22A	1	2.71	2.67	2.73	2.68	2.68
X24A	1	1.89	1.88	1.88	1.89	1.98
LG_X31	1	1.11	1.11	1.12	1.11	1.12

Table 182: Variance Inflation Test for Nation-wide Characteristic Price Index Model (Imputed Datasets / Full Sample / Year 2001)

VIF-TEST		Nation-wide CP.2001 Mix Model (Sub Sample)				
		GVIF^(1/2Df)				
Variables	df	in.mi01	in.mi02	in.mi03	in.mi04	in.mi05
C_X01	8	1.06	1.06	1.06	1.06	1.06
C_X14	4	1.50	1.49	1.50	1.50	1.49
C_X19	5	1.07	1.07	1.08	1.07	1.07
C_X21	2	1.67	1.65	1.67	1.66	1.66
C_X23	2	1.48	1.47	1.48	1.48	1.51
C_X2527	3	1.39	1.36	1.41	1.40	1.39
C_X29A	5	1.35	1.34	1.35	1.35	1.34
D_X17	1	1.21	1.18	1.21	1.18	1.21
D_X18	1	1.59	1.53	1.74	1.66	1.54
D_X30	1	1.13	1.11	1.14	1.12	1.13
D_X32	1	1.13	1.13	1.13	1.13	1.13
D_X35	1	1.24	1.23	1.23	1.24	1.24
LG_AGE1	1	1.24	1.23	1.23	1.24	1.26
LG_X06A	1	1.25	1.25	1.23	1.23	1.26
LG_X08B	1	1.13	1.12	1.14	1.15	1.14
X22A	1	2.71	2.67	2.72	2.67	2.67
X24A	1	1.88	1.87	1.87	1.89	1.98
LG_X31	1	1.11	1.11	1.12	1.12	1.12

Table 183: Variance Inflation Test for Nation-wide Characteristic Price Index Model (Imputed Datasets / Sub Sample / Year 2001)

A.8.6 Nation-wide Characteristic Price Index Model (Year 2002)

A.8.6.1 Residual Normality

Jarque-Bera Test					
	in.mi01	in.mi02	in.mi03	in.mi04	in.mi05
nw.cp.2002	146.1035	228.9614	174.3321	211.6174	183.7701
iqr.nw.cp.2002	61.8279	84.5892	74.0938	76.4269	72.4715

Table 184: Jarque-Bera Normality Tests Nation-wide Characteristic Price Index Model (Imputed Datasets / Full + Sub Sample / Year 2002)

Residual Skewness					
	in.mi01	in.mi02	in.mi03	in.mi04	in.mi05
nw.cp.2002	-0.1430	-0.2491	-0.1776	-0.2365	-0.1786
iqr.nw.cp.2002	-0.2355	-0.2697	-0.2436	-0.2732	-0.2478

Residual Kurtosis					
	in.mi01	in.mi02	in.mi03	in.mi04	in.mi05
nw.cp.2002	1.3289	1.6342	1.4445	1.5696	1.4879
iqr.nw.cp.2002	0.7578	0.8991	0.8494	0.8309	0.8342

Table 185: Descriptive Statistics for Residuals of Nation-wide Characteristic Price Index Model (Imputed Datasets / Full + Sub Sample / Year 2001)

A.8.6.2 Heteroscedasticity

Breusch-Pagan / Cook Weisberg Test					
	in.mi01	in.mi02	in.mi03	in.mi04	in.mi05
nw.cp.2002	0.1642	0.4366	0.9197	0.3051	0.7641
iqr.nw.cp.2002	0.0048	0.0116	0.0133	0.0200	0.0131

Table 186: Breusch-Pagan Heteroscedasticity Test for Nation-wide Characteristic Price Index Model (Imputed Datasets / Full + Sub Sample / Year 2002)

Goldfeld-Quant Test					
	in.mi01	in.mi02	in.mi03	in.mi04	in.mi05
nw.cp.2002	0.0746	0.0540	0.0420	0.0049	0.0369
iqr.nw.cp.2002	0.1354	0.1187	0.1406	0.0400	0.0473

Table 187: Goldfeld-Quant Heteroscedasticity Test for Nation-wide Characteristic Price Index Model (Imputed Datasets / Full + Sub Sample / Year 2002)

A.8.6.3 Linearity

RAMSEY RESET					
	in.mi01	in.mi02	in.mi03	in.mi04	in.mi05
nw.cp.2002	0.7182	0.0508	0.1022	0.1999	0.1069
iqr.nw.cp.2002	0.8490	0.3814	0.1908	0.8574	0.5089

Table 188: Ramsey Reset Linearity Test for Nation-wide Characteristic Price Index Model (Imputed Datasets / Full + Sub Sample / Year 2002)

Rainbow Test					
	in.mi01	in.mi02	in.mi03	in.mi04	in.mi05
nw.cp.2002	0.9980	0.9367	0.9978	0.9973	0.9819
iqr.nw.cp.2002	0.8900	0.4984	0.3226	0.9422	0.7464

Table 189: Rainbow Linearity Test for Nation-wide Characteristic Price Index Model (Imputed Datasets / Full + Sub Sample / Year 2002)

A.8.6.4 Multicollinearity

VIF-TEST		Nation-wide CP.2002 Mix Model (Full Sample)				
		GVIF^(1/2Df)				
Variables	df	in.mi01	in.mi02	in.mi03	in.mi04	in.mi05
C_X01	8	1.06	1.06	1.06	1.06	1.06
C_X14	4	1.36	1.33	1.34	1.34	1.35
C_X19	5	1.05	1.05	1.06	1.05	1.05
C_X21	2	1.74	1.74	1.75	1.73	1.73
C_X23	2	1.39	1.38	1.38	1.39	1.39
C_X2527	3	1.36	1.37	1.37	1.34	1.39
C_X29A	5	1.27	1.26	1.26	1.26	1.27
D_X17	1	1.21	1.20	1.23	1.22	1.20
D_X18	1	1.69	1.76	1.70	1.65	1.88
D_X30	1	1.11	1.10	1.10	1.09	1.09
D_X32	1	1.12	1.12	1.12	1.12	1.13
D_X35	1	1.18	1.16	1.17	1.17	1.16
LG_AGE1	1	1.18	1.17	1.17	1.19	1.19
LG_X06A	1	1.21	1.21	1.23	1.22	1.24
LG_X08B	1	1.12	1.14	1.14	1.15	1.14
X22A	1	2.95	2.91	2.97	2.92	2.87
X24A	1	1.70	1.69	1.67	1.68	1.72
LG_X31	1	1.12	1.13	1.12	1.13	1.13

Table 190: Variance Inflation Test for Nation-wide Characteristic Price Index Model (Imputed Datasets / Full Sample / Year 2002)

VIF-TEST		Nation-wide CP.2002 Mix Model (Sub Sample)				
		GVIF^(1/2Df)				
Variables	df	in.mi01	in.mi02	in.mi03	in.mi04	in.mi05
C_X01	8	1.06	1.06	1.06	1.06	1.06
C_X14	4	1.37	1.34	1.35	1.34	1.36
C_X19	5	1.05	1.06	1.06	1.06	1.06
C_X21	2	1.75	1.74	1.75	1.74	1.73
C_X23	2	1.39	1.38	1.38	1.39	1.39
C_X2527	3	1.36	1.37	1.37	1.34	1.38
C_X29A	5	1.27	1.26	1.26	1.27	1.27
D_X17	1	1.20	1.20	1.23	1.22	1.19
D_X18	1	1.69	1.76	1.71	1.65	1.88
D_X30	1	1.11	1.11	1.10	1.09	1.09
D_X32	1	1.12	1.13	1.13	1.13	1.13
D_X35	1	1.17	1.16	1.17	1.17	1.16
LG_AGE1	1	1.17	1.17	1.16	1.19	1.18
LG_X06A	1	1.19	1.19	1.21	1.21	1.22
LG_X08B	1	1.11	1.14	1.14	1.15	1.15
X22A	1	2.95	2.92	2.98	2.92	2.87
X24A	1	1.70	1.69	1.67	1.68	1.72
LG_X31	1	1.12	1.12	1.12	1.13	1.13

Table 191: Variance Inflation Test for Nation-wide Characteristic Price Index Model (Imputed Datasets / Sub Sample / Year 2002)

A.8.7 Nation-wide Characteristic Price Index Model (Year 2003)

A.8.7.1 Residual Normality

Jarque-Bera Test					
	in.mi01	in.mi02	in.mi03	in.mi04	in.mi05
nw.cp.2003	784.0315	857.1311	743.0358	671.0775	711.4796
iqr.nw.cp.2003	178.1463	194.7214	171.2345	157.4586	133.2549

Table 192: Jarque-Bera Normality Tests Nation-wide Characteristic Price Index Model (Imputed Datasets / Full + Sub Sample / Year 2003)

Residual Skewness					
	in.mi01	in.mi02	in.mi03	in.mi04	in.mi05
nw.cp.2003	-0.5625	-0.5744	-0.4915	-0.5053	-0.4886
iqr.nw.cp.2003	-0.3930	-0.3846	-0.3536	-0.3675	-0.3401

Residual Kurtosis					
	in.mi01	in.mi02	in.mi03	in.mi04	in.mi05
nw.cp.2003	2.5803	2.7241	2.5809	2.4047	2.4909
iqr.nw.cp.2003	1.1069	1.2027	1.1428	1.0487	0.9557

Table 193: Descriptive Statistics for Residuals of Nation-wide Characteristic Price Index Model (Imputed Datasets / Full + Sub Sample / Year 2003)

A.8.7.2 Heteroscedasticity

Breusch-Pagan / Cook Weisberg Test					
	in.mi01	in.mi02	in.mi03	in.mi04	in.mi05
nw.cp.2003	0.2876	0.2345	0.1628	0.1677	0.1938
iqr.nw.cp.2003	0.7866	0.4661	0.2013	0.2148	0.2505

Table 194: Breusch-Pagan Heteroscedasticity Test for Nation-wide Characteristic Price Index Model (Imputed Datasets / Full + Sub Sample / Year 2003)

Goldfeld-Quant Test					
	in.mi01	in.mi02	in.mi03	in.mi04	in.mi05
nw.cp.2003	0.9937	0.9941	0.9990	0.9997	0.9996
iqr.nw.cp.2003	0.9703	0.9783	0.9906	0.9867	0.9966

Table 195: Goldfeld-Quant Heteroscedasticity Test for Nation-wide Characteristic Price Index Model (Imputed Datasets / Full + Sub Sample / Year 2003)

A.8.7.3 Linearity

RAMSEY RESET					
	in.mi01	in.mi02	in.mi03	in.mi04	in.mi05
nw.cp.2003	0.0231	0.0219	0.0024	0.0802	0.0580
iqr.nw.cp.2003	0.0714	0.0342	0.0756	0.1237	0.2581

Table 196: Ramsey Reset Linearity Test for Nation-wide Characteristic Price Index Model (Imputed Datasets / Full + Sub Sample / Year 2003)

Rainbow Test					
	in.mi01	in.mi02	in.mi03	in.mi04	in.mi05
nw.cp.2003	0.9407	0.9988	0.9644	0.9220	0.9999
iqr.nw.cp.2003	0.7074	0.9454	0.7642	0.6849	0.9256

Table 197: Rainbow Linearity Test for Nation-wide Characteristic Price Index Model (Imputed Datasets / Full + Sub Sample / Year 2003)

A.8.7.4 Multicollinearity

VIF-TEST		Nation-wide CP.2003 Mix Model (Full Sample)				
		GVIF^(1/2Df)				
Variables	df	in.mi01	in.mi02	in.mi03	in.mi04	in.mi05
C_X01	8	1.06	1.06	1.06	1.05	1.06
C_X14	4	1.39	1.38	1.38	1.38	1.39
C_X19	5	1.08	1.08	1.08	1.08	1.08
C_X21	2	1.62	1.61	1.63	1.62	1.62
C_X23	2	1.36	1.36	1.36	1.37	1.36
C_X2527	3	1.35	1.33	1.34	1.35	1.33
C_X29A	5	1.31	1.31	1.31	1.31	1.31
D_X17	1	1.21	1.22	1.26	1.22	1.25
D_X18	1	1.56	1.54	1.54	1.60	1.49
D_X30	1	1.11	1.11	1.13	1.12	1.15
D_X32	1	1.06	1.07	1.06	1.05	1.06
D_X35	1	1.14	1.13	1.14	1.15	1.13
LG_AGE1	1	1.15	1.16	1.17	1.16	1.17
LG_X06A	1	1.26	1.24	1.25	1.23	1.23
LG_X08B	1	1.15	1.16	1.15	1.15	1.15
X22A	1	2.54	2.52	2.55	2.51	2.55
X24A	1	1.67	1.71	1.68	1.69	1.68
LG_X31	1	1.13	1.13	1.13	1.13	1.15

Table 198: Variance Inflation Test for Nation-wide Characteristic Price Index Model (Imputed Datasets / Full Sample / Year 2003)

VIF-TEST		Nation-wide CP.2003 Mix Model (Sub Sample)				
		GVIF^(1/2Df)				
Variables	df	in.mi01	in.mi02	in.mi03	in.mi04	in.mi05
C_X01	8	1.06	1.06	1.06	1.05	1.06
C_X14	4	1.38	1.38	1.38	1.38	1.38
C_X19	5	1.08	1.08	1.08	1.08	1.09
C_X21	2	1.62	1.61	1.63	1.62	1.62
C_X23	2	1.38	1.38	1.38	1.37	1.38
C_X2527	3	1.35	1.33	1.34	1.35	1.33
C_X29A	5	1.31	1.30	1.31	1.31	1.31
D_X17	1	1.21	1.22	1.25	1.22	1.24
D_X18	1	1.56	1.53	1.55	1.60	1.49
D_X30	1	1.11	1.11	1.13	1.13	1.15
D_X32	1	1.06	1.07	1.06	1.05	1.06
D_X35	1	1.14	1.13	1.14	1.15	1.13
LG_AGE1	1	1.15	1.16	1.17	1.16	1.16
LG_X06A	1	1.25	1.23	1.24	1.23	1.22
LG_X08B	1	1.15	1.15	1.14	1.15	1.15
X22A	1	2.53	2.51	2.54	2.51	2.54
X24A	1	1.69	1.73	1.70	1.69	1.70
LG_X31	1	1.13	1.13	1.13	1.13	1.15

Table 199: Variance Inflation Test for Nation-wide Characteristic Price Index Model (Imputed Datasets / Sub Sample / Year 2003)

A.8.8 Nation-wide Characteristic Price Index Model (Year 2004)

A.8.8.1 Residual Normality

Jarque-Bera Test					
	in.mi01	in.mi02	in.mi03	in.mi04	in.mi05
nw.cp.2004	3893.1868	3732.8247	3745.0371	3589.9553	3572.4022
iqr.nw.cp.2004	79.4521	59.7053	61.0524	70.1605	58.6863

Table 200: Jarque-Bera Normality Tests Nation-wide Characteristic Price Index Model (Imputed Datasets / Full + Sub Sample / Year 2004)

Residual Skewness					
	in.mi01	in.mi02	in.mi03	in.mi04	in.mi05
nw.op.2004	-0.7589	-0.7400	-0.7235	-0.6734	-0.6897
iqr.nw.cp.2004	0.0207	0.0386	0.0186	0.0449	0.0592

Residual Kurtosis					
	in.mi01	in.mi02	in.mi03	in.mi04	in.mi05
nw.cp.2004	4.4136	4.2976	4.3339	4.2697	4.2406
iqr.nw.cp.2004	0.6706	0.5742	0.5864	0.6243	0.5631

Table 201: Descriptive Statistics for Residuals of Nation-wide Characteristic Price Index Model (Imputed Datasets / Full + Sub Sample / Year 2004)

A.8.8.2 Heteroscedasticity

Breusch-Pagan / Cook Weisberg Test					
	in.mi01	in.mi02	in.mi03	in.mi04	in.mi05
nw.cp.2004	0.4046	0.6495	0.1909	0.1174	0.2844
iqr.nw.cp.2004	0.1543	0.2601	0.5901	0.6275	0.7125

Table 202: Breusch-Pagan Heteroscedasticity Test for Nation-wide Characteristic Price Index Model (Imputed Datasets / Full + Sub Sample / Year 2004)

Goldfeld-Quant Test					
	in.mi01	in.mi02	in.mi03	in.mi04	in.mi05
nw.cp.2004	0.1674	0.4185	0.4820	0.1494	0.6835
iqr.nw.cp.2004	0.9730	0.9968	0.9990	0.9980	0.9994

Table 203: Goldfeld-Quant Heteroscedasticity Test for Nation-wide Characteristic Price Index Model (Imputed Datasets / Full + Sub Sample / Year 2004)

A.8.8.3 Linearity

RAMSEY RESET					
	in.mi01	in.mi02	in.mi03	in.mi04	in.mi05
nw.cp.2004	0.0000	0.0000	0.0000	0.0000	0.0000
iqr.nw.cp.2004	0.0000	0.0000	0.0000	0.0000	0.0000

Table 204: Ramsey Reset Linearity Test for Nation-wide Characteristic Price Index Model (Imputed Datasets / Full + Sub Sample / Year 2004)

Rainbow Test					
	in.mi01	in.mi02	in.mi03	in.mi04	in.mi05
nw.cp.2004	1.0000	1.0000	1.0000	1.0000	1.0000
iqr.nw.cp.2004	0.9912	0.9297	0.8995	0.9992	0.9834

Table 205: Rainbow Linearity Test for Nation-wide Characteristic Price Index Model (Imputed Datasets / Full + Sub Sample / Year 2004)

A.8.8.4 Multicollinearity

VIF-TEST		Nation-wide CP.2004 Mix Model (Full Sample)				
		GVIF^(1/2Df)				
Variables	df	in.mi01	in.mi02	in.mi03	in.mi04	in.mi05
C_X01	8	1.07	1.07	1.07	1.07	1.06
C_X14	4	1.46	1.47	1.46	1.46	1.46
C_X19	5	1.11	1.11	1.11	1.11	1.11
C_X21	2	1.96	1.97	1.99	1.97	1.95
C_X23	2	1.59	1.60	1.60	1.59	1.60
C_X2527	3	1.31	1.31	1.33	1.35	1.32
C_X29A	5	1.36	1.36	1.35	1.35	1.35
D_X17	1	1.39	1.37	1.43	1.40	1.37
D_X18	1	1.53	1.53	1.55	1.68	1.55
D_X30	1	1.15	1.14	1.14	1.13	1.13
D_X32	1	1.12	1.12	1.11	1.11	1.11
D_X35	1	1.07	1.07	1.07	1.07	1.07
LG_AGE1	1	1.15	1.15	1.14	1.15	1.14
LG_X06A	1	1.26	1.26	1.28	1.25	1.26
LG_X08B	1	1.26	1.26	1.28	1.27	1.26
X22A	1	3.17	3.20	3.28	3.21	3.16
X24A	1	2.85	2.90	2.92	2.85	2.86
LG_X31	1	1.12	1.11	1.12	1.11	1.12

Table 206: Variance Inflation Test for Nation-wide Characteristic Price Index Model (Imputed Datasets / Full Sample / Year 2004)

VIF-TEST		Nation-wide CP.2004 Mix Model (Sub Sample)				
		GVIF^(1/2Df)				
Variables	df	in.mi01	in.mi02	in.mi03	in.mi04	in.mi05
C_X01	8	1.07	1.07	1.07	1.07	1.06
C_X14	4	1.46	1.47	1.46	1.46	1.46
C_X19	5	1.11	1.11	1.11	1.11	1.11
C_X21	2	1.95	1.96	1.98	1.96	1.94
C_X23	2	1.59	1.60	1.60	1.59	1.60
C_X2527	3	1.31	1.31	1.33	1.35	1.32
C_X29A	5	1.35	1.35	1.35	1.35	1.35
D_X17	1	1.38	1.37	1.43	1.40	1.37
D_X18	1	1.53	1.53	1.56	1.68	1.55
D_X30	1	1.15	1.14	1.15	1.13	1.13
D_X32	1	1.12	1.12	1.11	1.11	1.11
D_X35	1	1.07	1.07	1.07	1.07	1.07
LG_AGE1	1	1.14	1.15	1.14	1.15	1.14
LG_X06A	1	1.25	1.25	1.27	1.25	1.26
LG_X08B	1	1.25	1.25	1.28	1.26	1.26
X22A	1	3.15	3.19	3.26	3.20	3.15
X24A	1	2.84	2.88	2.91	2.84	2.85
LG_X31	1	1.12	1.12	1.12	1.12	1.12

Table 207: Variance Inflation Test for Nation-wide Characteristic Price Index Model (Imputed Datasets / Sub Sample / Year 2004)

A.8.9 Nation-wide Characteristic Price Index Model (Year 2005)

A.8.9.1 Residual Normality

Jarque-Bera Test					
	in.mi01	in.mi02	in.mi03	in.mi04	in.mi05
nw.cp.2005	14159.4572	25367.7343	26468.4363	11833.2265	24217.4603
iqr.nw.cp.2005	62.3385	57.4961	63.5002	57.3163	67.1668

Table 208: Jarque-Bera Normality Tests Nation-wide Characteristic Price Index Model (Imputed Datasets / Full + Sub Sample / Year 2005)

Residual Skewness					
	in.mi01	in.mi02	in.mi03	in.mi04	in.mi05
nw.cp.2005	-1.3904	-1.7075	-1.7340	-1.3976	-1.7113
iqr.nw.cp.2005	-0.1091	-0.0952	-0.0923	-0.1658	-0.0880

Residual Kurtosis					
	in.mi01	in.mi02	in.mi03	in.mi04	in.mi05
nw.cp.2005	10.9709	14.7508	15.0217	9.9656	14.3809
iqr.nw.cp.2005	0.7268	0.7027	0.7401	0.6476	0.7664

Table 209: Descriptive Statistics for Residuals of Nation-wide Characteristic Price Index Model (Imputed Datasets / Full + Sub Sample / Year 2005)

A.8.9.2 Heteroscedasticity

Breusch-Pagan / Cook Weisberg Test					
	in.mi01	in.mi02	in.mi03	in.mi04	in.mi05
nw.cp.2005	0.0007	0.0002	0.0002	0.0016	0.0001
iqr.nw.cp.2005	0.4628	0.1205	0.1580	0.1976	0.1090

Table 210: Breusch-Pagan Heteroscedasticity Test for Nation-wide Characteristic Price Index Model (Imputed Datasets / Full + Sub Sample / Year 2005)

Goldfeld-Quant Test					
	in.mi01	in.mi02	in.mi03	in.mi04	in.mi05
nw.cp.2005	0.9945	1.0000	1.0000	1.0000	1.0000
iqr.nw.cp.2005	0.0746	0.1963	0.1634	0.1144	0.1574

Table 211: Goldfeld-Quant Heteroscedasticity Test for Nation-wide Characteristic Price Index Model (Imputed Datasets / Full + Sub Sample / Year 2005)

A.8.9.3 Linearity

RAMSEY RESET					
	in.mi01	in.mi02	in.mi03	in.mi04	in.mi05
nw.cp.2005	0.0000	0.0002	0.0000	0.0029	0.0000
iqr.nw.cp.2005	0.0010	0.0006	0.0001	0.0232	0.0000

Table 212: Ramsey Reset Linearity Test for Nation-wide Characteristic Price Index Model (Imputed Datasets / Full + Sub Sample / Year 2005)

Rainbow Test					
	in.mi01	in.mi02	in.mi03	in.mi04	in.mi05
nw.cp.2005	1.0000	1.0000	1.0000	1.0000	1.0000
iqr.nw.cp.2005	0.9406	0.6058	0.8857	0.8602	0.7897

Table 213: Rainbow Linearity Test for Nation-wide Characteristic Price Index Model (Imputed Datasets / Full + Sub Sample / Year 2005)

A.8.9.4 Multicollinearity

VIF-TEST		Nation-wide CP.2005 Mix Model (Full Sample)				
		GVIF^(1/2Df)				
Variables	df	in.mi01	in.mi02	in.mi03	in.mi04	in.mi05
C_X01	8	1.11	1.11	1.11	1.12	1.12
C_X14	4	1.41	1.40	1.40	1.39	1.40
C_X19	5	1.15	1.14	1.14	1.14	1.14
C_X21	2	1.70	1.68	1.69	1.68	1.67
C_X23	2	1.56	1.55	1.58	1.55	1.55
C_X2527	2	1.41	1.40	1.39	1.41	1.41
C_X29A	4	1.32	1.32	1.32	1.32	1.32
D_X17	1	1.23	1.23	1.27	1.22	1.23
D_X18	1	1.12	1.11	1.09	1.13	1.11
D_X30	1	1.24	1.24	1.25	1.26	1.27
D_X32	1	1.19	1.21	1.20	1.19	1.19
D_X35	1	1.14	1.14	1.15	1.14	1.14
LG_AGE1	1	1.26	1.26	1.24	1.26	1.27
LG_X06A	1	1.22	1.21	1.23	1.20	1.21
LG_X08B	1	1.21	1.22	1.21	1.20	1.19
X22A	1	2.40	2.40	2.39	2.38	2.36
X24A	1	2.16	2.15	2.22	2.18	2.15
LG_X31	1	1.15	1.14	1.14	1.14	1.13

Table 214: Variance Inflation Test for Nation-wide Characteristic Price Index Model (Imputed Datasets / Full Sample / Year 2005)

VIF-TEST		Nation-wide CP.2005 Mix Model (Sub Sample)				
		GVIF^(1/2Df)				
Variables	df	in.mi01	in.mi02	in.mi03	in.mi04	in.mi05
C_X01	8	1.12	1.11	1.11	1.12	1.12
C_X14	4	1.42	1.41	1.41	1.40	1.41
C_X19	5	1.15	1.14	1.14	1.14	1.14
C_X21	2	1.71	1.69	1.70	1.69	1.68
C_X23	2	1.56	1.56	1.59	1.56	1.55
C_X2527	2	1.42	1.41	1.40	1.42	1.42
C_X29A	4	1.33	1.33	1.33	1.32	1.33
D_X17	1	1.23	1.23	1.27	1.22	1.23
D_X18	1	1.12	1.11	1.08	1.13	1.11
D_X30	1	1.25	1.25	1.26	1.27	1.29
D_X32	1	1.20	1.21	1.20	1.19	1.19
D_X35	1	1.15	1.15	1.16	1.15	1.14
LG_AGE1	1	1.26	1.26	1.24	1.25	1.27
LG_X06A	1	1.22	1.21	1.22	1.20	1.20
LG_X08B	1	1.20	1.21	1.21	1.19	1.19
X22A	1	2.41	2.41	2.40	2.39	2.37
X24A	1	2.17	2.16	2.23	2.19	2.16
LG_X31	1	1.15	1.14	1.14	1.14	1.13

Table 215: Variance Inflation Test for Nation-wide Characteristic Price Index Model (Imputed Datasets / Sub Sample / Year 2005)

A.8.10 Nation-wide Characteristic Price Index Model (Year 2006)

A.8.10.1 Residual Normality

Jarque-Bera Test					
	in.mi01	in.mi02	in.mi03	in.mi04	in.mi05
nw.cp.2006	7833.2488	8424.8152	9004.6956	8820.3996	8746.6006
iqr.nw.cp.2006	32.5049	3.3326	23.2771	46.8304	50.3614

Table 216: Jarque-Bera Normality Tests Nation-wide Characteristic Price Index Model (Imputed Datasets / Full + Sub Sample / Year 2006)

Residual Skewness					
	in.mi01	in.mi02	in.mi03	in.mi04	in.mi05
nw.cp.2006	-1.5593	-1.5437	-1.5781	-1.6064	-1.6373
iqr.nw.cp.2006	-0.0433	-0.0169	-0.0722	-0.1383	-0.1569

Residual Kurtosis					
	in.mi01	in.mi02	in.mi03	in.mi04	in.mi05
nw.cp.2006	14.0570	14.5598	15.1123	15.0512	14.9368
iqr.nw.cp.2006	0.9244	0.2898	0.7700	1.0896	1.1190

Table 217: Descriptive Statistics for Residuals of Nation-wide Characteristic Price Index Model (Imputed Datasets / Full + Sub Sample / Year 2006)

A.8.10.2 Heteroscedasticity

Breusch-Pagan / Cook Weisberg Test					
	in.mi01	in.mi02	in.mi03	in.mi04	in.mi05
nw.cp.2006	0.5716	0.2816	0.5331	0.5685	0.7716
iqr.nw.cp.2006	0.0176	0.0558	0.0094	0.0120	0.0003

Table 218: Breusch-Pagan Heteroscedasticity Test for Nation-wide Characteristic Price Index Model (Imputed Datasets / Full + Sub Sample / Year 2006)

Goldfeld-Quant Test					
	in.mi01	in.mi02	in.mi03	in.mi04	in.mi05
nw.cp.2006	1.0000	1.0000	1.0000	1.0000	1.0000
iqr.nw.cp.2006	0.9998	0.9980	0.9975	0.9986	1.0000

Table 219: Goldfeld-Quant Heteroscedasticity Test for Nation-wide Characteristic Price Index Model (Imputed Datasets / Full + Sub Sample / Year 2006)

A.8.10.3 Linearity

RAMSEY RESET					
	in.mi01	in.mi02	in.mi03	in.mi04	in.mi05
nw.cp.2006	0.1255	0.6263	0.2079	0.4159	0.1192
iqr.nw.cp.2006	0.1825	0.8393	0.2791	0.4683	0.0987

Table 220: Ramsey Reset Linearity Test for Nation-wide Characteristic Price Index Model (Imputed Datasets / Full + Sub Sample / Year 2006)

Rainbow Test					
	in.mi01	in.mi02	in.mi03	in.mi04	in.mi05
nw.cp.2006	0.9298	0.9845	0.8840	0.9916	0.9192
iqr.nw.cp.2006	0.0248	0.0673	0.0211	0.3030	0.0267

Table 221: Rainbow Linearity Test for Nation-wide Characteristic Price Index Model (Imputed Datasets / Full + Sub Sample / Year 2006)

A.8.10.4 Multicollinearity

VIF-TEST		Nation-wide CP.2006 Mix Model (Full Sample)				
		GVIF^(1/2Df)				
Variables	df	in.mi01	in.mi02	in.mi03	in.mi04	in.mi05
C_X01	8	1.15	1.15	1.15	1.16	1.15
C_X14	4	1.78	1.83	1.76	1.86	1.76
C_X19	5	1.24	1.24	1.24	1.25	1.23
C_X21	2	1.68	1.68	1.68	1.68	1.67
C_X23	2	1.73	1.72	1.73	1.74	1.72
C_X2527	2	1.48	1.48	1.47	1.48	1.49
C_X29A	4	1.73	1.76	1.71	1.82	1.71
D_X17	1	1.39	1.42	1.41	1.39	1.38
D_X18	1	1.26	1.24	1.23	1.24	1.28
D_X30	1	1.26	1.27	1.24	1.28	1.27
D_X32	1	1.18	1.20	1.18	1.19	1.17
D_X35	1	1.10	1.10	1.09	1.10	1.10
LG_AGE1	1	1.21	1.21	1.22	1.22	1.20
LG_X06A	1	1.22	1.23	1.24	1.20	1.23
LG_X08B	1	1.23	1.27	1.25	1.23	1.21
X22A	1	2.20	2.20	2.20	2.23	2.21
X24A	1	2.02	2.00	1.99	2.00	2.02
LG_X31	1	1.17	1.19	1.20	1.17	1.15

Table 222: Variance Inflation Test for Nation-wide Characteristic Price Index Model (Imputed Datasets / Full Sample / Year 2006)

VIF-TEST		Nation-wide CP.2006 Mix Model (Sub Sample)				
		GVIF^(1/2Df)				
Variables	df	in.mi01	in.mi02	in.mi03	in.mi04	in.mi05
C_X01	8	1.15	1.16	1.16	1.16	1.15
C_X14	4	1.78	1.82	1.76	1.85	1.75
C_X19	5	1.24	1.24	1.24	1.25	1.23
C_X21	2	1.68	1.68	1.68	1.68	1.68
C_X23	2	1.73	1.72	1.72	1.74	1.72
C_X2527	2	1.48	1.47	1.47	1.48	1.48
C_X29A	4	1.73	1.77	1.72	1.82	1.71
D_X17	1	1.39	1.42	1.41	1.39	1.38
D_X18	1	1.26	1.23	1.23	1.23	1.27
D_X30	1	1.26	1.27	1.25	1.28	1.27
D_X32	1	1.19	1.20	1.18	1.20	1.17
D_X35	1	1.11	1.11	1.10	1.11	1.11
LG_AGE1	1	1.22	1.21	1.22	1.22	1.20
LG_X06A	1	1.21	1.23	1.23	1.19	1.22
LG_X08B	1	1.23	1.27	1.25	1.23	1.21
X22A	1	2.21	2.21	2.20	2.23	2.21
X24A	1	2.02	1.99	1.98	2.00	2.02
LG_X31	1	1.17	1.19	1.20	1.17	1.16

Table 223: Variance Inflation Test for Nation-wide Characteristic Price Index Model (Imputed Datasets / Sub Sample / Year 2006)

A.9 Record Sheet for German Society of Property Researchers Meetings

gif-Erhebung regionaler Büromarktdaten
- Markt München -

Bitte beachten Sie beim Ausfüllen des Fragebogens
Erfassungszeitraum ist das Jahr 2006
Geben Sie die von Ihnen für die Berichtsregion erhobenen Daten an

Legen Sie allen Angaben die Mietfläche gemäß gif-Richtlinie MF-B zugrunde
Legen Sie die gif Definitionen zum Büromarkt zugrunde
- siehe dazu den Verweis auf die entsprechenden Paragraphen bei den Abfrageparametern

	Stadtgebiet	Umland	Gesamt
Umsatz			
Flächenumsatz durch Mieter (m²) (§6 und § 6.1 Def. zzgl. Kommentare)................	553,000	101,000	654,000
Flächenumsatz durch Eigennutzer (m²) (§6 und § 6.2 Def. zzgl. Kommentare)................	Erfassung erst ab 2007		
Mieten			
realisierte Spitzenmiete (Euro/m²/Monat) (§8.2a Def.)................	30.00		
realisierte Durchschnittsmiete (Euro/m²/Monat) (§8.2b Def.)................	15.22	9.82	14.25
Leerstand absolut/ Quote			
Leerstand (m²) (§7a Def. zzgl. Kommentare)................	1,073,200	548,600	1,621,800
- darunter Flächen zur Untervermietung (m²)................	Keine Angabe	Keine Angabe	Keine Angabe
Flächenbestand (m²) Fortschreibung* (§2 Def.)................	Einheitliche Angabe Q1 2007		
Leerstandsquote (%)................	7.7%	12.9%	8.9%
Baudynamik			
erfolgte Fertigstellungen 2006 (m²)................	85,000	19,800	104,800
absehbare Fertigstellungen 2007 (m²)................	124,000	24,000	148,000

Zum Flächenumsatz: Eigennutzer werden ab 2007 erfasst
Zum Leerstand: Die Angaben zu Untermietflächen waren sehr unterschiedlich bzw. wurden z.T. gar nicht erfasst.
Zum Flächenbestand: Die Marktteilnehmer werden sich im ersten Quartal auf eine einheitliche Flächenbestandszahl einigen. Die Leerstandsquote wurde auf Basis einer Fortschreibung des Vorjahreswertes ermittelt.

Alle Daten beziehen sich auf die in München nach wie vor übliche Praxis, überwiegend BGF als Flächenmaß zu verwenden. Das Verhältnis bei Neuanmietungen lag 2006 bei ca. 70:30 (BGF:gif). Über den Gesamtmarkt (Bestand) kann ein Verhältnis von ca. 85:15 angegeben werden.

München, den 13.01.2007
Brigitte Schmale / Rita Dafinger

A.10 Interview Protocol

Thema:	gif-Büromarktkennzahlen / gif-Moderationen
Interviewpartner:	Günter Muncke (langjähriger Leiter des gif-Arbeitskreis 2 Marktanalysen und Bedarfsprognosen)
Ort:	Hotel Adlon, Berlin
Datum:	20. September 2007
Dauer:	ca. 30 Minuten

Anmerkung: Im Folgenden handelt es sich nicht um ein wortgenaues Gesprächsprotokoll, sondern um ein Inhaltsprotokoll. D.h. die Antworten des Interviewpartners wurden sinngemäß aufgenommen und zusammengefasst.

Frage 1: Wer nimmt an den gif-Moderationen über die relevanten Büromarktdaten teil?

Antwort von Herrn Günter Muncke:

Die gif-Moderationen für den Jahresend-Datenabgleich der wesentlichen Büromarktkennziffern sind nach Standort bzw. Städten organisiert. Pro Standort wird vom gif Arbeitskreis II (Markt- und Bedarfsanalysen) jeweils ein neutraler Moderator ernannt.

An den gif- Moderationen nehmen die jeweils am Ort marktführenden Research- und Maklerunternehmen teil. Die Teilnehmerzahl ist von der Größe des Standorts abhängig. So werden beispielsweise in Berlin ca. 10, in München ca. 5, und in Frankfurt ca. 8 Teilnehmer eingeladen.

Für welche Städte eine gif-Moderation organisiert wird, ist von der Marktgröße und dem Vermietungsumsatz abhängig. So haben in der Vergangenheit auch gif-Moderationen für Dresden und Leipzig stattgefunden. Diese Städte sind jedoch wegen der geringen Nachfrage nach Büroflächen aus dem Jahresendabgleich wieder herausgenommen werden.

Frage 2: Wie erfolgt der Datenabgleich zwischen Diskussionsteilnehmern?

Antwort von Herrn Günter Muncke:

Der Datenabgleich zwischen den Diskussionsteilnehmern erfolgt unterschiedlich. Für manche Städte tauschen die Teilnehmer die im Jahr abgeschlossenen wichtigsten Mietverträge als Listen aus, während für andere Städte der Datenabgleich ausschließlich durch Diskussion erfolgt.

In der Regel tragen die Marktteilnehmer die aus ihrer Sicht vertretbaren globalen Kennziffern (d.h. Durchschnittsmiete, Spitzenmiete, Flächenumsatz, etc.)vor. Anschließend findet bei Diskrepanzen zwischen den Marktteilnehmern durch Diskussion der besonders bedeutsamen Transaktionen ein Annäherungsprozess statt. Hier werden die wichtigsten abgeschlossenen Mietverträge des vergangenen Jahres besprochen bzw. abgeglichen. Auf dieser Grundlage macht der neutrale Moderator am Ende der Diskussion einen Vorschlag.
Das Ziel dieser Diskussion ist es, einen Konsenswert unter den Teilnehmern zu finden. Die veröffentlichen gif-Zahlen repräsentieren also nicht unbedingt den rechnerischen Mittelwert.

Als Faustregel kann man annehmen, dass alle Mietverträge besprochen werden, welche 80% des Flächenumsatzes bilden. Kleinere Mietverträge (d.h. <500m²) werden üblicherweise nicht im Einzelnen berücksichtigt.

Frage 3: Dient ein Standardmietvertrag als Diskussionsbasis?

Antwort von Herrn Günter Muncke:

Definitorische Grundlagen sind die Mietflächendefinition nach gif-Richtlinie MF-B sowie die gif-Büromarktdefinitionen.

Eine Ausnahme bildet der Münchner Büromarkt. Hier findet überwiegend eine BGF-Mietflächendefinition Anwendung. Approximativ werden dann die Umsätze und Mietpreise auf gif-Definition umgerechnet. Hierbei stellt die Flächendefinition ein Politikum mit Diskussionspotential dar, da nach gif-Definitionen die durchschnittlichen Mietpreise und Spitzenmieten höher sind, jedoch der Flächenumsatz geringer ausfällt.

Aufgrund der Tatsache, dass die Teilnehmer in der Regel nicht alle Vertragsdetails kennen oder auch die Vertragsparteien vertrauliche Nebenvereinbarungen treffen, sind die gif-Zahlen als Nominalmieten, d.h. ohne Incentives oder andere Anpassungen, zu verstehen.

Frage 4: Wie wird der Büromarkt der Städte geographisch abgrenzt?

Antwort von Herrn Günter Muncke:

Laut gif-Definitionen werden die Büromärkte der einzelnen Städte nach den kommunalen Stadt- (Verwaltungs-)grenzen abgebildet. Innerkommunale Büromärkte müssen folglich getrennt betrachtet werden??. Dies bedeutet beispielsweise, dass Berlin und Potsdam nicht als ein Markt, sondern als zwei separate Büromärkte betrachtet werden.

Im Konsens können sich ansonsten die Marktteilnehmer auf die Einbeziehung von zusätzlichen Gebietsteilen im Umland verständigen, wenn ansonsten die Daten der „Kerngemeinde" transparent aufgezeigt werden. So haben sich die Diskussionsteilnehmer in Frankfurt darauf verständigt, dass auch Mietverträge berücksichtigt werden, welche für außerhalb der Stadtgrenze Frankfurts gehörende Büromärkte wie Offenbach-Kaiserlei oder Eschborn abgeschlossen wurden. Es findet sozusagen eine „gedankliche" Eingemeindung statt.

Eine Konsensfindung für innerkommunale Teilmärkte (z.B. Bankenviertel, Citylage) innerhalb der Städte kann bedauerlicherweise nicht stattfinden. Hier divergieren die Grenzen der Teilmärkte zwischen den Diskussionsteilnehmern zu stark. Außerdem wird der Aufwand für den Abgleich und die Rückrechnung der vergangenen Zeitreihen als zu hoch von den Diskussionsteilnehmern angesehen.

Frage 5: Gibt es einen Standardablauf für die gif-Moderation und die Ermittlung der Durchschnittsmieten?

Antwort von Herrn Günter Muncke:

Jeweils zu Jahresende verschickt der Moderator an die Diskussionsteilnehmer einen einheitlichen Erfassungsbogen. Dieser Erfassungsbogen, welcher die einzelnen Kennziffern auflistet und deren Definitionen spezifiziert, dient als Grundlage für die spätere Diskussion.

Anschließend werden die Teilnehmer zur Diskussionsrunde eingeladen. Früher fanden diese Gespräche Anfang Januar statt, mittlerweile finden diese schon bereits Ende Dezember statt.

In welchen Bahnen die Diskussion verläuft, ist nicht standardisiert und wird den Diskussionsteilnehmern überlassen. Die gif sieht ihre primäre Aufgabe an, die Makler- und Researchunternehmen zusammenzubringen, um die in der Vergangenheit teilweise beträchtlichen Abweichungen in der Marktberichterstattung zu verringern und damit das Vertrauen in die publizierten Daten zu erhöhen .

Frage 6: Gibt es Konfliktpotential zwischen den Teilnehmern?

Antwort von Herrn Günter Muncke:

Die gif stellt von vornherein klar, dass jeder Diskussionsteilnehmer eigene Kennzahlen publizieren kann. Ziel der gif ist es lediglich, die Bandbreite der Werte zu verringern und einen Konsenswert zu liefern.

Frage 7: Sind die Protokolle öffentlich einsehbar?

Antwort von Herrn Günter Muncke:

Es werden selbstverständlich Protokolle angefertigt. Diese sind jedoch nicht für Dritte einsehbar. Wichtig ist, dass durch die Teilnahme der wichtigsten Makler- und Researchunternehmen eine gewisse Transparenz entsteht.

Wie bereits erwähnt, die veröffentlichten gif-Kennzahlen repräsentieren nicht einen nach statistischen Grundsätzen ermittelten Wert, sondern eine Vereinbarung unter Fachleuten über einen statistischen Sachverhalt.

Exkurs Frankfurt
In den 90er Jahren gab es für das Marktgebiet Frankfurt ein Datenbankprojekt. Hier wurden von den einzelnen Maklerhäusern die registrierten Mietverträge eingetragen. Jedoch gab es große Differenzen, was Flächen-, Miet und Mieterangaben betrifft. Die Abstimmung war sehr komplex und führte dazu, dass letzten Endes doch nur etwa 60% aller registrierten Mietverträge abgeglichen werden konnten, also immer noch ein relativ großer „Graubereich" verblieb.

Frage 8: Welche Probleme bzw. offene Punkte stellen sich häufig während der gif-Moderationen?

Antwort von Herrn Günter Muncke:

In den gif-Diskussionsrunden wird häufig diskutiert, wie mit Mietverträgen umgegangen wird, welche Rücktrittsklauseln enthalten (bspw. im Rahmen von Projektentwicklungen). So kann es durchaus passieren, dass eine Vertragspartei von einem unterschriebenen Mietvertrag zurücktritt. Hier stellt sich die Frage, inwiefern solche Änderungen rückwirkend berücksichtigt werden (können), zumal der jeweilige Mietvertrag bereits in die veröffentlichten gif-Zahlen aufgenommen worden ist. Eine Veränderung der veröffentlichen Vorjahreskennzahlen findet seitens der gif nicht statt, möglicherweise aber bei einzelnen Marktteilnehmern mit gut organisierter Research-Abteilung.

A.11 Interregional Rent Change

A.11.1 Laspeyres Hedonic Office Rent Index (L-HORIX)

A.11.1.1 Annual Rental Growth Rate

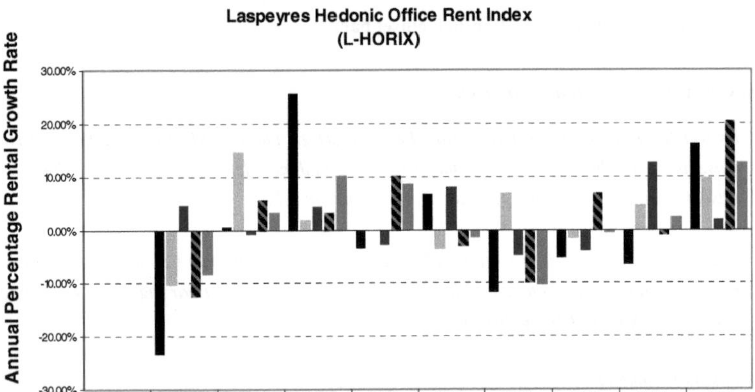

	1997	1998	1999	2000	2001	2002	2003	2004	2005	2006
Berlin		-23.20%	0.48%	25.45%	-3.42%	6.56%	-11.78%	-5.14%	-6.55%	16.18%
Düsseldorf		-10.32%	14.70%	1.84%	-0.15%	-3.64%	6.91%	-1.63%	4.48%	9.72%
Frankfurt		4.61%	-0.72%	4.46%	-2.68%	7.96%	-4.88%	-3.86%	12.57%	1.86%
Hamburg		-12.32%	5.68%	3.20%	10.23%	-3.11%	-9.85%	6.80%	-1.12%	20.31%
Munich		-8.39%	3.15%	10.14%	8.52%	-1.37%	-10.39%	-0.65%	2.37%	12.58%

Berlin Düsseldorf Frankfurt Hamburg Munich

Figure 56: Interregional Rent Change – Laspeyres Hedonic Office Rent Index – Annual Rental Growth Rate

A.11.1.2 Correlation Analysis

Correlation	Laspeyres Hedonic Office Rent Index (L-HORIX)				
	Berlin	Düsseldorf	Frankfurt	Hamburg	Munich
Berlin	**1.00**	0.09	0.00	0.47	0.64
Düsseldorf	0.09	**1.00**	0.68	0.72	0.59
Frankfurt	0.00	0.68	**1.00**	0.53	0.58
Hamburg	0.47	0.72	0.53	**1.00**	0.87
Munich	0.64	0.59	0.58	0.87	**1.00**

Table 224: Interregional Rent Change – Laspeyres Hedonic Office Rent Index – Correlation Analysis

A.11.2 Paasche Hedonic Office Rent Index (P-HORIX)

A.11.2.1 Annual Rental Growth Rate

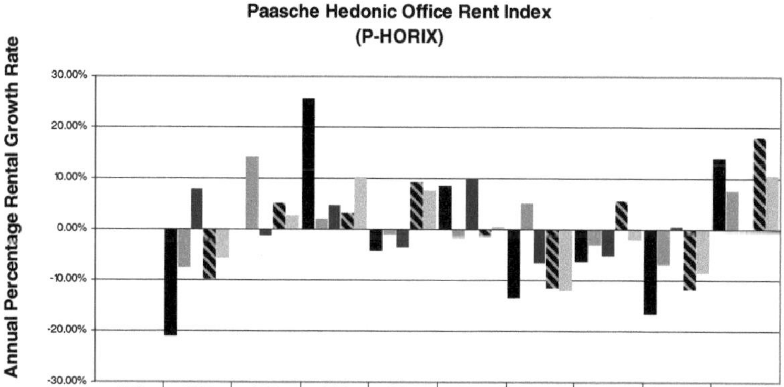

	1997	1998	1999	2000	2001	2002	2003	2004	2005	2006
Berlin		-20.86%	0.02%	25.53%	-4.22%	8.57%	-13.34%	-6.28%	-16.58%	13.95%
Düsseldorf		-7.59%	14.17%	1.91%	-0.97%	-1.83%	5.02%	-2.82%	-6.74%	7.61%
Frankfurt		7.79%	-1.18%	4.52%	-3.48%	10.00%	-6.57%	-5.02%	0.49%	-0.09%
Hamburg		-9.65%	5.19%	3.26%	9.32%	-1.28%	-11.45%	5.52%	-11.73%	18.01%
Munich		-5.60%	2.67%	10.21%	7.63%	0.49%	-11.98%	-1.85%	-8.61%	10.42%

Berlin Düsseldorf Frankfurt Hamburg Munich

Figure 57: Interregional Rent Change – Paasche Hedonic Office Rent Index – Annual Rental Growth Rate

A.11.2.2 Correlation Analysis

Correlation	Paasche Hedonic Office Rent Index (P-HORIX)				
	Berlin	Düsseldorf	Frankfurt	Hamburg	Munich
Berlin	**1,00**	0,31	0,40	0,68	0,81
Düsseldorf	0,31	**1,00**	0,25	0,48	0,48
Frankfurt	0,40	0,25	**1,00**	0,24	0,60
Hamburg	0,68	0,48	0,24	**1,00**	0,86
Munich	0,81	0,48	0,60	0,86	**1,00**

Table 225: Interregional Rent Change – Paasche Hedonic Office Rent Index – Correlation Analysis

A.12 Intertemporal Rent Change

A.12.1 Berlin

A.12.1.1 Annual Rental Growth Rate

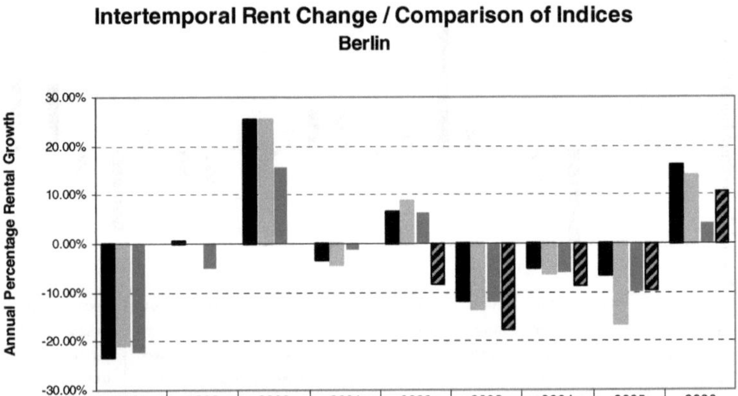

	1998	1999	2000	2001	2002	2003	2004	2005	2006
L-HORIX	-23.20%	0.48%	25.45%	-3.42%	6.56%	-11.78%	-5.14%	-6.55%	16.18%
P-HORIX	-20.86%	0.02%	25.53%	-4.22%	8.57%	-13.34%	-6.28%	-16.58%	13.95%
RD-ORIX	-22.39%	-5.04%	15.70%	-1.20%	6.24%	-12.09%	-5.90%	-9.94%	4.16%
GIF-ORX					-8.50%	-17.86%	-8.70%	-9.52%	10.53%

Figure 58: Intertemporal Rent Change – Berlin – Comparison of Indices – Annual Rental Growth Rate

A.12.1.2 Correlation Analysis

Correlation based on €/m²/month	L-HORIX	P-HORIX	RD-ORIX	GIF-ORIX
Laspeyres Hedonic Office Rent Index (L-HORIX)	1.00			
Paasche Hedonice Office Rent Index (P-HORIX)	0.88	1.00		
Rental Database Office Rent Index (RD-ORIX)	0.78	0.94	1.00	
German Real Estate Research Society Office Rent Index (GIF-ORIX)	0.81	0.86	0.90	1.00

Table 226: Intertemporal Rent Change – Berlin – Comparison of Indices – Correlation Analysis

A.12.2 Düsseldorf

A.12.2.1 Annual Rental Growth Rate

Intertemporal Rent Change / Comparison of Indices
Düsseldorf

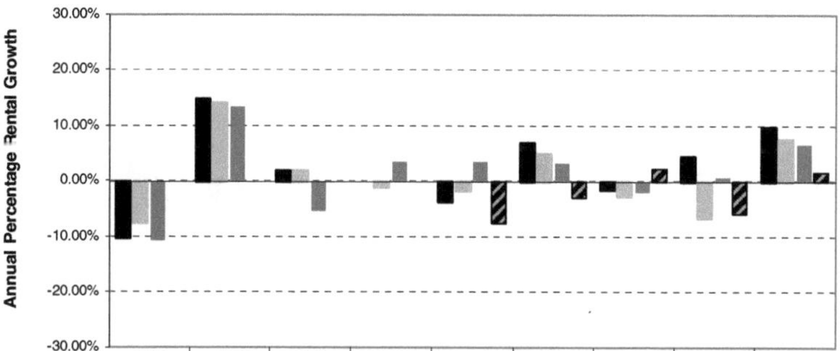

	1998	1999	2000	2001	2002	2003	2004	2005	2006
L-HORIX	-10.32%	14.70%	1.84%	-0.15%	-3.64%	6.91%	-1.63%	4.48%	9.72%
P-HORIX	-7.59%	14.17%	1.91%	-0.97%	-1.83%	5.02%	-2.82%	-6.74%	7.61%
RD-ORIX	-10.78%	13.37%	-5.48%	3.38%	3.39%	3.14%	2.13%	0.63%	6.68%
GIF-ORX					-7.59%	-2.99%	2.31%	-6.02%	1.60%

Figure 59: Intertemporal Rent Change – Düsseldorf – Comparison of Indices – Annual Rental Growth Rate

A.12.2.2 Correlation Analysis

Correlation based on €/m²/month	L-HORIX	P-HORIX	RD-ORIX	GIF-ORIX
Laspeyres Hedonic Office Rent Index (L-HORIX)	1.00			
Paasche Hedonice Office Rent Index (P-HORIX)	0.26	1.00		
Rental Database Office Rent Index (RD-ORIX)	0.88	0.38	1.00	
German Real Estate Research Society Office Rent Index (GIF-ORIX)	-0.58	0.51	-0.76	1.00

Table 227: Intertemporal Rent Change – Düsseldorf – Comparison of Indices – Correlation Analysis

A.12.3 Frankfurt

A.12.3.1 Annual Rental Growth Rate

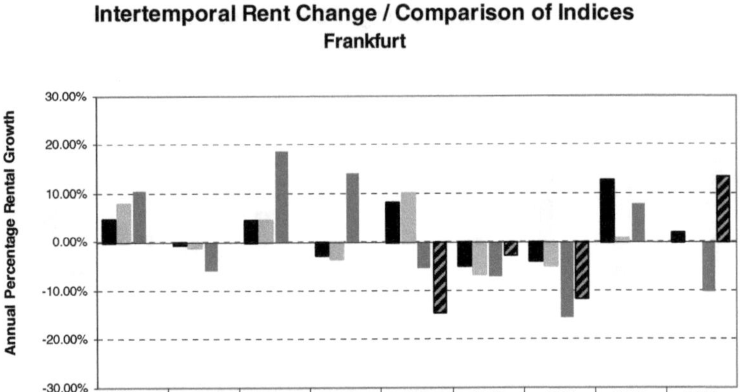

	1998	1999	2000	2001	2002	2003	2004	2005	2006
L-HORIX	4.61%	-0.72%	4.46%	-2.68%	7.96%	-4.88%	-3.86%	12.57%	1.86%
P-HORIX	7.79%	-1.18%	4.52%	-3.48%	10.00%	-6.57%	-5.02%	0.49%	-0.09%
RD-ORIX	10.39%	-6.01%	18.62%	14.07%	-5.46%	-7.06%	-15.58%	7.72%	-10.17%
GIF-ORX					-14.63%	-2.86%	-11.76%	0.00%	13.33%

Figure 60: Intertemporal Rent Change – Frankfurt – Comparison of Indices – Annual Rental Growth Rate

A.12.3.2 Correlation Analysis

Correlation based on €/m²/month	L-HORIX	P-HORIX	RD-ORIX	GIF-ORIX
Laspeyres Hedonic Office Rent Index (L-HORIX)	1.00			
Paasche Hedonice Office Rent Index (P-HORIX)	-0.06	1.00		
Rental Database Office Rent Index (RD-ORIX)	0.10	0.67	1.00	
German Real Estate Research Society Office Rent Index (GIF-ORIX)	-0.26	0.36	0.78	1.00

Table 228: Intertemporal Rent Change – Frankfurt – Comparison of Indices – Correlation Analysis

A.12.4 Hamburg

A.12.4.1 Annual Rental Growth Rate

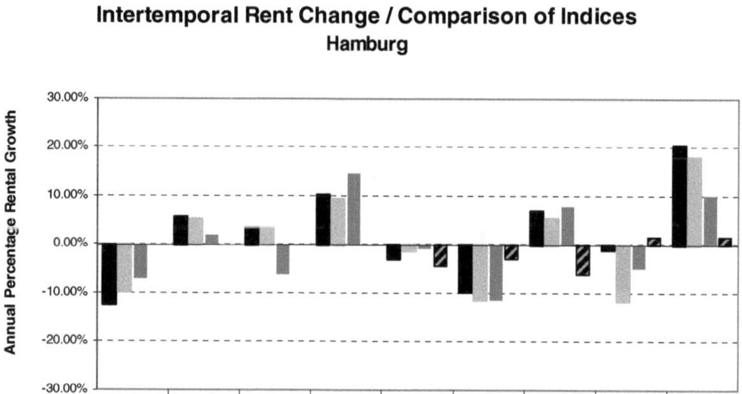

	1998	1999	2000	2001	2002	2003	2004	2005	2006
L-HORIX	-12.32%	5.68%	3.20%	10.23%	-3.11%	-9.85%	6.80%	-1.12%	20.31%
P-HORIX	-9.65%	5.19%	3.26%	9.32%	-1.28%	-11.45%	5.52%	-11.73%	18.01%
RD-ORIX	-7.13%	1.89%	-6.08%	14.59%	-0.79%	-11.38%	7.81%	-4.92%	9.99%
GIF-ORX					-4.35%	-3.03%	-6.25%	1.67%	1.64%

Figure 61: Intertemporal Rent Change – Hamburg – Comparison of Indices – Annual Rental Growth Rate

A.12.4.2 Correlation Analysis

Correlation based on €/m²/month	L-HORIX	P-HORIX	RD-ORIX	GIF-ORIX
Laspeyres Hedonic Office Rent Index (L-HORIX)	1.00			
Paasche Hedonice Office Rent Index (P-HORIX)	0.49	1.00		
Rental Database Office Rent Index (RD-ORIX)	0.73	0.74	1.00	
German Real Estate Research Society Office Rent Index (GIF-ORIX)	0.11	0.72	0.47	1.00

Table 229: Intertemporal Rent Change – Hamburg – Comparison of Indices – Correlation Analysis

A.12.5 Munich

A.12.5.1 Annual Rental Growth Rate

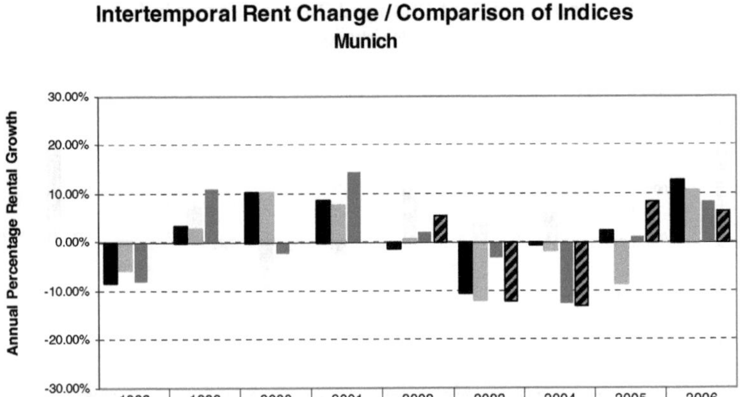

	1998	1999	2000	2001	2002	2003	2004	2005	2006
L-HORIX	-8.39%	3.15%	10.14%	8.52%	-1.37%	-10.39%	-0.65%	2.37%	12.58%
P-HORIX	-5.60%	2.67%	10.21%	7.63%	0.49%	-11.98%	-1.85%	-8.61%	10.42%
RD-ORIX	-7.99%	10.93%	-2.38%	14.42%	2.02%	-3.19%	-12.74%	1.09%	8.27%
GIF-ORX					5.49%	-12.14%	-13.16%	8.33%	6.29%

Figure 62: Intertemporal Rent Change – Munich – Comparison of Indices – Annual Rental Growth Rate

A.12.5.2 Correlation Analysis

Correlation based on €/m²/month	L-HORIX	P-HORIX	RD-ORIX	GIF-ORIX
Laspeyres Hedonic Office Rent Index (L-HORIX)	1.00			
Paasche Hedonice Office Rent Index (P-HORIX)	0.56	1.00		
Rental Database Office Rent Index (RD-ORIX)	0.73	0.69	1.00	
German Real Estate Research Society Office Rent Index (GIF-ORIX)	0.72	0.81	0.92	1.00

Table 230: Intertemporal Rent Change – Munich – Comparison of Indices – Correlation Analysis

Bibliography

Acock, Alan C. (2005): *Working with Missing Values*, in: *Journal of Marriage and Family*, Vol. 64, Iss. 4, pp. 1012-1028.

Allison, Paul D. (2000): *Multiple Imputation for Missing Data: A Cautionary Tale*, in: *Sociological Methods and Research*, Vol. 28, Iss. 3, pp. 301-309.

Alreck, Pamela / Settle, Robert (1985): *The Survey Research Handbook*, Homewood, IL 1985.

Anas, Alex / Arnott, Richard / Small, Kenneth A. (1998): *Urban Spatial Structure*, in: *Journal of Economic Literature*, Vol. 36, Iss. 3, pp. 1426-1464.

Anglin, Paul M. / Gencay, Ramazan (1996): *Semiparametric Estimation of a Hedonic Price Function*, in: *Journal of Applied Econometrics*, Vol. 11, pp. 633-648.

Archer, Wayne R. / Smith, Marc T. (2003): *Explaining Location of Suburban Offices*, in: *Real Estate Economics*, Vol. 31, Iss. 2, pp. 139-164.

Arge, Kirsten (2005): *Adaptable office buildings: theory and practice*, in: *Facilities*, Vol. 3/4, pp. 119-127.

ATIS Real (ed.) (2006a): *City Report Berlin 2006 Quarter 3*, 2006a.

ATIS Real (ed.) (2006b): *City Report Frankfurt 2006 Quarter 3*, 2006b.

ATIS Real (ed.) (2006c): *City Report Hamburg 2006 Quarter 3*, 2006c.

ATIS Real (ed.) (2006d): *City Report Munich 2006 Quarter 3*, 2006d.

ATIS Real (ed.) (2006e): *Office Market Report Germany 2006*, 2006e.

ATIS Real (ed.) (2007): *Office Market Report Germany 2007*, 2007.

ATIS Real (ed.) (2008): *Office Market Report Germany 2008*, 2008.

AtisReal (ed.) (2006): *Office Market Report Germany 2006*, 2006.

Backhaus, Klaus / Erichson, Bernd / Plinke, Wulff / Weiber, Rolf (2003): *Multivariate Analysemethoden - Eine anwendungsorientierte Einführung*, 10th Edition Ed., 2003.

Badeen, Dennis (1999): *On the limits of neo-classical eonomics in its modeling of human behaviour, motivation and economic totalities towards a self-critical model for economics*, Master of Arts, Trent University, Peterborough, Ontario 1999.

Ball, Michael (2003): *Is there an office replacement cycle?*, in: *Journal of Property Research*, Vol. 20, Iss. 2, pp. 173-189.

Ball, Michael / Lizieri, Colin / MacGregor, Bryan D. (1998): *The Economics of Commercial Property Markets*, 1st Ed., 1998.

Bao, Helen X.A. / Wan, Alan T.K. (2004): *On the Use of Spline Smoothing in Estimating Hedonic Housing Price Models: Empirical Evidence Using Hong Kong Data*, in: *Real Estate Economics*, Vol. 32, Iss. 3, pp. 487-507.

Bartik, Timothy J. (1987): *The Estimation of Demand Parameters in Hedonic Price Models*, in: *The Journal of Political Economy*, Vol. 95, Iss. 1, pp. 81-88.

Bartlett, E. / Howard, N. (2000): *Informing the decision makers on the cost and value of green building*, in: *Building Research & Information*, Vol. 28, Iss. 5/6, pp. 315-324.

Baßeler, Ulrich / Heinrich, Jürgen / Utecht, Burkhard (2002): *Grundlagen und Probleme der Volkswirtschaft*, 17th Ed., Frankfurt 2002.

Baum, Andrew / Turner, Neil (2004): *Retention rates, reinvestment and depreciation in European office markets*, in: *Journal of Property Investment & Finance*, Vol. 22, Iss. 33, pp. 214-235.

Beer, Michael (2006): *Hedonic Elementary Price Indices: Axiomatic Foundation and Estimation Techniques*, University of Fribourg Switzerland, Fribourg 2006.

Beidatsch, Kaja (2006): *Geographic Selection - Auswahl von Zielmärkten im Portfoliomanagement*, PhD, European Business School (ebs), 2006.

Bender, A. / Din, A. / Favarger, P. / Hoesli, Martin / Laakso, J. (1999): *Environmental quality perceptions of urban commercial real estate*, in: *Journal of Property Investment & Finance*, Vol. 17, Iss. 3, pp. 280-296.

Benjamin, John D. / de la Torre, C. / Musumeci, J. (1998): *Rationales for real estate leasing versus owning*, in: *Journal of Real Estate Research*, Vol. 15, Iss. 3, pp. 223-238.

Benjamin, John D. / Sa-Aadu, J. / Shilling, James D. (1992a): *Influence of Rent Differential on the Choice between Office Rent Contracts with and without Relocation Provisions*, in: *Journal of the American Real Estate and Urban Economics Association*, Vol. 20, Iss. 1, pp. 289-302.

Benjamin, John D. / Shilling, James D. / Sirmans, C.F. (1992b): *Security Deposits, Adverse Selection and Office Leases*, in: *Journal of the American Real Estate and Urban Economics Association*, Vol. 20, Iss. 1, pp. 259-272.

Berliant, Marcus / McMillen, Daniel P. (2006): *Hedonism vs. nihilism*, in: *Regional Science and Urban Economics*, Vol. 36, pp. 118-131.

Beyerle, Thomas (2006a): *Asset-Klasse Immobilien: neue Immobilienprodukte und ihre Analyse*, <www.degi.de/research/thema_d_monats/pdf/Thema_des_Monats_0604.pdf>, Access Date: 03.11.2007.

Beyerle, Thomas (2006b): *Immobilienmarktresearch in Deutschland - Eine Status-quo Analyse*, in: *Zeitschrift für immobilienwirtschaftliche Forschung und Praxis*, pp. 1-12.

Beyerle, Thomas (2007): *Neue Perspektiven - Marktreport Deutschland 2007*, Frankfurt 2007.

Bishop, Matthew (2004): *Essential Economics*, <http://library.books24x7.com.eproxy2.lib.hku.hk/toc.asp?bookid=15681>, Access Date: 06.04.2008.

Björklund, Kicki / Söderberg, Bo / Wilhelmson, Mats (2002): *An Investigation of Property Price Studes*, in: Wang, Ko /Wolveration, Marvin L. (eds.): *Real Estate Valuation Theory*, Vol. 8, 2002, pp. 64-93.

Bollinger, Christopher R. / Ihlanfeldt, Keith R. / Bowes, David R. (1998): *Spatial Variation in Office Rents within the Atlanta Region*, in: *Urban Studies*, Vol. 35, Iss. 7, pp. 1097-1118.

Bond, Shaun A. / Loizou, Pavlos / McAllister, Patrick (2005): *Lease Maturity and Initial Rent: Is there a Term Structure for UK Commercial Property Leases*, <http://www.reading.ac.uk/REP/fulltxt/2805.pdf>, Access Date: 03.11.2007.

Bone-Winkel, Stephan / Schulte, Karl-Werner / Focke, Christian (2005): *Begriff und Besonderheiten der Immobilie als Wirtschaftsgut*, in: Schulte, Karl-Werner (ed.): *Immobilienökonomie - Betriebswirtschaftliche Grundlagen*, Vol. Band 1, Ed. 3rd, Köln 2005, pp. 5-24.

Bortz, Jürgen (1999): *Statistik für Sozialwissenschaftler*, 5th Edition Ed., Berlin 1999.

Bottom, Connel / McGreal, Stanley / Heaney, George (1997): *Evaluating office environments using tenant organization perceptions*, in: *Facilities*, Vol. 7/8, pp. 195-203.

Bourassa, Steven C. / Hoesli, Martin / Sun, Jian (2006): *A simple alternative house price index method*, in: *Journal of Housing Economics*, Vol. 15, pp. 80-97.

Bowbrick, Peter (1994): *Limitations of Lancaster's theory of Consumer Demand*, PhD, Henley Management College, Oxfordshire 1994.

Bowles, Samuel / Gintis, Herbert (1993): *The Revenge of Homo Economicus: Contested Exchange and the Revival of Political Economy*, in: *Journal of Economic Perspectives*, Vol. 7, Iss. 1, pp. 83-102.

Boyd, Terry / Kimmet, Philip (2004): *Innovative Benchmarks for Built Asset Performance - The Triple Bottom Line Approach* at: Clients Driving Innovation International Conference: Sydney, Australia 2004.

Brachinger, Hans Wolfgang (2003): *True Hedonic Price Indices: Concepts and Estimation Problems*, <http://www.vfs.unizh.ch/papers/Brachinger.pdf>, Access Date: 03.11.2007.

Brade, Kerstin / Bobber, Michael / Schmitt, Alexander / Sturm, Verena (2005): *Immobilienmarketing*, in: Schulte, Karl-Werner (ed.): *Immobilienökonomie - Betriebswirtschaftliche Grundlagen*, Vol. 1, Ed. 3rd, Köln 2005, pp. 711-776.

Brand, J. (1999): *Development, implementation and evaluation of multiple imputation strategies for the statistical analysis of incomplete datasets.*, PhD, Erasmus University Rotterdam, Rotterdam 1999.

Brasington, David M. / Hite, Diane (2005): *Demand for Environmental Quality: A Spatial Hedonic Analysis*, in: *Regional Science and Urban Economics*, Vol. 35, Iss. 1, pp. 57-82.

Breidenbach, Marc (2005): *Real Estate Securitisation*, PhD, European Business School (ebs), Köln 2005.

Brueggeman, William B. / Fisher, Jeffrey D. (2007): *Real Estate Finance and Investments*, 13th Ed., New York 2007.

Brühl, Martin / Lizieri, Colin (1994): *Centralism vs Federalism - Implications for Regional Diversification*, in: *Journal of Property Valuation & Investment*, Vol. 12, Iss. 1, pp. 59-73.

Bruin, Anne de / Flint-Hartle, Susan (2003): *A bounded rationality framework for property investment behaviour*, in: *Journal of Property Investment & Finance*, Vol. 21, Iss. 3, pp. 271-284.

Buetow, Gerald / Albert, Joseph (1998): *The Pricing of Embedded Options in Real Estate Lease Contracts*, in: *Journal of Real Estate Research*, Vol. 15, Iss. 3, pp. 253-265.

BulwienGesa (2008): <http://www.riwis.de/riwis_online/>, Access Date: 05.03.2008.

BulwienGesa Online Databank (2008): <http://www.riwis.de/riwis_online/abfrage/tablelist_join.php3>, Access Date: 05.03.2008.

Case, Branford / Szymanoski, Edward J. (1994): *Precision in House Price Indices: Findings of Comparative Study of House Price Index Methods*, in: *Journal of Housing Research*, Vol. 6, Iss. 3, pp. 483-496.

CB Richard Ellis (ed.) (2006a): *Office Market Berlin Q3 2006*, 2006a.

CB Richard Ellis (ed.) (2006b): *Office Market Frankfurt Q3 2006*, 2006b.

CB Richard Ellis (ed.) (2006c): *Office Market Hamburg Q3 2006*, 2006c.

CB Richard Ellis (ed.) (2006d): *Office Market Munich Q3 2006*, 2006d.

CB Richard Ellis (ed.) (2007a): *Office Market Berlin 2007*, 2007a.

CB Richard Ellis (ed.) (2007b): *Office Market Frankfurt 2007*, 2007b.

CB Richard Ellis (ed.) (2007c): *Office Market Hamburg 2007*, 2007c.

CB Richard Ellis (ed.) (2007d): *Office Market Munich2007*, 2007d.

Chaplin, Russell (1998): *An ex post comparative evaluation of office rent prediction models*, in: *Journal of Property Valuation & Investment*, Vol. 16, Iss. 1, pp. 21-37.

Clapp, J.M. (1993): *Dynamics of Office Markets: empirical findings and research issues*, Washington D.C. 1993.

Clapp, John M. (1980): *The Intrametropolitan Location of Office Activities*, in: *Journal of Regional Science*, Vol. 20, Iss. 3, pp. 387-399.

Clapp, John M. (2003): *A Semiparametric Method for Valuing Residential Locations: Application to Automated Valuation*, in: *Journal of Real Estate Finance Economics*, Vol. 27, Iss. 3, pp. 303-320.

Clapp, John M. (2004): *A Semiparametric Method for Estimating Local House Price Indices*, in: *Real Estate Economics*, Vol. 32, Iss. 1, pp. 127-160.

Clauw, Frederik (2005): *The identification problem in estimating hedonic demand parameters: an overview*, <http://www.vve.be/nl/vveDag/3.5.%20clauw.pdf>, Access Date: 03.11.2007.

Clayton, Jim (1998): *Further Evidence on Real Estate Market Efficiency*, in: *Journal of Real Estate Research*, Vol. 15, Iss. 1/2, pp. 41-57.

Colett, David / Lizieri, Colin / Ward, Charles (2003): *Timing and Holding Periods of Institutional Real Estate*, in: *Real Estate Economics*, Vol. 31, Iss. 2, pp. 205-222.

Colin, J. (1995): *An economic basis for the analysis and prediction of local office property markets*, in: *Journal of Property Valuation & Investment*, Vol. 13, Iss. 2, pp. 16-30.

Colwell, Peter F. / Munneke, Henry J. (2006): *Bargaining Strength and Property Class in Office Markets*, in: *Journal of Real Estate Finance Economics*, Vol. 33, pp. 197-213.

Colwell, Peter F. / Munneke, Henry J. / Trefzger, Joseph W. (1998): *Chicago's Office Market: Price Indices, Location and Time*, in: *Real Estate Economics*, Vol. 26, Iss. 1, pp. 83-106.

Conniffe, Denis / Duffy, David (1999): *Irish House Price Indices - Methodological Issues*, in: *The Economic and Social Review*, Vol. 30, Iss. 4, pp. 403-423.

Crosby, Neil / Gibson, V. / Murdoch, Sandy (2003): *UK Commercial Property Lease Structures: Landlord and Tenant Mismatch*, in: *Urban Studies*, Vol. 40, Iss. 8, pp. 1487-1516.

Crosby, Neil / Hughes, Cathy / Murdoch, Sandi (2006): *Flexible Property Leasing and the Small Business Tenant*, in: *Journal of Property Research*, Vol. 23, Iss. 2, pp. 163-188.

Crosby, Neil / Murdoch, Sandy (2000): *The influence of procedure on rent determination in the commercial property market of England and Wales*, in: *Journal of Property Investment & Finance*, Vol. 18, Iss. 4, pp. 420-444.

Crosby, Neil / Murdoch, Sandy (2001): *Basis of rental value for performance measurement systems*, in: *Journal of Property Research*, Vol. 18, Iss. 2, pp. 123-139.

Curry, Bruce / Morgan, Peter / Silver, Mick (2001): *Hedonic regressions: misspecification and neural networks*, in: *Applied Economics*, Vol. 33, pp. 659-671.

D'Arcy, E. / Keogh, G. (1999): *The Property Market and Urban Competitiveness: A Review*, in: *Urban Studies*, Vol. 36, Iss. 5-6, pp. 917-928.

D'Arcy, E. / McGough, T. / Tsolacos, S. (1997): *National economic trends, market size and city growth effects on European office rents*, in: *Journal of Property Research*, Vol. 14, Iss. 4, pp. 297-308.

Davey, Adam / Shanahan, Michael / Schafer, Joseph L. (2000): *Correcting for Selective Nonresponse in the National Longitudinal Survey of Youth Using Multiple Imputation*, in: *The Journal of Human Resources*, Vol. 36, Iss. 3, pp. 500-519.

Day, Brett (2001): *The Theory of Hedonic Markets: Botaining welffare measure for changes in environmental quality using hedonic market data*, 2001.

De Lange, Nobert (1989): *Standortpersistenz und Standortdynamik von Bürobetrieben in westdeutschen Regionalmetropolen seit dem Ende des 19. Jahrhunderts*, Paderborn 1989.

Degener, Arne (2005): *gif e.V. stellt Definitionen zur einheitlichen Darstellung des Büromarktes vor*, in: *Der Immobilienbrief*, 04.03.2005, pp. 7-8.

Deka Bank (ed.) (2007): *Deka Immobilien Monitor Ausgabe Mai 2007*, 2007.

Demirtas, Hakan / Schafer, Joseph L. (2003): *On the performance of random-coefficient pattern-mixture models for non-ignorable drop-out*, in: *Statistics in Medicine*, Vol. 22, pp. 2553-2575.

Des Rosiers, Francois / Theriault, Marius / Villeneuve, Paul-Y (2000): *Sorting out access and neighbourhood factors in hedonic price modelling*, in: *Journal of Property Investment & Finance*, Vol. 18, Iss. 3, pp. 291-315.

Desyllas, Jake (2000): *The relationship between urban street configuration and office rent patterns in Berlin*, PhD, University College London, 2000.

Deutsche Gesellschaft für Immobilienfonds (ed.) (2008): *Neue Perspektiven - Marktreport Deutschland 2008*, Frankfurt 2008.

Deutscher Immobiliendatenbank (ed.) (2006): *DID German Commercial Propert Lease Trends 2006*, 2006.

Diehl, Bianca (2006): *Nebenbei sparen*, in: *Immobilienmanager*, Vol. 4, pp. 40-41.

DiPasquale, Denise / Wheaton, William C. (1992): *The Markets for Real Estate Assets and Space: A Conceptual Framework*, in: *Journal of the American Real Estate and Urban Economics Association*, Vol. 20, Iss. 1, pp. 181-197.

Dixon, T. / Marston, A. / Thomson, B. / Elder, B. (2003): *eBusiness and City of London office market*, in: *Journal of Property Investment & Finance*, Vol. 21, Iss. 4, pp. 348-365.

Dobberstein, Monika (2000): *Das prozyklische Verhalten der Büromarktakteure - Interessen, Zwänge und mögliche Alternativen*, in: *Working Paper of the Universitiy of Dortmund*, Vol. 2, pp. 1-16.

Donders, Rogier / Heijden, Geert van der / Stijnen, Theo / Moons, Karel G.M. (2006): *Review: A gentle introduction to imputation of missing values*, in: *Journal of Clinical Epidemiology*, Vol. 59, pp. 1087-1091.

Dowall, D.E. (1988): *Office Market Research: The Case for Segmentation*, in: *The Journal of Real Estate Development*, Vol. 4, Iss. 1, pp. 34-43.

Downs, Anthony (1993): *Cycles in Office Space Markets*, in: White, John R. (ed.): *The Office Building From Concept to Investment Reality*, 1993, pp. 153-169.

Downs, David H. / Slade, Barrett A. (1999): *Characteristics of a full-disclosure, transaction-based Index of Commercial Real Estate*, in: *Journal of Real Estate Portfolio Management*, Vol. 5, Iss. 1, pp. 95-104.

Drèze, Jacques H. / Hagen, Kare P. (1978): *Choice of Product Quality: Equilibrium and Efficiency*, in: *Econometrica*, Vol. 46, Iss. 3, pp. 493-513.

Dröge, Ferdinand (2005): *Handbuch der Mietpreisbewertung für Wohn- und Gewerberaum*, 3rd Ed., Munich 2005.

Drummer, Martin (2007): *BIP und Dax*, in: *Frankfurter Allgemeine Zeitung*, p. 42.

DTZ Research (ed.) (2005): *Newsletter - Der deutsche Büromarkt*, 2005.

DTZ Research (ed.) (2006): *DTZ Analyse der deutschen Büroimmobilienmärkte*, 2006.

DTZ Zadelhoff Tie Lung (ed.) (2006a): *Facts Düsseldorf Q2 2006*, 2006a.

DTZ Zadelhoff Tie Lung (ed.) (2006b): *Facts Q2 2006*, 2006b.

Dubin, Robin / Pace, Kelley R. / Thibodeau, Thomas G. (1999): *Spatial Autoregression Techniques for Real Estate Data*, in: *Journal of Real Estate Literature*, Vol. 7, pp. 79-95.

Dunse, Neil / Jones, Colin (1998): *A hedonic price model of office rents*, in: *Journal of Property Valuation & Investment*, Vol. 16, Iss. 3, pp. 297-312.

Dunse, Neil / Jones, Colin (2002): *The existence of office submarkets in cities*, in: *Journal of Property Research*, Vol. 19, Iss. 2, pp. 159-182.

Dunse, Neil / Jones, Colin / Orr, Allison / Tarbet, Heather (1998): *The extent and limitations of local commercial property market data*, in: *Journal of Property Valuation & Investment*, Vol. 16, Iss. 5, pp. 455-473.

Dunse, Neil / Leishman, Chris / Watkins, Craig (2002): *Testing for the Existence of Office Submarkets: A Comparison of Evidence from Two Cities*, in: *Urban Studies*, Vol. 39, Iss. 3, pp. 483-506.

Durrant, Gabriele B. (2005): *Imputation Methods for Handling Item-Nonresponse in the Social Sciences: A Methodological Review*, in: *ESRC National Centre for Research Methods Review Papers*, Vol. 2, pp. 1-37.

Eberhard, André (2007): *Europäische Büromärkte 4. Quartal 2006*, in: *Der Immobilienbrief*, Vol. 133, pp. 14-15.

Englund, Peter / Gunnelin, Ake / Hoesli, Martin / Söderberg, Bo (2004): *Implicit Forward Rents as Predictors of Future Rents*, in: *Real Estate Economics*, Vol. 32, Iss. 2, pp. 183-215.

Ertle-Straub, Susanne (2003): *Standortanalysen für Büroimmobilien*, PhD, University Leipzig, Leipzig 2003.

Evans, Allen W. (1995): *The property market: ninety per cent efficient*, in: *Urban Studies*, Vol. 32, pp. 5-29.

Evans, Allen W. (2004): *Economics, Real Estate and the Supply of Land* London 2004.

Evans, Michael K. (2003): *Practical Business Forecasting*, 2003.

Falk, Bernd (2002): *Immobilien-Handbuch: Wirtschaft, Recht, Berwertung*, 3rd Ed., Lansberg 2002.

Fama, E.F. (1970): *Efficient capital markets : a review of theory and empirical work*, in: *Journal of Finance*, Vol. 25, pp. 383-420.

FAZ (2001): *Die "immo-ebs"*, in: *Frankfurter Allgemeine Zeitung*, 22.06.2001, p. 55.

Federal Statistical Bureau of Germany (2008): <https://www-genesis.destatis.de/genesis/online>, Access Date: 13.04.2008.

Fenwick, David (2005): *Statistics on real estate prices: the need for a strategic approach*, in: *Bank of International Settlements Papers*, Vol. 21, pp. 368-382.

Fenwick, David / Ball, Adrian (2003): *The use of hedonic methods for quality-adjusted prices*, in: *IFC Bulletin*, Vol. 16, pp. 11-15.

Fichman, Mark / Cummings, Jonathin N. (2003): *Multiple Imputation for missing data: Making the most of what you know*, in: *Organizational Research Methods*, Vol. 6, Iss. 3, pp. 282-308.

Fisher, Jeffrey D. (1994): *Income Property Valuation*, 1994.

Fisher, Jerry / Gatzlaff, Dean / Geltner, David / Haurin, Donald (2004): *An Analysis of the Determinants of Transaction Frequency of Institutional Commercial Real Estate Investment Property*, in: *Real Estate Economics*, Vol. 32, Iss. 2, pp. 239-264.

Fletcher, Mike / Mangan, Jean / Raeburn, Emily (2004): *Comparing hedonic models for estimating and forecasting house prices*, in: *Property Management*, Vol. 22, Iss. 3/4, pp. 189-200.

Flüshöh, Christian / Stottrop, Daria (2005): *Büroflächenbestand - Grundlagen, Daten und Methoden*, PhD, Universtität Dortmund, Dortmund 2005.

Focke, Christian (2005): *Gewerbeimmobilien-Investments in Polen*, PhD, European Business School (ebs), 2005.

Fox, John (2006a): *The car Package*, <http://cran.r-project.org/doc/packages/car.pdf>, Access Date: 05.02.2007.

Fox, John (2006b): *The Companion to Applied Regression Package*, <http://cran.r-project.org/doc/packages/car.pdf>, Access Date: 03.11.2007.

Frankfurter Allgemeine Zeitung (2006): *Die Büronebenkosten steigen weiter*, in: *Frankfurter Allgemeine Zeitung*, p. 49.

Fraser, W.D. / Leishman, C. / Tarbert, H. (2002): *The long-run diversification attributes of commercial properties*, in: *Journal of Property Investment & Finance*, Vol. 20, Iss. 4, pp. 354-373.

French, Nick (2001): *Decision Theory and Real Estate Investment: An Analysis of the Decision-Making Processes of Real Estate Investment Fund Managers*, in: *Managerial and Decision Economics*, Vol. 22, Iss. 7, pp. 399-341.

French, Nick / Wiseman, G. (2003): *The price of space, the convergence of value in use and value in exchange*, in: *Journal of Property Investment & Finance*, Vol. 21, Iss. 1, pp. 23-30.

Gärtner, Markus (2007): *Preisspirale abwärts*, in: *Immobilienmanager*, Vol. 10, pp. 36-37.

Gat, Daniel (1998): *Urban Focal Points and Design Quality Influence Rents: The Case of the Tel Aviv Office Market*, in: *The Journal Real Estate Research*, Vol. 16, Iss. 2, pp. 229-247.

Gatzlaff, Dean / Geltner, David (1998): *A Transaction-based Index of Commercial Property and Its Comparison to the NCREIF Index*, in: *Real Estate Finance*, Vol. 15, Iss. 1, pp. 7-22.

Geltner, David M. / Miller, Norman G. / Clayton, Jim / Eichholtz, Piet (2007): *Commercial Real Estate Analysis and Investments*, Mason 2007.

Gerhard, Jan (2003): *Immobilienportfoliomanagement mit Immobilienindex-Derivaten*, PhD, European Business School, Köln 2003.

Gesellschaft für Immobilienwirtschaftliche Forschung (2007): *Deutsche Büromärkte weiter auf Erholungskurs - gif stellt Ergebnisse der Büromarkterhebung 2006 vor*, <http://www.gif-ev.de/publikationen/presse/pressemitteilungen/2007/GIF%20Buromarkterhebung%202006.pdf/view>, Access Date: 03.11.2007.

Gesellschaft für immobilienwirtschaftliche Forschung (gif) (2004): *Definitionssammlung zum Büromarkt*, in: p. 15.

Geßner, Silke (1997): *Immobilienindex im Bereich des Investmentmanagements*, Master of Business Administration, University of Leipzig, Leipzig 1997.

Gibler, Karen M. / Nelson, Susan L. (2003): *Consumer Behaviour Applications to Real Estate Education*, in: *Journal of Real Estate Practice and Education*, Vol. 6, Iss. 1, pp. 63-83.

Gibson, V. (2003): *Flexible working needs flexible space? Towards an alternative workplace strategy*, in: *Journal of Property Investment & Finance*, Vol. 21, Iss. 1, pp. 12-22.

Glascock, John L. / Jahanian, Shirin / Sirmans, C.F. (1990): *An Analysis of Office Market Rents: Some Empirical Evidence*, in: *Journal of the American Real Estate and Urban Economics Association*, Vol. 18, Iss. 1, pp. 105-119.

Glascock, John L. / Sirmans, C.F. / Turnbull, Geoffrey (1993): *Owner Tenancy as Credible Commitment under Uncertainty*, in: *Journal of the American Real Estate and Urban Economics Association*, Vol. 21, Iss. 1, pp. 69-82.

Gowdy, John M. / Polimeni, Raluca Iorgulescu (2005): *The death of homo economicus: is there life after welfare economics*, in: *International Journal of Social Economics*, Vol. 32, Iss. 11, pp. 924-938.

Greer, Gaylon E. (1993): *Investment Analysis for Real Estate Decisions*, 3rd edition Ed., 1993.

Grenadier, S.R. (1995): *Valuing lease contracts: a real-options approach*, in: *Journal of Financial Economics*, Vol. 38, pp. 297-331.

Griliches, Z. (1971): *Introduction: Hedonic Price Indexes Revisited*, in: Griliches, Z. (ed.): *Pirce Indexes and Quality Change*, Cambridge 1971, .

Gunnelin, Ake / Söderberg, Bo (2003): *Term Structures in the Office Rental Market in Stockholm*, in: *Journal of Real Estate Finance and Economics*, Vol. 26, Iss. 2/3, pp. 241-265.

Hahr, Henric (2006): *Technische Analyse von Büroimmobilien im Bestand*, PhD, University of Stuttgart, Stuttgart 2006.

Hall, John M. (1985): *Offices in a Modern Economy*, in: Marber, Paul /Marber, Paula (eds.): *Office Development*, London 1985, pp. 23-32.

Hanink, Dean M. (1996): *How "local" are Local Office Markets?*, in: *Real Estate Economics*, Vol. 24, Iss. 3, pp. 341-358.

Hanke, John E. / Reitsch, Arthur G. (2000): *Business Forecasting*, 2000.

Hansz, Andrew J. / Diaz III, Julian (2001): *Valuation Bias in Commercial Appraisal: A Transaction Price Feedback Experiment*, in: *Real Estate Economics*, Vol. 29, Iss. 4, pp. 553-565.

Hargity, Stephen E. / Yu, Shi-Ming (1993): *Property Investment Decisions - A quantative approach*, 1993.

Hassanain, Mohammad (2006): *Factors affecting the development of flexible workplace facilities*, in: *Journal of Corporate Real Estate*, Vol. 8, Iss. 4, pp. 213-220.

Haurin, Donald (2003): *US commercial real estate indices: transaction-based and constant liquidity indices* at: IMF/BIS Conference on Real Estate Indicators and Financial Stability: Washington, D.C. 2003.

Heckman, James / Matzkin, Rosa / Nesheim, Lars (2003): *Simulation and Estimation of Hedonic Models*, in: *CESifo Working Paper*, Vol. 1014, pp. 1-59.

Heerwagen, J. (2000): *Green buildings, organizational success and occupant productivity*, in: *Building Research & Information*, Vol. 28, Iss. 5/6, pp. 353-367.

Hendershott, Patrick. H. (1996): *Valuing properties when comparable sales do not exist and the market is in disequilibrium*, in: *Journal of Property Research*, Vol. 13, pp. 57-66.

Heyser, Hartwig (2006): *Bestimmungsgründe des Büromietzinses - Hedonische Mietpreise am Beispiel des Münchner Gewerbemarktes*, PhD, Alberts-Ludwigs-Universität Freiburg, Freiburg 2006.

Hill, Matthew (2003): *Financing corporate real estate: The impact of corporate real estate in the shareholder value equation*, in: *Briefings in Real Estate Finance*, Vol. 2, Iss. 4, pp. 313-325.

Hill, Robert J. / Melser, Daniel (2007): *Comparing House Prices Across Regions and Time: An Hedonic Approach*, in: *School of Economics UNSW Discussion Paper*, Vol. 2007-33, pp. 1-26.

Hodgson, Douglas / Slade, Barrett / Vorkink, Keith P. (2006): *Constructing Commercial Indices: A Semiparametric Adaptive Estimator Approach*, in: *Journal of Real Estate Finance Economics*, Vol. 32, pp. 151-168.

Hoesli, Martin / Giaccotto, Carmelo / Favarger, Phillipe (1997): *Three New Real Estate Price Indices for Geneva, Switzerland*, in: *Journal of Real Estate Finance and Economics*, Vol. 15, Iss. 1, pp. 93-109.

Hoesli, Martin / MacGregor, Bryan D. (2000): *Property Investment - Principles and Practice of Portfolio Management*, 1st Ed., Essex 2000.

Horton, Nicholas J. / Lipsitz, Stuart R. (2001): *Multiple Imputation in Practice: Comparison of Software Packages for Regression Models with Missing Values*, in: *The American Statistician*, Vol. 55, Iss. 3, pp. 244-254.

Huh, Serim / Kwak, Seung (1997): *The Choice of Functional Form and Variables in the Hedonic Price Model in Seoul*, in: *Urban Studies*, Vol. 7, pp. 989-998.

Hulten, Charles R. (2003): *Price Hedonics: A Critical Review*, in: *Federal Reserve Bank of New York Economic Policy Review*, Vol. September 2003, pp. 5-15.

Hutchison, Norman / Adair, Alastair S. / Leheny, Iain (2005): *Communicating Investment Risk to Clients: Property Risk Scoring*, in: *Journal of Property Research*, Vol. 22, Iss. 2-3, pp. 137-161.

Ibrahim, Joseph / Chen, Ming..Hui / Lipsitz, Stuart R. / Herring, Amy H. (2005): *Missing Data Methdods for Generalized Linear Models: A Comparative Review*, in: *Journal of the American Statistical Association*, Vol. 100, Iss. 469, pp. 332-346.

ifo Institut für Wirtschaftsforschung (2005): *Die volkswirtschaftliche Bedeutung der Immobilienwirtschaft*, in: *German Journal of Property Research*, Vol. Sonderausgabe, .

Ihlanfeldt, K. (1990): *The intrametropolitan location of new office firms*, in: *Land Economics*, Vol. 66, pp. 182-198.

International Monetary Fund (2004): *Compilation Guide on Financial Soundness Indicators - Chapter Nine Real Estate Price Indices*, <http://www.imf.org/external/np/sta/fsi/eng/2004/guide/chap9.pdf>, Access Date: .

Jaffe, Austin J. (1995): *Fundamentals of real estate investment*, 3rd Ed., 1995.

Janssen, C. / Soèderberg, B. / Zhou, J. (2001): *Robust estimation of hedonic models of price and income for investment property*, in: *Journal of Property Valuation & Finance*, Vol. 19, Iss. 4, pp. 342-360.

Janssen, Christian (2003): *Hedonic estimation of income multipliers*, in: *Property Management*, Vol. 21, Iss. 5, pp. 315-336.

Jedem, Ulrich (2006): *Immobilienrating - Überlegung zur Risikoeinschätzung bei Immobilien aus Sicht der Kapitalgeber*, PhD, Albert-Ludwigs-Universität zu Freiburg, Freiburg 2006.

Jefferies, Rodney L. (1994): *Lease Incentives and Effective Rents: A Decapitalization Model*, in: *Journal of Property Valuation & Investment*, Vol. 12, Iss. 1, pp. 21-42.

Jones Lang LaSalle (ed.) (2006a): *City Profile Berlin Update Q3*, 2006a.

Jones Lang LaSalle (ed.) (2006b): *City Profile Frankfurt Update Q3 2006*, 2006b.

Jones Lang LaSalle (ed.) (2006c): *City Profile Hamburg Update Q3 2006*, 2006c.

Jones Lang LaSalle (ed.) (2006d): *City Profile Munich Update Q3 2006*, 2006d.

Jones Lang LaSalle (ed.) (2007a): *City Profile Berlin Quarter 1 2007*, 2007a.

Jones Lang LaSalle (ed.) (2007b): *City Profile Düsseldorf Quarter 1 2007*, 2007b.

Jones Lang LaSalle (ed.) (2007c): *City Profile Frankfurt Quarter 1 2007*, 2007c.

Jones Lang LaSalle (ed.) (2007d): *City Profile Hamburg Quarter 1 2007*, 2007d.

Jones Lang LaSalle (ed.) (2007e): *City Profile Munich Quarter 1 2007*, 2007e.

Jones Lang LaSalle (ed.) (2007f): *Ökologische Nachhaltigkeit von Büroimmobilien*, Frankfurt 2007f.

Jonker, Nicole (2001): *Constructing quality adjusted price indexes: a comparison of hedonic and discrete choice methods* at: Issues in the Measurement of Price Indices: Frankfurt 2001.

Kain, John F. (1989): *Comments on The Economics of Architecture and Urban Design: Some Preliminary Findings*, in: *AREUEA Journal*, Vol. 17, Iss. 2, pp. 261-265.

Karakozova, Olga (2004): *Modelling and forecasting office returns in the Helsinki area*, in: *Journal of Property Research*, Vol. 21, Iss. 1, pp. 51-73.

Kauffmann, Albrecht / Nastansky, Andreas (2007): *Property market indices for periods below one year in Germany*, in: *German Journal of Property Research*, Vol. 2, pp. 55-71.

Kemp, Steven M. / Kemp, Sid (2004): *Business Statistuics Demystified*, New York 2004.

Kempf, Simon (2006): *Investigation of Influencing Factors determining Office Rents in German Metropolitan Areas - An empirical Analysis* at: ERES Conference: Weimar, Germany 2006.

Keogh, G. / D'Arcy, E. (1999): *Property Market Efficiency: An Institutional Economics Perspective*, in: *Urban Studies*, Vol. 36, Iss. 13, pp. 2401-2414.

Kling, John L. / McCue, Thomas E. (1987): *Office Building Investments and the Macroeconomy: Empirical Evidence, 1973-1985*, in: *Journal of the American Real Estate and Urban Economics Association*, Vol. 15, Iss. 3, pp. 234-255.

Knight, J. / Dombrow, J. / Sirmans, C.F. (1995): *A Varying Parameters Approach to Constructing House Price Indexes*, in: *Real Estate Economics*, Vol. 23, pp. 187-205.

Kofman, Paul / Sharpe, Ian G. (2003): *Using Multiple Imputation in the Analysis of Incomplete Observations in Finance*, in: *Journal of Financial Econometrics*, Vol. 1, Iss. 2, pp. 216-249.

Kokoski, Mary / Waehrer, Keith / Rozaklis, Patricia (2000): *Using Hedonic Methods for Quality Adjustment in the CPI: The Consumer Audio Product Component*, in: *Bureau of Labor Statistics (BLS) Working Papers*, Vol. 344, .

Kulish, Valdimir V. (2007): *Market efficiency and the phase-lagging model of the price evolution*, in: *Physica A*, Vol. 387, pp. 861-875.

Kuls, Nobert (2006): *Die Öko-Türme von Manhattan - In New York ist umweltverträgliches Bauen en vogue*, in: *FAZ Sonntagszeitung*, 28.05.2006, p. V13.

Kurzrock, Björn-Martin (2007): *Einflussfaktoren auf die Performance von Immobilien-Direktanlagen*, PhD, European Business School, Oestrich-Winkel 2007.

Laverne, Robert J. / Winson-Geideman, Kimberly (2003): *The Influence of Trees and Landscaping on Rental Rates at Office Buildings*, in: *Journal of Arboriculture*, Vol. 29, Iss. 5, pp. 281-290.

Leishman, C. / Dunse, N.A. / Warren, F.j. / Watkins, C. (2003): *Office Space Requirements: comparing occupiers' preferences with agents' perceptions*, in: *Journal of Property Investment & Finance*, Vol. 21, Iss. 1, pp. 45-60.

Li, Wenzheng / Prud'homme, Marc / Yu, Kam (2006): *Studies in Hedonic Resale Housing Price Indexes* at: Canadian Economic Association 40th Annual Meeting: Montréal, Canada 2006.

Lindner-Figura, Jan / Oprée, Frank / Stellmann, Frank (2005): *Geschäftsraummiete*, München 2005.

Lovells (2006): *Immobilienrecht*, <www.heuer-dialog.de/downloads/NewsletterImmobilienrechtSeptember20006.pdf>, Access Date: 03.11.2007.

Ludwig, Helge (2005): *Prognose von Gewerbemieten in Deutschland - Methodik und Umsetzung von Mietprognosemodellen für unterschiedliche Marktcharakteristika bei Gewerbeimmobilien*, TU Munich, 2005.

Lum, Sau Kim (2004): *Property price indices in the Commonwealth*, in: *Journal of Property Investment & Finance*, Vol. 22, Iss. 1, pp. 25-54.

Lützkendorf, T / Lorenz, D. (2005): *Sustainable property investment: valuing sustainable building through property performance assessment*, in: *Building Research & Information*, Vol. 33, Iss. 3, pp. 212-234.

Mackmin, David / Emary, Richard (2000): *The assessment of worth: the need for standards*, in: *Journal of Property Investment & Finance*, Vol. 18, Iss. 1, pp. 52-65.

Maier, Kurt M. (1999): *Risikomanagement im Immobilienwesen - Leitfaden für Theorie und Praxis*, Frankfurt 1999.

Makridakis, Spyros / Wheelwright, Steven C. (1989): *Forecasting Methods for Management*, New York 1989.

Malpezzi, Stephen (2002): *Hedonic Pricing Models: A Selective and Applied Review*, <http://www.bus.wisc.edu/realestate/pdf/pdf/Hedonic%20Pricing%20Models%20Survey%20for%20Maclennan.pdf>, Access Date: 03.11.2007.

Maurer, Raimond / Pitzer, Martin / Sebastian, Steffen (2001): *Konstruktion transaktionsbasierter Immobilienindizes: Theoretische Grundlagen und empirische Umsetzung für den Wohnungsmarkt in Paris*, in: *Mannheimer Manuskripte zu Risikotheorie, Portfolio Management and Versicherungswirtschaft*, Vol. 128, pp. 1-25.

Maurer, Raimond / Sebastian, Steffen (2000): *Immobilienindizes im Portfolio-Management*, in: *Working Paper Series: Finance & Accounting of Johann Wolfgang Goethe-University*, Vol. 52, pp. 1-24.

Mayer, Horst (2004): *Interview umd schriftliche Befragung*, 2nd Edition Ed., 2004.

McAllister, Patrick (2001): *Pricing short leases and break clauses using simulation methodology*, in: *Journal of Property Investment & Finance*, Vol. 19, Iss. 4, pp. 361-374.

McCann, P. / Ward, C. (2004): *Real Estate Rental Payments: Application of Stock-Inventory Modelling*, in: *The Journal of Real Estate Finance and Economics*, Vol. 28, Iss. 2, pp. 273-292.

McParland, Clare / McGreal, Stanley / Adair, Alastair (2000): *Concepts of price, value and worth in the United Kingdom - Towards a European perspective*, in: *Journal of Property Investment and Finance*, Vol. 18, Iss. 1, pp. 84-102.

Meija, Luis C. (1999): *Availability of Credit and Loan Default: A Look at the Commercial Mortgage Supply Cycle*, in: *Journal of Real Estate Research*, Vol. 18, Iss. 1, pp. 175-196.

Milionis, Alexandros (2007): *Efficient capital markets: A statistical definition and comments*, in: *Statistics & Probability Letters*, Vol. 77, pp. 607-613.

Mills, Edwin S. (1992): *Office Rent Determinants in the Chigago Area*, in: *Journal of the American Real Estate and Urban Economics Association*, Vol. 20, Iss. 1, pp. 273-287.

Mooradian, R.M. / Yang, S.X. (2000): *Cancellation strategies in commcercial real estate leasing*, in: *Real Estate Economics*, Vol. 28, pp. 65-88.

Morrell, Guy (1995): *Property indices: a coming of age*, in: *Journal of Property Valuation and Investment*, Vol. 13, Iss. 3, pp. 8-21.

Mueller, Glenn R. (1999): *Real Estate Rental Growth Rates at Different Points in the Physical Market Cycle*, in: *Journal of Real Estate Research*, Vol. 18, Iss. 1, pp. 131-150.

Munneke, H. / Slade, Barrett A. (2001): *A metropolitan transaction-based commercial price index: a time-varying parameter approach*, in: *Real Estate Economics*, Vol. 29, Iss. 1, pp. 55-84.

Neap, Halil Shevket / Celik, Tahir (1999): *Value of a Product: A Definition*, in: *International Journal of Value - Based Managent*, Vol. 12, Iss. 2, pp. 181-191.

Nesheim, Lars (2006): *Hedonic price function*, in: *Working Paper of Centre for Microdata Methods and Practice (CEMMAP)*, Vol. 18, pp. 1-25.

Nitsch, Harald (2006): *Pricing Location: A Case Study of the Munich Office Market*, in: *Journal of Property Research*, Vol. 23, Iss. 2, pp. 93-107.

Nitzan, Jonathan (1992): *Inflation and Restructuring - A Theoretical and Empirical Account of the U.S. Experience*, PhD, McGill University, Montreal 1992.

O'Mara, Martha A. (1999): *Strategic Drivers of Location Decisions for Information-Age Companies*, in: *The Journal of Real Estate Research*, Vol. 17, Iss. 3, pp. 365-386.

Orr, Allison / Dunse, Neil / Martin, David (2003): *Time on the market and commercial property prices*, in: *Journal of Property Investment & Finance*, Vol. 21, Iss. 6, pp. 473-494.

Oudshoorn, C.G.M. / van Buuren, S. / van Rijckevorsel, Jan (1999): *Flexible multiple imputation by chained equationss of the AVO-95 Survey*, in: *TNO Report*, .

Oven, Atilla / Pekdemir, Dilek (2004): *A Comparison between Office Rent Determinants of Istanbul and other Major Metropolitan Areas* at: 46th European Regional Science Association Conference: Porto 2004.

Pace, Kelley R. / Sirmans, C.F. / Slawson V., Carlos (2002): *Are Appraisers Statisticians?*, in: Wang, Ko /Wolveration, Marvin L. (eds.): *Real Estate Valuation Theory*, Vol. 8, 2002, pp. 31-43.

Pakes, Ariel (2002): *A Reconsideration of Hedonic Price Indices with an Application to PCs*, in: *National Bureau of Economic Research Working Paper*, Vol. 8715, pp. 1-47.

Pavlov, A.D. (2000): *Space-varying regressions coefficients: a semi-parametric approach applied to the real estate market*, in: *Real Estate Economics*, Vol. 28, pp. 249-283.

Pecar, Branko (1997): *Business forecasting for managment*, London 1997.

Persky, Joseph (1995): *Retropsectives - The Ethology of Homo Economicus*, in: *Journal of Economic Perspectives*, Vol. 9, Iss. 2, pp. 221-231.

Peto, Robert (1997): *Market information management for better valuations II: data availability and application*, in: *Journal of Property Valuation and Investment*, Vol. 15, Iss. 5, pp. 411-422.

Peto, Robert / French, Nick / Bowman, G. (1996): *Price and worth: developments in valuation methodology*, in: *Journal of Property Valuation and Investment*, Vol. 14, Iss. 4, pp. 79-100.

Plewka, Torsten (2003): *Derivative Instrumente für den Immobilienanlagemarkt - Eine Analyse der Funktionsfähigkeit von Immobilienderivativen und synthetischen Immobilienanlageprodukten*, PhD, University of Leipzig, Leipzig 2003.

Posner, Kenneth A. (1993): *In search of hidden value: Explicit and implicit options in real estate leases*, in: *Real Estate Finance*, Vol. 10, Iss. 2, pp. 47-54.

Pretorius, Frederick / Walker, Anthony / Chau, K.W. (2003): *Exploitation, Expropriatition and Capital Assets: The Economics of Commercial Real Estate Leases*, in: *Journal of Real Estate Literature*, Vol. 11, Iss. 1, pp. 3-34.

Pyhrr, Stephen / Roulac, Stephen E. / Born, Waldo (1999): *Real Estate Cycles and Their Strategic Implications for Investors and Portfolio Managers in the Global Economy*, in: *Journal of Real Estate Research*, Vol. 18, Iss. 1, pp. 7-68.

Ramsey, J.B. (1969): *Tests for Specification Errors in Classical Linear Least-Squares Regression Analysis* in: *Journal of the Royal Statistical Society. Series B (Methodological)*, Vol. 31, Iss. 2, pp. 350-371.

Redman, Arnold L. / Tanner, John R. / Manakyan, Herman (2002): *Corporate real estate financing methods: A statistical study of corporations' choices*, in: *Journal of Corporate Real Estate*, Vol. 4, Iss. 2, pp. 169-184.

RICS (2003): *Red Book*, 2003.

Ries, Robert / Bilec, Melissa (2006): *The Economic Benefits of Green Buildings: A Comprehensive Case Study*, in: *The Engineering Economist*, Vol. 51, Iss. 3, pp. 259-295.

RIWIS, 2007 (2007): <http://www.riwis.de/>, Access Date: 13.04.2008.

Robinson, Jon (1999): *Commercial lease terms and the property cycle*, in: *Facilities*, Vol. 17, Iss. 5/6, pp. 177-182.

Rohmert, Werner (2002): *Büromarkt-Maklerresearch - die Daten im Vergleich*, in: *Der Immobilienbrief*, July 2002, pp. 5-7.

Rohmert, Werner (2007): *Hauspreise und Hauspreisindex*, in: *Der Immobilienbrief*, Vol. 133, pp. 24-25.

Rohmert, Werner (2008): *Bleibt Immobilien-Research doch ein Ratespiel?*, in: *Der Immobilienbrief*, January 2008, pp. 12-13.

Rosen, Sherwin (1974): *Hedonic Prices and Implicit Markets: Product Differentiation in Pure Competition*, in: *Journal of Political Economy*, Vol. 82, Iss. 1, pp. 34-55.

Ross, Stephen A. / Westerfield, Randolph W. / Jaffe, Jeffrey (2002): *Corporate Finance*, 6th Ed., New York 2002.

Rottke, Nico B. (2007): *The Transaction-Based Real Estate Approach: A Paradigm for Interdisciplinary Real Estate Education* at: European Real Estate Research Society Conference: London 2007.

Rottke, Nico B. / Wernecke, Martin (2002a): *Management im Immobilienzyklus - Folge 3: Endogene Mechanismen*, <http://www.rem-institute.org/file/87/03_Management_im_Immobilienzyklus__Endogene_Faktoren.pdf>, Access Date: 03.11.2007.

Rottke, Nico B. / Wernecke, Martin (2002b): *Management im Immobilienzyklus - Folge 5: Vier Phasen des Immobilienzyklus*, <http://www.rem-institute.org/file/76/07_Management_im_Immobilienzyklus__Portfolio_Management.pdf>, Access Date: 03.11.2007.

Rottke, Nico B. / Wernecke, Martin (2002c): *Management im Immobilienzyklus - Folge 13: Immobilienmarketing*, <http://www.rem-

institute.org/file/82/13_Management_im_Immobilienzyklus__Marketing.pdf>, Access Date: 03.11.2007.

Rowland, Patrick (2000): *Pricing lease clauses - The prosepect on an art becoming science*, in: *Journal of Property Investment & Finance*, Vol. 18, Iss. 2, pp. 177-195.

Royal Institution of Chartered Surveyors / Centre for European Property Research *International Leasing Structures - Incorporating a comparative study*, in: Iss. 26, pp. 25-31.

Rudolf, Matthias / Müller, Johannes (2004): *Multivariate Verfahren*, Göttingen 2004.

Ryan, Sherry (2005): *The Value of Access to Highways and Light Rail Transit: Evidence for Industrial and Office Firms*, in: *Urban Studies*, Vol. 42, Iss. 4, pp. 751-764.

Sartori, Nicola / Salvan, Alberto / Thomaseth, Karl (2005): *Multiple Imputation of missing values in a cancer mortality analysis with estimated exposure dose*, in: *Computational Statistics & Data Analysis*, Vol. 49, pp. 937-953.

Schafer, Joseph L. (1997): *Analysis of incomplete multivariate data*, London 1997.

Schafer, Joseph L. (1999): *Multiple Imputation: a primer*, in: *Statistical Methods in Medical Research*, Vol. 8, pp. 3-15.

Schafer, Joseph L. (2001): *Multiple Imputation Models and Procedures*, <http://fetcher.fw-notify.net/0000000582138416841 6/mimodels.pdf>, Access Date: 03.11.2007.

Schafer, Joseph L. / Graham, John M. (2002): *Missing Data: Our View of the State of the Art*, in: *Psychological Methods*, Vol. 7, Iss. 2, pp. 147-177.

Schafer, Joseph L. / Olsen, Maren K. (1998): *Multiple Imputation for Multivariate Missing-Data Problems: A Data Analyst's Perspective*, in: *Multivariate Behavioural Research*, Vol. 33, Iss. 4, pp. 545-571.

Schafer, Joseph L. / Yucel, Recai M. (2002): *Computational Strategies for Multivariate Linear Mixed-Effects Models with Missing Values*, in: *Journal of Computational and Graphical Statistics*, Vol. 11, Iss. 2, pp. 421-442.

Schick, Jürgen Michael (2005): *Weiße Flecken in der Statistik*, in: *Immobilienwirtschaft*, April 2005, p. 20.

Schulte, Karl-Werner / Lee, Anthony / Paul, Eduard (2005a): *Wörterbuch Immobilienwirtschaft*, Wiesbaden 2005a.

Schulte, Karl-Werner / Rottke, Nico / Pitschke, Christoph (2005b): *Transparency in the German real estate market*, in: *Journal of Property Investment & Finance*, Vol. 23, Iss. 1, pp. 90-108.

Schulte, Karl-Werner / Wiffler, Matthias (2006): *Markttransparenz*, in: *Praxishandbuch Immobilienzyklen*, Köln 2006, pp. 415-435.

Shiers, David (1999): *The green development of commercial property* at: RICS Cutting Edge Conference: Cambridge 1999.

Shiller, Robert J. (2006): *Tools for Financial Innovation: Neoclassical versus Behavioral Finance*, in: *The Financial Review*, Vol. 41, pp. 1-8.

Shilton, Leon (1998): *Patterns of Office Employment Cycles*, in: *The Journal of Real Estate Research*, Vol. 15, Iss. 3, pp. 339-354.

Sing, Tien Foo (2005): *Impact of information and communications technology on real estate space*, in: *Journal of Property Investment & Finance*, Vol. 23, Iss. 6, pp. 494-505.

Sinharay, Sandip / Stern, Hal S. / Russell, Daniel (2001): *The Use of Multiple Imputation for the Analysis of Missing Data*, in: *Psychological Methdos*, Vol. 6, Iss. 4, pp. 317-329.

Sirmans, G. Stacy / Macpherson, David A. / Zietz, Emily N. (2005): *The Composition of Hedonic Pricing Models*, in: *Journal of Real Estate Literature*, Vol. 13, Iss. 1, pp. 3-43.

Sivitanidou, Rena (1996): *Do Office-Commercial Firms Value Access to Service Employment Centers? A Hedonic Value Analysis within Polycentric Los Angeles*, in: *Journal of Urban Economics*, Vol. 40, pp. 125-149.

Slade, Barrett A. (2000): *Office Rent Determinants During Market Decline and Recovery*, in: *Journal of Real Estate Research*, Vol. 20, Iss. 3, pp. 357-380.

Söderberg, Bo (2002): *A Note on the Hedonic Model Specification for Income Properties*, in: Wang, Ko /Wolveration, Marvin L. (eds.): *Real Estate Valuation Theory*, Vol. 8, 2002, pp. 157-180.

St. Lawrence, S. (2004): *Review of the UK corporate real-estate market with regard to availability of environmentally and socially responsible office buildings*, in: *Journal of Corporate Real Estate*, Vol. 6, Iss. 2, pp. 149-161.

Stanton, Richard / Wallace, Nancy (2002): *An Empirical Test of Contingent Claims Lease Valuation Model*, in: *Fourth Coming in the Journal of Real Estate Research*, pp. 1-27.

Tabachnick, Barbara G. / Fidell, Linda S. (2006): *Using Multivariate Statistics*, 5th edition Ed., 2006.

Thériault, Marius / Des Rosiers, F. / Joerin, Florent (2005): *Modelling accessibility to urban services using fuzzy logic - A comparative analysis of two methods*, in: *Journal of Property Investment & Finance*, Vol. 23, Iss. 1, pp. 22-54.

Thomas Daily (2007): <http://web.thomas-daily.de/core/article.html?articleId=391201&newContext=true>, Access Date: 18.03.2008.

Thomas Daily (2008): *Büromarkt: Nutzer lehnen höhere Mietpreise für "grüne Büros" ab*, in: .

Thomas, Matthias (1997): *Die Entwicklung eines Performanceindexes für den deutschen Immobilienmarkt*, PhD, European Business School (ebs), 1997.

Thommen, Jean-Paul / Achleitner, Ann-Kristin (1998): *Allgemeine Betriebswirtschaftslehre. Umfassende Einführung aus managementorientierter Sicht*, 1998.

Thomson, D.S. / Austin, S.A. / Devin-Wright, H. / Mills, G.R. (2003): *Managing value and quality in design*, in: *Building Research & Information*, Vol. 31, Iss. 5, pp. 334-245.

Triplett, Jack E. (2004): *Handbook on Hedonic Indexes and Quality Adjustments in Price Indexes* Paris France 2004.

Tu, Yong / Yu, Shi-Ming / Sun, Hua (2004): *Transaction-based Office Price Indexes: A Spatiotemporal Modeling Approach*, in: *Real Estate Economics*, Vol. 32, Iss. 2, pp. 297-328.

Turner, Neil / Thomas, Matthias (2001): *Property market indices and lease structures - the impact on investment return delivery in the UK and Germany: Part I*, in: *Journal of Property Valuation & Investment*, Vol. 19, Iss. 2, pp. 175-187.

Vandell, Kerry D. / Lane, Jonathan S. / Kain, John F. (1989): *The Economics of Architecture and Urban Design: Some Preliminary Findings*, in: *Journal of the American Real Estate and Urban Economics Association*, Vol. 17, Iss. 2, pp. 235-265.

Vermietungsdatenbank (2003): *Erläuterung zum Datenerhebungsblatt*, 2003.

von Auer, Ludwig (2004): *Overcoming Data Limitation in Hedonic Regressions*, <http://www.ipeer.ca/papers/Auer,Oct.12,2004.pdf>, Access Date: 03.11.2007.

Wallace, Nancy (1996): *Hedonic-Based Price Indexes for Housing: Theory, Estimation and Index Construction*, in: *FRSBF Economic Review*, Vol. 3, pp. 34-48.

Walzel, Barbara (2005): *Typologische Aspekte der Immobilienökonomie - Unterscheidung anch Immobilienarten*, in: Schulte, Karl-Werner (ed.): *Immobilienökonomie - Betriebswirtschaftliche Grundlagen*, Vol. Band 1, Ed. 3rd, Köln 2005, pp. 117-140.

Wang, Jing (2005): *Valuing Options in Commercial Real Estate Leases*, PhD, University of Hong Kong, Hong Kong 2005.

Wang, Peijie (2000): *Market Efficiency and Rationality in Property Investments*, in: *Journal of Real Estate Finance and Economics*, Vol. 21, Iss. 2, pp. 185-201.

Webb, Brain R. / Fisher, Jeffrey D. (1996): *Development of an Effective Rent (Lease) Index for the Chicago CBD*, in: *Journal of Urban Economics*, Vol. 39, pp. 1-19.

Webb, Brain R. / Miles, Mike / Guilkey, David (1992): *Transactions-Driven Commercial Real Estate Returns: The Panacea to Asset Allocation Models*, in: *Journal of* *the American Real Estate and Urban Economics Association*, Vol. 20, Iss. 1, pp. 325-357.

Wernecke, Martin (2004): *Büroimmobilienzyklen*, PhD, European Business School (ebs), Köln 2004.

Wheaton, William C. (1999): *Real Estate "Cylces": Some Fundamentals*, in: *Real Estate Economics*, Vol. 27, Iss. 2, pp. 209-230.

Wheaton, William C. / Torto, Raymond G. (1995): *Office Rent Indices and their Behaviour Over Time*, in: *Journal of Urban Economics*, Vol. 35, Iss. 2, pp. 121-139.

Wild, Bernhard / Autenrieth, Matthias (2008): *Greenbuidings*, in: *Immobilienmanager*, Vol. 03, pp. 14-17.

Wilson, Tom (1985): *Offices as an Investment*, in: Marber, Paul /Marber, Paula (eds.): *Office Development*, London 1985, pp. 121-132.

Wolverton, Marvin L. / Senteza, Jimmy (2000): *Hedonic Estimates of Regional Constant Quality House Prices*, in: *Journal of Real Estate Research*, Vol. 2000, Iss. 19, pp. 235-253.

Wuertz, Diethelm (2006): *The fMultivar Package*, <http://cran.r-project.org/doc/packages/fMultivar.pdf>, Access Date: 06.03.2007.

Wurtzenbach, Charles H. / Miles, Mike E. (1995): *Modern Real Estate*, 5th Ed., 1995.

www.emporis.com (2008):
<http://www.emporis.com/en/wm/ci/bu/sk/li/?id=100563&bt=2&ht=2&sro=1>, Access Date: 31.03.2006.

Wyatt, Peter (1999): *Can geographical analysis of property values aid business location planning?* at: The Cutting Edge: Cambridge 1999.

Zabel, Jeffrey E. (1999): *Controlling for Quality in House Price Indices*, in: *Journal of Real Estate Finance and Economics*, Vol. 19, Iss. 3, pp. 223-241.

Zhang, Paul (2001): *Multiple Imputation of Missing Data in Clinic Trials*, PhD, University of Toronto, Toronto 2001.

